The Jats

Their Role in the Mughal Empire

Girish Chandra Dwivedi

Prepared under the personal supervision of
Professor Ishwari Prasad M.A., L.L.B. D. Litt.
Professor Emeritus, University of Allahabad.

Editor
Dr. Vir Singh

Originals

(an imprint of Low Price Publications)
Delhi-110052

Distributed by
D.K. Publishers Distributors (P) Ltd.
4834/24, Ansari Road, Darya Ganj,
New Delhi-110002
Phones: 23278584, 23278368, 23261465,
e-mail: dkpd@del3.vsnl.net.in
visit us at: www.dkpd.com

First Published 1989

Corrected and Updated Edition 2003

ISBN 81-88629-08-1 (HB)

Published by
Originals
(an imprint of Low Price Publications)
A-6, Nimri Commercial Centre,
Near Ashok Vihar Phase-IV,
Delhi-110052
Phones: 27401672, 27452453
e-mail: lpp@nde.vsnl.net.in
visit us at: www.lppindia.com

Printed at
D K Fine Art Press P Ltd.
Delhi-110052

PRINTED IN INDIA

Contents

Preface

The Jats are located prominently in the North-West region of India. Renowned historians called them 'almost a nation' which excelled in agriculture and in battlefield alike. The Jats (may be Hindu, Muslim or Sikh) are true sons of the soil, which is why these patriots always stood in ancient as well as medieval times like rock in the face of invaders seeking to ravage the motherland. But the irony is that these patriots were branded as rebels by historians.

I feel happy that Dr. Girish Chandra Dwivedi has highlighted the dynamic role of the Jats during the later period of the Mughal Empire. This intensive study shows that an instinctive attachment to democratic ways and a sturdy independence have throughout been the chief characteristics of the Jats. In 1669 this race of warrior-agriculturists rose against the narrow and over-centralised despotic regime of Aurangzeb. The author asserts that besides an oppressive agrarian system and the religious policy of Aurangzeb, 'the adventurous disposition and martial character of Jats' has been the third major factor in rebellion. He elaborates further that 'probably not many agricultural communities possessed obstinate courage, indomitable spirit, heroic valour and tribal unity of Jats which were needed to transform a deep resentment into a military regime.' This powerful movement of the Jat-peasantry gave birth to strong leaders like Gokula, Rajaram and Chudaman. After critically examining the activities and situation prevailing in their times, the author describes in detail how Badan Singh assisted by his ablest son Surajmal laid the foundation of strong Bharatpur State.

History bears testimony to the fact that the Jats always rose against tyranny, injustice, economic and social exploitation and were never overawed by claims of racial or tribal superiority. Whenever the occasion arose they beat their ploughshares into swords and taking advantage of the decrepit political structure, they laid the foundations of their political power under several tribal chiefs. Maharaja Suraj Mal, the builder of Bharatpur, was by far the most resplendent star in the

Eighteenth century political firmament. He distinguished himself in war and diplomacy alike and earned the reputation of a strong and wise ruler, possessing administrative acumen and consideration for common weal. His rule extended over substantial portions of the modern States of Rajasthan, Haryana and Uttar Pradesh.

Though many erudite scholars like Prof. Jadunath Sarkar, Prof. Kalika Ranjan Qanungo, Prof. Satish Chandra, Prof. Irfan Habib have written extensively on the history of the Jats, there is a feeling that there are many gaps in these studies that come in the way of truly appraising the contributions of the Jats to the emergence of national ethos. The contribution of Dr. G.C. Dwivedi in this respect is outstanding.

Surajmal Memorial Education Society is encouraging scholars by providing various facilities to undertake research on different aspects of the history of the Jats and publishing works of eminent scholars. The Society is thankful to Dr. Rajiv Dwivedi, the elder son of late Dr. G.C. Dwivedi, who compared the two corrected copies of this work and supplied one copy to the Society. I wish to acknowledge with deep appreciation the serious effort put in by Dr. Vir Singh towards bringing out this revised edition. We are grateful to Originals(an imprint of Low Price Publications) for the personal interest that they took in bringing out this book.

Ram Niwas Mirdha
Chairman,
Surajmal Memorial Education Society

Editors Note

The present work arises out of the painstaking research work undertaken by late Dr. Girish Chandra Dwivedi, who was able to update the references after many years by correcting and rewriting many pages in the light of recent findings. Before the author could prepare the final copy for publication, he died at an early age of forty-one. As a matter of fact he left the work in the form of a cursorily revised draft which required an appreciable amount of labour to remove its blemishes.

Sh. Mahendra Singh Verma, resident of village Liberhedi in Saharanpur Dist. helped Dr. G. C. Dwivedi in compilation of the historical references related to the Jat traditions. Eventually, after the sad demise of Dr. Dwivedi, the manuscript of this monumental work came to Surajmal Memorial Education Society through Sh. Verma. On the recommendation of the academic committee the Society decided to publish it. I remember the scorching heat of June when I made a trip to Banaras, to meet Dr. Dwivedi's family and seek their permission for the publication of this work. Dr. Rajiv Dwivedi, the author's elder son, made my tough journey fruitful.

The work of casting it in a form fit for publication also devolved on my shoulders and I have done my level best to do away with the short comings in preparing the press copy without meddling with its thought content for which the credit rests with the author. It is for the scholars of history to judge the contents of this work, but I can say with confidence that we have lost in Dr. G.C. Dwivedi a great historian who had keen insight into the history of the Jats.

The response of scholars on its publication gave satisfaction to the Society. Prof. Irfan Habib, a great historian on Mughal India made a special mention in his book-*The Agrarian System of Mughal India* (1999, p-392, f.n.14), in his words: A detailed description of the various phases of the Jat rebellion is offered by Sh. Girish Chandra Dwivedi, '*The Jats: Their Role in the Mughal Empire*, New Delhi - 1989'. After thirteen years of its first publication in 1989, the Society felt the need to update this work.

The authenticity of any research work depends on the references and studies conducted. Footnotes of the work have been very carefully compared again and page numbers in as many as 34 references have been corrected as per the original work. Other than these, following corrections and changes have been made in the footnotes:

In Chapter I, f.n. 1, full French name of the Wendel's Memoires and other information relating to it has been deleted because it is given in detail in the title-Manuscript D. French-(I) in the Bibliography. In chapter I, the page nos. of references f. n. 2, 71 and 72, are not mentioned in the manuscript, they are, in fact, from the Introduction pages of *History of Aurangzeb III*, published by Govt. of India. In the third chapter, f.n. 62, of the Upendra Nath Sharma's work '*The New History of Jats*' the misprint of pp. 360-361 has been changed to 260-261. The author had not mentioned the page numbers of the following cited works and I had no time to trace them at the time of first edition. Now, I have traced them and written at proper places. *Akhbarat* (chapter II, f.n.68, 69 and 71-73), *Roznamcha* (chapter III, f.n.73); *Jai Singh* (chapter VI, f.n. 15); *Tarikh-e-Alamgir-Sani* (chapter VII, f.n. 38); *Memoires on Jats* (chapter IX, f.n. 19 and Appendix 5, f.n. 17); *Imad* (chapter XI, f.n. 29); *Supra* (chapter XIV, f.n. 10); *Mathura Gazette.* (Appendix 5, f.n. 12). In chapter I, f.n. 15 reference XXII-f is not traceable in the manuscript. This quotation is from Ibbetson, *The Punjab Castes*, and I have written its page number here. Wherever there are two publishers, of the same work, the name of the editors has been mentioned in the references for clarity. For example, *S.P.D.*, *Chachnama, Iqbalnama* and *Freedom Movement* etc. have two different editors. Abbreviation '*Raj.*' has been written in full *Rajwade* to avoid confusion with Rajasthan. Also the abbreviations of three books, which were left by the author but used by him, have been added.

Instead of changing the page numbers of this edition in *Supra* and *Infra* I have given the number of chapters and footnotes there to avoid difficulty in every edition. Besides correcting the page nos. of references in the footnotes and other minor errors, I have also done away with the numerous printing mistakes of the first edition.

In appendix 5 footnote number 12-a has been deleted. In one of the copy of the manuscript I found one para written by the author quoted from '*Brij Ka Itihas*' by Dr. Raghubir Singh. I have added its matter in footnote no. 20 and the order of the footnotes have been rearranged. Thus in appendix 5 footnotes are 26 instead of 24. Due to printing difficulty Hindi '*Sakhas*' were not given in the first edition.

Now all these '*Sakhas*' in chapter I, f.n. 75-79, 82 and chapter XII f.n.62 have been incorporated. In chapter IV, f.n. 53 also a poem from *Vansh Bhaskar* have been added with English translation.

The translation of *Wendel's French Memoires on Jats* has been corrected and done according to the English edition (1991) of the Memoires in the first sentence of introduction by Dr. G.C. Dwivedi. In chapter II the names of the matter of f.n. 39 have been rewritten in historical sequence for clarity as '*Brij Raj, Bhao Singh* and *Raja Ram's* associate *Ram Chehra* has perished'.

In this edition twenty seven footnotes based on recent findings clarifying and describing certain facts, names (Pratap Jat/Pratap Naruka) and places (Mendu/Mudsan, Jabra/Jawara, Jhajjar/Jhajhar) have been added to update the work, which are given in Roman numbers to differentiate with the footnotes of the author.

Sub-headings of the subject matter have been added with their page numbers with the name of every chapter in the contents of this edition to give clear glimpse of the subject to the reader. In the end of the book the addition of index of names and places will certainly be useful for researchers.

Under the dynamic leadership and guidance of Sh. Ram Niwas Mirdha, the Society has been organizing Seminars, Conferences and Workshops of National level on various topics relevant to the life and education of the rural people. *The Research and Publication Centre* of the Society has been undertaking the collection, preservation and publication of material on rural heritage of North-West India. The society has established a rich library on its campus for the use of research scholars. It also provides financial assistance to scholars in different Universities, who wish to pursue research on any aspect of Jat Community. Till now the Society has published fifteen books and given research scholarships for two students.

We feel immense pleasure and express our gratitude to Sh. OM PRAKASH CHAUTALA, Hon'ourable Chief Minister of Haryana, for providing sum of rupees five Lacs for the Research Centre of the Society for various Research and allied activities mentioned above. The Society looks forward for his constant encouragement in future also.

I am grateful to Sh. Ram Niwas Mirdha who reposed his trust in me and valuable suggestions of Dr. S. S. Rana, Vice- President of the Society and administrative support of Shri S. P. Singh, Secretary of the Soceity, which have been of immense help in this updated edition.

The diligent efforts of Sh. Manish Dagga (Vinayak Computers) and *Originals* (*an imprint of Low Price Publications*) have made this fine publication possible. I honestly hope that this corrected and updated work will provide a clean mirror of the Jat History to the research scholars and readers.

Dr. Vir Singh
Director
Research & Publication Centre
Suraj Mal Memorial Education Society

Abbreviations

Aftab Numa	:	Mirat-i-Aftab Numa.
Ahkam	:	Ahkam-i-Alamgiri by Inayatullah.
Ahwal	:	Ahwal-i-Salatin-i-Mutakherin.
Ajaib	:	Ajaib-ul-Afaq.
Amira	:	Khazan-i-Amira.
Aurangzib	:	J.N. Sarkar, History of Aurangzib.
Bangash Nawabs	:	Irwine, 'The Bangash Nawabs of Farrukhabad', J.A.S.B., Vol. XLVIII, Part I, 1879.
Bernier	:	Bernier, Travels in Mogul Empire, Trans. by A. Constable.
Bharatpur	:	Ram Pande, Bharatpur upto 1826.
Bishan Singh	:	K. R. Qanungo, 'Some Sidelights on the Career of Raja Bishan Singh Kachhwah of Amber', Proc. I.H.C., 1948.
Brij	:	Raghubir Singh, Brij Ka Itihas, I.
Br. Mus.	:	British Museum, London.
Dekkan	:	Jonathan Scott, Ferishta's History of the Dekkan, Vol. II.
D.C.	:	Delhi Chronicle.
Dirgh	:	Dirgh Nagar Varnan (Hindi Ms.) by Somnath.
Durrani	:	Ganda Singh, Ahmad Shah Durrani.
Elliot	:	Elliot and Dowson, History of India as told by its own Historians.
Fall	:	J.N. Sarkar, Fall of the Mughal Empire.
Fatuhat	:	Fatuhat-i-Alamgiri.
Franklin	:	The History of the reign of Shah Alam, London, 1798.
Freedom Movement	:	Mahmud Husain (ed.), A History of the Freedom Movement.
Gul	:	Gul-i-Rahmat.
Gulistan	:	Gulistan-i-Rahmat.
Hadiqat	:	Hadiqat-ul-Aqalim.

Ibrat	:	Ibratnama by Khair-ud-Din.
Imad	:	Imad-us-Saadat.
Iqbal	:	Iqbalnama.
Itihas	:	U. N. Sharma, Jaton ka Navin Itihas, Part I.
J. Records (Pers.)	:	Jaipur Records, J.N. Sarkar's Collection
J. Records (Pers.)	:	R.S.L. Transcripts, Sitamau.
Jaipur	:	M.L. Sharma, History of the Jaipur State.
Jats	:	K. R. Qanungo, History of the Jats, 1925.
J.A.S.B.	:	Journal of Asiatic Society of Bengal.
Kamwar	:	Muhammad Hadi Kamwar Khan by Tazkirat-us-Salatin-i-Chaghtai.
K. K.	:	Khafi Khan Muntakhab-ul-Lubab
Khuda Bakhsha	:	Khuda Bakhsha Library, Bankipur, Patna.
Maasir	:	Maasir-i-Alamgiri.
M.U.	:	Maasir-ul-Umra.
Malwa	:	Raghubir Singh, Malwa Main Yugantar. Purvakal.
Marathas	:	G.S. Sardesai, New History of the Marathas.
Memoires des Jats	:	Memoires de L'origine, accroissement (F.X. Wendel) et etat present de puissance des Jats dans L'Indostan II de Partie suite des Memoires des Pattans (Fr. Ms.).
Mirat	:	Mirat-i-Ahmadi.
Muharbat	:	Tarikh-i-Ahmad or Muharbat-i-Salatin-i-Durrania-O-Bhao O-Jangu-O-Sikhan.
Muzaffarnagar Rec.	:	Chowdhry Qabul Singh's (Shoram, Muzaffarnagar) collection.
Nadir Shah	:	James Fraser, The History of Nadir Shah.
Nur	:	Sayyid Nur-ud-Din Hasan's Life of Najib-ud-Daulah, Trans. by J.N. Sarkar in I.H.Q. (1933) and Islamic Culture (1933).
Oudh	:	A.L. Srivastava, The First Two Nawabs of Oudh.
Panipat	:	H.R. Gupta (ed.), Marathas and Panipat.

Panipat	:	T.S. Shejwalkar, Panipat : 1761.
Parties and Politics	:	S. Chandra, Parties and Politics at the Mughal Court.
Proc. I.H.C.	:	Proceedings of Indian History Congress.
Purandare	:	Purandare Daftar, ed. by K.V. Purandare.
R.S.L.	:	Raghubir Singh Library, Sitamau.
Raj Wade	:	Marathanchya Itihasachin Sadhanen, ed. by V.K. Rajwade and others.
Roznamcha	:	Roznamcha by Mirza Muhammad.
Rustam	:	Tarikh-i-Hind by Rustam Ali.
Samin	:	Ghulam Husain Samin's narrative. Trans. by William Irvine in Ind. And., 1907.
S.P.D	:	Selections from the Peshwas' Daftar, ed. by G.S. Sardesai.
S.P.D., New Series	:	Selections from the Peshwas' Daftar, New Series, Vol. I, ed. by P.M. Joshi.
Shah	:	Shah Waliullah Dehlavi Ke Siyasi Maktubat, ed. and Trans. by K.A. Nizami.
Shakir	:	Tazkira-i-Shakir Khan by Shakir Khan.
Shivdas	:	Shahnama Munawar Kalam by Shivdas Lakhanavi.
Shuja	:	A.L. Srivastava, Shuja-ud-Daulah.
Siyar	:	Siyar-ul-Mutakherin.
Somnath	:	Somnath Granthawali, Vol. I, Kashi.
Storia	:	Storia Do Mogor by Manucci, Trans. by Irvine.
Sujan	:	Sujan Charitra by Sudan.
TAH	:	Tarikh-i-Ahmad Shahi.
TAL	:	Tarikh-i-Alamgir Sani.

Acknowledgements

The present work owes its origin to the deep impression which Professor K.R. Qanungo's brilliant work, *History of the Jats*, created on me. Naturally, when I took up research my first desire was to work on the Jats. In this I was fortunate to receive encouragement from and the kind guidance of Dr. Ishwari Prasad, Professor Emeritus, University of Allahabad, the renowned historian who has had a legend of rare eminence for decades. He advised me to concentrate on the dynamic role of the Jats in the history of the later Mughals rather than attempt a narrative of the Jat in the history on the traditional lines. So I did, but I may hasten to add that I have confined myself mainly to the role of the Jats of Bharatpur, although, wherever the Jats of the other places have been referred to in the various original sources and a discussion of their role has been deemed relevant to our theme, they have not been left out.

I am greatly indebted for the valuable help received from diverse sources, institutions and individuals without whose co-operation this work could not have been brought to a successful close.

It is my pious duty to express my sincere thankfulness to my revered supervisor, Professor Ishwari Prasad. Despite his old age and a busy schedule, he allowed me the privilege of writing this thesis at his feet. He has been very kind and affectionate throughout and allowed me to tax him time and again to get the fullest advantage of his erudite scholarship. But for his affectionate patronage, encouragement, guidance and personal interest, this work could not have at all been completed.

I feel it a privilege to express my gratitude to Maharajkumar Dr. Raghubir singh of Sitamau. He generously provided me the fullest possible facilities to use his rich library.

I am also grateful to Professor S.H. Askari. Inspite of his old age and frail health, he took pains to guide me to the relevant material both in the Khuda Bakhsh Library and in his personal collection and discussed with me many passages from the original sources. Among the valuable material which he made available to me, I must here make a pointed reference to his personal typed copy of the translation,[1] of *Iqbalnama*, which he had prepared for publication.

I shall be failing in my duty if I do not allude to the encouragement and scholarly guidance which I have received from Professor Satish Chandra, Professor K.A. Nizami and Professor Irfan Habib. Prof. Nizami was extremely kind in providing me all possible help during my stay in Aligarh. No less kind were Dr. Paramatma Sharan and Dr. Ganda Singh, who took great interest in my studies and always extended relevant information whenever I made a request. I must also express my gratitude to Professor Lallanji Gopal, Dr. G.D. Bhatnagar and Dr. C.B. Kapoor, who have given me much of their precious time going through my script and suggesting valuable improvements. Had it not been for their personal interest and affectionate help, the work could not have been submitted in its present form.

I also owe deep gratitude to Chowdhary Richhpal Sing, ex-Secretary, All India Jat Maha Sabha, Shri Jagdeo Singh Sidhanti, President, Sarva—Khap Panchayat, Chowdhary Qabul Singh, Secretary Sarva-Khap Panchayat and Mr. Mahendra Singh Varma for placing at my disposal the documents of Jat history collected by them, some of which have not been used earlier. At one time or the other they also took the trouble of accompanying me to Jat areas for the collection of Jat traditions and the Sakhas.

For their sympathetic help in providing me the necessary facilities for work, I am also thankful to the librarians and the staff of the British Museum Library, India Office Library, R.S. Library , Sitamau, Khuda Bakhsha Library, Patna, Bharatpur State Museum Library, Hindi Sahitya Samiti Library, Bharatpur, Public Library, Bhartpur, B.H.U. Library, M.U.A. Library, Shibli Academy Library, Azamgarh, Kashi Vidyapith Library, etc.

Of my well-wishers, who have been of valuable help to me I would like to make a special reference to Dr. W.K. Lele, Reader in Marathi, B.H.U., Dr. H.C. Nayyar, Head of the Urdu Dept., B.H.U. and Miss Asha of Mauritius, who have helped me in utilising, the Marathi, Persian and French sources respectively. Dr. Mrs. K. Gopal, Shri M.P. Singh and Shri P.N. Saksena took great pains for me and deserve my thanks.

I shall never forget the debt of Professor S.M. Tiwary, Dean Faculty of Commerce and Business Management, B.H.U. (my uncle-in-law) and Mr. K. C. Tiwary (my brother-in-law) who have worked for me very hard indeed.

Girish Chandra Dwivedi

---

1. I may be excused for striking a very perosnal note here. When Prof. Askari suggested to me the Ms. of *Tarikh-i-Bharatpur*,[1] be remarked that Sir Jadu Nath Sarkar had asked him to utilize that Ms. for his research studies on the Jats. Prof. Askari added that he was happy on my taking up the subject and making a suitable use of the Ms.

1. This work is written by Anand Rai.—Editor.

Introduction

"...the Jats have...hurt so many people so that no one can be persuaded that they are capable of doing good or so much of it as to be praised" said F.X. Wendel, a French Jesuit some two hundred years ago.[1] Having stayed in India for about fifty years as a contemporary eye-witness to and a keen observer of the Indian political scene, he made the above remark while surveying the history of the Jats. But the general impression about the Jats has not been much different; a Jat is inadvertently taken to be incapable of being great. The popular conception has since persisted and unfortunately the Jat history could not draw to it the adequate attention of earlier historians.

Sir William Irvine's *Later Mughals* makes relevant references to the Jats, but the scope of his subject did not permit him to investigate the Jat history thoroughly. Professor K.R. Qanungo's *History of the Jats* is a pioneer work on the subject. By his erudite scholarship, he imparted respectability to and focussed our attention on the Jat history.

Pioneer works generally suffer from certain unavoidable handicaps. In case of Professor Qanungo, he was denied use of quite a lot of material available to us now. With the result, his narrative is patchy and conclusions are often one-sided and incomplete. Recently, two more scholars, U.N. Sharma and Ram Pande, have brought out two works on the history of the Jats. Both have followed the pattern of Qanungo.

However, the basic issues still remain more or less unresolved.

In his great and exhaustive works Sir Jadu Nath Sarkar does refer to the events of Jat history, but only to the extent they have any bearing on his central theme. The confusing panorama of the political history of the later Mughal period has received the discerning attention of two more senior historians, Professor A.L. Srivastava and Professor Satish Chandra. But, sterling though their contributions have been, their own treatment of the Jats is brief and casual. Their subjects being different, it could not be otherwise also.[2]

---

1. *Memoires des Jats* (Fr. Ms.), 38.

II. Translation of the author has been corrected and done according to English edition 1991 of the Memoires. It is Wendel's lefthanded compliment to the Jats, when Suraj Mal helped and saved Wazir Safdarjang from almost inevitable ruin in the Delhi Civil War in 1753.—Editor.

2. After the first draft of the thesis was ready we received in print, Dr. Ram Pande's Ph. D. thesis, *Bharatpur Upto 1826*. This work does not concentrate on the rule of the Jats in the history of the Mughal Empire and therefore differs from the

Thus when the Jats engrossed my attention I felt the necessity, even after the learned works of these scholars, to take up the study of the role of the Jats in the history of the Mughal Empire.

I would like to add a few words about the choice of the topic. It would be pretentious on my part to justify the desirability of local or regional history. It is obvious that for a proper understanding of the history of a big area like the Mughal Empire we require an intensive study of different local powers. In later Mughal history when the imperial authority was effective only over a restricted area, the cobwebs of history become very much entangled. The fierce factionalism at the Court, the foreign invasions, the self-aggrandisement of the officials and the rise of the indigenous powers, often at variance with each other, further complicate the situation. Of the last, the role of some powers has received careful study from the scholars. But not so in the case of the Jats. We now require a study of the role of the Jats in the Mughal history, and not merely a history of the Jats alone. Such a study is expected to facilitate a better understanding of not only the Mughal but also of the Jat history in its true perspective.

The earlier writings create an impression that the advent of the Jats affected only the fringes of the history of the Mughal Empire. We thought - and our study shows it - that they had an important role to play in the political arena of the day which increased in scope in course of time. Earlier the Jats were "not remarkable in Hindustan"[3] and yet by seventeen sixties they earned for themselves "a reputation never seen outside"[4]. This constitutes a fascinating phase in the annals of medieval India.

Driven to arms in deep discontent, the Jat insurrection in the beginning symptomized the general disaffection in the Empire, even though it had then a local application only. Attempts at their ruthless repression, without redressal of their genuine grievances, kindled the native fury of the Jats. Inwardly exasperated, the ferocious Jats and the kindred people rose again ultimately setting at naught the imperial authority in the province of Agra. An obscure people rising to great heights and swaying the destiny of a big region is not an ordinary phenomenon; when we know that it was achieved in a short period the significance of the story increases.

---

scope of our thesis. It is extremely painful for us to point out that most of the sources listed in the Bibliography do not appear to have been very judiciously and thoroughly tapped by him. In the case of both internal and external history of Bharatpur there is little appreciable improvement over the information in the earlier works. It would be distasteful for us to list various types of lapses in the use and interpretation of the different sources. Some instances may, however, be seen on pp. 55, 73, 75, 79, 85, 86, 96, 138, 155, 180, 191, 211, 255, 261, 285, 307, 308, 310, 322, 332, 382, 407 "and 415 (f. n.)."

3. *Memoires des Jats* (Fr. Ms.), 64.

4. *Ibid.*, 29.

Breakdown of imperial authority afforded a golden opportunity for predatory warfare. Uncontrolled by any higher authority and uninspired by any higher motive than opposing the Mughals, the individual headmen succumbed to "seduction of rich spirits". And yet they are not to blame. Disgruntled as they were, it was not possible to face the situation in any other way. Aurangzeb's mistaken policy was bearing fruits. In the post-Aurangzeb period, the powerful elements at the Court found it expedient to conciliate the Jats in order to retain power and to rejuvenate the declining Empire. The latter readily accepted their new role. Whatever be the juristic standpoint, they no longer remained plebeian rebels perpetually fighting against the imperialists, but became allies of one or the other Court faction. Side by side the Jats, conscious of their strength, availed themselves of the opportunities for expansion. With the stabilization of their power and position increased the dependence of the important Mughal grandees upon them. So much so that the imperial Wazir, Safdar Jung went more than half way to seek their ready cooperation in the imperial affairs. This further improved their status, fortunes and strength.

Getting virtual sanction from the Mughal Emperor, the Jat State became a reality. In view of the manifest imbecility and impotence of the Mughal Emperors in containing the expansionist powers elsewhere, there was little possibility of their retaining their grip over the region concerned. Hence, irrespective of the advent of the Jats, the supercession of the Mughal power in the area looked a foregone conclusion, especially when the ever encroaching formidable Marathas and ambitious Jai Singh were casting covetous glances over the area. The Jats forestalled the rest in the fray. Even though detrimental to the interests of the empire, their emergence guaranteed to the ruled peace, happiness and security and also prevented the Maratha peril from coming dangerously close to the Mughal capital. In the imperial wars outside their own region, they played the role of faithful feudatories. There is little to suggest that the ambitious Jats were interested in wiping out the Mughal Empire, although it would be equally wrong to say that they wanted its restoration to its former virility and strength.

The increasing involvement of the Jats in the Imperial affairs, if it contributed to their steady growth, also entangled them with the hostile powers, Marathas, Imad, Abdali and his Indian confederates. All this while, the Jats also wished to have a decisive say in the contemporary affairs, and to ensure their influence over Delhi's government. They enjoyed such a conspicuous position that in the struggle for supremacy over the Mughal Empire, their alliance and failing that their neutrality was coveted by both the Marathas and the Afghans. As the most powerful Indian potentate, the Jat King, Suraj Mal, occupied a key position in the settlement of the contemporary affairs in the post-Panipat period. The imperial Wazir-designate being his dependent, the Jat Raja desired to control through his installation the imperial government; although as a prudent man he would not risk a war on that score. Suraj Mal's death in 1763 marks the close of the brightest chapter of the Jat history; after him there was a gradual decline in their fortunes and glory.

The treatment of the subject under study has to face problems peculiar to itself arising out of the nature of the subject. It needs no stress that the mind of the people is better and more correctly revealed by their own writings. In case of the Jat people who generally do not have a respectable tradition of literary activity, the paucity of any systematic and complete history from their side causes difficulties to a student of their history. The non-Jat sources[5] do provide facts about the Jat activities. But an exclusive dependence on them is likely to result in an unbalanced view. From wherever culled, facts are sacred but inferences drawn on their basis are apt to be influenced by the human element. In interpretation of a given situation personal likes and dislikes and preferences and prejudices are bound to creep in. We have thus to be wary, critical and analytical, when handling such material on a people who were opposed to the Mughals.

Out information about the Jats and their activities comes mostly from the varied Persian sources - the Mughal Official documents, the Court histories, the general or provincial histories, biographical sketches written by the Mughal public servants or by the Muslim historians of stray places, etc.

Among these there are some (e.g. *Roznamcha, Iqbal, Tal.*, and *Siyar*) which generally take a judicious view of the Jats. But side by side there are some (e.g. J. *Records, Ahkam, K.K. Shah, M.U., Ahwal* and *Shah Alam Nama*), which, though valuable, are not always impartial in their assessment of the Jats.

Of necessity, much of the information had to be taken from the sides of those opposed to the Jats. Putting absolute reliance on the sources (falling in this category) and paraphrasing them, would not help us form the balanced view for our present subject. Due allowance has to be made for their place of origin and the bias and prejudices of the authors concerned. It is not that they are not important—in fact quite a number of these are our most vocal sources and but for them our picture would have remained grossly incomplete—yet they need to be critically assessed, separating chaff from the grain.

It may not be out of place to say a word about Fransoo's *Tawarikh-i-Hunud,* one of the mss. being used here, which, though written in Persian

5. The sources we are consulting here for the first time include *Tarikh-i-Bharatpur, Tawarikh-i-Hunud, Waqa-i-Bharatpur, Waqa-i-Jang-i-Bharatpur, Safinat-ul-Aish,* Letter of Safdar Jang to Suraj Mal, various works of Somnath and Devdutta's account. These and rest of the sources screened thoroughly by me in the context of the Jat history, have been listed in the Bibliography with brief comments about their merits and demerits wherever necessary.

stands out from other Persian sources. It does not suffer from complexes and prejudices found in a number of other Persian sources. Though a later work, its author, a foreigner, based it on the information derived from the indigenous sources and meant it to present to Captain Abraham Lockett.

The Marathi documents (amply used by us in the context of the Jat history) also are our extremely valuable source, being exactly contemporary despatches. But they cover only a period of roughly three decades. They begin referring to the Jats from seventeen thirties when the Marathas came into contact with the nascent Jat power. Conceding that the references to the Jats in them are incidental and brief and not always fair, made as they were by an expansionist people about a rising and ambitious people, a careful handling of these letters serves as a corroborative evidence besides supplying altogether new information on several points.

Wendel's French account of the Jats is a very valuable source for Jat history, especially because its author was a contemporary observer of things relating to the reigns of Suraj Mal and Jawahar Singh. After its minute perusal we found that it contains some useful details which somehow escaped the attention of the other historians. In assessing this narrative we have to keep in mind that it was meant for European readers and perhaps to help the English (E.I.Co.) in framing their policy. The proverbial apathy of the Occident for the Orient is easily discernible in it[6]. Wendel is also inclined to taking undue interest in recording scandals about the Jat chiefs[7]. This taints the details of his important work.

Among the meagre sources emanating strictly from the Jat side, the compilations of Devdutta and Kahna Ram, though otherwise useful, contain only a few references to the political history of the period within our purview. The works of Somnath, written under the Jat patronage give us an idea of the literary and cultural activities at the Jat Court and the patronage given there to men of letters. Yet Somnath has only a few casual references to the political activities of the Jats. His works were written in the tradition of the Charan poets of the era of the "Ritikal poetry". They therefore, suffer from the literary conventions attaching importance to exaggerated glory of one's patron. Sudan, the author of *Sujan Charitra,* was the contemporary of Somnath. *Sujan Charitra* was known to earlier scholars also but was uncharitably dismissed as not useful[8]. Being mostly an eye-witness account, this work has its own importance. At places Sudan corroborates other sources. However, wherever he gives information, not available in other sources, we have to assess it as coming from a man having access to, and well acquaintance

6. But Fransoo the author of *Tawarikh-i-Hunud* is free from this defect.
7. *Infra*, Appendix B foot note 8-10.
8. Prof. A.L. Srivastava, (*Oudh*, p. 294) who upholds its general historical veracity, is the solitary exception.

with it. Yet *Sujan Charitra* gives the detailed account of the exploits of Suraj Mal between 1745 and 1753 only. Besides, it has to be borne in mind that, Sudan being a poet, his details have been at places overwhelmed by poetic flourishes.

The works of Somnath and Sudan suggest that the Jat Kings may have got their regular and complete history written at their Court. Further, it need not be emphasized that they had Persian Munshis in their employment. That some members of the Jat royal family themselves had a good knowledge of Persian is also known to us. In addition, we learn from a Marathi despatch that Jawahar Singh maintained a personal diary in which he made daily entries[9]. But unfortunately such valuable documents have not come down to us.[10]

In the case of the martial people like the Jats, who attach much value to deeds of valour, there is a great likelihood of oral traditions originating and spreading. The *Sakhas* which are in the form of 'floating literature', owe their origin to a period contemporary to the events and personalities concerned. They have a respectability of their own, in as much as they depict the seamy side of history treasured through generations of professional singers. For a people like the Jat at least, whose own written records about themselves are meagre, their tradition deserves our attention when we reconstruct their past history. Yet tradition, howsoever rich, has its own limitations; it has to be accepted only after putting it to the test of historical scrutiny.

We take this opportunity to clarify a few points about our study. First, it is mainly the activities of the Jats of Bharatpur between 1658 and 1763 A.D. that have been discussed. *Memoires des Jats* refers to two more centres of the Jat power - Patiala (under Ala Singh) and Gohad (under the Ranas)[11]. The sources of the period accessible to us do not throw much light on the activities of the Jats of Patiala and Gohad. They do not seem to have taken any significant part in the contemporary politics. In moments of crisis the Gohad Jats sought help from the powerful Jats of Bharatpur and at times took pride in accompanying their senior brethren in their march. Second, herein our primary aim has been to emphasize the external policy of the Jats of Bharatpur. We have alluded to the incidents of their internal history only to the extent of their relevance to our theme, in as much as they help in understanding particular events of the external history, or clarify the factors operating in their origin.

In converting the Hijari dates we have used *Taqwim-i-Hijari-o-Isawi* by A. Mahamud Khalidi (Karachi : 1952), which is based on Wustenfeld-

9. *S.P.D.*, XXIX, 119.
10. In response to my query the ex-Maharaja of Bharatpur informed me (25th September, 1963), "Unfortunately we have very little material of the type that you require..."
11. *Memoires des Jats* (Fr. Ms.), 4 footnote.

Mahlersche Vergleichungs-Tabellen der Mohammedanischen and Christlichen Zeitrechnung by Edward Mehler (Leipzig: 1926).

JAT IN THE PRE-AURANGZEB PERIOD

The evidence of anthropometry, linguistics, customs and institutions put together lead us to surmise that in all likelihood the Jats are the progeny of the famous republican people mainly of the Vedic stock - of the ancient Sind and Punjab[12].

We do not have the means to form an accurate and comprehensive view of their past, from the early medieval times to the commencement of the reign of Aurangzeb when their brethren of Mathura and Bharatpur step by step rose to political prominence. Our sources contain only incidental and meagre information about the Jats.

Majmal-ut-Tawarikh refers to an interesting legend about the Jats and the Meds. It says that both these people, the descendants of Ham, lived in Sind on the banks of the river Bahar. They indulged in mutual warfare. It so happened that the Jats overpowered the distressing Meds. But realizing the futility of a continuous struggle both the Jats and the Meds begged King Dajushan (Duryodhan) to appoint a King to rule over them and thereby ensure perpetual peace. The King nominated his sister Dassal (Duhsala), who governed them with wisdom. But despite its riches, dignity and greatness, there was no Brahman or wise man in the country. Hence from all over Hindustan thirty thousand Brahmans along with their families were sent there by her brother. They settled there and in time Sind became flourishing. The Queen later on made over a small portion of her realm to the Jats and appointed one of them, Judrat, as their chief. She made a similar provision for the Meds also[13]. This narrative would imply that the people designated as the Jats were present at the time of the war of Mahabharat. We, however, do not find the name Jat mentioned in the Mahabharat. As such, this account involving the mythological figures cannot be regarded to be historically accurate.[14]

---

12. For origin of the Jats their customs, usages, institutions habits etc. See my article, '*The Origin of the Jats*'. Also see Kashi Prasad Jaiswal, *Andhkar Yugin Bharat* (trans. Ram Chandra Varma), Kashi: Samvat 2014, p. 392; A.H. Bingley, *Sikhs* (Simla: 1899), p.12.
13. *Majmal-ut-Tawarikh* in Elliot, I, 104-105.
14. The above narrative including the despatch of the Brahmans to Sind seems to reflect the orthodox views of the time. The Jats displayed little enthusiasm in upholding the canons of orthodox religion and rigid caste system. *Chachnama* (Elliot, I, 187) observes, "There is no distinction among them (the Jats) of great and small"; *Zafarnama* (Elliot, III, 491) states, "they (the Jats) had cast aside all the restraints of religion", Qanungo, *Jats*, 24; Hutton, *Caste in India*, 33 with which Hindusim had come to be identified. It is likely that finding it difficult to endorse the socio-religious laxity of the Jats the orthodox elements invented this fanciful story, which is devoid of historical significance and validity, vide Qanungo, *Jats* 27.

Chachnama gives us a comparatively detailed information about the Jats of the lower Sind (especially of Brahmanabad) in relation to Rai Chach and Muhamad Bin Qasim. It says that after the subjugation of the fort of Brahmanabad Rai Chach "humiliated the Jats and the Lohanas and punished their chiefs". He imposed stern and disgraceful regulations on them. He ordered:

That they should never wear under-garments of shawl, velvet, or silk, but they might wear their outer-garments of silk, provided they were of a red of black colour: That they should put no saddles on their horses, and should keep their heads and feet uncovered: That when they went out they should take their dogs with them: That they should carry firewood for the kitchen of the chief of Brahmanabaḍ. They were to furnish guides and spies and were to be faithful when employed in such offices. They were to live in amity with Sarband, Son of Ahkam, and if any enemy came to invade the territory, or fight with Sarband, they were to consider it incumbent on them to assist him and steadily adhere to his cause. He thus finished his labours and established his rule. If any person showed rebellion or hostility, he took a hostage and exacted penalties until he should amend his conduct.[15]

Chachnama does not specify the causes of this unusual treatment but it is not difficult to surmise them. Resentful of external interference, and sensitive to autocracy the self-governing Jats have, from earliest times, mostly showed an instinctive attachment to democratic ways.[16] They were indifferent to the rigidity and exclusiveness in the socio-religious structure and generally had a natural apathy to the monarchical form of government, facts which gradually came to the forefront in the Hindu society under the hegemony of the Gupta Kings and thereafter[17]. In such a state of affairs, Chach, a high caste Brahman might have harboured a feeling of abhorrence for the defiant and unorthodox Jats.[18]

---

15. *Chachnama* in Elliot, I, 150-151.
16. Bingley's (*Sikhs* 11-12); U.N. Sharma, *Jaton Ka Navin Itihas* (Jaipur: 1977), 38.
17. K.P. Jaiswal, (Trans. Ram Chandra Varma), *Andhkar Yugin Bharat*, 391; R.C. Majumdar, *Corporate life in Ancient India*, 165-167.
18. It is interesting to observe certain basic similarities between the way of life which Manu ordained for low people and the treatment which Chach meted out to the Jats of Brahmnabad. Moreover, although there is no specific information in the Arabic and Persian sources about the Jats accepting Buddhism at that period, we have positive knowledge about the prevalence of Buddhism at the period in the Indus Valley (vide M. Habib, "The Arab Conquest of Sind", *Islamic Culture* Jan. 1929), in which the Jats formed the bulk of the population. Hence, it is not unlikely, that the Jats had definite leanings towards Buddhism, which was more agreeable to their ways and practices.[III]

III. Taking note of these similar ways and practices, Dr. Dharma Kirti, a modern Buddhist has written a book जाट जाति प्रछन्न बौद्ध है। (1999 Ed., New Delhi)

Basically peasant communities do not fit in Varna System. Their hardwork or labour in the fields puts them in the Sudra category, while their agriculture

It is also likely that the years long[19] stubborn resistance by the Jats and others to Chach during the latter's siege of Brahmanabad provided him the immediate provocation for adopting the repressive measures.

Chachnama refers to the Jats again at the time of Muhammad Bin Qasim's invasion of Sind. Following a query from the conqueror about the position of the Jats under Chach and Dahir, Sisakar, the minister of the fallen King, apprised him of the restrictions imposed upon them. The minister added that it, was incumbent upon them to supply escorts and conduct parties and serve as guides. If any injury befell a person on the road they had to answer for it. The minister went on that these people 'have the disposition of savages and always rebelled against their sovereigns. They plunder on the roads and within territory of Debal all join with them in their highway robberies'.

Having heard this, Qasim retained the same regulations against the Jats[20] of the eastern areas but not against those of the western, who, probably as mercenaries, had joined the invader against the oppressive Dahir.[21]

Other casual references to the Jats appertain to their obstructing the path of foreigners, a fact in some cases confirmed by the traditional

---

profession categorises them the Vaishya and when they fight in the battlefield definitely they are warrior class. If we peep through the thin curtain of exaggerated and biased portion of *Chachnama*, it also indicates that the Jats were cultivators, labourers (Supplying wood to royal kitchen) and these famous swordsmen were protecting Prince Sarband against invaders and guarding highways. *Chachnama* (Islamabad, 1982) p. 100, 166-167.

It is to be noted that restrictions were imposed on the defiant Jats including Summeras and Sammas tribes by the Brahman rulers- Chach and Dahir in Lohana territory in lower Sind only, whereas in northern territories held by the Vassal Buddhist Chiefs, the Jats were free from all restrictions. The overthrow of Brahman rule by the Arabs changed the socio-political atmosphere in lower Sind also and the Jats became political assertive as is evident from the Jat revolt against Sultan Mahmood in 1025 A.D.—Editor.

19. *Chachnama* in Elliot, I, 147.
20. *Ibid.*, 187.
21. Mirza Kalich Beg's translation of *Chachnama* quoted by Qanungo, *Jats*, 28. Despite the treatment accorded to the Jats by Chach and the Arab conquerer being similar, their approach and the underlying circumstances were basically different. The policy of Chach, "an implacable foe of the Jats" (Qanungo, *Jats*, 28), was characterized by feelings of hostility and vengeance. Muhammad Bin Qasim, on the contrary, was mainly governed by the dictates of expediency. The Arab generally retained the Hindu officials and duly respected their counsels on various matters. In keeping with it the Arab general continued the harsh measures against the Jats of Lahana" (according to Prof. Habib "most backward and savage section of the race") but spared the rest inhabiting other regions (Vide - M. Habib, 'The Arab Conquest of Sind', *Islamic Culture* October, 1929, 600, 601, footnote) such as Sawandi. (See *Chachnama* in Elliot, I, 190). As the Arabs generally maintained status-quo, it can safely be presumed that Chach's stern regulations also applied only to a section of that people.

accounts and persisting tradition of the Jats. *Kamil-ut-Tawarikh* notices the Jats seizing upon the roads of Hajar and plundering the corn of Kaskar. They had "planted posts in all directions towards the desert". At the orders of the reigning khalifa, Ajif bin Isa marched against them (219 A.H. - 834 A.D.). He was busy suppressing their chief Muhammad bin Usman for seven months. After killing many of the Jats, Ajif is said to have carried twenty seven thousand of them (including women and children) to Baghdad.[22]

Futuh-ul-Buldan alludes to the Jats having sway over the territory of Kikan. Amran, the governor of Sind, (sometime after 221 A.H. - 836 A.D.) attacked and subjugated them[23]. According to *Tabqat-i-Akbari,* Mahmud of Ghazni undertook his seventeenth expedition in 417 A.H. against the Jats (of the region of the Jud hills) who had molested his army on its return from Somnath. Mahmud is said to have organised a fleet of 1400 boats, while the Jats could gather 4,000 boats (or 8,000 according to some). A naval fight ensued between the two at Multan, in which most of the Jats were drowned. The rest were slain.[24]

Tarikh-us-Subuktigin describes that two or three thousand mounted Jats attacked the Ghazanvide commander Tilak (425 A.H. - 1034 A.D.) "chiefly for the purpose of seizing his property and money", when he was persuing the rebel, Ahmad Nialtigin in the lower Panjab. They carried away his son and subsequently killed Ahmad also. The Jats returned his son and the head of the deceased only after getting a portion of the promised "reward".[25]

Taj-ul-Maasir refers to the rising of the Jats of Haryana (588 A.H. - 1192 A.D.) under Jatwan, following the defeat of Prithwi Raj Chauhan. Jatwan besieged the Muslim garrison at Hansi. Hearing about it, Qutb-ud-Din hurriedly moved against the Jats. Jatwan raised the siege to confront Qutb-ud-Din, but was beaten after a sanguinary fight[26]. We are told that in Samvat 1252 (1195 A.D.) a meeting of the Sarva Khap Panchayat (Federal clan council of the Jats and other kindred people of Upper Doap, Haryana and the neighbouring areas) was held in a forest between the villages of Bhoju and Banera under the chairmanship of Rao Vijay Rao of the village, Sisauli. This meeting decided among others to raise a big militia "to defend the sarva Khap area against a

---

22. *Kamil-ut-Tawarikh* in Elliot, II, 247-248.
23. *Futuh-ul-Buldan* in Elliot, I, 128.
24. *Tabqat-i-Akbari* quoted in Elliot, II, Note D 477-478.
25. *Tarikh-us-Subuktgin* in Elliot, II, 132-133.
26. *Taj-ul-Maasir in* Elliot, II, 217. The Allahabad edition of Elliot's volume does not contain the following page (i.e. 218). As such, we have supplemented the above incident from Prof. Qanungo's *History of the Jats,* 33, which contains extracts from *Taj-ul-Maasir*, taken from the former edition of Elliot's history.

suspected attack by Muhammad Ghori and to protect the area from botandplunder".[27]

The Jat rose again when Timur invaded India. *Malfuzat-i-Timuri* testifies to his satisfaction over killing 2,000 Jats of a village Tohna near Sarsuti. He found them "demon like", "robust", "marauding" and "as numerous as ants, and locusts".[28] We learn that in order to hold deliberations over the problem of his invasion, a Sarva Khap Panchayat meeting was held in Samvat 1455 (1338 A.D.) in the forest of Chaugama under the presidentship of Deo Pal Rana. It passed the resolutions that they should "vacate the villagers, sending the children and women to the forests and that the able-bodied persons should take up arms and destroy the army of Timur".[29] The Panchayat militia harassed the forces of Timur, while they were advancing from Meerut towards Hardwar. In the process the former lost 6,000 men.[30]

Another invader Babar found the Jats inhabiting a tract between Mil-ab and Bhera mountains. He remarks: If one go (sic. goes) into Hindustan the Jats and Gujars always pour down in countless hordes from hill and plain for loot in bullock and buffalo...When we reached Sialkot, they fell in tumult on poor and needy folks who were coming out of the town to our camp, and stripped them bare. I had the silly thieves sought for, and ordered two or three of them cut to pieces.[31]

It is said that in response to Rana Sanga's call a Jat militia of 5,000 from the Upper Doab and another from the Brij participated in the battle of Sikari against Babar.[32]

Tarikh-i-Sher Shahi speaks of one redoubted Jat chief named Fateh Khan who ravaged the country of Lakhi Jungle and the road from Lahore to Panipat. Haibat Khan, the governor of the Panjab, crushed Fateh Khan and his associates.[33]

As is to be seen the Jats later opposed, to their worth, Nadir Shah (at Karnal) and Ahmad Shah Abdali (at Manupur). These examples suffice to show their tendency of opposing the foreign invaders. K.R. Qanungo rightly remarks:

They (the Jats) have shown in all periods - whether against Sultan Mahmud of Ghazni, or against Nadir Shah and Ahmad Shah Abdali -

---

27. Kanha Ram (Hindi Ms.) in possession of Chowdhary Qabul Singh of Shoram Muzaffarnagar 4-5. An entry of Bhadon, Samvat 1254 (August-September, 1197) in this Ms. (6) claims that a big Jat militia fought (near Meerut) and repulsed the Turkish forces. But the date and the result of the conflict are doubtful. Habibullah, *Foundation of Muslim Rule in India,* 62, 81 (footnote 38).
28. *Malfuzat-i-Timuri* and following it *Zafarnama* in Elliot, III, 248-249 and 491.
29. Kanha Ram (Hindi Ms.), 13.
30. *Ibid.*
31. *Memoires of Babur,* quoted by Qanungo, *Jats*, 33.
32. Kahna Ram (Hindi Ms.), 15.
33. *Tarikh-i-Sher Shahi* in Elliot, IV, 398-399.

the same propensity to fall upon the rear of a retreating army underterred by the heaviest odds, or the terror-inspiring fame of great conquerors. When encountered they showed the same obstinate and steady courage unmindful of the carnage on the field or of the miseries that were in store for them after defeat.[34]

Side by side they also resorted to pillage and plunder. Yet it would be too much to conclude that the whole Jat people were professional robbers or "a race of thieves"[35] or that they took to robbery as a permanent mode of living. The cradle land of the Jats - Sind and the Panjab- witnessed great political disorders and chaos during the period. The dynastic changes, the self-aggrandisement of high officials, and the intermittent foreign invasions put premium upon an efficient government. Administrative instability followed and this offered opportunities to the centrifugal forces to raise their heads. Essentially warlike, the Jats like many others did not lag behind. The unsettled conditions of the time held out to them irresistible temptations for satisfying their greed and asserting their tribal independence. Their tendency of resisting the invaders was pronounced but they were not well organised. Thus their military activities were, of necessity, confined to surprise raids, which seem to have been largely confused with plunder and robbery. On the one hand, the Jats laid their hands upon merchandise and on the other defied the authority and in course of time attempted to carve out their self-governing tribal spheres of influence. The reference in *Tarikh-i-Firuz Shahi*[36] that they along with other tribes established *mandals* "union of several villagers or tribes for a common object and mutual assistance"[37] - is significant in this context.

Another aspect of the activities of the Jats was their availability as mercenaries. This may have been partly responsible for the general impression of their being always lawless. We have already noticed that a section of the Jats was employed as mercenaries by Muhammad bin Qasim. Another instance of their being so employed relates to the times of Razia. The Jats of the Panjab were among the mercenaries recruited by her to reoccupy the throne.[38]

Ibn Khurdadba tells us that the Jat inhabitants skirting the route from Kirman to Mansura were entrusted with keeping watch over the route.[39] On the authority of *Chachnama* we have seen that in the times of Dahir the Jats served as escorts and were responsible for the safety of travellers.

---

34. Qanungo, *Jats*, 30.
35. *Memories des Jats* (Fr. Ms.), 45 footnote.
36. *Tarikh-i-Firuz Shahi* in Elliot, III, 245.
37. Qanungo, *Jats*, 32 footnote.
38. Habibullah, *The Foundation of Muslim Rule in India*, p. 265.
39. Ibn Khurdadba in Elliot, I, 14.

The traditional accounts of the Jats record that on many occasions the Sarva Khap Panchayat of the Jats and others met to express its deep resentment against the administrative oppression, unjust restrictions and humiliating exactions on ground of religious discrimination. In some cases they reportedly resolved to oppose the Muslim administration in case the oppressive measures were not withdrawn.[40] We do not have means to ascertain the dates and details of the resolutions of the Sarva Khap Panchayat. They may yet reflect the general attitude of the Jats towards the contemporary affairs.

Yet another significant aspect of their activities, which has often been ignored, is their proverbial association with agriculture. It is true that almost all the authorities barring *Chachnama* do not mention their agricultural pursuits. But there is a great agricultural tradition among them. *Chachnama* preserves a significant reference in this regard. It explicitly mentions that "the agriculturists in this part of the country (Sawandi region) were Jats".[41] This may be taken to suggest their association with the soil, though they might not have been exclusive tillers in other areas. It is not without significance to note that they presently inhabit some of the most fertile areas. This may suggest that the agriculturist Jats preferred to migrate to the areas where they could continue their traditional mode of life. About the Jats of the Upper Doab and the neighbouring places we have their own traditional accounts to indicate their continued deep attachment to their time-honoured profession.[42]

40. For details see Kanha Ram (Hindi Ms.), 6, 8-9, 12, 14.
41. *Chachnama* in Elliot, I, 190.
42. For details see Kanha Ram (Hindi Ms.), 7, 10, 12-14.

I

The Jat Uprising of 1669

Paradoxical though it might appear and strange though it might seem, the Jat uprising of 1669 under Gokul occurred at a time when the Mughal government was by no means weak or imbecile. In fact this period of Aurangzeb's reign witnessed the climax of the Mughal Empire.[1] During the early medieval period frequent breakdown of law and order often induced the Jats to adopt a refractory course.[2] But, with the establishment of the Mughal rule, law and order was effectively established and we do not come across any major Jat revolt during the century and a half preceding the reign of Aurangzeb.

CAUSES OF THE REVOLT

The underlying causes of the Jat revolt of 1669 have not been properly analysed so far. Historians have generally ascribed the said rebellion to Aurangzeb's religious discrimination and the oppression of local officers.[3] These, however, seem to have been the contributory causes but neither the sole nor the dominant factors which precipitated the revolt. Long before Aurangzeb even the bigotry of Firuz Tughluq and Sikandar Lodi[4] did not provoke the Jats for any such rebellion. It leaves the impression that religious persecution of the Emperor was not responsible for the Jat insurrection. When *Jiziya* was imposed ten years later, it did not create a similar stir among the Jats and the outrageous conduct[5] of the imperial officers seldom provoked a revolt of this magnitude. Hence, the real causes of the Jat rebellion of 1669 lay deeper than have been assigned to it so far.

---

1. J.N. Sarkar, *History of, Aurangzib* (Calcutta: 1912), I, Introduction, XI-XIII; F.X. Wendel, *Memoires des Jats,* 10.
2. For details, Sarkar, *Aurangzib*, I, Introduction, XXVIII f.
3. K.R. Qanungo, *History of the Jats* (Calcutta: 1925), 34; Sarkar, *Aurangzib*, III, 291-294; vide also Gokul Chandra Dikshit, *Brajendra Vansha Bhaskar* (Agra: 1983 V.S.), 11; Y.P. Shastri *Jat Kshatriya Itihas* (Hardwar; 1944), 73-76; Thakur Deshraj, *Jat Itihas*, 629; U.N. Sharma, *Itihas*, 88 ff.
4. For treatment of the Hindus under Firuz Tughlug, see *Tarikh-i-Firozshahi,* in Elliot, (Allahabad edition), III, 365-377 and for destruction of temples by Sikandar Lodi, see *Tarikh-i-Daudi*, in Elliot, IV, 447.
5. Niccolao Manucci, *Storia Do Mogor,* trans. William Irvine (Calcutta: 1966), II, 424; Bernier, *Travels in Mogul Empire,* trans. A. Constable (Delhi: 1968), 231, Satish Chandra, *Uttar Mughal Kalin Bharat Ka Itihas,* 10.

One of the main causes may be sought in the changed nature and scope of the Mughal government under Aurangzeb[6] which was detrimental to the democratic and tribal way of life of the Jat fraternity. Akbar assiduously tried to build a comprehensive state based on religious and social freedom, respect for village autonomy and willing acquiescence of the people at large.[7] The nature of the Mughal despotism generally retained its previous character under Jahangir.[8] In spite of Shahjahan's intolerant attitude in the beginning, the government in his times also displayed a "sense of justice" and kept the interests of the people in its view.[9]

But, with the accession of Aurangzeb, the comprehensive nature of the state gradually yielded to a narrow and overcentralized despotic regime.[10] A despotic system rests upon the personality of the ruler which motivates the entire administrative machinery.[11] Aurangzeb was gifted among other qualities with an astonishing industry, a dogged perseverance and an indomitable will. This bred in him a deep distrust of an intolerance for others, a narrow outlook, a "one track mind" and a passion to personally "supervise every minute detail of administration."[12] Theoretically, the basis of the despotism remained the same as under Akbar, but in practice Aurangzeb's personal character and his ideal of the state moulded it into an over centralized autocracy.[13] The enlightened and generous outlook of Akbar caring for all his people alike,[14] gave way to a narrow political outlook.

The over-centralized set-up, accompanied by the narrow outlook of the ruler, was naturally antagonistic to the tribal and democratic outlook of the Jats. An instinctive attachment to democratic ways and a "sturdy independence" have throughout been their chief characteristics.[15] They have a pronounced aversion to external interference and have been accustomed to self governance of their internal affairs.[16] The tendency to settle everything pertaining to their

---

6. Sarkar, *Auranzib*, I, Introduction, XV.
7. Beni Prasad, *History of Jahangir* (London: 1930), 88 ff.
8. *Ibid.*, 444f.
9. B.P. Saksena, *History of Shahjahan of Delhi* (Allahabad: 1938), 269, 271 and 296.
10. Sarkar *Aurangzib* (Calcutta: 1924), V, 455-457, 477f., see also III, 216.
11. J.N. Sarkar *Mughal Administration* , 11, 16 and 254.
12. For details see Sarkar, *Aurangzib*, I, Introduction, XV, vol. V. 1, 2, 455ff., also *studies in Mughal India* (Calcutta: 1919), 60-63, *Anecdotes of Aurangzeb* (Calcutta: 1925), 59, 107; *Storia*, II, 309, 366 and 371; Ishwari Prasad, *A Short History of Muslim Rule in India* (Ist ed. Allahabad), 728ff.
13. M. Athar Ali, *The Nobility Under Aurangzeb* (Asia Publishing House: 1966), 95; Sarkar, *Aurangzib*, V, 477ff., Vol. III, 248-264 et passim; *Mughal Administration*, 18; H.G.Keene, *The Mughal Empire* (London: 1866), 27; Ishwari Prasad, *op. cit.*, 721 and 732.
14. A.L. Srivastava, 'Akbar's Theory of Kingship'. *Journal of Indian History*, 1962.
15. *The Punjab Castes*, 102.
16. A.H. Bingley, *Sikhs* (Simla: 1899), 11, says, "From the earliest times, Jats have been remarkable for their rejection of the monarchical principle and their strong partiality for self governing commonwealth".

daily life in accordance with their cherished ideals has been, and still is, in vogue among them. Unfortunately, we do not have any contemporary written evidence about the Jats of the Mathura region during the time of Aurangzeb. But the evidence of their tribal and democratic practices has come down to us in respect of certain other regions.[17] The Jats being a homogeneous people, it would not be unfair to believe that those in perview also breathed almost, the similar spirit. Giving due regard to their tradition customs and laws, Akbar issued two *firmans,* dated 8th Ramzan, 987 A.H. and 11th Ramzan, 989 A.H. granting internal freedom to the clan-councils of the Jats of the Upper Doab region in religious matters and "to carry out their functions according to their ancient customs and laws".[18] Akbar's sagacious policy seems to have been followed until the time of Shah Jahan. Jahangir sometimes showed the top Jat leaders the unique favour of calling them to his audience and giving *khilats.*[19] But Aurangzeb, reversed this policy. He "restricted the activities" of their customary institutions. This, along with his religious fanaticism, created "concern" among the Jats. They discussed the issue in a meeting at Chhaprauli (1718 V. S.) and decided to protest against the new laws and pleaded for the reversion of the policy of the Delhi Court.[20] We have no information about Aurangzeb's specific treatment of the Jats of Mathura. But, on the basis of his dealings with the Jats of the Uper Doab region, it may be inferred that the former also suffered a similar encroachment upon their cherished customary rights was by itself a matter of resentment for the tribal Jats. And, as it came after the spell of Akbar's liberal treatment, the feeling of resentment must have been deep and strong. The courageous Jats, who had reminisences of their republican past and who still retained that spirit, could hardly afford to remain quiet before an immensely centralized system based on a narrow outlook which threatened to devour their traditional tribal and democratic ways.

---

17. The clan groups of the Jats of the Upper Doab region managed their own affairs, military, political, religious, social and economic, in medieval times. M.C. Pradhan, *The Political System of the Jats of Northern India* (Oxford: 1966), chapter IV, V. The Jats of Rajputana and central and eastern Panjab had organised small republics; Bingley, *Sikhs*, 1.
18. Akbar's *farmans* quoted by M.C. Pradhan, *op. cit.*, 97.
19. Mandate of Jahangir, dated 3rd Rabi I, 1030 A.H. referred to by M.C. Pradhan, *op. cit.*, 98, 112.
20. Kanha Ram (Hindi Ms., Muzaffarnagar Records), 17; The date of the meeting is, however, wrong because by that time (i.e. 1661 A.D.), the *Jiziya*, referred to in the proceedings of the Federal Council meeting, had not been imposed.

Probably, not less significant was the role of the economic factors in leading the Jat peasantry to rebellion. In actual operation the Mughal revenue assignment system was extremely harmful to the interests of the peasants and the Empire itself.[21] As the proprietor of land, the Emperor assigned a certain piece of land to the officials in lieu of their pay and also to enable them to defray the expenses over their troops, on condition of their paying a sum to the Emperor out of the surplus revenue. Such grants were called *jagirs.*[22] Since they were mainly grants of revenue out of which the holders (who were usually *mansabdars*) maintained their quota of troops for the Empire, the tendency was to fix revenue at the highest possible rate almost equal to the surplus produce.[23] Even this high rate went on increasing with the passage of time.[24] Under the circumstances, the peasants were financially hit very hard.[25] They were usually left with the barest minimum needed for supporting their lives.[26]

What added further to the hardships of the cultivators was the frequent transfer of the *jagirs* to different assignees. The *jagirdars* held their *jagirs* at the pleasure of the Emperor. Bhimsen remarks, "There is no hope of a *jagir* being left with the same officer next year."[27] This constant insecurity of the tenure of office proved unfortunate in two ways. Firstly it offered little incentive to the holders to exert for alleviating the distress of their tenantry. Instead it led them to employ all possible tactics to extort money from the peasantry.[28] Secondly, quite often at the time of the transfer the hard hit peasants of the same *jagir* were pressurised to pay the same sum twice, first to the collectors of the outgoing *jagirdar* and then to those of the incoming one. Thus this system ended in a "mad looting" of the peasants by the rival collectors.[29] The consequences were worse if a *jagir* was farmed out. Bhimsen points out, "when a *jagirdar* sends a collector to his *jagir*, he first takes an advance from the latter by way of loan. This collector, on arriving in the village, fearing lest a second man who had given a larger loan to the *jagirdar* was following (to supplant him), does not hesitate to collect the rent with every oppression".[30]

---

21. Bernier, 225-226; Sarkar, *Auranzib,* V. 452-453.
22. Bernier, 224.
23. Irfan Habib, *The Agrarian System of Mughal India* (Bombay: 1963), 318f.
24. *Ibid*, 320.
25. Bernier, 230.
26. I. Habib, *op. cit.*, 319, Sarkar, *Mughal Administration*, 80.
27. *Dilkusha* by Bhimsen, quoted by Sarkar, *Aurangzib,* V, 453; Bernier, 227.
28. I. Habib, *op.cit.*, 320; Bernier, 227.
29. Sarkar, *Aurangzib,* V, 446-447,, 452-453; I. Habib, *op.cit.*, 268.
30. *Dilkusha, op.cit.*, V, 453; Khafi Khan also testifies to the oppression of the revenue collectors in his time. *Khafi Khan*, I, 157-158.

If the report of Khan-i-Dauran to Aurangzib is any indication, the lot of the peasants attached to *Khalisa* was by no means better either.[31] And if the peasants refused to pay the revenue, very severe punishment was meted out to them. At times they were left with no other option than to sell their women, children and cattle, or to run away from their home to avoid extermination through-ill-treatment.[32] It is not that the Mughal government did not take measures to prevent their exploitation. But the measures were often inadequate and the officers generally discovered a way out to perpetuate their unusual excesses.[33] Thus the grievances of the peasantry generally went unredressed.[34]

In its actual operation Mughal assignment system became extremely "ruinous to the peasants and ultimately harmful to the interests of the Empire".[35] The exploitation by the collectors increased as the time went on.[36] At last a stage was reached when "excessive acts of oppression" by the officers could lead some of the peasants to shifting their hand from plough to the sword,[37] as happened in the case of the Jats following the atrocities of Abdun Nabi. We know it on the testimony of Shah Waliullah that "the cultivators of the villages between Delhi and Akbarabad were of the Jat caste".[38] Wendel also refers to the rack-renting of the tenants but is not sure if the Jats resorted to lawlessness around Agra as a retaliation against oppression or as a means to gratify their lust for further gains.[39]

Against this background, it was quite natural for the Jats to ventilate their resentment over the prevailing assignment system as agriculture occupied the uppermost place in their life. "To be a Jat is to be a ploughman",[40] is the testimony of the French Missionary F.X. Wendel, who lived among the Jats under study for quite a long time.

---

31. See the report quoted by Sakar, *Studies in Mughal India*, 223-224.
32. Bernier, 205, 226, 227; *Storia*, II, 423; I. Habib, *op.cit.*, 322-329. The burden of the prevailing systems of giving presents and the sale of governments, also ultimately fell upon the agricultural classes. Sarkar, *Mughal Administration*, 84f., *Aurangzib*, V, 467; Bernier, 230.
33. I. Habib, *op. cit.*, 273 ff; Bernier, 225, 231, 235; Sarkar, *Mughal Administration*, 80-81, *Aurangzib*, III, 291f. M. Athar Ali (*op.cit.*, 150) adds, "He (Aurangzib) was prepared to forgive or overlook any disobedience to his orders where his own military interests were not involved."
34. I. Habib, *op.cit.*, 247 and 297; Sarkar, *Mughal Administration*, 80-81.
35. Sarkar, *Aurangzib*, V, 452.
36. I. Habib, *op.cit.*, 324.
37. *Storia* (II, 424) says, "Sometimes these *faujdars* commit excessive acts of oppression, which cause rebellion and bring on battles". I, Habib, *op.cit.*, 329.
38. *Siyasi Muktubat* of Shah Waliullah Dahlavi, (Pers. Text and Urdu trans. by Prof. K.A. Nizami, 2nd ed., Delhi), 2.
39. *Memoires des Jats* (Fr. Ms.), 3.
40. *Ibid.*

The author of *Maasir-ul-Umra* seems to represent the official attitude when he remarks that the Jats of Mathura and Agra pretended to be agriculturists.[41] Modave, a keen French observer who visited India (1774-76), did not, however, fail to be impressed by the industry and voluntary attachment to and skill in agriculture which the Jats of Bharatpur displayed. Modave remarks, "The Jats are, in general, good men and would occupy themselves voluntarily in agriculture and the arts if they were not obliged almost always to keep themselves under arms.....One thing in my judgement does honour to the industry of the Jats; if is that......the plain is not as much abandoned as might be imagined and the fields there are better maintained than one would have expected.[42]

It is obvious that an oppressive system goes hard with the agriculturists. Its sharp reaction among the Jats, culminating into a rebellion, appears to have been because of their adventurous disposition and martial character.[43] Probably not many agricultural communities possessed obstinate courage, indomitable spirit, heroic valour and tribal unity of the Jats which were needed to transfer a deep resentment into a military resistance. The Jats had been a race of warrior agriculturists. A close look into their past reveals that they were as keen to promote agriculture as to manufacture good arms and to receive military training.[44] They highly disapproved of the enhanced revenue, the levying of "harmful taxes" and "looting by government tax collectors". They were prone to opposing such things and other oppressions even by force, if the occasion demanded.[45] This may explain better why in face of similar provocations other weak agricultural communities remained more or less inactive while the Jat peasants unsheathed their swords.

An auxillary factor for the Jat rebellion was the circumstantial collusion between the Jat cultivators and the Jat *zamindars*.[46] The *zamindars* often displayed a tendency to disobey the Mughal government. In applying force against neighbours and in defying the imperial authority

---

41. *Maasir-ul-Umra*, (trans. H. Beveridge and B. Prasad (Calcutta: 1941), I, 436.
42. Modave's French account, trans. by Sarkar, *Islamic Culture*, XI, 1937, 387-388.
43. I. Habib's general statement (*op. cit.*, 330) that by inclination the mass of the people were anything but warlike does not entirely hold good in case of the Jats at least.
44. See the decision of the Federal Council meeting (held on 10th Asarh, 1256 V.S., under the presidentship of Hari Pal Rana at Tikri) of the Jats of the Upper Doab, in Kanha Ram (Hindi Ms.), 7.
45. See council decisions dated 1256 V.S. (Tikri), 1344 V.S. (Sikarpur), 1383 V.S. (Sisauli) and 1547 V.S. (Baraut), in Kanha Ram (Hindi Ms.), 7, 10-12, 14.
46. For full discussion about the *zamindars* in general see I. Habib, *op. cit.* 136-189, 334-338.

they had their own motives of self-aggrandisement.[47] But the nature of their struggle against the Mughals before the reign of Aurangzeb was more defensive and passive in character. For various reasons, however, it did not remain merely defensive for long.[48] Manucci draws attention to this change, "Usually there is some rebellion of the *rajaha* and *zamindars* going on in the Mughal kingdom".[49] Thus, with their peculiar set of grievances, the *zamindars* and cultivators joined hands to oppose a common foe. We see Gokul and the subsequent Jat *zamindars* providing leadership to the rank and file.[50] But the association between the early Jat *zamindar* leaders and their Jat followers must have been of a precarious nature. If the general practice of the numerous *zamindars* of the Empire is an index, Gokul and his predecessors[51] also might have pressed their usual *zamindari* rights[52] over the Jat peasantry thereby displeasing the latter. Apart from it, the Jats, more than any other people, are reputed to be deeply attached to personal freedom and to resenting external control.[53] These factors must have come in the way of a cohesive union between the *zamindars* and the peasants. But it seems that they gradually got over them.

It is against this background that the part played by Aurangzib's religious bigotry in the Jat rebellion may best be appreciated. By nature Aurangzeb was an orthodox man. He had claimed the Empire as "the champion of pure Islam."[54] As an Emperor he cherished the vision of a Muslim State. He had set his heart upon governing his composite Empire in accordance with the tenets of orthodox Islam.[55]

---

47. According to the writer of the Agyapatra (c. 17th century; quoted in Indian History Congress Proceedings, V, 405) the *zamindars* were eager "to acquire new possessions bit by bit and to become strong....and to seize (land and power) forcibly from some and to create enmities and depredations against others." Manucci (*Storia*, II, 405) also says, "Usually the viceroys and the governors are in a constant state of quarrel with the Hindu Princes and *zamindars*-with some because they wish to seize their lands; with others to force them to pay more revenue than is customary". Also see I. Habib, *op. cit.*, 334.
48. I. Habib, *op.cit.*, 338.
49. *Storia*, II, 434.
50. I. Habib, *op.cit.*, 341.
51. Hereditary succession to *zamindari* was a general law in the Mughal Empire, I. Habib. *op.cit.*, 154.
52. For *zamindari* rights see I. Habib, *op.cit.*, 136ff.
53. Bingley, *Sikhs*, 90-91; D. Ibbetson, *The Panjab Castes*, 102. The statements of both these are illustrative of the whole Jat people, "The Jat was not very submissive to his chiefs." "Jat", *Encyclopaedia Britannica*, XII.
54. Sarkar, *Aurangzib*, III, 81.
55. *Ibid.*, III, 81; S.R. Sharma, *Religious Policy of the Mughal Emperors* (Bombay; 1962), 132 and 152.

Aurangzeb pursued a fourfold course with regard to his religious policy, namely, promotion of Islamic practices, regulations against the Hindus, conversions to Islam, and destruction of temples. Although he made a cautions start, his fanaticism increased with the passage of time.[56] His supreme object was to make both Muslim and non-Muslim conform to the orthodox Holy Law.[57] Hence, he issued regulations aiming at suppressing the un-Islamic ceremonies and encouraging Muslim ways among the people at large.[58] They corresponded to Islam but contained little which was substantially prejudicial to any religion.

But certain other promulgations were provocative to the Hindus. The revival of pilgrimage tax is a case in point. In 1665, restrictions were imposed on the public celebration of the Hindu festivals of Holi and Diwali.[59] In 1668, the Hindu fairs were prohibited in the Empire. In 1665, *discriminative* duties were imposed upon the Hindus. They were ordered to pay 5% while the Muslims merely 2.5% duty on their goods. In 1667, the Muslims were totally freed from this burden.[60] The same discrimination was practised in respect of the taxes on the produce from gardens.[61]

These steps, apart from being a source of revenue, were intended to pressurise the Hindu into accepting Islam. In addition, Aurangzeb adopted seductive methods to attract the non-Muslims to Islam. He offered posts, money grants, public honour and even amnesty as rewards for embracing Islam.[62]

Above all Aurangzeb embarked upon the policy of temple demolition, here he displayed his characteristic subtlety of approach. Early in 1659 he declared that his Canon Law prohibited the construction of new temples but did not ordain the demolition of the old ones.[63] Gradually he opened

---

56. S.R. Sharma (*op.cit.*, 122) is of the opinion that the presence of Raghunath Das, Jai Singh and Jaswant Singh applied "a restraint upon his (Aurangzeb's) religious enthusiasm."
57. Sharma, *op.cit.*, 109; also 'Aurangzeb's Religious Policy *Indian Historical Quarterly*, III, 81. We would trace here the course of his religious policy only until the outbreak of the Jat rebellion in 1669.
58. For details see Sharma *op.cit.*, 107-115; Sarkar, *Aurangzib*, III, 81-90; *Storia*, II, 3-6.
59. *Mirat-i-Ahmedi* by Ali Muhammad Khan, (trans. by M.R. Lokhandwala Gaekwad Oriental Series, No. 146, 223; Manucci (*Storia*, II, 144), however, claims that Holi was stopped altogether.
60. *Mirat*, 237; *Storia*, II, 55-56 and 389; *Maasir-i-Alamgiri* by Muhammad Saqi Mustaid Khan (Pers. text, Bib. Ind. Series), 530.
61. For details see Sharma, *op.cit.*, 142, 144; Sarkar, *Aurangzib*, III, 275-279.
62. Sharma, *op.cit.*, 170; Sarkar, *Aurangzib*, III, 276.
63. The original *farman* in this respect in the name of *faujdar* of Banaras is preserved in the Bharat Kala Bhawan, Banaras Hindu University.

out. The temple of Somnath was razed to the ground early in his reign.[64] In 1665, he ordered to redemolish the repaired temples of Gujrat which had once been destroyed by him during his viceroyalty of the province.[65] He next ordered the pulling down of all the newly constructed temples in Orissa. In 1669, he fully unmasked himself. In that year he issued a general order for the destruction of the Hindu schools and temples and the suppression of their teaching and religious practices throughout the Empire.[66] Several temples pulled down in the wake of this order included those of Malarna and Vishwanath.[67] Thus, within a short span of 11 years, Aurangzeb reversed the liberal and tolerant approach of Akbar. While Akbar's liberalism had secured him the willing co-operation of his people, Aurangzeb's bigotry created mounting discontent among the suffering non-Muslims.[68]

Mathura, the birth centre of the Jat rising, suffered heavily in Aurangzeb's reign. This venerated place of Hindu worship was naturally an object of annoyance to Aurangzeb. He appointed Abdun Nabi, "a religious man", as *faujdar* of the place to "suppress the Hindus". This officer amassed, through questionable means, cash worth 93,000 *mohars* and thirteen lakhs of Rupees and valuables worth four and a half lakhs.[69] Abdun Nabi demolished a temple in the city and upon its ruins erected a Jama Masjid in 1661-1662. Next, in pursuance of Aurangzeb's order, he removed the stone railing of the famous temple of Keshava Rai in 1666.[70]

All these acts must have provoked the Jats further. We know that during the Sultanate danger to or suppression of their religion generated disaffection among them.[71] There is no reason to believe that a more systematic religious persecutions by zealot Aurangzeb did not offend the religious feelings of the Jats. Generally speaking, the Jats have never been orthodox in their religious belief.[72] They do not bother about the philosophical or the ethical nuances of religion, but the outward ritualistic aspects do commonly touch them. Hence, measures like the closing of fairs and festivals and desecration of religious places could not but have caused concern among them.[73]

---

64. *Ahkam-i-Alamgiri*, by Inayetullah (R.S.L. Pers. Ms., hereafter referred to as Ahkam), I, 10a.
65. *Mirat*, 231 and 233.
66. *Maasir*, 81; *Storia*, II, 143.
67. For details of temple destruction see Sharma, *op.cit.*, 130-133; Sarkar, *Aurangzib*, III, 265-267, 280-282.
68. Sharma *op.cit.*, 132-133.
69. *Maasir*, 83 and 73.
70. Sarkar, *Aurangzib*, III, 293.
71. *Ibid*, Aurangzib, I, Introduction, XXX.
72. *Ibid*, XXII, XXIII; Shastri *op.cit.*, 121; J.H. Hutton, *Caste in India*, 33.
73. Deshraj (*op.cit.*, 126-127), rightly points out that fairs and festivals occupy an important place in the life of the Jats; Shastri, *op.cit.*, 121.

The religious bigotry of Aurangzeb and the consequent sufferings of the non-Muslims, however, had not assumed full proportions by 1668-1669. Jiziya, orders for the exclusion of the Hindus from public officers and even the destruction of the temple of Keshava Rai at Mathura followed later. And yet the Jats under Gokul unfurled the banner of revolt.

The 'floating literature', or the "*Sakhas*"[74] as they are called among the Jats and other local people, refers to the visit of Samarth Guru Ram Das[75] who exhorted the Jats for insurrection.[76] He urged them to meet excess with excess.[77] He also impressed upon them that tyranny is a sin but to tolerate tyranny is a greater sin.[78] Having been urged and inspired by the Guru, Gokul took a vow to save the Hindus from destruction and rose in rebellion.[79]

No doubt, an implicit reliance cannot be put on an evidence of the natureof "*Sakhas*" alone. 'Floating literature,' is passed on from one generation to another orally and as such is subject to exaggeration and change in the process. However, considering the character of the Jats, it is difficult to reject the testimony of the "*Sakhas*" altogether. Few would acknowledge, much less a Jat, anybody's superiority for nothing. Besides, there is a very strong and persistent tradition among the Jats about the visit and activities of the Samarth Guru in the Jat areas.[80] The traditional account as preserved by Devdatta also avers that Ram Das came and exhorted the Jats to throw off the Mughal Yoke.[81] The teachings and philosophy of Samarth Guru are not the matter under study but it is very well known that he was a religious preacher of a different brand. He did not subscribe to a life negating philosophy. He was vitally interested in

---

74. The "*Jogis*" sing these "*Sakhas*" on '*ektara*' on festive occassions. The author listned to and collected these *Sakhas*" from various *Jogis* of Haryana and western U.P.
75. "*Sakha*" एक शक्ति पैदा हुई दक्षिण में वो उत्तर में आई,
बाह्मण के घर जन्म लिया फेर साधु वेष धारा
समर्थ गुरु की पदवी पाकर भारत का तारा।
76. Sobha Ram *Jogis* "*Sakha*".
बड़े-बड़े वीरों से विद्रोह के नाम अपने सामने प्रण लिया,
आर्य हिंद यह आर्य देश हमारा है।
77. "*Sakha*" धर्म बचाओ, देश बचाओ, यही वचन सबसे प्यारा है।
जुल्म को जुल्म से रोको, यह मेरा सबको कहणा।
78. "*Sakha*" जुल्म करना पाप घणा, जुल्म का शेणा पाप बड़ा।
79. "*Sakha*" गोकुल योद्धा ने पहला बिड़ा पान का आण चबाया।
गुरु ने हाथ धर उसके सिर पर नूं उसे समझाया।।
80. In course of my wide tour of the Jat area (Western U.P. and Haryana) I heard from elderly Jat people stories associating different local places with the Guru's sojourn. His interest in wrestling warlike activities and his journey in the company of his followers are characteristically typical of the Guru. The common Jats have to this day preserved the liveliest memorial of the Guru and his activities in the Jat area.
81. Devdatta (Hindi Ms., Muzaffarnagar Records), 12-13, side note.

contemporary problems facing the society and the country. His visit and exhortation seem to have considerably influenced Gokul and his followers.

The Jats being restive, fuel was ready. Only fire was needed and it was, according to the "*Sakhas*", provided by Ram Das.[82] K.R. Qanungo observes that in the revolt of 1669 "one flare of the mighty conflagration kindled throughout India by the missionary zeal of the Emperor" and revived the "Hindu Nationalism.[83] Thus religious factors played an appreciable part in the Jat insurrection.

The economic causes, although important, may not be over-emphasized.[84] The vices in the operation of the assignment system did not multiply overnight in the reign of Aurangzeb. Their increasing tendency was discernible even before him. But when the tightening grip of Aurangzeb threatened the age-old democratic and tribal traditions of the Jats, the economic factors made their weight felt heavily.

From the foregoing discussion it may be concluded that the Jat rebellion of 1669 was essentially the result of the political provocation, aggravated by the economic discontent and set ablaze by the religious persecution.

THE OUTBREAK OF THE REBELLION

The Year 1669 witnessed, the bursting forth of the pent up fury of the Jats into a very powerful revolt under the inspiring leadership of Gokul,[85] the *zamindar* of Tilpat. A remarkable feature of this rebellion was its composite character. Though the Jats counted for its majority and provided leadership to it, it consisted of other local people as well such as, Mev, Mena, Ahir, Gujar, Naruka, Panwar and others.[86] The rebels gathered at the village of Sahora (about 6 miles from Mathura). Abdun Nabi, the *faujdar* of Mathura, attacked them. At first he appeared to be gaining ground, but in the middle of the fighting he was killed on 12 May, 1669 (21st Zil-Hijja, 1079 A.H.)[87] Overjoyed at this success, Gokul

---

82. "*Sakha*" सारे देश में सूखा इंधण बिछा पड़ा है, आग लगावन चाहिए।
आग लगा दो मेरे वीरों आगे आवणा चाहिए।

83. Qanungo, *Jats*, 36 and 37.

84. I. Habib (*op.cit.*, 338-342), attributes the Jat rising only to economic factors and totally dismisses the others.

85. *Maasir*, 93; *Fatuhat-i-Alamgiri* by Ishwar Das Nagar (R.S.L. Ms.) 53 a; *Tazkirat-us-Salatin-i-Chaghtai* by Muhammad Hadi Kamwar Khan (R.S.L.Ms.) II, 166; *M.U.*,I, 437, and 618. Without mentioning by name, Wendel also refers to Gokul and his rebellion. *Memoires des Jats* (Fr. Ms.), 9. About Gokul it is said that his original name was Ola and he was the son of Roria Singh of Sinsini. Gokul settled first near Mahaban and finally at Tilpat, as the *zamindar*. Vide Ganga Singh, *Yadu Vansh*, I, *Bharatpur Rajvansh Ka Itihas* (Bharatpur: 1967), 43; U.N. Sharma, *Ittihas*, I, 89f.

86. Ganga Singh, *op.cit.*, I, 64-65.

87. *Maasir*, 83; *Roznamcha* also known as *Ibratnama* by Mirza Muhammad (R.S.L.Ms) 133; Kamwar (Pers. Ms.), II, 163; *M.U.*, I, 437 and 618.

ravaged the *paragana* and town of Sadabad (24 miles from Mathura) in the Doab.[88] The turbulance spread to Agra District also whereto Radandaz Khan was sent (13th May-22nd Zil-Hijja) with a force to put down the rebels. Aurangzeb appointed Saf Shikan Khan as the new *faujdar* of Mathura.[89] As arms failed to prevail, diplomacy was resorted to. The Mughal government offered to forgive Gokul provided he surrendered his spoils. But Gukul spurned the offer. On the other side, as the situation was assuming serious proportions, the Emperor had to proceed (28th November-14th Rajab, 1080 A.H.) in person to the disturbed area. On his way, on 4th December (20th Rajab) Aurangzeb learnt of the circumstances of rebellion in the villages of Rewara, Chandarakanta and Sarkhud (Sarkharu?). He despatched Hasan Ali Khan to attack these places. Till noon the insurgents fought with bows and muskets. Getting desperate thereafter, many of them, having performed the *Jauhar* of their women, fell upon the Khan. A fierce fight raged till the evening in which many imperialists and 300 rebels were killed. Hasan Ali Khan returned to the Emperor, taking 250 male and female prisoners. Aurangzeb was pleased with his performance. He made him the *faujdar* of Mathura in place of Saf Shikan Khan who had obviously failed in suppressing the rebels.[90]

Under Hasan Ali Khan, were placed 2,000 *barqandaz* troops, 1,000 archers, 1,000 musketeers, 1,000 rocketmen, and 25 pieces of cannons. Amanulla, the *faujdar* of the environs of Agra, was also ordered to help Hasan Ali. The latter immediately got engaged in quelling the rebellion. In January 1670, Gokul, with 20,000 Jat and other followers, rushed forward to face the imperialists at a place 20 miles from Tilpat. Both the sides suffered many casualties in the battle in which the Jats, despite showing utmost bravery, could not cope with the trained Mughals and their artillery. They retreated to Tilpat. Hasan Ali followed them and besieged the fortalice. Fighting continued for three days in which muskets and bows were used by the contestants. On the fourth day, the royalists charged the besieged from all sides and having made a breach in the walls entered Tilpat. Then ensued a sanguinary conflict. The Jats displayed their reckless courage and undaunted valour. The experienced Mughals gained the day but not before losing 4,000 men. Of the vanquished 5,000 lay dead, while 7,000 were arrested. Gokul, with his two associates including 'Sonki' (Udai Singh Singhi),[91] was captured

88. *Maasir*, 93; *M.U.*, I, 437 and 618; cf. *Fatuhat*, (pers. Ms.), 53a.
89. *Maasir*, 83 and 84; *M.U.*, I, 618, II, 673.
90. *Maasir*, 91-92; Also *Kamwar* (Pers. Ms.), II, 166; Sarkar, *Aurangzib*, III, 294.
91. It is related that his full and correct name was Udai Singh Singhi. He was the uncle of Gokul and lived in *Mauza* Girsa. Vide Ganga Singh, *op.cit.*, I, 43.

alive through the efforts of Shaikh Razi-ud-Din, the *Peshkar* of Hassan Ali. They and other prisoners were presented to the Emperor. Being furious, he ordered Gokul and Singh to be cut limb on the *Chabutara* of the *Kotwali* (Agra). Other captives either met the fate of their leader or were put in chains.[92]

The overthrow of their leader dampened the spirits of the followers of Gokul. Hasan Ali Khan dealt with them sternly. For a few months more he kept on slaying, capturing and plundering the rebels and their families and demolishing their strong fortresses along both banks of Yamuna. Not long after, the last vestiges of the insurrection disappeared and peace was re-established in the region for some time. On 6th April, 1670 (25th Zi-qada, 1080 A.H.)), Aurangzeb granted audience to Hasan Ali and highly praised him for his distinguished services.[93]

AFTERMATH OF THE REBELLION

Never before in the history of the Mughal Empire had the standard of such a formidable rebellion been raised by the Jats as was done by those of Mathura under Gokul in 1669. Although the rebellion failed, it had considerable, though indirect, repercussions upon the future course of the Jat History and in the long run upon the Mughal Empire itself. The crushing defeat of the Jats in 1669 was not without a lesson. It exposed to them certain strategic flaws in their ways of fighting. They had seen their 20,000 gallant brethren being easily routed by the Mughal forces in a face to face combat. It must have been laid bare to them that, in the absence of proper military training and sufficient equipment their reckless courage and obstinate valour alone would not prove effective against the mighty Mughal army. Besides, the fall of Tilpat within the short duration of three days must have pointed out to them the hopeless vulnerability of their defence and its corresponding implications. The military tactics of Raja Ram and Churaman II clearly indicate that the Jats had benefited from the failure of 1669.

They gradually turned to making a change in their existing military methods. The subsequent Jat leaders grew alive to the efficacy of discipline and proper equipment in warfare. There developed an increasing tendency to build their forts in the fasteness of dense *jungles* capable of withholding the onslaught of powerful armies. Likewise they avoided the rashness of Gokul in inviting pitched battles with the mighty Mughals.

Gokul's rebellion also gave to the posterity an inspiration of political nature, namely, the usefulness of working under a united leadership.

---

92. *Fatuhat* (Pers. Ms.), 53a-53b; *Maasir*, 93-94; Kamwar (Pers. Ms.), II, 166; *M.U.*, I, 437 and 618.
93. *Maasir*, 100; *Roznamcha* (Pers. Ms.), 133.

We know that the Jats had the reputation of being impatient of any external control. Although success did not crown them in 1669, it was, perhaps, heartening for them to perceive that their joint efforts could gather so powerful a momentum as to disturb even the Mughal Emperor, compelling him to rush to the disturbed region. On the other hand, it was disheartening to them that the effectiveness of their resistance withered away once their chief leader Gokul, was no more. This seems to have emphasized to the Jats the advantage to working unitedly under a common leader. Although progress in this direction was necessarily slow, in due course it proved to be of considerable political importance to them. Once their combined efforts proved fruitful under later leaders and bright future prospects appeared ahead, their circumstantial union assumed a little fixed character. Consideration of common benefit might also have been instrumental in leading the tribal and democratic Jats to prefer, accept, and finally adopt the institution of kingship. To such circumstances may be traced the genesis of the Jat state of Bharatpur and the eventual emergence of the principalities of Patiala, Nabha and Jhind which were republican until recently.[94]

In the light of the above considerations it seems that from the viewpoint of the long term interests of the Jats, Gokul's abortive exertions were no less significant than the more fruitful struggles of Raja Ram and Churaman II. The brighter careers of these two have dimmed the image of Gokul, whose full importance has not been duly appreciated so far.[95] The circumstances in which they worked were not altogether similar. Gokul had to face more formidable odds than the two later fortunate Jat leaders. It is doubtful whether, even with their better organising capacity, their success could have been assured in Gokul's circumstances. It is difficult to resist the conclusion that though Gokul failed, his failure paved the way for the subsequent success of Raja Ram and Churaman II.

Prior to the Jat uprising, other revolt had taken place in a different part of the Empire.[96] But they were not so powerful and the places of their occurrence were comparatively too distant from the Capital. The rebellion under Gokul was, however, quite different. From the point of view of time, dimension and place it was the first fierce repudiation of the authority of Aurangzeb under his very seat. Though such an evidence is not forthcoming, the possibility cannot be ruled out that his audaciousness provided a stimulus to the later rebels such as the Satnamis.

---

94. Bingley, *Sikhs*, 12.
95. According to Qanungo (*Jats*, 39) Gokul "Watered" the newly-sprouted seedling of liberty in the heart of the Jats. But Sir Denzil Ibbetson (The *Panjab Castes*, 102) writes, "Sturdy independence" has been one of their Strongest characteristics". The Jats have always clung to liberty.
96. For minor risings vide Sarkar, *Aurangzib*, III, 21ff.

Aurangzeb's harsh policy itself seems to have duly contributed in fostering rebellious spirit among the Jats. Although with his overwhelming power he succeeded in suppressing the first Jat insurrection, the resentment underlying it not only lingered on but also probably received fresh provocation from his imprudent attitude. It is a fact that an autocratic regime cannot hope to survive if rebellions are not resolutely crushed. Occurring under the very shadow of the imperial Metropolis, the Jat revolt had additional ground for being crushed sternly, in that it might serve as a deterrent against similar eruptions. However, in the future interests of the Empire, the reasons justifying strict measures also warranted at the same time the removal of their just grievances and their pacification. It was for the first time that they had defied the imperial power in such large numbers in an organised way.[97] Aurangzeb did very little to reconcile them beyond despatching 200 horsemen to protect the village crops and preventing the soldiers from oppressing the villagers or taking any child captive.[98] He was anxious, no doubt to relieve the peasantry in general of the economic distress but his repeated *farmans*, as we have seen above, remained generally ineffective.

Aurangzeb pursued a course which seems to have estranged the Jats further. He wrecked terrible vengeance upon them. Apart from the treatment meted out to 7,000 captors, the family of their leader, Gokul, was forcibly converted to Islam. Gokul's daughter was married to Shah Quli Chela and his son renamed Fazil.[99] Even after the fall of Gokul the Mughal forces kept on imprisoning and plundering the Jats. Not content with it, as it were, Aurangzeb broke loose his fury upon the temple of Keshava Rai. It was levelled to the ground (during the month of Ramzan, 1080 A.H.--13th January to 11th February, 1670) and a mosque was built upon its site. Its idols were desecrated and later buried under the footsteps of the Begum Sahiba mosque at Agra. The name of Mathura was changed to 'Islamabad' and that of 'Brindaban' to 'Mominabad'. The temples and idols of the rest of the holy places in the Brij were gradually destroyed.[100] This added insult to injury. The affront inflicted upon the families of their leader and kinsmen must have outraged the feelings of the entire tribe in whose social consciousness and tribal sentiments have always been uppermost. It appears that Aurangzeb, despite his

97. The Jats were turbulent for some time. But this state was not a little due to the local oppression *Storia*, II, 77; Sarkar, *Aurangzib*, III, 291-292; *Muttra Gazetters*, 194; Also see Z. Faruki, *Aurangzib*, and His times (Bombay: 1935), 124.

98. *Maasir*, 92.

99. *Ibid.*, 94, Kanwar (Pers. Ms.), II, 166; *M.U.*, I, 437.

100. *Maasir*, 95-96; *Storia*, II, 143; Kamwar, II, 167; Raghubir Singh, *Brij*, I, 163; Faruki (*op.cit.*, 125), who is generally apologetic for Auranzeb, also thinks that the demolition of the temple was a retaliatory measure.

shrewdness, failed to appreciate properly the character of the Jat people, who are normally moderate, light-hearted and not unmanageable, unless of course when excited.[101] Modave is emphatic on the point that Bharatpur Jats "are in general goodmen" who follow their peaceful pursuits "not obliged almost always to keep themselves under arms."[102] Such were generally the people whom Aurangzeb had to deal with. There is basis to believe that they might have been largely pacified and the chances of their subsequent lawlessness minimized, had he displayed a little caution and foresight in his dealings with them. But Aurangzeb lacked that "warm generosity of the heart" and "chivalry to fallen foes" which had enabled Akbar to win the people's affection and praise.[103] It can hardly be called an act of political wisdom on his part to have tried to put down the warlike and stubborn Jats in a ruthless manner. Probably, Aurangzeb was too obstinate, vindictive and blind[104] to visualize this, as in some other cases, the evil consequences of leaving such a hardy people deeply annoyed in the neighbourhood of the Capital. So long as the Emperor had a firm grip over the north, the Jats remained subdued but as soon as it loosened, their pent up fury was let loose and they resumed their lawless course with added vigour. Thus the policy of Aurangzeb towards them defeated its very object and in the long run proved harmful for the Empire. It has been rightly remarked that "a little indiscretion and persistence in a wrong policy" converted "peaceful husbandmen (Jats) into flaming warriors", as it did "friends (Rajputs) into foes."[105] Ironical though it may sound, it appears that the persistence of the defiant attitude among the Jats and the eventual emergence of their political power were, thus, in no mean measure, due to the impolitic and vindictive attitude of Aurangzeb himself.[106]

---

101. Ibbetson, *op.cit.*, 102, Bingley, *Sikhs*, 91-94.
102. *Supra*, Ch. I, f.n. 42.
103. Sarkar, *Studies in Mughal India*, 62.
104. Sarkar, *Studies in Mughal India*, 44.
105. A.B. Pandey, *Later Medieval India* (Allahabad; 1963), 247.
106. U.N. Sharma, *Itihas*, 90; Raghubir Singh, *Brij*, 164.

II

Breakdown of Mughal Administration and the Fresh Jat Eruptions (1680-1707)

The decade following Gokul's rebellion corresponded with the period of a strong Mughal government. Aurangzeb with the bulk of his forces was present in the north. The vast resources of the Mughal Empire were as yet free from that great strain to which they were subjected later on (the second half of Aurangzeb's reign). The chivalrous Rajputs were not yet alienated from the Emperor and were adding to his strength. Some rebellions and wars did occur in these years that distracted the attention of the government, but the Emperor generally succeeded in tiding over the difficulties. The Satnamis were repressed into silence. Guru Tegh Bahadur was captured and killed and the situation in the Panjab was brought under control for the time being. Force and diplomacy worked together in improving the Mughal position against the intractable Afghans. The Bundela leader, Chhatrasal, could not be contained, his defiance had yet to assume serious proportions. The Mughal arms suffered a rebuff at the hands of Shivaji, the developments in the south were not serious enough to produced any effect upon the north or the fate of the Mughal Empire in general. Likewise, the failure of the imperialists in establishing permanent roots in the Assam[1] against the Ahoms did not reflect upon the general situation in the Empire. Thus, Aurangzeb was generally successful in dealing with all of his possible enemies.

However, this period of effective control over the political affairs in the north also witnessed his growing religious persecution. Temple destruction went on briskly in the Empire, the Hindus were excluded from the public offices and the much hated *Jizya* was reimposed. Such steps caused increasing bitterness among the non-Muslims and tended them to rebellion. Apparently, the policy of Aurangzeb was preparing a background for the impending storm in the north.

The Jats, though simmering with discontent, were constrained to remain quiet during these ten years. It is not difficult to trace the reasons

1. For details of the above developments see Sarkar, *Aurangzib*, III, 4, 183-191, 228-244, 298-301, 313-314, V. 395ff.

for their general passivity. The bitter memory of their ruthless suppression by the imperialists had yet not faded completely from their minds. They must have been deterred also by Emperor's general success against his enemies. Then again, it is also likely that the Jats as yet were not able to make good their heavy loss, suffered during the preceding encounter with the Mughals. Finally, they were perhaps disinclined to repeat the folly of a rash collusion with the Emperor, more so at a time when he had northern India tightly under his grip.

The Jats were obviously looking for a suitable opportunity. This was provided by Aurangzeb's departure from the north and his subsequent involvement in the unending Deccan Wars.[2] The time rolled on and yet the Emperor with his best lieutenants and the bulk of his army remained involved in the distant south. This began to wear out the revenue, the army, and the prestige of the Mughal arms as well. The north, inwardly agitating owing to the policies of Aurangzeb, was left in the hands of mediocre officers. With depleted strength, they found it increasingly difficult to cope with the widespread unrest among the people. All this worked to shatter the administrative framework. A mighty wave of rebellion swept through Rajputana, Agra, Bundelkhand, the Punjab, Malwa, Bihar and the extreme north-west.[3]

The brief spell of an uneasy clam prevailing among the Jats was broken in the early eighties, when they rose in arms again. Its leaders changed, tactics varied and its fortunes fluctuated but the revolt once restarted was henceforth a continuous process, ultimately resulting in the overthrow of the Mughal authority in the *suba* of Agra and the establishment of Bharatpur State.

RISE OF BRIJ RAJ

The first leader of whom we are informed was Brij Raj of Sinsini (16 miles north-west of Bharatpur).[4] In all likelihood, it was this Brij Raj whom Manucci refers to as the leader, "oldest in age and the greatest in authority", of the peasants of Agra. Who raising their heads had withheld revenue due to the imperial treasury.[5] In order to force these villagers to pay, Aurangzeb sent Multafat Khan, the *faujdar* of the environs of Agra, with a strong force. Multafat Khan attacked a village, where the rebels had rallied together. Their leader first assured the Khan but later incited his people against him. "Resolved to die rather than pay revenue", they came out and fought with

---

2. *Storia*, II, 300, *Roznamcha*, 133; *Memoires des Jats* 10; *M.U.*, I, 437.
3. For details see Sarkar, *Aurangzib*, V, 359ff.
4. *Imperial Gazetteer*, VIII, 75. It spells his name as "Brijh" which is a mistake for Brij Raj, who was the son of Khan Chand. See Sudan, Sujan *Charitra* (Kashi ed.), Ganga Singh, *op.cit.* 47, U.N. Sharma, *Itihas*, I, 100f.
5. *Storia*, II, 209.

such desperation that the force of the *faujdar* was routed. After humiliating him they set free Multafat Khan who succumbed to his wounds on 26th June, 1681 (19th Jamadi II, 1092 A.H.).[6]

Brij Raj also plundered passers-by and convoys on the roads. In 1682, a Mughal contingent pursued him upto his stronghold, Sinsini, which was put to siege. The Jat chief somehow succeeded in sending away his women from the fortress but was himself killed alongwith his son, Bhao Singh, while defending it.[IV] Sinsini fell into the hands of the enemy. Having fled from Sinsini the family of Brij Raj sought safety in a small and obscure mud fort (5 miles from Bayana). Here one of the wives of Bhao Singh gave birth to a posthumous son, named Badan Singh. It is after the name of this personage that the *garhi* is still known as 'Badangarhi'.[7]

RISE OF RAJARAM JAT (c. 1682-1688)

The next chief of whom we hear is the famous Raja Ram Jat of Sinsini.[8] He was the son of Bhagwat alias Bhajja Singh, the brother of Brij Raj.[9] The absence of Aurangzeb and his best troops from the north and the sloth and weakness of the local officers provided Raja Ram the opportune moment.[10] Obviously, there was little prospect of that counterblast of the Mughals which had disappointed the Jats in 1669-1670. The changed political situation around seemed to ensure for them a fair amount of success in their refractory course.

Raja Ram displayed a capacity to learn from the past and an insight into the exigencies of the present. He could infer from Gokul's example that lack of training and proper equipment, pitched contest against the powerful Mughal army and weak Jat defences were the precise reasons of the Jat debacle in 1669-1670. His reorganisation bears testimony to it that he tried to remove these glaring defects. He knew that the gallant Jats could give an impressive account of themselves under one leader. With this end in view he allied his Sinsinwara clansmen with the Sogaria

---

6. *Ibid.*, 209-210; *Maasir,* 209; *M.U.*, II, 282.

IV. Also, *Odier*, 3/25; *Waqa Rajasthan,* 2/45; Gokal Chandra Dixit, *Brajendra Vansh Bhaskar*, 18; *Sahyog* March 15, 1945; Jat Jagat cited by U.N. Sharma, *Itihas*, I, 186, f.n.28.—Editor.

7. *Odier Settlement Report, Bharatpur,* referred to by Ganga Singh, *op.cit.*, 47-48; Somnath, *Dirgh Nagar Varnan,* (Kashi Nagari Pracharini, Hindi Ms.) 3, *Ras Peeushnidhi* and *Madhav Vinod* in *Somnath Granthawali* (ed. by Sudhakar Pande, Kashi, 1971 A.D.), 3, and 318, presents an exaggerated picture of the qualities of Bhao Singh.

8. *Maasir*, 311; *Fatuhat* (Pers. Ms.), 131b; *Memoires des Jats* (Fr. Ms.), 9.

9. *Sujan*, 5; Ganga Singh, *op.cit.*, 32 and 48; U.N. Sharma, *Itihas*, I, 100f.

10. *Storia*, II, 300; *Roznamcha* (Pers. Ms.) 133-134; *M.U.* I, 437; *Memoires des Jats* (Fr. Ms.), 9.

Jats under Ramachehara, who possessed the castle of Sogar[11] (4 miles south-east of Bharatpur). He fraternised with the Jats of Sidgiri region[12] (Bayana, Rupbasaia). He also befriended the Jats of Ranthambhor against the Amber ruler, Ram Singh.[12a] On the basis of the contemporary despatches it can unmistakeably be deduced that Raja Ram proved a great rallying point and a great number of the Jats were united under his leadership.[13] Next, he began to organise his followers from the military point of view. He gave them military training and equipped them with fire-arms. He organised them into regiments placed under different captains. Simultaneously, he impressed upon the self-willed and freedom loving Jats, the necessity of remaining disciplined and obeying their captains. Thus he imparted to them the semblance of a regular army.[14] He gave similar attention to the strengthening of his defence, for he must have seen how Tilpat was easily stormed for lack of proper defence and thus sealing the fate of the Jat rising under Gokul. Raja Ram, therefore, built his forts in dense deep *Jungles* and surrounded them with mud ramparts. The forest-infested environs and the mud walls rendered them stronger[15] than was the chief stronghold of Gokul. These forts served as bases for operations and refuge as also places for dumping the booty. As is apparent from his tactics, Raja Ram stuck to the traditional mode of the Jat warfare, popularly known as "*Dhar*" (Guerilla) system. All through he avoided positional warfare with the Mughals and confined himself to sudden and intrepid attacks. This ensured him maximum benefit with minimum loss.[16] As would be seen in the following pages, these changes proved beneficial and gradually contributed to the success of the Jat rebellion.

Having thus prepared himself, Raja Ram began to organise raids in the countryside of the *Suba* of Agra. The Jats hovered on the roads and plundered the carvans and the travellers. The *Subadar* of Agra, Safi Khan was virtually besieged in the Agra fort. Along with the other rebels the Narukas, the Panwars, the Gujars and the Mevs-they practically closed the roads for normal traffic between Dholpur and Delhi, and Agra and Ajmer via Hindaun and Bayana. How deep was the consternation created by

11. *Memoires des Jats* (Fr. Ms.), 9, 10.
12. *Vanshbhaskara*, 2886.
12a. Ram Pande, *Bharatpur*, 8, 10.
13. *Infra*, See Ch. II, Estimate of Raja Ram.
14. Qanungo, *Jats*, 40; U.N. Sharma (*Itihas*, I, 104-105) claims that Aurangzeb summoned Raja Ram to Delhi, where he was properly received and was granted "the *gaddi* of Mathura and a *jagir* consisting of 575 villages". He, however, cites no contemporary authority in support of it.
15. *Memoires des Jats* (Fr. Ms.) 10, also footnote 11.
16. *Ibid.*, 9-10.

the insurgents would be clear by one instance that in an important place like Mathura no place except Jama Mosque was deemed safe.[17] Raja Ram also tried to ransack Akbar's mausoleum at Sikandara. But his attempt was foiled by the local *faujdar*, Mir Abul Fazl. He confronted the rebels at a place, 10 miles from Sikandara. The *faujdar*, succeeded in repulsing them, though in the process, he was seriously wounded and a number of his troops also perished. Raja Ram also suffered heavy casualties. Aurangzeb rewarded the *faujdar* with the title of Iltifat Khan, increasing his *Mansab* by 200 *sawars.* Unsuccessful at Sikandara, Raja Ram then fell upon Shikarpur and grabbed rich booty from the place. Therefrom, he retired towards Ratanpur.[18]

Raja Ram's mischief and disturbances went increasing.[19] This worried the Emperor. On 3rd May, 1686 (19th Jamdai II, 1097 A.H.), he appointed Khan-i-Jahan Bahadur Zafarjang, Kokaltash in order to punish the rebels. Despite his strenuous efforts, however, Khan-i-Jahan failed to capture any of the Jat strongholds or to punish the people.[20] Therefore, he ordered his son, Muhammad Azam, to proceed against the Jats. But he had only reached Burhanpur (July, 1687) when more pressing needs of Golconda compelled Aurangzeb to recall the Prince. Thereafter, Bidar Bakht was sent (December, 1687) to assume supreme command in the Jat war, while Khan-i-Jahan was to act as his deputy.[21]

Meanwhile, Raja Ram showed greater audacity. He fell upon the Mughal commander, Aghar Khan. The Khan with his retinue was enroute from Kabul to Bijapur when the Jats attacked him near Dholpur and fled away capturing many bullocks, carts, horses and women. The general gave them a hot chase but was killed in the ensuing skirmish along with his son-in-law and 80 other men. Two hundred Jats were killed in the action.[22] The psychological gain from this

---

17. *Fatuhat* (Pers. Ms.), 131b, 132b; *Storia*, II, 300; *Roznamcha* (Pers. Ms.), 134; *Memoires des Jats* (Fr. Ms.), 10-11; *M.U.*, I, 437; Qanungo, 'Some Sidelights on the Career of Raja Bishan Singh Kachhawaha of Amber', *Proceedings of Indian History Congress,* 1948, XI.
18. *Fatuhat* (Pers. Ms.), 131b-132b.
19. *Ibid.*, 132b.
20. *Maasir,* 274; *Fatuhat* (Pers. Ms.), 132b; *Roznamcha* (Pers. Ms.), 133; *Muntakhab-ul-Lubab*, II by Khafi Khan (Bib. Ind. Series), 395; Kamwar (Pers. Ms.), II, 223; *M.U.*, 1,437; *Memoires des Jats* (Fr. Ms.), 10. According to Abul Fazl Mamuri, Aurangzeb sent Khan-i-Jahan "Ostensibly in order to crush the Jats but really to rid the Deccan of his presence", as he was "suspected of being friendly wth the Marathas". Vide *Tarikh-i-Aurangzeb,* referred to by M.A. Ali, *The Mughal Nobility under Aurangzeb*, 103-104.
21. *Maasir*, 298-299, 311; *Roznamcha* (Pers. Ms.), 133; *K.K.* II, 395; *Kamwar* (Pers. Ms.), II, 231; *M.U.*, I, 437-438.
22. *Fatuhat* (Pers. Ms.), 164b; K.K. (II. 395) adds that Aghar Khan succeeded in rescuing his women, but was shot dead while besieging a fortalice; *M.U.*, I, 155; Sarkar, *Aurangzib*, V, 297-298.

audacious act was much more than the material one. Their success in killing and routing the reputed suppressor of the frontier Afghans must have whetted the audacity of the Jats. They carried their depredations further. Early in 1668, Raja Ram attacked Mahabat Khan, who on his way to Lahore was encamped near Sikandara. A fierce fight ensued in which Raja Ram was finally overpowered and driven back after losing 400 men. The casualties on the other side included 150 dead and 40 wounded.[23]

After a short while, Raja Ram reappeared at Sikandara and taking advantage of the delay in coming of Shaista Khan, the governor-designate of Agra, he attacked and plundered Akbar's mausoleum. The Jat leader carried away the precious articles of gold and silver, carpets, lamps etc. and destroyed what he could not carry. According to Manucci the Jats dragged out the bones of Akbar, threw them angrily into fire and burnt them. Muhammad Baqa (the Naib of Khan-i-Jahan) who was then at Agra, did nothing to frustrate the rebels. As a punishment, therefore, his *mansab* was reducted by 500 and that of Khan-i-Jahan by 1000 sawars.[24] The Jats also ransacked the villages, set aside for the support of Taj Mahal. Some Jats ravaged the environs of Khurja, while others captured the local Mughal officers at Palwal.[25]

One noteworthy fact is that the local Mughal officials and soldiers in general, winked at the disobedience of the Jats and even secretly entered into collusion with them to share the booty grabbed by them.[26] It is also to be noted that Muhammad Baqa, the deputy of Khan-i-Jahan at Agra, had remained inactive while Raja Ram robbed Akbar's tomb. This exasperated Aurangzeb and he reduced the deputy's *Mansab* by 500 and that of Khan-i-Jahan by 1000 *sawars.*[27] Meanwhile, the daring and audacity of the Jats alarmed Aurangzeb and he ordered Raja Ram Singh (who was at Kabul) to chastise Raja Ram. But due to his sudden death the Raja could not resume his charge.[28]

Raja Ram, on the other hand, persisted with his refractory activities. His strength and resources now began to attract the attention of others.

---

23. *Fatuhat* (Pers. Ms.), 132a.132b.
24. *Storia*, II, 300; *Fatuhat* (Pers. Ms.), 132b-133a.
25. Pande, *Bharatpur,* 7.
26. To give one instance, Fazil Khan, a Mughal official at Agra, was ordered to escort the royal treasure to the river Chambal. He, however, secretly informed the Jats about it and on demand even supplied them with ammunition. Thereafter, the said treasure was plundered according to the pre-meditated scheme. Qanungo, *Jats,* 342; *Jaipur Records* (Sarkar's collection, R.S.L. Sitamau transcriptions) number of pages cited here, VII, 335; cf. *Memoires des Jats* (Fr. Ms.), 11.
27. *Fatuhat* (Pers. Ms.) 132b-133a.
28. *Ibid*, 133a.

During these days the existing feud between the Chauhans and the Shekhawat Rajputs over disputed land in Bagtharia (22 miles north-east of Alwar) and some other *parganas* had erupted into an open war. The Chauhans appealed to Raja Ram for help, while the Shekhawats implored the help of Murtaza Khan, the Mughal *faujdar* of Mewat. Bidar Bakht, Rao Raja Anirudh Singh of Bundi and Maharao Kishor Singh Hada joined the *faujdar* and the Shekhawats. A severe battle was fought near Bijal. Opposite Raja Ram was the Hada Chief upon whom he inflicted a crushing defeat. Anirudh Singh himself could not stand before the Jat onset. He became nervous and fled along with his troops. When the battle was in its full fury the gallant Raja Ram led a fierce charge against the centre, consisting of the Mughals. Meanwhile, a Mughal musketeer, who had hidden himself in a tree, fired Raja Ram at his chest. He fell down from his horse and died immediately (Wednesday, 4th July, 1688-15th Ramzan, 1099 A.H.). His fall signalled the defeat of the Chauhans. Raja Ram's head was severed from the body and later on presented to Aurangzeb in the Deccan (5th September-19th Zi-Qada, 1099 A.H.). Ramchehara was captured alive in this battle. He was subsequently beheaded and his head was publically exposed at Agra.[29]

ESTIMATE OF RAJA RAM

Thus perished Raja Ram. As a leader of men and as a soldier, organiser and tactician, he was certainly more capable than any other preceding Jat Chief. His influence upon the contemporary history has not been properly assessed so far. It was he and not Churaman II who, first of all, endeavoured to transform his warrior followers into more or less disciplined troopers. The number of his regulars could not have been big but the credit of laying the foundation of a regular army, equipped with firearms must be given to him. Then again, he highlighted the efficacy of the guerilla tactics and proper defences by building the mud fortresses in dense *Jungles*. It is apparent that his dashing attacks in the presence of larger Mughal forces not only restored the shaken morale of his people but also infused in them a vigour that enabled them to withstand temporary reverses later on.

Raja Ram aimed at, and succeeded also in forging, a joint front of his brethren, as Churaman also did later on. But whereas Churaman through his indiscretion failed to preserve that unity, Raja Ram, through his tact and resourcefulness, maintained it. Disunity among the Jats did raise

29. *Ibid.*, 134a-135a; *J. Records*, XII, 1, 7; *Maasir*, 311-312; *M.U.* I, 438; cf. *Kamwar* (Pers. Ms.), II, 231; *Memoires des Jats* (Fr. Ms., 11-12) says that Raja Ram succumbed to his wounds, sustained while being pursued; M.L. Sharma *Kota Rajya Ka Itihas*, 207-209.

its head after his death, but it was not due to his policy but due to the disappearance of his rallying personality. A contemporary report (8th August, 1688-20th Shawwal, 1099 A.H.) about this disturbed period testified to it[30]. From this standpoint it would appear that as a leader of his people Raja Ram possessed better talents than Churaman. Raja Ram had deeper penetration into the individualistic and clan-conscious temperament of the Jats. If his dealings with the Sogaria and Ranthambhore Jats are a pointer, Raja Ram gave due deference to them and tried to strengthen his leadership by winning their gratitude and reposing confidence in them. It is true that Churaman II achieved far greater success than Raja Ram, who owing to his untimely death could not carry his policy and work to its logical conclusion. His mission was still in the offing. Yet, he should not be deprived of due credit for laying down certain policies which facilitated the task of his successors including Churaman. At least the fortune that he amassed proved to be of immediate and definite help to them.[31] There is a little room for suspicion that by his stress upon a common leadership, the unity of various Jat clans, a regular force and a modified strategy for the Jat defence, Raja Ram gave a new and useful direction to the Jat affairs. It would not be off the mark to point out that, had Raja Ram lived longer, he might have taken winds out of Churaman's sails. Hence, there is insufficient ground to support the view[32] that Raja Ram's work left no trace behind.

The steps undertaken by Raja Ram leave an impression that he wanted to throw off the Mughal yoke and he entertained the dream of regional independence. His premature end, coupled with the relentless pressure of the imperialists later, shattered such political ambitions for the present. Yet it is apparent that the measure of success that Raja Ram achieved during his life-time and the legacy that he bequeathed to the posterity proved in a corresponding degree detrimental to the interests of the Mughal Empire. So long as he was alive, he openly repudiated and practically eclipsed the Mughal authority in a big part of the *suba* of Agra. He held lawless sway over an area stretching from Delhi to the Chambal. His bands intermittently indulged in predatory activities. The Mughal officers failed to contain them. So great was the dread exercised by him that the contemporary opinion rated the feat of killing of Raja Ram alone as equivalent to the capture of Sinsini and killing of the Jats.[33] The perturbed Aurangzeb deputed one general after the other,

30. *J. Records*, Sarkar's coll. (Pers. Ms.), XII, 3, 7; Raghubir Singh in *Brij*, 166.
31. *Memoires des Jats* (Fr. Ms.), 9.
32. Sarkar, *Fall of the Mughal Empire*, II (Calcutta: 1934), 426.
33. *J. Records*, Sarkar's coll. (Pers. Ms.), XII, 3.

to crush him and his Jats but to no avail. Even Bidar Bakht with his big forces was in effective against the recalcitrants.

It is obvious that his persistent defiance often resulting in an utter rout of the reputed generals like Aghar Khan or in the object helplessness of great commanders like Khan-i-Jahan seriously undermined the prestige of the Mughal arms, so well established by Hasan Ali Khan in 1669-70. Though, taking advantage of the dissensions caused by Raja Ram's death, the imperialists temporarily repressed the Jats, the former awe and respect for the Mughal arms could not be restored and they resumed their offensive soon afterwards under Churaman.

It needs no stress that their successful defiance encouraged other insurgents also. The royal highway passing through Delhi and Agra had been completely blocked by the Jat rebels. At a time when Aurangzeb was engrossed in unending Deccan wars, this blockade was bound to cause him deep anxieties.[34]

Raja Ram's rebellion, besides making the political and military situation in the *suba* of Agra, also had its repercussions on the financial condition. There were areas wherefrom no revenue collection had been made for some time. To give one instance, we learn from a letter to Bishan Singh that, owing to the disturbance created by the Jats, the *mahals* of *kol* and Islamabad had been "ruined" and no revenue could reach the exchequer from them.[35] There is ground to suppose that more or less the same situation prevailed in other parts affected by the Jat rebellion. We do not have records to check the exact financial loss to the Mughals. Even if it did not materially affect them it must have been a source of concern to them. The loss to individual wayfarers must have been indeed severe as they generally lacked military protection.

It would not be inappropriate here to consider one aspect of the Jat revolt under Raja Ram as also other Jat leaders. In the wake of their military activities, Raja Ram and his bands perpetrated loot and plunder on the royal highways and in the countryside. Plunder assured enrichment in an easier and faster way. No doubt, this fact played its part in tempting people to the lawless course.[36] Notwithstanding, the point of plunder in the Jat movement cannot be magnified. To conclude that it was the sole motivating factor or booty as such was its ultimate goal, is to oversimplify the facts of the situation.[37] The harshness and

34. *Memoires des Jats* (Fr. Ms.), 11.

35. *J. Records*, Sarkar's coll. (Pers. Ms.), IX, 58-59, also 375; Qanungo, 'Bishan Singh', *Proc. I.H.C.*, XI, 171.

36. *Memoires des Jats* (Fr. Ms.), 9.

37. Satish Chandra, *Parties and Politics at the Mughal Court*, 1707-1740 (Aligarh: 1959), Introduction, 34. Habib, *op.cit.*, 341.

exactions of the local officers and the robbery by their neighbours, Gujars and the like, also goaded the Jats into a predatory life. Likewise, the terrible retaliation by the Mughals in 1670 must have tended them to the same direction. The Jats had seen their houses and religious places being demolished, their property plundered, their women molested and males tortured by the Mughal soldiers. Stubborn and warlike as they were, they could not accept all this meekly. So when they got their opportunity they paid their enemies in the same coin. Further, the inadequate measures for safety of the war materials and royal treasure sent to the Deccan through the *Brij* country offered them a natural temptation for plunder.[37a] Finally, with limited means at their disposal the Jat chiefs, political ambitions understandably channelized in sudden and intrepid attacks, which besides enriching their material resources, also served to weaken the imperial authority. Thus it would appear that the predatory activities of the Jats were more circumstantial than instinctive and were employed by their leaders largely to serve as a means to an end rather than to be an end in themselves.

IMPERIAL OPERATIONS AND THE FITFUL ACTIVITIES OF THE JATS: (1688-1695)

The unity among the Jats that Raja Ram was able to build up, seemed to crumble down after his death.[38] We do not corne across any capable supreme leader among them during the interregnum between his death and the ascendancy of Churaman II. The contemporary news-reports, which throw a flood of light on this period, refer to several petty Jat leaders springing up and creating disturbances in different quarters.

Besides the exit of Raja Ram's towering personality, two other probabilities may be suggested for the Jat activities being fitful in the period. First, as we shall see, the imperialists, especially Bishan Singh's forces operated vigorously against the insurgents from 1688 to 1695. They were at work throughout besieging the forts and fighting the rebels in different directions in the province of Agra. This increased pressure compelled the rebels to operate in nooks and corners. Secondly, the absence of a competent and inspiring leadership also tended to scatter their movements.

Choosing a successor capable of accomplishing the unfinished work of Raja Ram was not so easy. Brij Raj, Bhao Singh and Raja Ram's associate Ram Chehra had perished. Fateh Singh[39], the son of Raja

---

37a. Raghubir Singh in *Brij*, 164.

38. *J. Records*, Sarkar's coll. (Pers. Ms.), XII, 7, 3.

39. *J. Records*, Sarkar's coll. (Pers. Ms.), IX, 356; *Ahkam* (Pers. Ms.), II. 206a.

Ram does not appear to have been a promising youth. Amidst the circumstances, Raja Ram's aged father, Bhajja Singh of Sinsini assumed the leadership of the Jats,[40] while Raja Ram's other son, Jorawar Singh took up as his deputy.[41] But it can be reasonably inferred on the basis of the Vakil reports,[42] that the successor of Raja Ram lacked his efficiency and resourcefulness. He could not carry on Raja Ram's policy of uniting the Jats under one leadership. It caused a setback to the newly emerging forces of unity and gradually the deeprooted clan feeling reasserted itself. Several petty leaders, heading one clan or the other sprang up. One noteworthy feature of the coming years is that the repression of the Jats and their lawlessness continued side by side. When the imperial arms turned towards one direction, they created turbulence in the other. When chastised, they fled to renew the disturbances elsewhere. This state of affairs generally persisted till 1695.

BISHAN SINGH'S OPERATIONS AGAINST THE JATS

It has been mentioned above that Aurangzeb had appointed Raja Ram Singh to undertake the Jat war. But he died. Thereafter, Bishan Singh endeavoured through his *Vakil* to procure from the Emperor his patrimony, the *faujdarship* of Mathura and the charge to uproot the Jats.[43] Bishan Singh gave an undertaking to the Emperor to crush the Jat recalcitrants and capture their main stronghold, Sinsini. Aurangzeb agreed and bestowed upon the Rajput Prince the title of Raja, the *tika* of Amber, a *Khilat* and mansab of 2000/2000 *do aspah.* The Emperor appointed him (30th April, 1688-9th Rajab, 1099 A.H.) *faujdar* of Mathura with repeated orders for the "general massacre" of the Jats. He was also granted the *zamindari* of Sinsini and other Jat *mahals* and was promised further promotion and grant if he succeeded in his task. The Emperor also issued an oral order (to the Amber Vakil, Kesho Rai) to the effect that the foremost duty of Bishan Singh was the "extirpation of *Jat-i-badzat* (the Jat of evilbreed)".[44]

Bishan Singh's keenness for his new job cannot be explained merely on the ground of his longing for earning distinction and a high *mansab*

---

40. William Irvine, *Later Mughals*, I, 322; Qanungo, *Jats*, 43; Ganga Singh, *op.cit.*, 55; Dr. Pande (*Bharatpur*, 10) claims that Fateh Singh succeeded Raja Ram as overall leader. This does not appear to have been the case. The testimony of Kamwar Khan (*Kamwar*, II, 231) leads us to infer that Fateh Singh became the leader after the fall of Sinsini and the arrest of Jorawar Singh.
41. *Akhbarat* (J. Records), 19 Rabi-us-sani; *Kamwar* (Pers. Ms.II, 231) thinks that Jorawar was the brother of Raja Ram. Also see Ganga Singh, *op.cit.*, 55.
42. *J. Records*, Sarkars's coll. (Pers. Ms.), XII, 7.
43. *J. Records*, Sarkars's coll. (Pers. Ms.), VII, 276, 314.
44. *Ibid.*, VII, 314-315 also 103, 107, 317, 320, IX, 370, 341, XII, 1-5, 7-8, 11; *J. Records*, Sitamau coll. (Pers. Ms.) I, 7-8; *Fatuhat* (Pers. Ms.) 133a; Qanungo, 'Bishan Singh', *Proc. I.H.C.*, XI, 170, 171.

like his father and grandfather.[45] Other factors also lay underneath it. Enmity with the Jats he had inherited from his predecessor, Ram Singh and he must have been anxious to settle the old score. Moreover, the Jats had already penetrated into and seized some land belonging to him. Their expansion was detrimental to the socio-economic interests of the Rajputs. Therefore, Bishan Singh did not relish the Jat ascendancy on the borders of his state. Lastly, the Raja was seeing in this enterprise an opportunity of extending his territorial possessions also.[46]

On the other side, Aurangzeb's choice of the Raja for the onerous task was an exquisite piece of his political craft and shrewdness. The Emperor, perceived in Bishan Singh's eagerness a possible chance of the destruction of the Jat miscreants. By picking him Aurangzeb placed a mighty thorn in the side of the Jats and sharpened the feud between the Kachhawahas and the Jats. For more than three decades (until the installation of Badan Singh) the heaviest blows to the infant Jat power were inflicted by the Amber house. There was yet another aspect of the Emperor's decision. In view of his designs over Amber,[47] it is not improbable that the weakening of the Kachhawaha power was the other cherished desire which Aurangzeb hoped to fulfil out of Bishan Singh's present assignment. In any case, if the struggle continued for some time, as would not have seemed unlikely, it would open a new front of confrontation for the two concerned and thus drain out much of their energy. Thus, Aurangzeb was attempting to play off two strong neighbours against each other.

To pick up the thread of our narrative, Bishan Singh, though appointed in the life time of Raja Ram to 'kill or capture' him, delayed operations even after his death. This delay displeased the Emperor and Bishan Singh's Court *Vakil*, Kesho Rai had time and again to face angry enquiries at the court. We have several letters addressed to Bishan Singh wherein the Raja is repeatedly asked to undertake at once the assigned task and subjugate the Jats and capture Sinsini before the arrival of Bidar Bakht with the same intention and thereby win the Emperor's favour, honour and wide acclaim. Yet, the Raja delayed the operations to the embarrassment of his *Vakil*.[48] At last Bishan Singh arrived at Mathura (August, 1688). His presence on the scene with 10,000 cavalry and 20,000 infantry infused a new life in the punitive operations. The death of

---

45. Contra see Sarkar, *Aurangzib*, V, 300; Qanungo, *Jats*, 43.
46. Pande, *Bharatpur*, 10; U.N. Sharma, *Itihas*, I, 126.
47. Qanungo, 'Bishan Singh', *Proc. I.H.C.*, XI, 169 and 170; U.N. Sharma, *Itihas*, I, 118f., 127f.
48. *J. Records*, Sarkars's coll. (Pers. Ms.), VII, 107-109, XII, 1-3, 5, 8, 10.

Raja Ram had greatly eased the difficult task of the imperialists.[49] It is interesting to learn from a contemporary report that some of the Jats sued for the royal favour through the Amir-ul-Umra.[50] The Mughals took full advantage of such dissensions among the enemies.

In September, 1688, Bidar Bakht laid siege to Sonkh (a fortress on way to Sinsini from Mathura). A section of the Jats assembled near Gokul tried to create a diversion there and thereby relieve the Mughal pressure on Sonkh. However, Hari Singh, the general of Bishan Singh defeated the rebels inflicting heavy losses. Sonkh finally fell after a siege of four months.[51]

Sinsini, the chief stronghold of the rebels, had long been the main target of the Mughals. But operations in its thick environs severely taxed them. In 1689, Bidar Bakht's troops, that had been sent to besiege it, were themselves besieged. The Jats obstructed the supplies of the enemy and the Raja was required to exert for the continued supply of provisions to the Prince.[52] Bishan Singh had engaged a body of the Jats under Partap and placed it in his vanguard. But while he proceeded to join the Prince at Sinsini, Partap defected him and joined his brethren. Though Bishan Singh meant to break off one bone by striking it against the other, such developments annoyed Bidar Bakht and he lodged false complaints that the Raja was in secret collusion with the Jats.[V] The Amber agent had to remind the Raja to put up utmost exertions and to appoint one resourceful *Vakil* in the Prince's retinue to please him.[53] In fact, throughout his Jat campaign Bishan Singh had to fight on two fronts, against the Jats as also against his Court opponents who were

---

49. *J. Records*, Sarkars's coll. (Pers. Ms.), 3; Qanungo, 'Bishan Singh', *proc. I.H.C.*, XI, 171; *Fatuhat* (Pers. Ms.), 136a.
50. *J. Records*, Sarkars's coll. (Pers. Ms.), VII, 343, 344.
51. Qanungo, *Diggi*, 53, 79, 80 quoted by U.N. Sharma, *Itihas*, I, 129, 130; Qanungo, 'Bishan Singh', *Proc. I.H.C.*, XI, 171.
52. *J. Records*, Sarkars's coll. (Pers. Ms.), VII, 353-354.
V. G. C. Dwivedi confuses Pratap Jat with Pratap Singh Naruka (other than Rao Pratap Singh Naruka founder of Alwar state). According to contemporary Persian day-to-day reports of the Diggi House, the account given here is related to Pratap Singh Naruka, *Zamindar* of Barahi in the *Pargana* of Baroda. He was a notorious rebel in Kama-Pahari-Mewat region. He allied to the Jat rebels. Mughal court issued urgent orders to Bidar Bakht and Bishan Singh to crush him. But Bishan's general Hari Singh won over Pratap Naruka to the imperial side and made him the commander of Kachhwaha army at the time of the siege of Sinsini. Prince Bidar Bakht made it a grievance to Bishan Singh that he brought the bandit chief Pratap Singh Naruka to the imperial camp as the commander of the van of his army. After the fall of Sinsini we see his son engaged in lawless activities again. Thus we do not find any Pratap Jat who was heading a body of the Jats against Sinsini. K.R. Qanungo, *History of the House of Diggi*, 57, 71-73, 90; also Sheet No. 61.—Editor.
53. *Ibid.*, VII, 337-340, XII, 5-6.

fabricating stories about him. But remaining unperturbed, he cooperated with Bidar Bakht.

Meanwhile, the Jat through their guerilla tactics, continued to harass the imperialists. They frequently surprised the enemy camp and cut off the grain convoys and water carrying parties. This resulted in the scarcity of food and fodder. Prices rose very high. Animals died in large numbers and soldiers lay prostrated with hunger. But the besiegers kept up spirits. At last after four months of untold sufferings they succeeded in carrying their trenches to the main gate of the fortress, Having cleared the *jungle* around, they tightened the siege, mounted guns on raised platforms and laid mines. The Jats, however, foiled their first attempt. Getting intelligence of the whole things, their garrison blocked the opposite side of the mine with mud and stones. Hence, instead of blowing the wall, the mine, when fired, drove back, killing many of the artillerymen and the supervising Mughal officers. Then, another mine was laid under the wall in a months time. It was fired successfully, blowing a portion of the wall and the defenders atop. The Mughal-Rajput combine assaulted the fort (end of January, 1690) after 3 hours of fierce fighting. The determined Jats sold their lives dearly. One thousand five hundred of them perished or were wounded, while on the other side 200 Mughals and 700 Rajputs were killed or wounded. Of the remaining defenders, some were captured (along with Jorawar Singh) and killed while the others fled. The Emperor learnt of the fall of Sinsini on 15th February, 1690 (16th Jamadi I, 1101 A.H.) from the letters of the newswriters.[54] The fall of Sinsini fulfilled the cherished desire of both the Mughals and Bishan Singh. On the other hand, it obviously caused a great setback to the Jats. Among the notables Fateh Singh of Sinsini and Churaman managed to escape.[55] It is quite probable that with the end of Jorawar Singh of Sinsini, that Jat fugitives rallied under them. But at a time when the jubilant imperialists were keeping up pressure and the hard pressed Jats were being chased from one place to the other, it is unlikely that either of them was able to consolidate his position to be justly called the overall leader of the then scattered Jats.[56] At best, they actually headed only a faction of the Jats during these days.

We learn from an *arzi* of Kesho Rai (2nd April, 1690 3rd Rajab, 1101 A.H.) that the Emperor ordered the Prince and the Raja to make

54. *Fatuhat,* 136a-137a; *Maasir*, 334 (differing in details); cf. *Kamwar*, II, 231; Ganga Singh, *op.cit.*, 58; Jorawar Singh, his wife and children having been imprisoned were first taken to Mathura and finally presented to Aurangzeb in the Deccan. They were brutally slain and their limbs thrown to dogs. Qanungo, *Diggi*, 97, quoted by U.N. Sharma, *Itihas*, I, 142, also see 139ff.

55. *J. Records*, Sarkars's coll., IX, 356.

56. Raghubir Singh in *Brij*, 165; Ganga Singh, *op.cit.*, 60.

all possible efforts to slay the Jat rebels and to capture the rest of their fortresses.[57] Early in 1690[58], Hari Singh had been ordered to march against the powerful Jat chief, Amar Singh, who owned two forts, Khair (16 miles north-west of Aligarh) and Ranth (8 miles east of Khair). After a prolonged fight, Hari Singh succeeded in capturing these forts and expelling Amar Singh. The latter sought shelter with another powerful Jat leader, Nanda Jat, who was supreme in a tract stretching form Hathras and Mursan to Mahaban. Amar Singh's two prominent *sardars*, Birju and Taula who had gone into hiding in Arnia near Khurja, were arrested later on.[59]

On the other side of the Yamuna, the Jat rebels had flocked to and fortified various *garhis,* Sogar, Awar, Kasot, Sonkh, Pingora, Sewar, Dahara, Chakora, Undera, Bachhamadi, Chiksana, Ratanpur, Bhatawali and others. Besides the prominent Fateh Singh, Churaman and Nanda Jat, the other rebel leaders were Partap, Durga, Balram Jat, Jagman, Banarasi, Bansahana, Lodha, Bukna and Maujia.[60] As and when they got opportunity they indulged in lawless activities. To give a few examples, at this time (1690) Partap and Durga were creating trouble around Malpura, whose *zamindari* was granted to Hari Singh.[61] Balram Jat having fled (c. November, 1690) from the Raja's camp made a fort in *Mauza* Samuna (in *parganah* Ibrahimabad) his abode and ravaged the nearby *mahals.* He expelled the local *mutsaddis* and established his sway over them.[62] Churaman made Rasulpur his base and raided the adjacent territory, while Fateh singh operated from the fort of Pingora (14 miles south-west of Bharatpur).[63] The reports of such renewed depredations and Bishan Singh's delay in repressing the rebels infuriated Aurangzeb. He reprimanded the Raja and reduced his *mansab* by 500 *zats* and 1,000 *sawars* (1690).[64]

However, Bishan Singh did not lose heart. Combining diplomacy with valour, the Raja and his general, Hari Singh continued their fight against the Jats. In January, 1691, Bishan Singh sent Hari Singh to attack Awar and he himself moved towards Sonkh. On 21st May 1691, the Kachhwahas captured Sogar with a surprise attack. Achala and Rustam Sogaria were

---

57. *J. Records*, Sarkars's coll., IX, 198-199.
58. U.N. Sharma, *Itihas*, I, 144.
59. Qanungo, 'Bishan Singh' *Proc. I.H.C.*, XI, 171.
60. *J. Records*, Sarkars's coll. (Pers. Ms.), IX, 42, 356, and 330 (Hindi Letter); VII, 337 Sitamau coll., I, 9; Qanungo, 'Bishan Singh', *Proc. I.H.C.*, XI, 172.
61. *J. Records*, Sitamau coll. (Pers. Ms.), I, 9.
62. *J. Records*, Sarkars's coll. (Pers. Ms.), 1, 9, Sarkar's Coll. IX, 42-44.
63. Ganga Singh, op.cit., 60; Pande, *Bharatpur*, 11.
64. Qanungo, 'Bishan Singh', *Proc. I.H.C*, XI, 172.

stayed at Sogar. This place was surrounded by small *garhis* of Sonkh, Awar, Rarah, Sewar, Noh and Dahra. These were situated in impenetrable *jungles*. The Rajputs cleared the *jungles* and put several villages on fire. But the Jats held on. One day the Rajputs fell upon Sogar at a time when its gate was kept open for admitting provisions. Disguising themselves as labourers, some Rajput soldiers entered the fortress, while ten main troops arrayed outside the gate. Then they killed all those who opposed them. Five Hundred rebels were captured. The news of the fall of the *garhi* was sent to the Emperor along with its golden key.[65]

Bidar Bakht was subsequently recalled to the Deccan (December-1691).[66] Bishan Singh, however, stayed behind to carry on the work of suppressing the Jats. After Sogar, the Kachhawahas attacked Awar which was defended by Raja Ram and Alia. The siege here dragged on for ten months. Hari Singh had to be vigilant on ten sides. First, he had to cope with those rebels who emerging from the nearby *garhis*, surprised the besiegers. At the same time he had to confront their roving bands also. Inspite of these difficulties the Rajputs succeeded in capturing the *garhi* in February, 1692.[67]

The capture of these main strongholds did not materially improve the situation. The Jat rebels remained active throughout. Kanha Naruka, Ram Singh Pawar, Sheo Singh Pawar and Harkishan Chauhan co-operated with them. Troubles now stirred up in the Hindaun-Bayana region. The Jat and Rajput insurgents harassed the local *karories and amils* and exacted the revenue from the people. *Maasir-i-Alamgiri* tells us that Kamal-ud-Din Khan, the *faujdar* of Hindaun-Bayana tried to chastise the rebels in that quarter. In lieu of his services the Emperor increased his mansab by 500 *zat* (30th November, 1692).[68]

Kasot (7 miles to the north of Sogar) and Pingora (14 miles to the south-west of Bharatpur) were the next targets of the Kachhwahas. Around September, 1692, they captured Kasot. However, they experienced greater hardships in wresting Pigora from Fateh Singh (early in October) who fled to Sonkh Gujar. In view of its strategic position the castle of Pingora was not demolished. Instead the Kachhwahas chose to encamp there.[69] The *faujdari* of Hindaun and Bayana was granted to Bishan Singh (August, 1692). Subsequently, on 10th December his *mansab* was increased by

---

65. The letter of Kesho Rao, 20th Jan, 1691; *Fatuhat* (Pers. Ms.) 137a-137b. It is, however, wrong in stating that Sogar was captured only a day after Sinsini; *Maasir*, 340; *Kamwar* (Pers. Ms.), II, 237; U.N. Sharma, *Itihas*, 1, 48, 150, 151, 152.
66. *Maasir*, 344.
67. Qanungo, *Diggi*, 102-105; U.N. Sharma, *Itihas*, I, 156f.
68. *Akhbarat* (J. Records), IX, 345; *Maasir*, 351; Qanungo, *Diggi*, 102,106.
69. *Ibid.*, Qanungo, *Diggi*, 105.

500 Sawar and he was made the *faujdar* of Bhusawar also. As is evident from Aurangzeb's repeated orders, the obvious purpose of these new assignments and promotion was that the Raja should exert utmost for the extirpation of the rebels. However, side by side, his opponents, the Amir-ul-Umra, Kamal-ud-Din and others were busy maligning him. It was wrongly reported that the Raja was unwilling to suppress the rebels and capture their forts, that he shared one third of the booty of the plunderers and that Jagman, Fateh Singh and Churaman had resettled in their original homes. Though Bishan Singh refused such allegations, it annoyed the Emperor and he threatened to reduce his (Raja's) *mansab*. Thus Aurangzeb made the Raja confront the Jats "sometime by cajolery and more often by threats."[70]

To resume, during the siege of Pingora the Jats, who had assembled at Bhatavali (10 miles to the north of Pingora), harassed the Rajputs.[VI] Retaining their base there, they intended to obstruct the march of the Kachhawahas to the important castle of Sonkh. In the middle of December, 1692 Bishan Singh despatched a section of his army to Kathumar area, and he himself moved towards Bhatavali. A severe action took place near Sonkh Gujar (10 miles to the north west of Bhatavali) between Hari Singh and the rebels led by Fateh Singh and Churaman. In the end, the Jat chieftains fled towards Bayana and Rupbas. The Rajput[VI] general then directed an assault on Sonkh, which he caputured on 9th January, 1693. The Kachhwahas followed up this success by easily wresting the *garhis* of Raises (12 miles to the south of Sonkh) and Bhatavali (in February) from the Jats, Barora (19th April) from their associates the Narukas, and Garhi Kesra (in June) from the Chauhans. During the next six months the Raja's forces remained busy subduing the Panwars and Jat rebels and capturing their small *garhis*, Jharoti (6 miles to north-west of Bhusawar), Barah (10 miles to east-west of Jharorti), Saidpur Khairora (7 miles to south-east of Bhusawar), Mahua, Matan, Mahun etc. Meanwhile, some miscreants had gathered at Rarah (7 miles to north-east of Bharatpur). Gaj Singh attacked and captured it (September, 1693), though the defenders escaped.[71] There was, however, no rest for Bishan Singh. Pressed in one area, the rebel chieftains, Churaman, Ani Ram and others now raised their heads in the south-western region of Agra. Chaikora (8 miles to the south of Sikri),

70. Qanungo, 'Bishan Singh', *Proc. I.H.C.*, XI, 172; Meghraj to Bishan Singh, 28 January 1693, Also *J. Records*, IX, 356-357.

VI. Rajput means 'Kachhawahas' at both places because other Rajput clans—Naruka, Pawar and Chauhan were with the Jats and Rathor were also against Kachhawahas. Thus one clan cannot represent the whole body of the Rajputs.—Editor.

71. *Akbarat,* IX; Qanungo, *Diggi*, 106-108, 110-113, 116-123.

the castle of Maujea Jat, served as the base for their renewed activities. Bishan Singh, therefore, decided to besiege this *garhi.* But the Jat leaders had slipped away before he could do so. Hari Singh pursued them upto Sainpur but he failed to catch them. The Jat leaders, crossing the Parvati river, sought refuge in Ratanpur and Intai. Meanwhile seeing the concentration of the imperialists at Chaikora the local Jat Sardars retreated to Sarsoda (7 miles to the south-west of Chaikora) and resumed lawlessness in its environs. Hari Singh overpowered them in two encounters making five hundred of them captives including Alia's son Nand Ram (in the third week of March 1694). All of them were mercilessly slain on the road, to serve as a deterrent for the other insurgents. On 14th April, the Rajputs decamping from Chaikora shifted to the castle of Khorsa (4 miles to the west of Khanua). A fierce engagement took place there in which the rebels were finally pushed back. The Rajputs then assaulted the *garhi.* Subsequently they remained busy chastising the Jats but their leaders slipped to the *garhis* of Bachhamadi (4 miles to the east of Bharatpur), Undera (3 miles to the east of Bachhamadi) and Chiksana (1 mile to the south of Undera) situated in the deep *jungles.* Hari Singh rushed to the area and circled. He finally converged on Chiksana (c. May). A bloody encounter occurred there in which the Jat women[VII] also displayed their reckless courage in the battle field. However, the Rajputs ultimately prevailed over the rebels. Both sides sustained heavy losses. Numberous Jats were captured and later slain on Agra-Bharatpur road. But the ring leaders eluded Bishan Singh once more.[72]

The Jadon castle of Ratanpur (4 miles to the south-west of Sir Mathura) situated amidst hillocks and dense forest, north of the Chambal rankled in the minds of the imperialists. Most of the prominent Jat chieftains expelled from their castles (Churaman, Aniram and others from Sinsini; Lodha, Bukna and others from Sogar; Nand Ram, Alia Vijai Ram etc. from Awar; Jagman, Banarasi from Sonkh; Maujia and others from Chaikora) had flocked there. Discussions about the plan to arrest them were held with Raja Kalyan Singh Bhadauria (in whose *faujdari* lay the region of Ratanpur). It was decided that the imperialists should march to Ratanpúr via Bayana. But the Jat, Jadon and Gujar rebels getting an inkling of their plan, gathered at Bargaon (3 miles to the west of Jagnair) to engage the advancing imperialists and at the same time to cut off their supplies and create troubles in the rear. Postponing the original

---

VII. The leader of these women was Longshree, B.S. Bhargava, *Rajputana Ka Itihas,* 118-119 cited by, Ganga Singh, *Itihas,* p. 39.—Editor.

72. *Akbarat,* IX; *Diggi,* 125, 127-129, 132-134; U.N. Sharma, *Itihas,* 167-173.

plan Hari Singh attacked and overpowered the rebels at Bargaon and its environs (in May 1694). A fierce fight took place at Richhua (2nd week of May) in which over two thousand Jats fell fighting bravely. There after the Kachhawaha troops attacked Ratanpur (1st week of June). Following an action the castle fell, but the rebel chieftains fled crossing the chambal and thus dodged the Raja again.[73]

Meanwhile, the troubles had been brewing up in the trans-Yamuna, *parganas* of Mahaban Jalesar and Sadabad. Nand Ram Jat had built a strong fort at Jawara (2 miles to north-east of Mursan) and surrounded it with a network of small *garhis*, Kihrari (6 miles to the north of Mahaban), Jagsana (2 miles to the north of Kihrari) etc. Fraternizing with the Nohbar Jats of Noh (6 miles to the north-east of Jalesar) he plundered the above *parganas* and created lawlessness there. The Emperor ordered Bishan Singh and Hari Singh to crush Nanda and other Jat miscreants. The Raja, however, submitted that in the event of Itiqad Khan retaining the *faujdari* of Mahaban the responsibility of the rebels rested with the Khan and not with him. But these procrastinations proved futile. The Kachhawaha troops crossed the Yamuna and capturing Anore Garhi Kihara and other *garhis* laid siege to Jawara (1st week of March, 1695) Hari Singh, was, however, killed (5th April) while leading an assault. Thereupon Bishan Singh assumed command and through the efforts of Gaj Singh, Jawara was captured (2nd week of May) but Nanda's sons escaped.[74, VIII]

By now, the incessant chase of the intractable Jats had completely worn out Bishan Singh. He found himself "at sea with the Jats"[75], now that his brave general, Hari Singh had also died. Few would deny that from the viewpoint of actual results, the Jat war proved to be a miniature of Aurangzeb's war against the Marathas. "General massacre" and "extirpation" of the Jat rebels were the avowed objectives with which the imperialists had waged a seven year long strenuous warfare against them. They covered a big area, stretching from Mewat to the Chambal and from Hathras to the borders of Jaipur, in course of their operations. In the process they, no doubt, captured 52[IX] rebel strongholds, slew or drove away thousands of the rebels from them and imposed a curb on

---

73. *Akhbarat*, U.N. Sharma, *Itihas*, 172-176; Qanungo, 'Bishan Singh', *Proc. I.H.C.* XI, 172.

74. Meghraj to Bishan Singh, 30 January 1695; Qalnungo, *Diggi*, 140-147, 157; 'Bishan Singh', *I.H.C.* XI, 172; U.N. Sharma, *Itihas*, 176-179

VIII. Also *Itihas*, 130, 136-139, 143-145.—Editor.

75. Qanungo, 'Bishan Singh', *Proc. I.H.C*, XI, 172; cf. *Roznamcha* (Pers. Ms.), 134; *Shah*, 2.

IX. K.R. Qanungo mentions 50 *garhis*, *History of the House of Diggi*, 122.—Editor.

their activities. Nevertheless, as in the case of the Marathas in the south, the daring of the Jats could not be suppressed.[76] Let alone their whole body, even all the Jat leaders could not be exterminated. Manucci hits the truth when he says that the imperialists merely succeeded in making the Jats retreat.[77] Even this success was of a precarious nature. Overpowered in one quarter, the rebels would rally forth in the other to resume their lawless activities. The rebels were possessed of an irrepressible spirit and the collusion of the local *zamindars* and their agents[78] further emboldened them in their nefarious course. This hide and seek, which continued for the better part of these seven years, eventually overwhelmed Bishan Singh. Undeniably, he scored greater success than most of the other imperial generals had. But this proved only a partial one and even that he could not achieve without greatly impairing his forces and "ruining the land".[79, X] The Jat war must have disillusioned the ambitious Amber Raja. As its upshot, the existing feud between the Amber House and the Jats must have been sharpened.

Because of the Jat depredations[80] as also the long-drawn-out military operations, several areas were rendered desolate. This coupled with the frequent interference by the rebels, adversely reacted on the proceeds to the imperial treasury. We have contemporary evidence to show that there were certain *mahals* where from at one time or the other, not a single dime could be realized for the exchequer.[81]

The Emperor had reasons to be worried over the pernicious developments so close to the capital. The contemporary despatches show his pre-occupation with the Jat problem. The fact that the Jats had remained unsubdued even after long exertions added to his predicament. At last he was forced to depute (9th May, 1695) no less a personage than Prince Shah Alam himself to cope with the situation.[82, XI]

---

76. *Roznamcha* (Pers. Ms.), 134; U.N. Sharma, *Itihas*, 182; cf. *M.U.*, I, 438; *Shah*, 2.
77. *Storia*, II, 301; *Memoires des Jats*, (Fr. Ms.) 12. Its author, however, makes (at the same place) a contradictory and evidently misleading statement that a long period of peace and order followed the death of Raja Ram Jat.
78. *J. Records*, Sarkar's coll. (Pers. Ms.) XII, 113, VII, 335.
79. *Storia*, II, 301; Bishan Singh incurred a huge debt of 50 lakhs due to the Jat war, Vide U.N. Sharma, *Itihas*, I, 177.

X. See also Qanungo, *History of the House of Diggi*, 111.—Editor.

80. *J. Records*, Sarkar's coll. (Pers. Ms.), IX, 58, 241, 340, 342, VII, 85.
81. *Ibid.*, IX, 42-43, 58, 241, 342, 362, 375.
82. *Maasir*, 372-373; *M.U.*, I, *438*.

XI. Raja Ram Singh and his minor grand-son Bishan Singh were appointed to a dangerous command for keeping the Kheber Road safe and open for the imperialist. After the death of Raja Ram Singh in 1688 at Kohat in Kabul, Bishan Singh was transfered to Mathura on the condition to crush the Jats. On his failure Bishan Singh was again sent back to previous command where he died on 19th December 1699 A. D. in Darband in Kabul. K.R. Qanungo, *The History of the House of Diggi*, 25, 29, 43, 122.—Editor.

RISE OF CHURAMAN II

It stands to reason to believe that the rebuff sustained by the Jats reacted upon the future prospects of Fateh Singh, who otherwise being the son and heir of the distinguished Raja Ram, must have enjoyed a unique position among his clansmen. Obviously, failure was anathema in the eyes of the Jats, who measured the efficacy and ability of a leader in terms of his success. It could hardly be otherwise in a society wherein the bonds of political attachment to a superior leader were still to be strengthened. Thus, getting sceptical about his capabilities the Jats discarded Fateh Singh[83] in favour of Raja Ram's cousin, Churaman II,[84] who was unquestionably more capable than Fateh Singh. We learn from *Ahkam-i-Alamgiri* that Fateh Singh later fell somehow into the hands of the Mughals. At first kept at Lahore, he was afterwards taken to Agra. Aurangzeb seduced him to embrace Islam by promising to set him free and also to reward him with a suitable *mansab*. Failing that, Fateh Singh was ordered to be vigilantly kept in prison as before.[85] We have already noted that Bhao Singh[86] had died earlier and Jorawar Singh was killed after the fall of Sinsini (1691). The aged Bhajja Singh also seems to have perished. The disappearance of these prominent Sinsinwaras from the scene must have also faciliated the emergence of Churaman II as the supreme leader.

---

83. *Muttra Gazetteer* (Drake-Brockman: 1911), 197; Also Ganga Singh, *op.cit.*, p. 64.
84. Till now, only one Jat chief by the name of Churaman was known to us. *Fransoo*, in his invaluable Persian account to the Bharatpur ruling family, *Tawarikh-i-Hunud* 14b (my personal Micro Film copy made from the original in British Museum, London Pers Add. 19, 501) which he based, among others, on the reliable testimony of the Persian Munshis of the Jat Court, throws new light in this direction. While giving the geneaology of the Sinsinwara Jat chiefs, this foreigner indicates that there had been two leaders bearing one and the same name of Churaman. The Churaman with whom we have been familiar so far, was the fifth in order of descent from his first name sake *i.e.* Churaman I, who was the son of Rathpal. Fransoo specifies that Churaman II was one of the sons of Bhunta (?) seems to be a slip for Brij Raj). The other son mentioned by him is Bhao Singh, the father of Rup Singh and Badan Singh.

    It is commonly acknowledged that Raja Ram and Churaman (Precisely Churaman II) were brothers (See *J. Records*, Sarkar's coll. IX, 356; *Fatuhat*, 135b; Sarkar, *Aurangzib*, V, 302; Qanungo, *Jats*, 45; Pande, *Bharatpur*, 11). Yet Fransoo does not include Raja Ram among the brothers of Churaman. In fact he is silent about this Raja Ram. This omission seems extremely significant and indirectly supports the belief that Raja Ram and Churaman II were not real brothers but cousins; the former being the son of Bhajja Singh, while the latter that of Brij Raj. Both Bhajja and Brij, are uncritically believed to be one and the same man by Dr. Pande (*Bharatpur*, 5). Actually they were the sons of Khan Chand, See Ganga Singh, *Itihas*, 32-33; Gokul Chandra Dikshit, *Brijendra Vansha Bhaskar*, 6.
85. *Ahkam* (Pers. Ms.), II, 206a-206b. Afterwards, he was set free, for his name figures in the early activities of Badan Singh.
86. Wendel, *Memoires des Jats*, (Fr. Ms., 12) makes Bhao Singh live on even after 1707. This is wrong. Had he been alive all these years, the local news reporters and the Amber agents must have taken note of him also along with the other Jat leaders.

The departure of Shah Alam and Bishan Singh from the province of Agra in 1696,[87] obviously provided the opportune moment to Churaman to makeup the losses, consolidate his position and carry forward the work of Raja Ram. Bold, practical, unscrupulous and rapacious, Churaman II possessed a good capacity for organisation and for making clever use of his opportunities which he was lucky to enjoy almost throughout his career.[88] About his early career it is said that he engaged 500 horsemen and 1,000 footmen. Nanda Jat, the father of Bhure Singh and grand father of Daya Ram, joined him with 100 men.[89] The Mewatis under Bayzid Khan, the Khuntelas of Sonkh, the Sogarias under Khem Karan and Bargujars under Hathi Singh of Dahana also joined him.[90] Churaman robbed the wayfarers and carvans on the royal highways. He strengthened his bands with musketeers and carvalry. Step by step the number of his followers increased to 14,000.[91] Meanwhile, as a number of the Jat castles had been occupied or demolished by the imperialists, Churaman built new forts in the impenetrable *jungles*, for the purposes of defence and preservation of booty. In it he was aided by the hidden wealth of his ancestors including Raja Ram.[92] Among the new forts he built a formidable one at Thun (11 miles to the west of Deeg) in a low marshy and thickly wooded tract. According to Shivdas, Thun was surrounded by so thick a *jungle* of thorny bushes that even the birds found it difficult to pass through it. Its rampart was as high as 'heaven', while the moat around was so deep that water burst up from the bottom.[93]

Side by side his predatory activities went on unabated. He plundered first, the countryside of Agra and then Kota, Bundi, Hindaun and Bayana.[94] He seized the wealth and places of the weaker ones. Attending to his job with "great perfection", Churaman rose "higher and higher" and gradually became most redoubtable in his neighbourhood.[95]

---

87. *Maasir*, 382.
88. For full details See, Ch. IV. Character and estimate of Rao Churaman II; Also Qanungo, *Jats*, 45-46.
89. *Imad-us-Saadat* by Ghulam Ali Khan Naqawi (Gaekwad Library, B.H.U, Ms.) 83.
90. *Akhbarat* Muhammad Shah's reign (R.S.L. Sitamau transcript) XXIII, 82; *Shahnama Munawwar Kalam* by Shivdas Lakhanavi (ed. by S.H. Askari, Patna, 1968) 16, 17 and 84; *Iqbalnama*, Anon. (English trans. by S.H. Askari.) Pages from his typed transcript cited. 23 and 24; Ganga Singh, *op.cit.*, 69, U.N. Sharma, *Itihas*, 197.
91. *Imad* (Pers. Ms.), 83; *Memoires des Jats* (Fr. Ms.), 12.
92. *Memoires des Jats* (Fr. Ms.), 12.
93. *Shivdas*, 19; *Iqbal*, 23; *Memories des Jats* (Fr. Ms.), 14.
94. *Memories des Jats* (Fr. Ms.), 13; Imad (Pers. Ms.), 83; Also Ganga Singh, *op.cit.*, 69.
95. *Memories des Jats* (Fr. Ms.), 14.

It is needless to emphasize that the loss of Sinsini, the ancestral place[96] of those, who were providing leadership to the Jat fraternity, rankled in the Jat bosom. About the year 1704 Churaman recaptured Sinsini from the Mughals, though not by the might of his sword but by gold. Accepting substantial amount from the Jats, Devi Singh, the fort commandant, handed over Sinsini to them. The Jats seized all the imperial effects including two big guns, eighteen *rahkalahs*, stores of lead and gunpowder and other articles.[97] Obviously, the loss of Sinsini was as distressing to the Mughals as its re-occupation was heartening to the Jats. Mirza Muhammad says that Churaman re-occupied all those forts which had earlier been lost to the Mughals.[98]

This flare up grieved Aurangzeb. What must have added to his worries was the fact that the royal treasure amounting to rupees 30 lakhs (realized from Bengal and other places) lay accumulated at Agra and it had to be sent safely to the Deccan.[99] Deeply censuring the *nazim* of Agra for his manifest carelessness, the Emperor repeatedly ordered him to put up utmost exertions to immediately re-capture Sinsini, "extinguish the fire of rebellion and plunder" and "eradicate the name and vestige" of the Jats rebels from the land.[100] Mukhtar Khan the *nazim* of Agra had given an undertaking (22nd Zil Hijja?) to the Emperor "to annihilate" the Jats within two years, if he was granted rupees ten lakhs for recruiting additional troops, 1500 *sawars* (at the monthly salary of rupees 25 per *sawar*) and 2,000 footmen (at the monthly allowance of rupees 4 per footmen) for the purpose.[101] Mukhtar Khan was advanced rupees one lakh from the Agra treasury. The *faujdars* of the *suba* of Agra and Delhi along with 5,500 *sawars* were also deputed for crushing the Jats.[102]

The imperialists laid siege to Sinsini in 1705. But it proved arduous again and dragged on. The surprise attacks of the Jats coupled with the rains impeded its progress. The Jats completely destroyed three of the

96. *Tawarikh-i-Hunud* (Pers. Ms.), 13b-14a; Dikshit (op.cit. 17-18) and U.N. Sharma (*Itihas*, 185-186) think that Brij Raj assuming the leadership, had recovered Sinsini but he later died alongwith Bhao Singh while defending it against the Mughals and that afterwards old Bhajja Singh tried to recapture it but failed and subsequently died out of this shock in 1702. This, however, looks doubtful. The reality is that Brij Raj had died before Raja Ram's assumption of the Jat leadership. As for Bhajja, the father of Raja Ram, even if he was not dead by now, he must have grown too old to withstand the rigours of warfare.
97. *Ahkam* (Pers. Ms.), I, 7b, 67b, 73b, II, 203a, 205b.
98. *Roznamcha* (Pers. Ms.), 134.
99. *Ahkam* (Pers. Ms.), I, 36b, II, 204b.
100. *Ibid.*, II, 203b, 204a, 205b, also I, 69a, 73a.
101 *Ahkam* (Pers. Ms.), I, 69b, II, 203b.
102. *Ibid.*, I, 78b, II, 203, 204a, 204b.

five big Mughal cannons deployed to storm the fort and rendered another unworkable by inserting an iron bar inside the barrel. All these days they continued to be supplied with provisions from outside.[103] The *nazim* initially found himself helpless against the tenacious Jats.[104] Aurangzeb had earlier commanded the experienced Bidar Bakht to proceed on to the scene and take revenge from the Jats for their misdeeds. Besides those mentioned above, the Prince was ordered to take with him Kalyan Singh Bhadauria and Jai Singh of Amber. But due to his illness and other pre-occupations Bidar Bakht could not depart and had to stay in Malwa during the rainy season.[105]

Mukhtar Khan, however, clung on to his business and on 9th October, 1705 (2nd Rajab, 1117 A.H.), he succeeded in reducing Sinsini. The news of the fall of the fortalice alongwith its golden key was sent to the Emperor. In reward for his services Mukhtar Khan got an addition of 500 *zat* to his existing rank.[106] The Prince was now ordered to cancel his departure. Mirza Muhammad adds that the *nazim* recaptured other forts also from the hands of Churaman.[107]

What a glaring contrast in the situation! No Jat power worth the name existed when Aurangzeb had ascended the throne, but by the time of his death, the Jat power, if not the Jat state, had certainly come into existence. The Jats, fundamentally agriculturists, were converted into unpacified and unsubdued foes of the Mughal authority, ready to wrest any advantage that the troubled times might offer to them. Such a change in the attitude of a people whose one prominent section under Hathi Singh Jat helped Aurangzeb at a critical stage on his march to contest the Crown of Hindustan,[108] must have added to the agony of his last days.

---

103. *Ibid.*, I, 36a, 77b-78a, also 72b, II, 201b, 203b, 204a.
104. *Ibid.*, I, 77a.
105. *Ibid.*, I, 7, 23b, 69a, 70a, 74b, 75b, 77a, 78b. 87b; Also *J. Records,* Sitamau coll. (Pers. Ms.), I, 22, 23 and 25. Parichit Rai to Jai Singh, 15 Rajab year 49.
106. *Maasir*, 498; *Akham* (Pers. Ms.), I,79a, *J. Records,* Sitamau coll. (Pers. Ms.), I, 27; Kumbh Karan to Jai Singh in 1705 (1117 A.H.).
107. *Roznamcha* (Pers. Ms.), 134.
108. Ishwar Das (*Fatuhat*, Pers. Ms., 23a) relates that when Prince Aurangzeb, on his way to oppose Dara, came to the fords of the Chambal, he found them barred by the opposite entrenchment. He was ignorant about other ferries, while the waters were deep. This perturbed Aurangzeb. At this critical juncture Hathi Singh Jat, the *zamindar* of Gohad, came forward to lead his troops to a neglected ford (Kanira), where from Aurangzeb crossed the Chambal. Though by itself and small incident, it in one stroke turned the scales against Dara. He had to hurry up for the Capital, leaving heavy artillery behind which greatly weakened his position.

III
The Decline of the Mughal Empire and the Rise of the Jat Power (1707-1720)

The Jat power under the leadership of Churaman II took a big leap forward during the rule of the imbecile successors of Aurangzeb. It is outside our scope to dwell in detail upon the events of the Empire in the succeeding decades. However, it would be worthwhile to keep in view the broad facts and trends of the period which formed the background of the rapid advance of the Jats.

THE DECLINE OF THE MUGHAL EMPIRE

Aurangzeb's policy and conduct rudely shook the foundations of the Empire. He left behind a host of serious problems for his weak successors to deal with people highly agitated. As an upshot of his Deccan warfare, the general administration was weakened and the state of finances also became chaotic. The crisis in the *jagirdari* system and the degeneration of the nobility were yet other problems bequeathed by him to his weak successors.[1]

His immediate successor, Bahadur Shah, though abler than those that followed him could not check the worsening situation. After him started a chain of indolent, dissolute and incompetent rulers, incapable of evoking either respect or fear.[2]

To make matters worse, scramble for power and *jagirs*, personal affiliations with one or the other contestants for the Crown and ethnic and religious considerations combinedly worked to accentuate discord, and factionalism in the ranks of the Mughal nobility. The Emperor, often aligned with some faction, ceased to be a unifying force and fomented secret plots instead. By the end of Aurangzeb's reign two rival factions had emerged; the first consisted of Asad Khan and Zulfiqar Khan, while

---

1. For details see Sarkar, *Aurangzib*, V, 436ff; Satish Chandra, *Parties and Politics*, Introduction, also 22.
2. For details see Satish Chandra, *Parties and Politics*, 22-23, 56-60; Irvine, *Later Mughals*, I, 136-140, 241 and 396.

the other comprised of Firoz Jang, Chin Qillich, Hamid Khan and others. Both these groups although at cross purposes with each other, nurtured a common grudge over their exclusion by Bahadur Shah from the Wizarat—an office which gradually became the focal point of the Court-politics. Having won the Crown for Jahandar Shah, Zulfiqar Khan acquired that coveted office, and in the process real power, to the resentment of the other aspirants. He endeavoured to conciliate the Marathas, Rajputs and the Jats and thereby "bridge the gulf" between them and the Empire. But soon the Sayyid brothers supplanted him. Factional politics dominated the reign of Farrukh Siyar. The Emperor and his sycophants hatched plots to get rid of the dominating Sayyids, while the latter attempted to retain their supremacy. The Sayyids courted the friendship of the powerful Hindu elements including the Jats in order to retain power as also to earn their goodwill and thereby rejuvenate the Empire. Farrukh Siyar's murder and the pro-Hindu policies offered a pretext to their rivals to construe the Sayyid's acts as being dangerous for the monarchy, Islam and all the nobles. Soon they were overthrown. But this brought no change in the basic issues and the general situation. The administrative condition went from bad to worse. Bankruptcy stared in the face of the government. The *jagirdari* system headed for a crash, endangering the whole edifice of the *mansabdari* system.[3]

The break-down of the imperial authority and the resultant chaos paved the way for, and in turn was accentuated by, the foreign invasions and internal aggression. The centrifugal forces, active since the times of Aurangzeb, received fresh stimulus. To give a few glaring examples, Chhatrasal, flagrantly defying the Mughal authority, seized the royal lands. The Sikhs under Banda rose in arms and ravaged a large tract around Sirhind. The Marathas, through their persistent incursions affecting a very wide area violently shook the roots of the Mughal Empire.[4] Some imperial governors the Nizam, Murshid Quli Khan, Saadat Khan and Abdus Samad-themselves contributed to the dismemberment of the Empire by carrying out their separate kingdoms.[5]

Others were not slow in emulating the examples set by the Mughal grandees. Two adjacent centres of the Afghan power came to the forefront, the first was of the Bangash Pathans at Farrukhabad and the other of the Rohillas in Katehar. The Rajputs also exploited the imperial weakness to expand their territories. Jai Singh Sawai entertained the ambition of

---

3. For details see Satish Chandra, *Parties and Politics*, 57-60, 79-84, 116, 117, 174-176 and 256; Irvine, *Later Mughals*, I, 138-139, 334-336; II, 131-132 and 134.
4. For details see Irvine, *Later Mughals*, I, 93-121, 307-320, II, 163-167, 170-185 and 229ff.
5. Sarkar, *Fall*, I, 42, 181-182.

bringing under his domination the region from the Sambhar lake to Agra and thence to the Narmada. Though this could not materialize, he made worthwhile addition to his patrimony all the same. Similarly, the Jodhpur Rajas cast covetous glances upon their neighbouring lands. They eventually annexed some areas lying in the Mughal *suba* of Gujrat.[6] Petty chiefs were busy in capitalizing the impotence of the Mughal government. Ashub aptly remarks, "every *zamindar* became a Raja and every Raja a Maharaja".[7] The Mughal Emperors, on the other hands, were reduced to mere figureheads, and their Empire, destitute of its former virility, grandeur and extent, was fast heading towards its doom.

It was this state of affairs amidst which Churaman II and his successors shaped their policy and conduct, which we shall examine below.

PRECARIOUS DETENTE BETWEEN THE MUGHALS AND THE JATS

The Mughal-Jat relations entered into a new stage after the death of Aurangzeb. Until then both the government and the Jats had displayed inveterate hostility and repugnance towards each other. After Aurangzeb the changing circumstances obliged both sides to dilute their former intransigence. Consequently, for the first time during the Mughal rule, the Jats came to be actively and directly associated with the imperial affairs. This was destined to have considerable repercussion especially upon the history of the Jats.

Expediency and political sagacity induced the Mughals to placate the Jat chief, Churaman II. The geographical proximity of the Jat country and their growing military importance made the Jat support worth obtaining both for the contestants of the imperial Crown and the factional leaders of the Mughal Court. Conviction also tended the Mughals in the same direction. The Mughal government after 1707 generally pursued a lenient policy, shunning the sternness and inflexibility of the days of Aurangzeb. This reversal of the policy was a welcome relief to the Jats. It held out prospects of the growth of their infant power. The astute Churaman perhaps calculated that a display of loyalty to the throne would allay the Mughal suspicions and provide him opportunities to strengthen his position. The hope of winning rewards inclined him to join one or the other claimant to the Mughal throne or the powerful nobles. His participation in the imperial affairs must have been equally motivated by his rapacious habits. Plunder and

6. For details see Sarkar, *Fall*, I, 42, 181ff: Raghubir Singh, *Malwa Main Yugantar Purva Kal* (Indore: 1938), 199; Satish Chandra, *Parties and Politics*, 186-187.
7. Ashub quoted by Satish Chandra, *op.cit.*, 187; Also *Siyar-ul-Mutakherin*, trans. John Briggs (London: 1832) I, 208.

booty were too alluring for him to remain indifferent to the imperial wars in his neighbourhood. Self-aggrandisement, therefore, remained the keynote of Churaman's relations with the Mughal government as before, when he had been its sworn enemy. Thus it may safely be said that more under the pressure of the circumstances than by deliberate policy both the Mughal government and the Jats were obliged to soften their attitude towards each other.

The death of Aurangzeb in 1707 caused a deadly contest between Muazzam and Azam for the Crown of Hindustan. The rivals faced each other in the battlefield of Jajau. Mirza Muhammad tells us that Bahadur Shah, in an attempt to muster up as big an army as possible, despatched assuasive messages to Churaman, asking him to present himself with his force. Responding to the royal summons, Churaman came with two to three thousand *sawars* and waited on Bahadur Shah[8]. This version of Mirza Muhammad dispels the impression that Churaman went to Jajau of his own "to pillage the vanquished."[9] The audacious Jat, however, did not forget to turn the discomfiture of the enemy to his advantage. In the thick of the fight he slipped away and vigorously plundered Azam's baggage. Finally he departed grabbing goods, cattle, treasure and precious jewels.[10] It seems that Churaman taking advantage of the situation following Jajau, recaptured Sinsini and resumed depredations around Mathura on the Delhi-Agra Road. As a result the traffic on the road was completely stopped for two months and hundreds of travellers including the wife of Amin-ud-din Sambhali got stranded. In August 1707, troops were sent to chastise the Jat plunderers.[11] The Wazir, Munim Khan, however, found it expedient to ignore his misdeeds. He once again called and on 16th September presented Churaman before the Emperor. Bahadur Shah conferred upon him the *mansab* of 1,500 *zat* and 500 *sawar* and entrusted to him the charge of the road between Delhi and Agra.[12]

The year 1707, particularly marked an epoch in the early career of Churaman. In its wake, it brought to him honour, power and immense riches, such as "his predecessors had not acquired (even) in a lifetime."[13] It secured for him admission to the proud ranks of the imperial

8. *Roznamcha* (Pers. Ms.), 134f.
9. Contra see Irvine, *Later Mughals*, I, 322; Qanungo, *Jats*, 48; Pande, *Bharatpur*, 13, U.N. Sharma, *Itihas*, I, 200.
10. *Roznamcha*, 135; *Bahadur Shah Nama*, 164; K.K.II, 668; *M.U.* I, 438.
11. *Akhbarat*, 13 August, 1707; *Dastur-ul-insha* quoted by Irvine, *Later Mughals*, I, 321, footnote; *Memoires des Jats*, 13.
12. *Roznamcha* (Pers. Ms.), 135; *Bahadur Shah Nama*, 164; K.K. II,, 668-669, 776; *M.U.*, I, 438.
13. *M.U.*, I, 438; Also *Majma-ul-Akhbar* in Elliot, VIII, 360. R. Pande (*op.cit.*, 14) is wrong in his statement that Churaman was given the charge from Delhi to Chambal.

mansabdars. A confirmed rebel was suddenly exalted to the zenith of a Mughal peer, officially entrusted with the charge of a part of the imperial highway. It obviously enhanced his image among the local people who must have rallied round him in greater numbers. In the changed situation Churaman revised his tactics. Partly moved by the conciliatory attitude of the new administration and partly by his own keenness to have more opportunities for advancement, he chose to display loyalty to Bahadur Shah.[14] However, loyalty with him was more a matter of convenience than of conviction. Thus, he would help the Mughal government but at the same time incite his people to connive at the lawless course. Probably, getting a hint from him the Jats had refortified Sinsini. Bahadur Shah, therefore, sent Raza Bahadur to reduce it. On 2nd December, 1707, a bitter fight ensued in which 1,000 Jat were killed. Raza Bahadur demolished the fortress, seizing then carts worth of weapons from the vanquished.[15]

CHURAMAN HELPS THE GOVERNMENT

In keeping with his new policy, Churaman apparently chose to be passive on the Sinsini affair. Similarly, in the next few years, he applied a restraint on his predatory habits, though local malefactors sometimes indulged in plundering on the roads.[16] Mirza Muhammad emphatically adds that henceforward till the defeat of Jahandar Shah (*i.e.* from September, 1707 to January, 1713) he devoted himself to the imperial service and did not permit any obstructions on the road."[17] Early in 1708, he helped the local *naib faujdar*, Rahim-ul-la Khan, in suppressing the local Afghan rebels. Having attacked the village of Thiravali (5 miles to the east of OL) he accompanied the Khan in an expedition against the Billochi rebels of Shergarh (20 miles to the north of Mathura). They resisted the invaders for three days but ultimately turned their backs, promising to make over a property worth two thousands to the Jat. This further enhanced his image as a powerful chief. Little wonder, therefore, that greater recognition awaited Churaman. In July, 1708, Jai Singh had occupied Amber, expelling the local *faujdar*, Sayyid Hussain Khan. Thereupon, Bahadur Shah sent re-inforcements to him for recovering

---

14. K.R. Qanungo's view (*Jats*, 48) that Churaman remained faithful for fear of Bahadur Shah's government being "fairly strong", is untenable. It was unquestionably weaker than the preceding one and even that falied to make Churaman faithful to the Mughals.
15. Irvine, *Later Mughals*, I, 322.
16. *Ibid*., 321, footnote.
17. *Roznamcha*, 135. Wendel's assertion (*Memoires des Jats, 13*) about his constant and wide spread disorders in Bahadur Shah's reign cannot be accepted in face of Mirza Muhammad's opinion to the contrary.

that place. In this context Hussain Khan sought the help of the redoubtable Churaman. The Khan sent him money to recruit troops for the purpose. The Jat leader responded and collecting a big force, moved to Narnaul where Hussain Khan had been living ever since his expulsion. About the same time (*i.e.* the end of September) Jai Singh appealed to Churaman to detach himself from the Sayyid and thereby co-operate with him (the Raja) against the Mughals, who were out to destroy the Hindus. In return, the Raja assured him to expel his opponent, Jaitra Singh, from the *pargana* of Kaithwada. Churaman, thereafter, diserted the Sayyid. However, this was not necessarily due to his "veneration for the Hindu sentiments."[18] It is also to be borne in mind that he had already recruited a big force of his own out of the Mughal resources. Besides, he had got Jai Singh's assurance about Kaithwara and taking advantage of it he eventually (in November, 1708) wrested that place from Jaitra Singh. Thus, once his interest appeared to have been served, the clever Jat thought it foolish to burn his fingers unnecessarily in the impending Rajput war. More so, it was sure to annoy Jai Singh and in turn endanger his prospects at Kaithwada. Thus, what he precisely did was that on some pretext he withdrew, leaving Hussain Khan to his own fate. Later, he sent a very humble message to Jai Singh calling himself the Raja's "own servant", he intimated that he wished to see him (Jai Singh) personally and that he never desired to oppose him. Further he assured Jai Singh of his 'services' to do the needful in the Mathura region.[19] This episode incidentally, depicts Churaman at his real self.

From Sayyid Hussain Khan's camp Churaman proceeded to Kama, where Raza Bahadur, the local *faujdar* was preparing to fight the local Rajput *zamindar*, Ajit Singh. The latter withholding the payment of revenue had expelled the local officers and openly challenged the Mughal authority in that area. His turbulent ways caused worry to both the local *faujdar* as well as to the ambitious Churaman, whose chief stronghold, Thun, lay so close to Kama. Hence, both these united and with a big force (about 18,000) attacked Ajit Singh who confronted the enemy with about 10,000 horses and gunners. A bitter fight ensued near Kama in which the Rajput artillery played a major role in repulsing the Jats and the Mughals. The jubilant rebels pursued their enemies upto Khoh (about 8 miles to the south). After three days (*i.e.* 7th October, 1708) they rallied again and then charged the Rajputs. The Mughal-Jat

---

18. U.N. Sharma (*Itihas*, I, 217) infers it.
19. Jaitra Singh (of Kaithwada)—Jai Singh; Kishan Singh and Zalim Singh-Jai Singh—Jai Singh, Phalgun Badi 2 Samvat 1765, both quoted by Bhatnagar, *Sawai Jai Singh*, 41, also see (for details of Husain Khan's struggle with the Rajputs) 38 ff; Irvine, *Later Mughals*, I, 67ff.

combine initially appeared to gain advantage. But the Rajputs, fighting gallantly re-emerged victorious in the end. Many on both sides were killed and wounded. Raza Bahadur was also killed. Churaman and his men, who had been surrounded by the Rajputs towards the end, sallied out against the besiegers. He, however, received wounds from a sword cut delivered by a Rajput soldier, while he was on his way to Thun.[20]

About two months later, (December 1708) Churaman with 6,000 horses joined Mir Khan, the *faujdar* of Narnaul and passing through Sonkh-Sonkhari, attacked the rebel Rajputs. Jai Singh Naruka of Jawali, offered them a stiff resistance.[21]

It is said that Chura's brother Ati Ram, who was a friend of the Naruka, mediated a settlement between Churaman and the Naruka and hence, further operations were given up.[22]

Hereafter, there is a gap of about twenty one months (January, 1709-October 1710) in our information of Churaman's movements. Perhaps these days he was silently busy in expanding and consolidating his hold. Sometime in October, 1710, possibly on being summoned he presented himself to Bahadur Shah (ca. October, 1710) somewhere near Delhi,[23] when the Emperor was on his march against Banda. He was placed under Muhammad Amin Khan, who had been ordered to capture Sarhind. Subsequently, serving the Wazir faithfully, he took part in the campaigns at Sandhaura and Lohagarh.[24] The Wazir, who had shown his favours, died in February, 1711 and this exposed him to the pressures of the Court. We learn from the *Akhbarat* that the fortress at Halena being built by his brother, Ati Ram, would be demolished.[25] It is not clear whether or not this was carried out, Churaman, however, moved on with the Emperor to Lahore.

---

20. *Akhbarat,* Kartik Sudi 5, Samvat, 1765 (7 October, 1708) quoted by U.N. Sharma, *Itihas*, I, 215, 212-215; Kamwar, II, 315.
21. M.L. Sharma, *Jaipur*, 138.
22. U.N. Sharma, *Itihas*, I, 217. He, however, cited no authority in his support.
23. There is some confusion with regard to the date and place of Churaman's arrival of the imperial camp. Irvine (*Later Mughals,* I, 323 and 106) and following him U.N. Sharma (*Itihas*, 222) make Churaman join the Emperor both at Ajmer and near Delhi. His having gone opposite to such a distant place as Ajmer looks against the fitness of things. That Churaman, having joined at Ajmer, later left and rejoined near Delhi, has not been, indicated by them either. Hence, his joining at Ajmer looks doubtful. *Maasir-ul-Umra*, though a later source, states (I, 438) that Churaman joined when"the line of march passed near their (The Jat's) houses." This impliedly supports our view that he joined the Emperor somewhere near Delhi. Qanungo (*Jats*, 48) and R. Pande (*op.cit.*, 14f.) altogether ignore this issue.
24. *K.K.* II, 669 and 670; *M.U.*, I, 438; Irvine, *Later Mughals*. I, 323; R. Pande (*op.cit.*, 15, footnote 1) cited Mirza Muhammad as his lone original authority for Churaman's participation in the Sikh expedition. But Mirza Muhammad makes no statement supporting it.
25. *Akhabarat*, 24 July, 1711.

In the battle of Lahore (March, 1712) consequent upon the death of Bahadur Shah, the Jat leader sided with Azim-ush-Shah. Therein he looked after the supplies to the Prince's camp. Churaman and the *banjaras* had promised to maintain regular supplies. He carried out his pledge faithfully and the Prince looked satisfied. However, largely due to his conceit and evasive tactics Azim-ush-shan was defeated and killed. Thereafter, plundering the Camp, Churaman, apparently made his way home. Providence smiled over him again. Though the contestant whom he had joined, lost the race for the Crown, he was pardoned by the victor, Jahandar Shah. Probably through the intercession of the new Wazir, Zulifqar Khan, whose pro-Hindu leanings were evident, he was presented a *khilat* and re-instated in his *mansab*.[26] This leniency reflected the general policy of Jahandar Shah's government. We know that soon after Jahandar's coronation, Farrukh Siyar had also proclaimed himself Emperor of Patna. Impliedly it meant that the war of succession was not really over yet. Side by side, the new Wazir too had his opponent at the Court. Both the Emperor and the Wazir, thus stood in need of help among others of the Hindu elements also. Besides, their co-operation was deemed necessary to strengthen the declining Empire also. Hence, compulsion and policy induced the government to be considerate towards the redoubted Churaman who had grown into "*the de facto ruler*" of the entire region stretching from Delhi to the Chambal.[27]

The Emperor sent order to Churaman and several Rajput Rajas to join Prince Azi-ud-Din, who had been deputed to Agra to watch the movements of Farrukh Siyar. But all of them procrastinated. Azi-ud-Din was subsequently defeated at Khajuha (November, 1712). This alarmed Jahandar Shah. Early in December, making fulsome promises he sent a *farman* to Churaman to reach Agra with his men against Farrukh Siyar. Churaman came with a big force and fought on the side of the Emperor at the battle of Agra (January 1713). But once his cause appeared to have been lost, the audacious Jat felt no qualms of conscience in plundering the rear of his professed master. He went back to Thun carrying treasures, many elephants and camels together with their baggage. He did not spare the camp of the victor either. The Jats so thoroughly looted it that Farrukh Siyar could not find anything better than a filthy screen and a small wooden platform to sit on, while receiving the homage of his officials.[28]

---

26. Murtaza Hussain, *Hadiqat-ul-Aqalim* (Nawal Kishore ed.), 129; S. Chandra, *Parties and Politics,* 76, 122; Irvine, *Later Mughals,* I, 167.
27. *Memoires des Jats,* 13; Qanungo, *Jats,* 49; Irvine, *Later Mughals,* I, 322.
28. *Akhbarat,* 29 October, 29 November, 2 December, 1712; *Roznamcha,* 1351 *Jahandar Nama* and *Mirat-i-Waridat,* quoted by Irvine, *Later Mughals,* I, 232, 234, 244 and 223. Also K.K., II, 776; cf. Qanungo, *Jats,* 49; cf. *Memoires des Jats,* 13.

INVOLVEMENT IN THE COURT POLITICS

The high-handedness and the daring of Churaman looked dangerous to and justly infuriated Farrukh Siyar.[29] Early in his reign, he appointed Raja Chhabela Ram, his personal adherent and a brave soldier, as the governor of Agra, his birthplace. The Emperor ordered him to proceed at once beyond the Yamuna and crush the Jats, leaving Raja Girdhar Bahadur in charge of the *suba* of Allahabad. Raja Mohkam Singh and Gandhar Singh were placed under him.[30] The Raja, however, delayed in taking the field against the Jats. Meanwhile, the latter persisted with their widespread depredations, even though Farrukh Siyar was fully secure on the throne. Becoming conscious of his power, Churaman's pride crossed all bounds and he showed scant regard to the local officials. By employing tricks he as usual evaded paying the *peshkash*. His bands plundered the way farers, sparing not even the royal *peshkhana*, if it had not troops to guard it.[31] It is evident that his motives in doing all this were to detract Chhabela Ram from his job and thus gain time to strengthen himself and also to extract more concessions from the government. The task before the Raja was difficult indeed. Inspite of it, he addressed himself to it in an earnest way. He mustered additional forces and gave a months' salary in advance to enthuse the soldiers. His subsequent efforts against the recalcitrants showed some results. At least in some areas (such as Fatehpur Sikri), he succeeded in suppressing them and bringing the situation under control. Traffic on the nearby roads was also restored.[32] It seems that side by side, by promising to procure them *mansabs*, the Raja tried to win over some of the powerful associates of Churaman to his side. However, his plans did not come off and he increasingly found it difficult to cope with the Jats. In fact, he had to fight on two fronts, the one against the Jats and the other against his Court opponents (the Sayyids) who were secretly patting Churaman and other chiefs.[33] Apparently pressed by the Raja, Churaman and his close relations begged the Emperor's pardon through the Raja's opponents though they didn't agree to demolish their *garhis*. Chhabela Ram's enemies on one hand, pleaded for Churaman and on the other accused the Raja of 'idleness' in suppressing him.[34] This coupled with

29. *Ajaib-ul-Afaq* (R.S.L. Ms.), 56; Also Memoires des Jats, 14.
30. *Ajaib*, 37, 56 and 82; *Roznamcha*, 135 and 51; Kamwar, II, 391, 395.
31. *Ajaib*, 55-56, 59, 82, 123; *Memoires des Jats*, 13.
32. *Ajaib*, 55, 56, 60, 123.
33. We come across an interesting disclosure that Churaman was secretely presented with a horse and a few cloth rolls by some official. Vide Ajaib, 122; Also see Satish Chandra, *Parties and Politics*, 123.
34. *Ajaib*, 123, 124 and 55, 58.

the talk of his transfer pained Chhabela Ram and he wrote to the Emperor, "I am pleaded over His Majesty's desire of my transfer. This would be my good fortune, if His Majesty thinks like that. The person, who dares to accomplish the difficult task of suppressing Churaman Jat, may be granted an imperial *farman* so that he might extirpate him. However, it must be enquired from him as to how long will he take (to accomplish the task)? This will automatically reveal his boastfulness." The Raja added "whosoever is appointed to fulfil this task (of uprooting Churaman), shall himself fail in his efforts."[35]

Chhabela Ram hit the truth, for, despite his long exertions of four months, he himself failed in suppressing Churaman mainly because of "the obstacles" placed by the Wazir and the Mir Bakshi. Chhabela Ram was, therefore, replaced by a willing Khan-i-Dauran, also a native of Agra, as the governor of that province.[36] Chhabela Ram's struggle against the Jats brings certain facts to the forefront, which deserve our attention. For the first time, disharmony over the Jat problem was reflected in the Mughal government. The Wazir and the Mir Bakshi, both topmost officials, were secretly patting Churaman, while the Emperor determined to subdue him. It was a strange development as no inner conflict with regard to the attitude towards the Jats had hitherto been visible at the highest level. The Sayyid's secret encouragement to Churaman at this stage may properly be appreciated in the light of their early differences with Farrukh Siyar and their opposition to Chhabela Ram. It would be relevant to mention here that in the very first month of his reign, differences sprang up between the fickleminded Farrukh Siyar and the Sayyids. The appointment of Chhabela Ram as the *diwan* of the *khalisa* without the consent of the Wazir, Abdullah Khan, accentuated them further. Chhabela Ram secretly made complaints against the Sayyids. They, therefore, "retaliated by secretly supporting" Churaman against him.[37] Their present role must have impressed upon the Jat leader that he could look forward to them for protection and also for realizing his personal ambitions. On the other side, it seems probable that in Churaman the Sayyids saw a useful ally and by their underhand dealings, proving helpful to the Jat, they were the first to take steps to allure him to their side. It is, then, from this stage, that the genesis of the Sayyid-Jat alliance and the Jat problem becoming one of the crucial issues of the factional politics at the Mughal Court, may reasonably be traced.

35. *Ibid.*, 57 and 58.
36. *Roznamcha*, 135-136, 51; Also, Kamwar, II, 400.
37. Satish Chandra, *Letters of a King-Maker of the Eighteenth Century*, 28, footnote, I. It is interesting to note that the Sayyids burst into joy when they got the news of the death of Chhabela Ram (October, 1719). See Kamwar II, 455.

The new governor of Agra, Khan-i-Dauran, knew that to crush Churaman by force of arms was an extremely difficult task. By temperament also he was more a man of diplomacy than of war.[38] Hence, he sought recourse to conciliation and diplomacy rather than force in dealing with the Jat problem. He sent several letters to Churaman, asking him to present himself before the Emperor. Churaman agreed and on 25th September, 1713 (16th Ramzan, 1125 A.H.), arrived at Barahpula. Raja Bahadur Rathora, son of Azimush-Shan's maternal uncle, was sent to receive him. On 20th October, he marched in at the head of 3,000 to 4,000 *sawars.* Khan-i-Dauran advanced in person to receive and conduct him to *Diwan-i-Khas.* The Jat leader presented 21 *mohars* and two horses to the Emperor. Farrukh Siyar granted him the title of 'Rao Bahadur Khan' alongwith a *khilat* and an elephant. His *mansab* was also increased. Three others (presumably including Khem Karan Sogaria) accompanying him, were also given the *khilats.* The charge of the royal highway from Barahpula (Delhi) to the Chambal was given to Churaman.[39] It is said that at the request of the Mir Bakhshi he was also granted five *parganas,* Baroda Meo (Nagar), Kathumar, Akhaigarh (Nadbai), Au and Helak, as *jagir.* Khem Karan jat was given the title of "Bahadur Khan" and assigned the *jagir* consisting of the *parganas* Rupbas, Bharatpur, Malah, Aghapur, Barah and Ikran.[40]

Criticizing the royal favours, the author of *Roznamcha* observes, "the disobedient and quarrelsome" Churaman was "thus flattered". The Emperor, however, was mistaken, if by showing these favours, he expected that Jat to mend his ways. Soon Churaman exploited his position to usurb the imperial territories and strengthen his power. The Mewatis and other local people and the *zamindari* veered round him and his authority and control became exceedingly strong. Grievous complaints were made to the Emperor that he harshly

---

38. *Roznamcha,* 136. *Siyar* quoted by Satish Chandra, *Parties and Politics,* 211-212, footnote.

39. *Akhbarat,* 11, 15, Ramzan (20, 24 September), 11, Shawwal (20 October); *Roznamcha,* 136; Kamwar, II, 399; Irvine, *Later Mughals,* I, 223; Satish Chandra, *Parties and Politics,* 123; U.N. Sharma, *Itihas,* 237-239.

40. *Muttra Gazetteer,* 197; cf. *Tarikh-i-Bharatpur,* 4a; Baldeo Singh, *Tawarikh-i-Bharatpur,* 18 and others quoted by U.N. Sharma, *Itihas,* 239, 243. Quoting Deshraj, *Jat Itihas,* 568, 556, 557 as his principal source U.N. Sharma (*Itihas,* 242-243) concludes that on the appeals of Churaman the Sayyids procured the *jagir* of Tuksan, Bara, Simdhari, Chhotua, Kotapatti etc. for Thenua Jat chief Bhure Singh. He also believes in that Khuntaile Jat chieftains (Hathi Singh of Sonkh, Fauda Singh of Arig and Sita Ram of Pathena) were given the titles of '*Faujdar*', *jagirs* and lands on *ijara.* He claims further that the other kith and kins of Churaman received numerous villages and *pattis* on *ijara.*

exacted the road dues (*rahdari*)[41] and meddled with the affairs of the rightful *jagir*-holders. Thus he advised the *zamindars* of *pargana* Sahar not to pay their dues to the *jagirdars*. According to another report (of March 1716), he exacted as *nazrana* rupees two each from all the *mansabdars* and *zamindars* of *pargana* Thun. His followers infested the roads, waylaid the carvans and the passers-by and ravaged the *jagir* and *khalisa*, spreading ruin and insecurity upto the Capital. To cite a few instances, in June-July 1715, the reports reached that he plundered the villages of the *parganas* of Kama, Sahar, Fatehpur Sikri, Mewat and Agra. Later on in October, his bands looted the villages of Wati and Dhulhera in the *parganas* of Mathura and Sikri, threatening the latter in the process. In March, 1716, Churaman frustrated Izzat Khan, the *faujdar* of Mewat, in his effort to restore order in that quarter. Moreover, he secretly manufactured arms and ammunition and fortified his *garhis* including Thun.[42] In all probability, Wendel's undated statement that Churaman "plundered several ministers of the Court" and "attacked..the revenue sent from the provinces", refers to this period.[43]

JAI SINGH'S JAT EXPEDITION: SIEGE OF THUN (SEPTEMBER 1716 - MAY 1718)

The reports of Churaman's increasing turbulence enraged the Emperor and he once more resolved to extirpate" him. But to find out a 'valiant' person, capable enough to undertake this arduous task, was a real problem for him.[44] At last he turned his thoughts to Sawai Jai Singh, who himself bore a grudge against the Jats. It may be recollected that a hereditary feud existed between the Jaipur ruler and Churaman and his followers. The latter offered renewed provocation to the Raja by despoiling some parts of his own state as well.[45] In September 1715, Farrukh Siyar ordered Jai Singh to present himself at the Court from Malwa. At length to the response to the repeated and urgent summons, he turned up on 25th May 1716 and undertook to "the great pleasure" of the Emperor, the responsibility of leading the Jat expedition.[46]

---

41. It should, however, be borne in mind here that not only in his but in others cases as well, '*rahdari*', a government charge in certain areas, had become a common instrument of oppression for the merchants and wayfarers. See *Zahir-ud-Din Malik, Muhammad Shah* (unpublished thesis) 247.
42. *Roznamcha*, 136; *Akhbarat*, 14, 16, April, 20, 28 June, 18 July, 16 October, 2 November, 1715, 16, 20, 29 March 1716; *Shivdas*, 16, 17, 18; *Iqbal*, 22, 23, 24; *Memoires des Jats*, 14; *M.U.I*, 439; Qanungo, *Jats*, 51; Irvine, *Later Mughals*, I, 321, footnote, 323; U.N. Sharma, (*Itihas*, 244-248) at places appears to be apologetic about Churaman's depredations.
43. *Memoires des Jats*, 13.
44. *Roznamcha* 136.
45. *Memoires des Jats*, 14; U.N. Sharma (*Itihas*, 250), however, thinks that Churaman had offered no provocation to Jai Singh ever since 1708.
46. *Kamwar*, II, 417, 418; *Roznamcha*, 136. Irvine, *Later Mughals*, I, 324.

We may pause here to take note of an underlying aspect of the present expedition. That Churaman's contumacy and lawlessness offered immediate and main provocation to the Emperor, is quite obvious and needs no elucidation. Yet, this alone is not sufficient to explain the Emperor's decision. To an appreciable degree it was linked with the Court politics. The estrangement between the Emperor and his Wazir, the Sayyids went on increasing and Farrukh Siyar attempted to get rid of his domineering ministers, while the latter endeavoured to retain and strengthen their hold by winning more adherents. It is significant to note that the Emperor did not consult the Wazir about Churaman's affairs. Nor did he make any hint to him about his desire to despatch Jai Singh against him.[47] This a revealing fact of the situation, pointing to the prior emergence of an understanding between the Sayyids and Churaman. It may partly account for Jai Singh's delay in complying with the repeated royal orders, even when his heart was inwardly set at the destruction of the Jats. Churaman's affairs assuming a factional nature, Jai Singh wanted to avoid, as far as possible, being entangled in the Court rivalries. Apparently, Farrukh Siyar wished to attain three objects simultaneously to destroy Churaman, to deprive the Sayyids of a strong partisan and to win over Jai Singh to his side, by holding out to him the bait of command in the Jat war.[48]

Early in September, 1716, the Emperor gave formal orders to Raja Jai Singh to proceed against the Jats.[49] Maharao Bhim Singh Hada of Kota, Budh Singh of Bundi; Gaj Singh Kachhwaha of Narwar, Chhatrasal Bundela, Durgadas Rathore, Rao Indra Singh and others were ordered to join Jai Singh. The latter was presented with a splendid *khilat* and an elephant. He was also given rupees 40 lakhs to meet the expenses. At this time Sanjar Khan and Shamsher Khan were sent in advance with 1,000 Walashahi troops to Palwal (36 miles south to Delhi) for the purpose of keeping communications open and providing convoys from that place to Hodal on one side and to Faridabad on the other.[50] On 15th September (9th, Shawwal), Jai Singh started on the auspicious day of Dashehra.[51] Jai Singh commanded a big army consisting of about 50,000 cavalry and more of infantry.[52] Promising to procure for him a *mansab*, the Raja

47. *Roznamcha*, 175-176.

48. Satish Chandra, *Parties and Politics*, 123; Pande, *Bharatpur*, 16 and 17.

49. *Roznamcha*, 137; *Ahwal-i-Salatin-i-Mutakherin*, Anon. (R.S.L. Ms.) 59, *Siyar*, I, 139; *Memoires des Jats*, 14.

50. *Shivdas*, 16; *Iqbal*, 22-23; Ahwal, 59; Siyar, I, 139. V.S. Bhatnagar, *Jai singh*, 77.

51. *Roznamcha*, 137; *Shivadas*, 16; Iqbal, 23; *Ahwal* 59; *K.K.*, II 776; *Memoires des Jats*, 14; *Siyar*, I, 139; *M.U.*, I, 439; *Majma-ul-Akhbar* in Elliot, VIII, 360.

52. *Shivdas*, 16 and 25; *Iqbal*, 23; *Memoires des Jats*, 14 says that the big numbers gave the impression as if Jai Singh "was going to conquer a whole kingdom."

won over Bayzid Khan Mewati " a trusted follower of Churaman" and placed him to lead his vanguard.[53]

On getting the news of the Raja's coming, Churaman dispersed guerilla contingents under his son, Mohkam Singh, and his nephews, Badan Singh and Rup Singh to harass and intercept the invaders. When Jai Singh reached near Kama (14 miles south of Deeg, 24 miles south-west of Thun), Badan Singh, taking 2,000 horses, surprised Bayzid Khan, on 15th October, 1716. Bayzid was wounded in the fight. But Badan Singh had to fall back after the arrival of Rajput re-inforcements. Jai Singh fixed his base camp at Kama. A few days later (end of October), he occupied Radhakund (4 miles, north of Gowardhan) and prepared to press the enemy on two sides.[54] As Jai Singh moved on, the local Jat population, evacuating their dwellings, scattered to other places or repaired to Thun, where Churaman lay "determined to defend himself to the last."[55] The fort of Thun, with its lofty remparts, a very deep ditch and thickly-wooded environs, was rendered fairly strong. Churaman had stored provisions sufficient for several if not altogether 20 years. On the eve of the siege he asked the merchants to evacuate Thun leaving their goods and property behind. He assured them of compensation if he emerged victorious.[56] Besides his own warrior tribesmen, Churaman had about 12,000 professional *sanyasi* fighters in his stronghold. He also employed many Afghans of Shahjahanpur and Bareilly at three rupees per day. This apart, he enjoyed the support of the local people including the Mewatis,[57] who were ready to harass the imperialists through guerilla tactics.

In the second week of November, 1716, the imperialists moved closer to Thun. On 9th instant, Rup Singh with 2,000 horses fell upon the advance guards of the Raja. A severe action ensued near Thun in which Rup Singh was wounded and his brother Ani Ram fell, fighting bravely. The same day, Jai Singh fixed his camp near Thun and began efforts to besiege the forts.[58]

Broadly Jai Singh's problem was two fold; first, he had to steer his way through the impregnable and thorny *jungles* to Thun to invest it

53. *Shivdas*, 17; Iqbal, 24.
54. *Akhbarat*, 16, 18, 19, 29, 27 October, 1716.
55. *Memoires des Jats*, 14-15.
56. *Shivdas*, 19-20 and *Iqbal*, 26-27, assert that it was not Churaman but *Jai Singh* who asked the traders to move away from them. This looks funny. The truth is rather the other way round. Vide Irvine, *Later Mughals*, I,324; Qanungo, *Jats*, 52.
57. *Shivdas*, 16, 17, 18; *Iqbal*, 23, 24; *Akhbarat*, 20 October, 1716; Satish Chandra, *Parties and Politics*, 124.
58. *Akhbarat*, 9, 21 November, 1716, Kamwar, II, 418.

effectively, secondly, at the same time he had to cope with the surprise attacks of the Jats. The task was indeed a difficult one, but remaining unperturbed, the Raja put up great exertions from the very beginning. He began to clear the *jungles* and make trenches, *sabats* and posts to station his selected troops.[59] But the Jats taking shelter in the *Jungles* and nearby *garhis* often engaged and harassed the assailants. Thus, Muhkam singh attacked the Raja's forces near Bahaj (Bahore, 9 miles west of Gowardhan) and after a little fight, drove them back. Again on 11th December, 1716, was reported another fierce contest at Thun, in which the Raja overpowered the Jats.[60] But the overall progress was very slow, which irritated the Emperor. On 13th March, 1717, he wrote disapprovingly that though seven months had elapsed since the Raja's appointment, Thun had not been "invested (even) from one side, not to speak of its conquest... the Jats come out under its (*jungle's*) shelter and attack the royal army."[61] He ordered the Raja to make vigorous efforts to reduce Thun and Deeg. To speed up the process, before the onset of the monsoon (May-June, 1717) a large (said to throw a ball weighing a Shahjahan maund) and 84 smaller cannons were sent to Jai Singh at Thun from Delhi through the deputy Governor of Agra, Nusrat Yar Khan. In addition 300 maunds of gunpowder, 150 maunds of lead and 500 rockets were ordered to be sent from Agra. About the same time, following the orders, Abdus Samad Khan, the governor of Lahore and Sayyid Khan-i-Jahan, the governor of Ajmer, reached Delhi. However, the idea of sending Abdus Samad was dropped and Khan-i-Jahan, the maternal uncle of the Sayyids, was ordered to go to Thun, outwardly to help but really to frustrate Jai Singh, as his subsequent actions prove.[62]

The overall situation, however, did not materially change with the arrival of the fresh enforcements. Jai Singh could suppress neither the tenacious defenders nor the audacious robbers. Gallant Rup Singh and Muhkam Singh with their guerilla forces continued to resist successfully, the assailants. In the second week of December, 1717, the Rajputs attacked (Bhusawar, south of Thun), then defended by Chura's brother, Ati Ram. Rup Singh and Muhkam Singh, leading succour fought desperately but were overpowered. The Jats, then, fell back to Jharsauli to offer resistance to the south of Thun. In such continual fighting both sides 'suffered heavy losses'. Inspite of the presence of the Raja's army,

59. *Shivdas*, 17; Iqbal, 23; *Roznamcha*, 175; *Ahwal*, 59.

60. *Akhbarat*, 17, 21 November 1716; Kamwar, II, 418; U.N. Sharma, *Itihas*, 258ff.

61. J. Records (Add. Pers. II, 143) quoted in *Parties and Politics*, 124-125.

62. *Kamwar*, II, 418, 421; *Shivdas*, 17-18; *Roznamcha*, 137; *Iqbal* 24; *Ahwal*, 59; *Siyar*, I, 139; *M.U.*, I, 439; *K.K.* (II, 777) says that Khan-i-Jahan lay inactive for a few months outside the capital. Also U.N. Sharma, *Itihas*, I, 260-261.

the roads and the countryside were also not cleared of the plunderers. To cite one instance, a group of the Jat and the Mewati freebooters attacked a merchant *carvan* near Hodal and carried away merchandise worth rupees 20 lakhs.[63]

The siege had now dragged on for eighteen months with little prospect of an imminent success. Thick *jungles*, frequent surprise attacks of the Jats, hostility of the local population, secret encouragement to the Jats from the Court and dearness of the supplies caused by the famine[64] presented impediments in the way of Jai Singh. In November, 1717, he was replaced by Muhammad Amin Khan as the governor of Malwa. This affected his resources at a time when he from his own pocket was spending a lot in the Jat campaign. Hence, this added further to his difficulties. Earlier in January, 1718, he submitted to the Emperor that he humbled the enemy in most of the encounters, but the incitement and encouragement from "the persons close to His Majesty" emboldened the Jats. Owing to it, the Raja confessed, his campaigning had borne no fruits.[65] To some extent Jai Singh was correct, for we learn that at the instance of the Wazir, Abdullah Khan, Khan-i-Jahan espoused the cause of Churaman, secretly supplying him with provisions and gunpowder.[66] Yet the prolonged warfare began to tell upon the resources of Churaman. Getting straitened, the Jat chief made overtures to Abdullah Khan through his agent at Delhi, offering to pay 50 lakhs, 30 lakhs as *peshkash* and 20 lakhs as present to the Wazir.[67]

On the other side, Farrukh Siyar was under the impression that the Raja would speedily crush the Jats, but his failure even after the lapse of such a long time, "displeased" him. Meanwhile, Abdullha Khan also kept harping on the failure of the Raja. He represented in a taunting manner, that "extirpation of Churaman was beyond the capacity and strength of the Raja" (Jai Singh).[68] He reminded the Emperor that a year and a half had passed by and a huge amount of money, (two

---

63. *Shivdas*, 17-18; *Iqbal*, 23, 25; *Akhbarat*, 5, 6, 9 *Muhrram*, as quoted by U.N. Sharma *Itihas*, I, 267; Also *K.K.* II, 777; Ahwal, 59; *Siyar*, I, 139.
64. *Shivdas*, 16, 18; *Iqbal*, 23-26; *Roznamcha*, 175.
65. *Kamwar*, II, 425.
66. *Roznamcha*, 176 and 175.
67. Shivdas, 20, 25; Iqbal, 27. Both these, however, give the impression that it was with this offer that Churaman won over a disinterested Abdullah Khan to his side. It does not appear convincing. At best their version may be taken to mean that following this (offer, Abdullah took greater interest in his case. Also see *K.K.* II, 777; *Ahwal*, 59 *Siyar*, I, 139; *M.U.*, I, 439; *Majmaul-Akhbar* (in Elliot VIII, 360-361) confuses Abdullah Khan with Husain Ali.
68. *Roznamcha*, 176.

crores) had already been spent and that the monthly expenses of Jai Singh were very heavy. Yet, "upto the time nothing has been concluded, and God alone knows when it (the Raja's campaign) would come to an end". Further, the Wazir informed that through his agent Churaman had begged pardon and offered to present himself before the Emperor along with his wife, sons and nephews and to pay 30 lakhs as *peshkash.*[69] This, however, was not enough to relent the Emperor. In addition, he insisted for an assurance from Churaman that Thun and Deeg would be defortified and they would never be repaired and that he along with his sons and nephews would serve the Emperor elsewhere in the province of Agra. At length the helpless Emperor yielded, though still unwillingly, to the Wazir's suggestion. In March 1718, pardoning Churaman, he ordered for the termination of the Jat campaign.[70] On behalf of the Emperor, Abdullah Khan wrote to Khan-i-Jahan to "console" Churaman and, giving him his "word" and protecting his (Chura's) property, conduct him safely to the Court along with his sons, brother and newphews.[71] It is striking to note that in keeping with Churaman's specific request[72] Jai Singh, the first man on the spot, was excluded from the peace-negotiations, which were carried through Khan-i-Jahan. A separate flattering *farman* was sent to the Raja, appreciating his exertions, but asking him, at the same time, to stop hostilities at once as "promise and written agreement" had been sent to Churaman following his overtures.[73] These underhand developments greatly hurt the Raja, now that he believed that success was within his grasp. But he obeyed the orders and suspended the fighting.[74] Khan-i-Jahan comforted Churaman. The latter presented to the Sayyid and the Raja two horses each of Iraqi and Arabian breed. Churaman took Khan-i-Jahan inside his fort and showed him the provisions and war material in his stores.

Subsequently, the Jat chief set out in the Sayyid's company with his sons, brother and nephews for the Court.[75] Reaching Delhi on 31st March,

69. *Shivdas*, 20 and 25; *Iqbal*, 27; *Roznamcha*, 137, 176; Satish Chandra, *Parties and Politics*, 125.
70. *Farman*, March, 1718 and *Farman*, Kapatdwara, 185, quoted by V.S. Bhatnagar, Jai Singh, 80.
71. The copy of the farman in *Shivdas*, 21 and 20; *Iqbal*, 28 and 27; *Roznamcha*, 176; Also *K.K.*, II, 777; Ahwal, 59.
72. See *Ahwal*, 59; *Siyar*, I, 139.
73. The substance of the farman is given by *Shivdas*, 21-22 also 20; *Iqbal*, 28-29 also 27; *Roznamcha*, 176.
74. *Shivdas*, 22; *Roznamcha*, 176; *Iqbal*, 29; Also *K.K.*, II, 777; *Ahwal*, 59; *Siyar*, I, 140. The first part of the description of this siege in *Memoires des Jats*, 15 is accurate in so far as it clearly puts that in the reign of Farrukh Siyar. But it mistakes its end with the second and successful siege of Thun.
75. *Shivadas*, 22; *Iqbal*, 29.

1718 (10th Jamadi I, 1130 A.H.), Churaman directly went to the Wazir and took up his residence close to his palace. This friendliness between them afflicted the heart of the Emperor and "strengthened the roots of (his) discord (with the Wazir)".[76] On 9th April, 1718 (19th Jamadi I) Churaman was formally presented to the Emperor by the Wazir, Abdullah Khan. Churaman presented 1,000 *asharfis*, while his son, Muhkam Singh and two nephews, Rup Singh and probably Badan Singh presented 500 *asharfis* each. They were favoured with special *khilats* and horses. Other associates of the Jat chief were given ordinary *khilats.*[77] Wendel asserts that Churaman received from the Emperor the title of 'Fateh Sihgh' with the appointments like the small Rajas.[78] The terms of the treaty were finalised through Abdullah Khan. On 20th April, the Wazir submitted to the Emperor that a *peshkash* of 50 lakhs in cash and goods fixed up on Churaman to be paid in successive instalments. Farrukh Siyar gave his approval.[79]

However, both the Emperor and Jai Singh were inwardly raging at the course of events. In May, 1721, Jai Singh made one feeble attempt to settle his score with Churaman. He "pressurised" him to pay the *peshkash* and to surrender other forts. Moving a step further, Farrukh Siyar ordered for their speedy conquest.[80] Little did he realize that under the circumstances the prospects of the conquest of the Jat forts had not increased. Meanwhile, Churaman had managed to pay 30 lakhs to the imperial treasury.[81] At length Jai Singh, withdrawing his forces from Thun, returned to the Court on 19th May (29 Jamadi II) 1718. Next Month, he presented to the Emperor, the keys of the Jat forts of Thun and Jharsauli,[82] although as the subsequent events show, this surrender was effective on paper only.

CONSEQUENCE OF JAI SINGH'S EXPEDITION

Jai Singh's Jat campaign was an event of considerable importance. The fact that Churaman had withstood his vigorous military pressure,

76. *Kamwar*, II, 426-427; *Ahwal*, 59; *Siyar*, I, 140; Also see *K.K.*, II, 777.
77. *Kamwar*, II, 427; *Roznamcha*, 178 and 137; *Shivdas* 22 and 25; *Iqbal*, 30; Also Shah, 2. U.N. Sharma, (*Itihas*, I, 271) claims that the mansab of Churaman was increased, and the "high and decorative medal of Omra" was also granted to him.
78. *Memoires des Jats*, 84.
79. *Kamwar*, II, 427. Satish Chandra (*Parties and Politics*, 125) and following him Dr. Pande (*Bharatpur*, 21) say that Churaman surrendered Deeg etc. As the subsequent narrative would reveal, this surrender was effective on paper only.
80. Farman, Kapatdwara, 18/185; quoted by U.N. Sharma, *Itihas*, I, 272.
81. *Shivdas*, 25-26, quoting *Kamwar*, Sharma (loc cit, 272) mentions that Churaman paid 50 lakhs. So far as we are able to infer Kamwar merely states about amount having been fixed up on Churaman.
82. *Kamwar*, II, 427; Farman Kapatdwara, 19/163, quoted by Sharma, loc. cit, 272; Also, *Roznamcha*, 179; *Shivdas*, 23; *Iqbal*, 30; *K.K.* II, 777.

made him "renowned".[83] Besides, it affected the factional politics at the imperial Court. Precisely, Churaman's affair worsened the already strained relations between the Emperor and the Sayyids and soon became the "main subject" of their dissension. Visibly annoyed, Farrukh Siyar refused to Churaman to grant audience a second time.[84] The Emperor's rupture with the Wazir became open especially following Jai Singh's claim that but for Abdullah Khan's tendentious support Churaman would have been either arrested or forced to flee into the *jungle*, in another month's time.[85] Shivdas tells us that the Emperor, being induced by his sycophants, ordered Abdullah Khan to deliver "the mischief fomentor" Churaman and Ratan Chand to the government. But the Wazir refused saying that if he so desired, Churaman could be sent back to his home. This "infuriated" the Emperor and he began to think of "seizing and killing" the Wazir.[86] This incident played its own part in the immediate recall of Hussain Ali by Abdullah Khan from the south[87] and subsequent deposition of Farrukh Siyar.

Jat war also deepened ill-will between the Sayyids and Jai Singh[88] and inspite of his reluctance eventually embroiled the Raja in the Court-politics. Incensed at Abdullah Khan's intrigues which prevented him from reaping the fruits of his labour, the Raja hereafter became an implacable foe of the Sayyids. On the other hand, their common grudge against the Sayyids helped to bring Farrukh Siyar and Jai Singh closer. It is noteworthy that when every other important noble crossed over to the side of the Sayyids, Jai Singh stood off and refused to toe their line until the end.[89]

The present episode also sharpened the hereditary feud between the Jaipur house and the Jat chiefs. Strengthened with the Sayyids support, Churaman not only thwarted the Raja's military efforts but made him swallow diplomatic humiliation. The dual rebuff must have left the Raja burning with the fire of revenge. As for Churaman, Jai Singh's ardour for the Jat war gave another proof of the hostility of the Amber Rajas towards the emergence of the Jat power. This led him to develop close relations with Raja Ajit Singh, who assured him of security against Jai Singh.[90]

---

83. *Memoires des Jats*, 16.
84. *K.K.* II, 777; *Ahwal*, 59; *Siyar*, I, 140 and 138; *M.U.*, I, 439.
85. *Roznamcha*, 194; Also *Siyar*, I, 140; Irvine, *Later Mughals*, I, 337, 345.
86. *Shivdas*, 24; Iqbal, 31; *Roznamcha*, 194.
87. Abdullah Khan wrote a letter to his brother, dwelling upon the serious developments over the affairs of Churaman and Ratan Chand. *Shivdas*, 25-26; *Iqbal*, 32-34.
88. *Roznamcha*, 175-176, 228.
89. Irvine, *Later Mughals*, I, 371.
90. M. Mitra, *Ajit Singh*, 250 (quoting Qaiyo, Hist. Ess, 60, 63); Qanungo, *Jats*, 57.

The astute Jat thus attempted to counteract the hostility of one Rajput Raja with the friendship of the other.

Lastly, Jai Singh's expedition brought Churaman closer to the Sayyid brothers who saw in him "a new and useful partner" to their cause.[91] Their lenient policy towards the powerful Hindu elements facilitated such a development. It is to be noted, however, that hitherto the Sayyids' role in the Jat affairs was more in the nature of harming their opponents than protecting the Jats. But the process was now reversed in so far as Abdullah Khan, besides manoeuvring to help Churaman with materials, manipulated for him almost on favourable terms in a situation more difficult than in the past. Personal gratitude and self-interest, thus, actuated him to strengthen "the chain of unity and concord" with the Sayyids.[92] He became one of their closest adherents and allies[93] and in the process attained greater honours and fame. We know, that, besides retaining power, the Sayyids, through their friendship with the local powers, aimed at making the State broad based.[94] Judging from this stand point, Churaman's association with the Wazir and the Mir Bakshi imparted a new though spurious significance to his activities. Besides his alliance with those who held the reigns of the government, impliedly meant that for all practical purposes he had ceased to bear a rebel in the eyes of the Mughal government.

There is, however, the other side of the picture also. The way an established rebel (the Jat) was admitted to the royal favours against the will of the Emperor bore ill for the already declining Mughal authority.[95] While it sustained Churaman in his contumacious course,[96] it obviously left an ominous precedent also for likeminded people. Moreover, the Jat war cost the imperialists much in terms of money, material and time and yet the power of Churaman could not be crushed. In addition, the absence of Jai Singh during these two years from Malwa gave suitable opportunity to the Marathas to realize *chauth* and establish their hold in the province.[97]

CHURAMAN AS THE ALLY OF THE WAZIR AND THE MIR BAKSHI

Henceforward, the history of Churaman was merged with the history of the Sayyid brothers. He either, stayed with them or reported himself

---

91. Jonathan Scott, Ferishta's *History of the Deccan*, London: 1794, *K.K.*, II, Part V, 150.
92. *M.U.*, I, 439.
93. *Sahifa-i-Iqbal* (Aligarh University Hist. Dept. Library Ms.) 4a; *Shivdas*, 76 and 90; *Memoires des Jats*, 84; *Siyar*, I, 271; *M.U.*, I, 439; Qanungo, *Jats*, 53, 54.
94. Satish Chandra, *Parties and Politics*, 128-129.
95. *Shah*, 2.
96. *Majma-ul-Akhbar*, in Elliot, VIII, 361.
97. *K.K.*, II, 781; *Selections from the Peshwas' Dafter* ed. by G.S. Sardesai, XXX, 17a, 17b.

at their first call, and actively participated in most of the activities of his benefactors. Churaman's affair, as noted above, increased the strife between Farrukh Siyar and Abdullah Khan. Fearing assassination, the Wazir ceased to move out and also gave up attending the Court. He also summoned his brother, Husain Ali, from the Deccan. The latter's approach terrified Farrukh Siyar into conciliating Abdullah Khan. The Emperor paid him a visit and exchanged vows and promises. The next day (9th December, 1718) Abdullah Khan appeared at the Court and made the customary offerings. But all this gave a false covering to their mutual enmity.[98] That very afternoon the imperial gunners under Tika (or Bika) Hazarai clashed with the soldiers of Churaman and Ajit Singh, resulting in casualties on both sides. Abdullah Khan's mansion slightly escaped being attacked. Only the coming-on of night stopped the fight after three hours. The next morning Ghazi-ud-Din Khan (the Mir Atish), Said Quli Khan Qul and Sayyid Najm-ud-Din Ali Khan intervened and pacified the opponents, Farrukh Siyar sent Zafar Khan to offer apologies to Ajit Singh.[99] During these stormy days Farrukh Siyar made a bid both to pacify his powerful foes and to grant further favours to his supporters. The latter included Jai Singh, who was angry with Abdullah Khan, for his role in the matter of Churaman. For fear of the Wazir, however, the Emperor hesitated to reward Jai Singh. He, therefore, first tried a reconciliation between the Wazir and the Raja and thus, sent Zafar Khan to persuade Jai Singh to see Abdullah Khan (30th December, 1718). He agreed and paid a visit to the Wazir. Soon after the Wazir and then the Emperor himself paid visits to the Raja (5th, 6th January 1719). Yet, there was hardly any improvement in their mutual relations.[100]

In the following days the events headed fast towards the deposition of Farrukh Siyar (February, 1719), in which Churaman helped his benefactors. The Sayyids with their associates including the Jats took possession of the fort and the palace. In sheer desperation the Emperor unsuccessfully implored Ajit Singh to help him escape through the unoccupied eastern side of the Delhi fort facing the Yamuna. When Abdullah Khan heard of it he entrusted the charge of guarding that crucial place to his confidant, Churaman, so that none would escape. The Jat chief with his relations and troops took position there and devotedly executed his task. He got hold of the keys of all the gates including those of the palace. When Itiqad Khan advised against

98. *Kamwar*, II, 433; *Roznamcha*, 219, 237-238.
99. *Roznamcha*, 219; *Kamwar*, II, 433; *K.K.*, II, 800. Both K.R. Qanungo and Ram Pande, have somehow missed this incident.
100. *Roznamcha*, 227-228; Irvine, *Later Mughals*, I, 364-365.

surrendering the keys to Farrukh Siyar, he pleaded his helplessness in the matter. Scolding Itiqad for his present misfortune, Farrukh Siyar expelled him from Diwan-i-Khas and he hid himself in the *harem*. Soon after, he was dethroned, blinded and imprisoned to make room for the Sayyids' creature, Rafi-ud-Darjat.[101]

A couple of months later, Churaman rendered yeoman service to Hussain Ali Khan during the latter's siege of the Agra fort, following the enthronement of a rival Emperor, Neku Siyar, by Mitra Sen Nagar and the fort garrison (8th May, 1719). This rebellion posed a serious challenge to the dominance of the Sayyids. The rebels expected help from Jai Singh, Chhabela Ram and Nizam-i-Mulk. Anticipating danger, Ghairat Khan, the new governor of Agra, and Samandar Khan, the commandant designate of Agra fort, were earlier hurried off to Agra. They were, however, opposed by the rebels. Getting this news the Sayyids immediately despatched Churaman, Raja Bhim Singh and others to re-inforce Ghairat Khan.[102] Later, Husain Ali himself marched from Delhi reaching Agra early in July. About this time Churaman was given the charge of the imperial highway between Barahpula (Delhi) and Gwalior.[103] The Jat chief rushed to Agra with Govind Singh Jat and the sons of Nanda Jat. During the siege, he maintained his position at an entrenchment near the fort on the side of the Yamuna. He entered into negotiations with the hardpressed besieged and devised his own mode of conduct. The fort garrison took him and his namesake, Churaman Hazari (in the service of Hussain Ali), inside the fort, where, on a pot of the Ganga water, a solemn oath was taken about Prince Neku Siyar and his nephew Mirza Asghari being made over to the Jat chief along with a cash amount of rupees 50 lakhs. The princes and the amount were to be taken to the country of Raja Jai Singh. However, Churaman took the Prince and

---

101. *Roznamcha*, 243-246; *Shivdas*, 37 and 38; *Kamwar*, II, 438-441; *Iqbal*, 47-49; *K.K.*, II, 813, 814-816; *Memoires des Jats,* 84 adds that Churaman and Ajit Singh captured much booty on this occasion. R. Pande's (*Bharatpur*, 22) description of Churaman's doings in 1719 is misleading. U.N. Sharma (*Itihas*, 278) citing *Umara-i-Hunud* concludes that Churaman held one hand and Ajit Singh the other while enthroning Rafi-ud-Darjat. This cannot be accepted in view of the several other weightier sources and modern scholars Irvine (*op.cit.* I, 389), M. Mitra (*Ajit Singh*, 209) etc. referring instead to Abdullah Khan having done so. Likewise, he makes a doubtful claim that the Jats sided with the Marathas in the clashes on 18th February. To the best of our information they did not do so. Even Irvine (*op.cit* I, 382ff) who reproduces the incident so minutely, nowhere mentions Jats here. Sharma displays a tendency to uncritically relate, at places too prominently, the Jats with the contemporary events.

102. *K.K.* II, 823-828; *Memoires des Jats,* 84; *Shivdas*, 39ff; *Iqbal*, 50ff.

103. Kam Raj, *Ibratnama*, 68a, quoted by Irvine, *Later Mughals,* I, 413 f.n., also 422; Satish Chandra, *Parties and Politics*, 150.

the gold to Husain Ali Khan, who kept the former in his custody but gave them oney, an elephant, a special *khilat* and a *mansab* of 5,000 to the Jat.[104] After this the two Churamans entered into a compact with the Buxaria Hazaris to open the gates of the fort. Churaman Jat allowed the families of the Buxarias to come out safely as per agreement. On 2nd August, 1719 both the fort and Neku Siyar were captured by Husain Ali.[105]

Shortly afterwards, the Emperor, Rafi-ud-Daulah, followed his predecessor to the grave and the Sayyids now enthroned Prince Roshan Akhtar (Muhammad Shah) in their camp at Bidyapru (6 miles north of Fatehpur Sikri). Two days later, (20th September, 1719) Churaman waited upon the new Emperor and made an offer of 9 *mohurs* to him.[106] In return the Jat chief received a special *khilat.*[107]

In September, 1720, Churaman deputed his son,[108] Muhkam Singh to join Husain Ali Khan on his march towards the Deccan against Nizam-ul-Mulk. About this time (c. August, 1720), in appreciation of his valuable services, Husain Ali promised to Churaman to procure for him the title of Raja[109] after his return from the Deccan. However, when the army reached near Toda Bhim Husain Ali fell (28th September) to a conspiracy hatched by his adversaries.[110] His chief adherents, including Muhkam were captured. Despaired of his life the Jat offered to embrace Islam. But Muhammad Shah did not think it prudent to accept it. Instead he gave him a *Khilat* and allowed him to go home.[111] The clamency shown to Muhkam Singh stands in deep contrast to the disgraceful treatment meted out to certain other supporters of the Sayyids.[112] This gesture of the Emperor was apparently intended to win over Churaman to his side. With the same purpose promises of great favours were also made to him. The circumstances having changed, Churaman himself found it expedient for the present to submit to the Emperor.[113] He led the return march of

---

104. *Shivdas*, 44; *Iqbal,* 56; *Memoires des Jats,* 84 says that the Prince in question was Ali Zafar, the brother of Neku Siyar. An ealier authority *Kamwar*, II, 449 also says that the Prince was his brother; *K.K.*, II, 836; cf. *Later Mughals*, I, 424-425, 414.
105. *Shivdas*, 44; *Iqbal*, 56; *Kamwar*, II, 449-450.
106. *Kamwar*, II, 451, 453-454; Claiming to have followed this authority Dr. Pande (*Bharatpur,* 22) states that the Jat offered five Mohurs through Ghairat Khan. In fact, it was Ghulam Ali who offered the present that day.
107. *Kamwar*, II 454.
108. See *Shivdas*, 72 and 67; *M.U.*, I, 439.
109. Irvine, *Later Mughals*, II, 214; Following him, Qanungo, *Jats*, 55.
110. *Shivdas*, 70; *Kamwar*, II, 471; *K.K.*, II, 904; *Iqbal*, 79-80; For details see Irvine, *Later Mughals*, II, 51ff.
111. *Shivdas*, 72.
112. *Ibid.*, Also *K.K.*, II, 909.
113. *Shivdas*, 76, *Ahwal*, 105; Irvine, *Later Mughals*, II, 68.

the Mughal army northwards towards the Yamuna. He prevailed upon the Emperor to abandon his scheduled route, running through his *zamindari*. Instead, he took the army across the territory of his foe, Jai Singh,[114] later (October), Khem Karan Sogaria, a powerful Jat chieftain, joined the imperial cavalcade near Barsana. He was placed in the rearguard.[115] Incidentally, it may be inferred from Muhammad Qasim's account that Khema Jat had strained relations with the Sayyids at least for over a year. This may account for their despatching Dilawar Ali Khan to reduce Fatehpur, a fort held by Khema, during Husain Ali's siege of Agra.[116] It is not clear how far this incident influenced Khema's present decision.

Meanwhile, Abdullah Khan, having heard of the tragic end of his brother, resumed his march to Delhi. The Jat and the Mewati plunderers harassed him as he marched on to Faridabad.[117] He enlisted fresh troops and thereafter, taking Muhammad Ibrahim, the rival Emperor, with him, he marched to Bilochpur to confront Muhammad Shah.[118] In response to the Sayyids secret letters Churaman and many other followers of the Sayyid, deserted Muhammad Shah and joined him before the battle.[119]

Churaman's motives in rejoining Abdullah Khan have not always been judged very fairly. There is not enough ground to suspect his "devotion and gratitude" to the Sayyid.[120] Acknowledging in unequivocal terms his deep gratitude and indebtedness to the munificence of the Sayyids, Churaman himself confessed before Muhammad Amin Khan (in Muhammad Shah's camp) that they, "have conferred on me such benefits that if I had a thousand lives and a thousand times my wealth, I would have offered up all, including my family and children on their behalf.[121] Irvine believes that his decision was based on the argument that in case of Abdullah Khan's defeat, pardon could be more easily secured from Muhammad Shah than on the contrary.[122] There is an inherent contradiction in this contention. There was better scope of an easier pardon from Abdullah Khan, who had all along upheld pro-Jat and pro-Hindustani policies, than from his Mughal opponents, the main reason of whose rallying against the Sayyids was the latter's pursuance of the above policies.[123] The fact that Churaman refrained from going straightaway to his patron after the

114. *Shivdas*, 76.
115. *Shivdas*, 86-87.
116. Qasim's *Ibratnama*, 283, referred to in *Later Mughals*, I, 429.
117. Kamwar, II, 471; Also *Shivdas*, 80; *Iqbal*, 80.
118. *Shivdas*, 82ff., *K.K.*, II, 914-918; *Kamwar*, II, 471; *Iqbal*, 85, 87-88; *Ahwal*, 104.
119. *Shivdas*, 92, 87 and 90; *K.K.*, II, 919; *Iqbal*, 88; *Ahwal*, 104.
120. Contra see Qanungo, *Jats*, 56.
121. Qasim quoted in *Later Mughals*, II, 68.
122. Irvine, *Later Mughals*, II, 81.
123. *supra*, p. 74.

murder of Hussain Ali is not difficult to explain. The fear arising from the presence of the huge enemy forces at the back of his territory, their scheduled march on the route passing through it, and the uncertainty of the movements of Abdullah Khan, dissuaded him from such course. It is clear that amidst the circumstances, only a person unmindful of the realities could have committed the indiscreet folly of providing added provocation to the imperialists.[124] As it was, Churaman took the most expedient step. In joining Muhammad Shah, he not only cleverly disarmed his suspicions but also managed to safeguard his *taaluqas* from being molested by the Mughal army, which should have been the case had Churaman done otherwise. In the process he availed himself of the opportunity to unite with his patron, Abdullah Khan. Thus it would appear that Churaman's presence in the royal camp was a temporary device to avert a possible danger. All this leave little scope to suspect his loyalty to the Sayyid. As we shall see, he clung to him until his cause was irredeemably lost.

While coming over to Abdullah Khan along with his brother and son, Churaman carried off three elephants and some camels to present to the Sayyid. But be returned him two elephants and camels as gifts.[125] The author of *Iqbalnama*, who was present in the battle of Hasanpur (2-3, November, 1720,13-14 Muharram) narrates: he (Churaman) gave the advice (to Abdullah Khan) against the expediency of commencing the fight that day (13th Muharram, 1131 A.H.). He talked much about stopping the rot impressed upon Sayyid Abdullah Khan that he would harass the opposite army by hundred kinds of deceit and tricks and highway robbery and would make difficult task easy. But his suggestion was not accepted.[126] Abdullah Khan, however, "deputed" Churaman's troops, riding swift mares, to hover in the rear of Muhammad Shah's camp. Killing many enemy soldiers, Churaman with a contingent of 200 musketeers fought his way into the camp from the west. But Raja Raj Bahadur of Kishangarh, Raja Gopal Singh Bhadauria and others pushed him back. Some of the Jats fell on the south and grabbed a part of the baggage. Zafar Khan, Muzaffar Khan and Muhammad Khan Bangash confronted them and forced them back again. The Jats then attacked Mir Mushrif and Alwi Khan Tarin of Lucknow on the east but were repulsed after a fight. Their raids created great confusion and many camp followers and traders in "sheer panic" jumped in the nearby Yamuna. The Jats commanded as its western bank and whosoever fled

124. cf. Qanungo, *Jats*, 55.
125. *K.K.*, II, 919; *Ahwal*, 104, 105; *M.U.*, I, 439; Scott, *Dekkam*, II; 180.
126. *Iqbal*, 88.

to that side did not escape being plundered. Persisting with his unexpected attacks, Churaman laid his hands on many baggage packed bullocks and camels grazing on the sandy mound on the river side. At one stage he passed by Muhammad Shah, who himself shot four arrows at Churaman and despatched a strong force against him. Meanwhile, Abdullah Khan, despite heavy desertions from his side, fought gallantly, but was wounded and imprisoned. Mughal soldiers started plundering the camp of the Sayyid. Churaman also joined them. In the end he went back to his country, grabbing a rich booty which included 1,000 bullocks and many camels loaded with goods and the records of the imperial Almoner's department.[127]

---

127. *Iqbal*, 95-96; *Shivdas*, 90-91 and 92; *Kamwar*, II, 471-472; *K.K.*, II, 930-931; *Ahwal*, 105 and 109; *Tarikh-i-Hind* (by Rustam Ali, R.S.L. Sitamau Ms.) 488-489; *Siyar*, I, 271-273; *Memoires des Jats*, 84; *M.U.*, I, 439-440; Irvine, *Later Mughals*, II, 85ff.

IV

The Mughal Jat Relations After the Fall of the Sayyids (1720-1722)

In befriending Rao Churaman II, the Sayyids had visualized to utilize a rising power for perpetuating their control on the government. But fate had decreed otherwise. One time "King Makers", now they could not stand even their own ground, and with their overthrow, Churaman was deprived of a gracious patronage, which had not only rescued him from difficult situations but had also raised him to the pinnacle of such power and prestige as he could not have ordinarily dreamt of. He was now exposed to the inescapable fury of the Mughals, which his alliance with the detested Sayyids had only served to heighten. It may not be far from truth to say that opposition to Churaman was, to a great extent, part and parcel of the general opposition to the Sayyids. The suppression of Ajit Singh,[1] another Sayyid adherent, is a case in point. The common adversity brought the old associates, Churaman and Ajit Singh, still closer. They now entered into an alliance, promising armed support to each other in hour of need. Hence, in 1721, Churaman despatched his son, Muhkam Singh, to Ajmer at the head of a contingent for the aid of the Raja against the Mughals. He also attempted (about September, 1721) to obstruct Saadat Khan on his march from Agra to Delhi to lead the Mughal forces against Ajit Singh.[2] The Jat Chief also established close relations with Chhatra Sal Bundela, whom he had an occasion to meet as a co-fighter during the Mughal campaign at Lohagarh (1710). Sometime in 1721 (c. April-May), Churaman sent aid, probably on request to Chhatra Sal in his encounter with Diler Khan, the deputy of Muhammad Khan Bangash.[3]

---

1. For details see *Shivdas*, 117ff.
2. M.Mitra, *Ajit Singh*, 250 (Basing on Hist. Essays); Irvine, *Later Mughals*, II, 110, 121. Qanungo, *Jats*, 57.
3. Irvine, *Later Mughals*, II, 121; Also *Shivdas*, 101ff. Following Irvine, Qanungo, *Jats*, 57.

SAADAT KHAN'S FIRST OPERATIONS AGAINST THE JATS (FEBRUARY-SEPTEMBER, 1721)

Soon after the removal of the Sayyids (three months after the battle of Hasanpur) the Jats felt the pressure of the Mughals. Saadat Khan, who had played a leading part in the overthrow of Husain Ali Khan, was rewarded with the governorship of Agra (October, 1720).[4] In February, 1721, he took leave from the Court to look after his new assignment. The Jats of Mathura were proving intractable, so he took the field against them and forced the rebels to take shelter in their fortresses. Then he besieged them and succeeded in capturing four of them situated near Mathura. A number of the defenders were put to the sword; Saadat Khan also lost 400 men in the process. Pleased with this news, the Emperor sent him a congratulatory message with a *Khilat* and a jewelled dagger.[5]

However, he could not personally follow up his success, as he was temporarily recalled to help suppress Ajit Singh. In his absence his deputy, Nilkanth Nagar, took up his unfinished task. With a force of 10,000 horses and more of infantry he attacked Jat villages in the environs of Fatehpur Sikri and penetrated as far as Pichuna (8 miles south of Bharatpur). Here he captured some villagers and their animals. But when he was returning Muhkam Singh and Shardul Singh of Halena whom Churaman had deputed earlier, fell upon him with a force of six thousand on horse and foot (16th September, 1721-5th Zil-Hijja). Though his army was double in strength, Nilkanth could not cope with the valiant Jats and was beaten. In course of the fight he received bullet shot and fell down dead in the '*hauda*' of his elephant. Those who could manage, escaped, while the rest surrendered their horses and arms and became prisoners in the hands of the Jats. Muhkam Singh, taking all the elephants, the captives and other goods, went to his place and obtained money in the form of fine from every prisoner according to his status.[6]

Meanwhile, an internal storm, largely the offshoot of Churaman's own impudence and indiscretion, had been brewing among the Sinsinwara Jats. A section of the Jat chieftains under Badan Singh was opposed to Churaman's rough behaviour, inordinate love of plunder and deceitful and aggressive tactics. It stood and pressed for a peaceful and systematic policy of expansion accompanied by friendlier relations

4. A.L. Srivastava, *First Two Nawabs of Oudh* (Lucknow: 1933), 24.
5. *Siyar*, I, 315; Srivastava, *Awadh*, 27-28, Qanungo as also R. Pande have overlooked the above episode. This may account for the latter's wrong impression (*Bharatpur*, p.24) that Saadat Khan moved to Agra only after the death of Nilkanth Nagar.
6. *Shivdas*, 121-122, 125; *Siyar*, I, 328; *Iqbal*, 106; *Pathena Raso* quoted by Ganga Singh, *op.cit.*, 88-91.

with the neighbours and the Mughal court. However, Churaman, acting rashly imprisoned Badan Singh.[7] This made other Jats suspicious about his ulterior designs and they insisted for Badan Singh's release. At last Churaman had to bow down and he set Badan Singh free (about 1721).[8]

SAADAT KHAN'S SECOND OPERATIONS (SEPTEMBER 1721-1722)

Obviously, these developments widened the rift in the Jat leadership. Badan Singh after his release proceeded to Agra to make a common cause with Saadat Khan, who after the route of his deputy was ordered to proceed at once to the rebellious area. On his arrival Badan Singh approached him. Saadat Khan found it prudent to win him over to his side and hence gave him a *khilat* and a chain of elephants.[9] We learn from *Sujan Charitra* that Saadat Khan established intimacy with Badan Singh's brother, Rup Singh also.[10] About this time (c. 17th September—10th October, 1721-6th to the end of Zil Hijja, 1133 A.H.) Churaman committed suicide by swallowing the deadly poison[11] and the leadership

---

7. Qanungo, *Jats*, 57; V.S. Bhatnagar, *Jai Singh,* 102b; Tod, *Rajasthan*, 652 (differing in details; Ganga Singh, *op.cit.*, 88-90. Though none of these quote any authority in support of them, their generally similar contention seems to be correct in the light of Badan Singh's flight to Saadat Khan and other developements. They are, however, silent about Badan Singh's second activity. U.N. Sharma (*Itihas*, 303-305), generally agreeing with the above, emphasizes here, Badan Singh's insistence on the division of Chura's "extensive state". He speaks of Badan Singh's flight to Saadat Khan but is silent about his arrest on this occasion.
8. Qanungo, *Jats*, 57. According to a local tradition, the decision of Churaman to get Muhkam Singh married in a Deshwar family of Kailuri (2 miles to the south-west of Jatauli) further provocated the supporters of Badan Singh and they threatened to break off all social contacts with him. Also see Ganga Singh *op.cit.*, 90.
9. *Shivdas*, 122.
10. *Sujan*, 60.
11. The authorities accessible to us furnish different versions about the time and manner of Churaman's death. Of the relevant authorities on the Jats, Fransoo completely ignores the subject, while Wendel (*Memoires des Jats,* 15, 84 and 1f.n.) makes uncertain observation that he died either during or just before Jai Singh's second expedition (i.e. Sept.-Oct., 1722), reportedly poisoned by Muhkam Singh. Partly agreeing with Wendel, *Rustam* (495) suggests his death during Jai Singh's war. *Siyar (I, 329)* and *Majma-ul-Akhbar* (in Elliot, VIII, 361) show Churaman living at the commencement of Jai Singh's war. But they differ regarding the manner of his death. *Siyar* says that upon Badan Singh's desertion, Muhkam reproached Churaman for the extremities suffered by the besieged. Thereupon, Churaman swallowed poison and expired. *Majma-ul-Akhbar* relates that when Badan Singh helped Jai Singh to open the fort of Thun, Chura becoming desperate burnt himself in the fort Magazine. These sources obviously do not help us much. *Shivdas* (118-119) a contemporary author, who ends his account at the completion of the 4th regnal year of Muhammad Shah's reign, does speak of Chura's death but not of Jai Singh's war, clearly implying thereby that Chura had died before that event, more precisely towards the close of the fourth regnal year. Still more precise is the

now passed on his eldest son, Muhkam Singh[12]. Saadat Khan commenced his second campaign under the guidance of dissident Jat brothers. The Khan had a name for bravery and determination and though for long he made all possible efforts, he failed to chastise the Jats led by Muhkam Singh. The inaccessibility and strength of the Jat strongholds and their guerilla tactics foiled his diplomacy and valour alike.[13] Possibly, Badan Singh went back disappointed sometime during Saadat Khan's operations.

CHARACTER AND ESTIMATE OF RAO CHURAMAN II

Before proceeding further with the study of the Mughal-Jat relations, it would not be out of place to pause here and form an estimate of

---

corroborative testimony of *Tarikh-i-Muhammadi* (quoted in *Later Mughals*, II, 122f.n.). According to it Chura passed away in Zil-Hizza, 1133 A.H. (*i.e.* between 12 Sept-10th Oct., 1721). Khafi Khan (II, 944) seems to indirectly support it when he refers that Chura died before the commencement of Saadat Khan's second campaign (*i.e.* late in Sept., 1721). Significantly, *Kamwar Khan* (II, 483), though silent about the date of the death, does mention that Thun was defended against Jai Singh by his sons and not by Chura himself. Thus, if he does not clearly endorse, he does not contradict either, the weighty evidence of contemporary Shivdas, *Tarikh-i-Muhammadi* and impliedly Khafi Khan. As we have noted above Chura issuing instructions to Muhkam and Shardul on the day of their action against Nilkanth *i.e.* 16th Sept., it becomes clear that he died after that date *i.e.* between 17th Sept. and 10th Oct., 1721.

As regards the manner of his death, Shivdas states the one of his relations, a wealthy man, expired childless. The brethren summoned and handed over to Mukhan Singh all the deceased's riches and the *zamindari*. Chura's second son, Zul Qaran, pressed for his share also. A verbal dispute followed between the two. Zul Qaran collected his men and engaged Muhkam in his house. Meanwhile, Chura having been informed about the affair, went there to pacify his sons. But Muhkam spoke abusingly and became ready to fight his father. In anger and anguish Chura swallowed the deadly poison, which he always carried with him. He went to a nearby garden and lay down dead. After a long time had elapsed the people sent to enquire about, found him dead. Of the other authorities, relevant here, Kamwar ignores this issue, while Khafi Khan, by merely announcing it, suggests a natural death. Without specifying the underlying cause, *Tarikh-i-Muhammadi* does support, though in brief, Shivdas's reference to the tussle between Chura's sons, Tham Singh(?) and Muhkam and Chura's unsuccessful bid at their reconciliation. But it differs from Shivdas in so far as it makes Chura perish in the fighting itself. This part of its story is not confirmed by any other source, whereas Shivdas's version of suicide through poison finds its endorsement in the current local tradition also. The latter adds that having swallowed poison at Thun, Chura galloped on to a village, Nautha (5 miles south of Nadbai) where he lay unconscious under a Peepal tree. He expired shortly after the arrival of the search party on the spot. There is a *Chabutara*, nearby a Peepal tree in Nautha, which the popular belief links with the name of Churaman II.

12. *Memoires des Jats*, 16; *Tawarikh-i-Hunud*, 14a; *Siyar*, I, 329; Alexander Dow, *The History of Hindustan* (London: 1812), II, 352.
13. cf. *Shivdas*, 123, 125 and 127; *K.K.*, II, 944-945; *M.U.*, I, 426-427 and 440 (merely reproduced Khafi Khan)

Churaman and his work. Rao Churaman II was one of those men of history to whom destiny proved remarkably unsparing and bounteous. *Majma-ul-Akhbar*, though a later work, aptly sums up,"... his good fortune proved like waters richly fertilizing the field of his successful career in life..."[14] More due to the combination of fortuitous circumstances than to his own endeavours, he rose from the depths of a despised rebel to the enviable height of a *Panchhazari Mansabdar* and the uncrowned king of the region between Delhi and the Chambal. Stars smiled upon him right from the dawn of his eventful career. It was his luck as a chief Fateh Singh failed and hence the leadership was devolved on him, though he did not directly descend from the famous Raja Ram. Further, his tenure as the Jat chief coincided with the waning Mughal power. This offered him golden opportunities to fulfil his designs. Besides, it is noteworthy that, although he was not negligent in his turbulent ways, again and again he received royal favours. To crown all, he was extremely fortunate in gaining the favour of certain influential nobles of the day.

Our authorities speak very little of his character. An inference may, however, be drawn on the basis of his performance. Ambitious, bold and rapacious, Churaman II was cunning to an unusual degree. Certain traits of his character suggest that as a person he was complex. His movements after the murder of Husain Ali reflect his coolness and foresight, but the case of his suicide reveals his impulsiveness. His relations with the Sayyids and Ajit Singh illustrate his sense of devotion and gratitude. At the same time his conduct in the wars of succession generally testifies to his being unscrupulous and deceitful. Similarly, while his treatment of his nephew, Badan Singh, smacks of his intransigence and imperious disposition, the way he held back in face of extreme provocation from his eldest son, Muhkam Singh, speaks of his occasional resignation and self-restraint. Churaman displayed a passionate love for money and plunder throughout his life. Example of occasional loot were not wanting among the Jats either before or after him. But no other Jat leader of his calibre had ever given himself to plunder to this extent. In the process he set a bad precedent for his followers. By his misdeeds he, as also some others, heaped such infamy on the Jat community as could not be completely removed even by the noble deeds of illustrious Suraj Mal. These, coupled with his rough tactics, also turned a section of his own people against him. Little surprise then, that this aspect of his life brought him severe condemnation—severer than in case of any other Jat leader - from the contemporary and later writers. He has been denounced as "the mischief fomentor"[15], "accursed wretch", "rascal", "good-for nothing-fellow",

14. *Majma-ul-Akhbar* in Elliot, VIII, 360; Francklin, *The History of the Reign of Shah Aulam* (London: 1798), 51.
15. *Shivdas*, 16 and 24.

"belonging to the race of traitors", "notorious freebooter",[16] "demon of the waste"[17], "rogue" "one of the hereditary disloyal persons",[18] "robber chief",[19] "evil-minded one",[20] "practised plunderer"[21] and so on. And yet, it must be conceded that such phrases in the absence of due emphasis on some of his good qualities, only demonstrate the biased approach of most of the authors. They give the impression as if he had no other quality or no other mission in life except incessant plunder. So far as Churaman's loot in course of wars was concerned, it must be remembered that it was in keeping with the general practice of the age.[22] The examples of the Mughals, Marathas and even Rajputs indulging in it can easily be multiplied. Much of the criticism of Churaman by his contemporaries reflected the official view-point. As it was, most of them repeatedly hit only on one aspect—however bad—of his life, ignoring the other side of his activities.

Churaman was a good soldier, a fine tactician and a diplomat of considerable merit. If no brilliant exploits are associated with his name, he could certainly boast of having thwarted his enemies more than once. His successful defence of Thun against Raja Jai Singh stands out as his masterpiece. Churaman was a skilful military organiser too. The interest he evinced in training, equipment and expansion developed the Jat army into a reckonable force. He also improved upon the system of Jat defence by building strong mud-forts like Thun well provided with arms and ammunitions. By his skilful handling of his opportunities and resources as well as his high associations, Churaman grew extremely strong. He became the "de facto ruler and law giver" of the entire population under his sphere of influence.[23] Yet, there is insufficient ground to style him as "great revolutionary" or "great epoch maker" and to equate his relentless plundering with "a revolution"[24] and so on.

The Jat power made rapid progress during his leadership. Essentially Machiavellian in approach, he could change postures to serve his end. An implacable rebel till the end of Aurangzeb's reign, he later found it

---

16. *K.K.* in Elliot, VIII, 511, 512, 514, 515 and 532.
17. *Iqbal*, 88.
18. *Ahwal*, 105.
19. *Imad*, 83, Qanungo, *Jats*, 47-48.
20. *M.U.*, I, 438.
21. Irvine, *Later Mughals*, I, 231.
22. *Tarikh-i-Ahmad Shahi* (my own micro-film copy, from the originl in British Museum, Br. Mus. Or. 20005), 133b, preserves a significant remark of Malharrao Holkar, reflecting the general tendency of the soldiers. Upon Imad's objection against the Maratha loot (in 1754) Malhar spoke, "These are soldiers. They always do it."
23. Qanungo, *Jats*, 45, 49.
24. U.N. Sharma, *Itihas*, 185, 188, 201, 308.

convenient to profess loyalty to the Mughal throne. In turn he, for the first time, gained the royal favours. But he reverted to his old ways and tried to fish in troubled waters during the reign of Farrukh Siyar. Efforts at his suppression were tried but failed and in the end Churaman received additional concessions. However, the concessions offered from a position of apparent helplessness defeated their very objective. Instead of making Churaman sincerely loyal, they made him conscious of his mischief potential and thus eventually whetted his contumacious designs. Side by side the dictates of self-interest drew him closer to the mighty Sayyids and the latter themselves, for reasons already explained, extended their support to Churaman to the point of infuriating Farrukh Siyar. With the Emperor demanding his annihilation and the Wazir and the Mir Bakhshi offering him full protection, the Jat problem in general and Churaman's case in particular assumed interesting dimensions. More so, when the Emperor himself by virtue of his bickerings about and patronage to equally questionable persons like Itiqad Khan, looked like behaving almost as a factional leader. Thus, the policy towards the Jats became a factional issue at the Court.

The role of Sayyids in the ascendancy of Churaman has not been properly brought out. Besides what we have described at the relevant places, it is to be noted that for the first time in the history of Jats, a chief could attain such heights as to become an ally and close confidant of an imperial Wazir and a Mir Bakhshi. To their patronage, more than to any other single factor, Churaman owed, his spectacular rise - a debt which he openly acknowledged. He received all that he could perhaps aspire for, except the title of Raja, which though promised, could not be conferred upon him due to the murder of Husain Ali. In return, the grateful Jat served them with devotion till their end. This was a pleasant exception in a career otherwise marred by unrivalled cunning and deceit. However, his association with the Sayyids was not an unmixed blessing. It gave an added provocation to their opponents as already mentioned.

It has been argued that the work of Churaman "left no trace" behind and Badan Singh "had to begin everything from the very foundations".[25] This does not appear to be entirely correct. Undeniably, Churaman II did not prove himself to be a farsighted statesman. He lacked that vision, prudence and spirit of accommodation, which were necessary in a successful leader of a tribal and democratic people like the Jats. Though born and brought up among them, he failed to appreciate their susceptibilities. As a result, despite his resources and status he could not weld them into a compact and homogeneous unit or state. On the

25. Sarkar, *Fall*, II, 426.

contrary, unrest and rift came to the forefront even during his lifetime. In the circumstances, Badan Singh had to considerably overhaul his system and devise sagacious policies for the creation of the Jat state. Nevertheless, it would be unfair to deny Churaman his due recognition. By leaving an armed force, numbering 14,000 quite a few strong mud forts, considerable wealth and people conscious of their potentiality, he contributed a good deal towards the emergence of the Jat state. All his shortcomings admitted, the general condition of the Jats at the time of his death was better than it was at his assumption of their leadership. Except depletion in his rank and followers, the rest of his long life's work was intact, when his son, Muhkam Singh stepped into to fill up his place. As we shall see, Jai Singh's victory over the latter, no doubt, inflicted a blow to the rising Jat power. But Churaman cannot be held solely responsible for whatever happened after his death. Likewise, it would be much to presume that his achievements were obliterated and the *zamindari* as it finally passed on to Badan Singh wore altogether a deserted look, with no vestiges of preceding leaders' sustained efforts. In any case Churaman's much-talked-about treasures escaped Jai Singh,[26] and turned out to be of much use to Badan Singh.[27] Similarly, a single military set-back could not have shattered the Jat spirit and self-confidence worked up during the days of Churaman. If even this much survived, it was of no mean value to his successors for self-confidence is a pre-requisite for the rise and growth of a people.

'RAJA' MUHKAM SINGH (C. SEPTEMBER-OCTOBER, 1721-18 NOVEMBER, 1722)[XII]

Muhkam Singh succeeded his father to the leadership. Fransoo, while giving the genealogy of the Jat rulers, mentions him as the first Raja, who set up his Raj at Thun.[28] It appears, however, that he himself adopted the title of the Raja.[29]

Ill-tempered, domineering and pugnacious, young Muhkam Singh was incapable as a leader.[30] He is believed to have forcibly occupied the vacant leadership, much against the then prevalent custom among the Jats. A majority of the Jat leaders, (apparently headed by Badan Singh) did not approve it. They also disliked his intemperance and wished to

---

26. *K.K.* II, 945-946; *M.U.*, I, 440.
27. *Memoires des Jats*, 18; Jadunath Sarkar (*Fall*, II, 430) himself admits it.
XII. Contra see Rajpal Singh, the period (1721—Nov.1722) covered by this heading belonged to Churaman as he was alive at this time. *Rise of the Jat Power*, pp. 36-42.—Editor.
28. *Tawarikh-i-Hunud*, 14a and 14b.
29. Dow, *Hindustan*, II, 352.
30. *Siyar*, I, 329; For his character see *Appendix, A.*, *Tawarikh-i-Hunud*, 16b.

sack him.[31] This situation precipitated an internal crisis again. Getting jealous of Badan Singh's "bravery and ability", Muhkam Singh threw that chief into prison at Khoh (6 miles north west of Deeg). He posted two guards outside his cell, preventing both ingress and egress, instructing them not to admit anybody to him.[32] This was thus Badan Singh's second imprisonment within a short time. The maltreatment at the hands of Muhkam Singh ultimately strengthened his cause. Fransoo adds that as many as 22 prominent *sardars* (said[33] to be Raja Ram's son, Fateh Singh of Ajan, Anup Singh of Arig, Ati Ram's son, Shardul Singh of Halena, Gujars of Sihi and Helak, *Purohit* Kalu Ram and Lalji of Barsana and others), who loved Badan Singh for his "good behaviour", appealed to Muhkam Singh to release his cousin but he refused. At length they sought the intervention of Muhkam's guru, Makhan Das Bairagi. Moved by the entreaties, the Bairagi ordered his disciple to set Badan free. Muhkam reluctantly yielded to the command of his guru, saying, "I know for definite that your holiness has now passed on the sovereignty of Brij from me to the hands of Badan Singh". Thus, securing his freedom, the latter returned to his *jagir* Kumbher and began devising plans for ejecting the hated leader. Ultimately his thoughts turned to Jai Singh and he went to that Raja to seek his help in the matter. By his devoted services and courage he gained "closeness and status" with the Raja. Then he insisted upon him to invade and destroy insolent rebel, Muhkam Singh, holding out the temptation that thereby his (Raja's) "rule will prevail in the Brij country". Jai Singh agree to it.[34]

At a time when Muhkam's strength was dwindling owing to the widening discord, he and his brother Zul Qaran further provocated the Mughals. They created widespread turbulence in their neighbourhood. They committed depredations on the royal highway, and despoiled the village and towns. Expelling the revenue officials, they illegally realized revenue from the *khalisa* and *jagir mahals.* Saadat Khan failed all through to chastise the insurgents. All this caused deep anxiety to the government, as is evident from a *farman* addressed to Nizam-ul-Mulk, wherein he is ordered to tackle this and other pressing problems.[35]

---

31. Ganga Singh, *op.cit.*, 93; Also *Tawarikh-i-Hunud*, 15a.
32. *Tawarikh-i-Hunud*, 14b-15a. He does not take note of his first captivity by Churaman. In fact he omits all relevant details about that leader; Also *Imperial Gazetteer*, VIII, 75; *Madhava Jayati* by Somnath, quoted by U.N. Sharma, *Itihas*, 310.
33. U.N. Sharma, *Itihas*, 304, 310.
34. *Tawarikh-i-Hunud,* 15a-17a; Also Dikshit, *op.cit.*, 29; Tod, *Rajasthan*, 652 (in details differing); cf. *K.K.*, II, 945; *M.U.*, I, 440; *Memoires des Jats,* 16; *Imperial Gazetteer*, VIII, 75. U.N. Sharma (*Itihas*, 310-311) says that before going to Jai Singh, Badan Singh met Rati Ram Jat of Jargavan (8 miles south of Bhasawar) and married his son, Suraj Mal with that chieftain's daughter, Hansia.
35. *Shivdas*, 123, 125 and 127; Also *Kamwar*, II, 484; *M.U.*, I, 440; *Tawarikh-i-Hunud,* 16b.

JAI SINGH'S SECOND EXPEDITION (AUGUST-NOVEMBER, 1722)

At last, Jai Singh, who himself was keen for undertaking the task, received orders to march for the second time against the Jats. On 9th April, 1722 (4th Rajab), Raja Girdhar Bahadur, Arjun Singh of Orchha, Ajit Singh of Kaman and others were placed under him.[36] A force of 14,000 to 15,000 horsemen, artillery and ammunition was under his charge. Rupees two lakhs were given to him for necessary expenditure.[37] On 19th August, 1722, (18th Zi-qada) Jai Singh and Muzaffar Khan were ordered to be ready for their departure. The Bakhshis were required to make up an expeditionary force of 50,000 horsemen.[38] On 22nd August (21st Ziqada) Jai Singh was appointed governor of Agra (vice Saadat Khan) and *faujdar* of Mathura. The territories under Jat occupation were granted to him as *jagir*. Some more nobles - Sayyid Muzaffar Khan (Jai Singh's deputy at Agra), Hamid Khan, Iradat Mand Khan and Muhammad Khan Bangash— were posted to serve under the Raja. Now he marched and when he was still on his way to Thun, Badan Singh coming from Deeg, met him once more, and offered him presents. Jai Singh reciprocated the gesture by presenting, a shield and a sword.[39]

As on the first occasion, Jai Singh began by cutting down the jungles and pushing his trenches forward. The Jats made frequent, though unsuccessful sorties, resulting in casualties on both sides. On 15th October, 1722 (15th Muharram), it was reported at the Court that the skirmishes were taking place daily at Thun, where Muhkam Singh stood bravely to meet the assailants.[40] On 21st October, 1722, the Court received the reports of the fall of enemies three outlying fortesses and resulting increasing despair of the enemies. A big cannon, 300 *bans*, 500 maunds of gun-powder and leads and 100 *rahkalas*, on demand were ordered to be sent from the imperial arsenal.[41] Muhkam Singh had earlier appealed to Ajit Singh for help. Accordingly, on a promise to pay Rupees three lakhs in advance and meet daily expenses he sent a force under Vijay Raj Bhandari. It came upto Jobnair (26 miles north-west of Jaipur) and

---

36. *Kamwar*, II, 480; Also *K.K.*, II, 945; *Rustam*, 495; *M.U.*, I, 440; *Majma-ul-Akhbar* in Elliot VIII, 361.
37. *K.K.*, II, 945.
38. *Kamwar*, II, 482; Also see *Rustam*, 495; *Majma-ul-Akhbar* in Elliot VIII, 361.
39. *Kamwar*, II, 482; *Tazkira-i-Shakir Khan* by Shakir Khan (R.S.L Sitamau Ms.), hereafter referred to as Shakir,2; *Memoires des Jats*, 84; *Siyar*, I, 329 (Its English translation mentions "Ajit Singh Sevai", which is an obvious slip for Jai Singh Sawai); Scott, *Dekkan*, II, 187; Zahir-ud-Din Malik *Muhammad Shah* (unpublished thesis, Muslim University Aligarh), 171; *Dastur Qaumwar*, VII, 435 and Farman (Kapatdwara), 160, 27/36 quoted by U.N. Sharma, *Itihas*, 313—315.
40. *Kamwar*, II, 483; *K.K.*, II, 945; *Rustam*, 495; *M.U.*, I, 440.
41. *Kamwar*, II, 483; Also *M.U.*, I, 440.

encamped there (October, 1722).[42] Meanwhile, Badan Singh guided Jai Singh to the vulnerable spots in the defences of the fort of Thun. He also seduced many of Muhkam's captains to cross over to the side of the Raja. Having resisted the imperialists for two months Muhkam now lost heart and decided to escape from the fort. But before that he laid out a death-trap for the enemy. He dug up mines in the fort and spread gun powder on their floor. Then carrying as much treasure as possible he made off in the darkness of night (c. 8th November) to Ajit Singh at Sambhar. Next morning the Raja wanted to enter the fort. But Muhkam's flight, despite abundance of supplies in Thun, convinced Badan Singh of the leader's treachery. He, therefore, dissuaded the Raja from going inside the fort and thereby prevented a major disaster. Hardly had Jai Singh decided otherwise when the fort mines began to explode, "hurling the stones through the sky". Jai Singh expressed his gratefulness to Badan Singh for having wisely saved his own and his associates' lives.[43] Hectic attempts to trace out the much publicized treasures of Churaman were made but in vain. The city and fort of Thun were demolished and the soil was ploughed by asses by Jai Singh to make it detestable in public eyes.[44] On 10th November, 1722 (11th Safar, 1135 H.) Jai Singh's *Vakil*, Jag Ram conveyed to the Emperor the welcome news of the conquest of Thun and the flight of the sons of Churaman, presenting him 500 *mohars* on his master's behalf. Muhammad Shah ordered the Raja to arrest Muhkam and his family members.[45]

A few days later, Jai Singh entered into an agreement with Badan Singh in his camp at Thun. The Raja placed a turban on his head. The French missionary says that he also bestowed upon the Jat chief the title of "Raja of Birch (Brij)", the *teeka*, the *nishan*, the *naqqara* (kettle-drum) and the five-coloured flag (which was that of the Rajas of Jaipur also). But Badan Singh took no other title except that of the "*Thakur*".[46]

---

42. Pancholi Rai Chand - Jai Singh, 28, October, 1722, Jaipur Archives, quoted by V.S. Bhatnagar, *Jai Singh*, 103; M. Mitra, *Ajit Singh*, 250.
43. *Tawarikh-i-Hunud*, 17a-18b, Also *Kamwar*, II, 484, *K.K.* II 945; *Rustam*, 495; *Memoires des Jats*, 15, 16; *Siyar*, I, 329; *M.U.* I, 440; *Majma-ul-Akhbar*, in Elliot, VIII, 361.
44. Thun was, however, rebuilt, though on a different site, well before Wendel's arrival in the Jat country. See *Memoires des Jats,* 15. Side note *Tawarikh-i-Hunud* (19b) relates an interesting incident that during the Maratha invasion of Bharatpur (1754) Malharrao, in order to assuage Muhkam Singh, ploughed the site of the former Thun with elephants and sowed pearls.
45. *Kamwar*, II, 484; *K.K.*, II, 945-946; *Memoires des Jats*, 15; *Tawarikh-i-Hunud*, 18b; *M.U.*, I, 440; *Majma-ul-Akhbar* in Elliot, VIII, 361; Scott, *Dekkan*, II, pt. V, 187; *Bhaskar*, 3081; Zahir-ud-Din Malik, *Muhammad Shah*, 172.
46. *Memoires des Jats*, 16 main body and footnote; Also see *Rustam*, 495, *Dastur Qaumwar*, VII, quoted by U.N. Sharma, *Itihas*, 321; *S.P.D*, XXX, 124; *Siyar*, I, 329-330; *M.U.*, I, 440; *Majma-ul-Akhbar* in Elliot, VIII, 361.

Generally corroborating Wendel, Fransoo adds that the right of coinage and the *kotwali* of the sadar (Agra) was also given to Badan Singh.[47] In May 1723, the Emperor ordered Jai Singh to give some portions of the *zamindari* of Churaman to Badan Singh and thus he acknowledged his leadership. Following a written agreement in June, 1725, Jai Singh formally made over to the Jat chief the lands of Churaman on the condition of his paying an annual tribute of rupees eighty three thousand to Jaipur.[48] According to Fransoo the tracts assigned to Badan Singh consisted of Mathura, Vrindaban, Mahaban, the parganas of Hissar, Chhata, Kosi, Hodal etc. yielding a total revenue of 50 to 60 lakhs.[49] He apparently includes here those areas also which only gradually came under the possession of Badan Singh. Thus, the new Jat chief started his career as a feudatory of the Jaipur Raja. It is interesting to note here that the great Suraj Mal, even in the heyday of his power when he far outstripped the Jaipur King, Madho Singh, formally behaved himself as the vassal of the Raja.[50, XIII]

CONSEQUENCES OF JAI SINGH'S SECOND EXPEDITION

Jai Singh's second Jat expedition was no less remarkable than the first one. The conquest of Thun and the other forts fulfilled the cherished desire of the Mughals as well as the Jaipur chief. The Emperor expressed his great pleasure by ordering the beating of drum continuously for three days.[51] Jai Singh avenged his former disgrace and at the same time gratified the long-standing desire of the Jaipur rulers (as also of the Mughals) to humble the recalcitrant Jats. It added also to his fame and fortune.[52] His political ambition to establish personal overlordship over the Jats also seemed to have been realized. Likewise, the humility and submissiveness of the new Jat chief must have tickled his typically Rajput notion of social superiority as well.

A deeper insight, however, cannot but reveal the shallowness of the achievement. It has to be conceded that Jai Singh thrived upon the

---

47. *Tawarikh-i-Hunud*, 18b.
48. *Kapatdwara papers*, 73, quoted by V.S. Bhatnagar, *Jai Singh*, 103; U.N. Sharma, *Itihas* 321-322.
49. *Tawarikh-i-Hunud*, 18b.
50. See *Tawarikh-i-Hunud*, 63; *Sujan*, 36; Qanungo, *Jats*, 60; Contra see Pande, *Bharatpur*, 30-31.
XIII. More details for the period 1722-1725 see Rajpal Singh, *Rise of the Jat Power*, pp. 36-42.—Editor.
51. *Kamwar*, II, 484; *Memoires des Jats*, 84; side note.
52. In reward for his services the Raja received the titles (in June 1723) of "Rajah-i-Rajeshwar, Shri Rajadhiraj, Maharaja Sawai Jai Singh". See Irvine, *Later Mughals*, II, 124.

mutual discord and enmity among the Jat fraternity, as is evident from a traditional local saying.[53, XIV] It is open to dispute whether without Badan Singh's help and guidance, the Rajput could have succeeded so quickly or comfortably. This naturally makes dim the glory of Jai Singh's victory. Even this victory was of precarious nature. In the ultimate analysis, what he succeeded in destroying was the power of the sons of Churaman and not the Jat power as such. The loss sustained by the Jats was, thus, more ostensible than real.[54] The imperialists attained little beyond reducing or destroying a few Jat forts and putting to flight the existing leader, Muhkam Singh. Paradoxical though it may sound, their victory turned out to be a boon in disguise for the Jats. It only forced the deficient and unpopular Muhkam to make room for the capable Badan Singh, who raised Jats glory to unprecedented heights. In the process, he showed himself to be more dangerous than Muhkam or even his father, for the Mughal authority, in the *suba* of Agra at least. In respect of the Jaipur house also, if not Badan Singh or his son (Suraj Mal), certainly his grandson (Jawahar Singh), proved a potential source of anxiety and trouble to his Jaipur contemporary.[55] Yet the irony was that the Mughal Emperor and Jai Singh themselves had facilitated as well as sanctioned the elevation of Badan Singh. Keeping these cross currents in view, Wendel appeared to be lamenting, "But it was Jai Singh himself who undid what he had done himself".[56] Thus, whatever might have appeared at the moment, in reality there was not much for the Court to feel jubilant over, or contended about the episode.

As an upshot of this war the relations between the new Jat leadership and the Kachhwahas on the one hand and the Rathors on the other underwent a transformation. While in the case of the Kachhwahas the former enmity gave way to amity, coolness and ill-will were bound to supersede the earlier warmth between the Jat leadership and the Rathors, following Ajit Singh's act of extending asyslum to Muhkam Singh.

---

53. "They wanted to takeover Delhi and Agra, but due to brother's enmity lost their own Thun."

XIV. लेन चहति हे दिल्ली आगरा घर की थून दई।
बंधु बैर अनबन के कारण कैसी कुमति ढई।। -

ब्रजेन्द्र वंश भास्कर, p. 30

जयसिंह बदन जट्टहिं संहेत, बहुभव दिवाय थूनहि समेत।
है साह हिंतु मुहकम हराम, यातें पलाय गय धन्व धाय।।

वंश भास्कर, p. 3080-81.—Editor.

54. Satish Chandra, *Parties and Politics*, 178-179; Contra see Sarkar, *Fall*, II, 426.

55. *Memoires des Jats*, 16.

56. *Ibid*.

CHARACTER AND ESTIMATE OF MUHKAM SINGH

Muhkam Singh gained experience of warfare and politics as a helper to his father, Rao Churaman II. Like Rup Singh he distinguished himself as a brave and energetic warrior on several occasions. He held his *guru*, Makhan Das Bairagi in high esteem but he showed himself wanting in love for his family. He shared his father's attachment to a predatory life. As a person he was offensive, jealous and selfish and thus he apparently created more enemies than friends. He nurtured high ambition yet he lacked vision and purpose to sustain it. Likewise, however, bold and daring, he did not possess heroic fortitude to overcome moments of peril.

Muhkam's tenure in office was too short to enable us to judge him properly as a leader. His incapability, however, is evident. Imperious and self-indulgent, he failed to inspire confidence in his own people. He foolishly clung to the policies, disapproved of even during the lifetime of his father. Therefore, the rift which he had inherited from his father widened under him and several chieftains having deserted him, helped the imperialists in putting him to flight. Thereafter, Muhkam Singh lived as a fugitive for more than half a century. Recapture of his patrimony with external help remained the object of his activities till well past the reign of Badan Singh. To seek help he approached Ajit Singh, Malharrao Holkar, Imad-ul-Mulk, the Emperor Ahmad Shah and others and in the process apparently caused deep anxieties to the Jat rulers. Besides, his intrigues obviously influenced the Jat policy towards the personages concerned and vice versa. At last, disappointed from all sides poor Muhkam stood a suppliant at the gates of Raja Suraj Mal and Raja Ranjit Singh. Both, especially the former, generously provided for him. In the end Muhkam went to Ajmer where he died at a fairly ripe age in presence of Jiwa Ram Jat, the Mukhtar of Suraj Mal.[57]

---

57. For details of Muhkam's subsequent career see *Memoires des Jats*, 1, footnote; *Tah.* 94b, 98b, 102b-103b, 106b-107a, 131b; *Tawarikh-i-Hunud*, 19b-20a, 26a; *S.P.D.* XXX, 134. II, 23, XXVII, 83; *M.U.*, I, 440; Also see Appendix A.

V
Emergence of Jat Kingdom : Policy and Measures (1723-1756)

The emergence of Thakur Badan Singh as the leader of the Jats, marks the dawn of a new era in their history. It signalled the ascendancy of the forces of stable conquest and steady growth over those of dubious and erratic expansion.[1] However, the situation that he inherited was difficult,[2] if not "almost hopeless".[3] Far from being a homogenous unit,[4] the Jats, so accustomed to clannish and individual independence, were broadly divided on policy matters into two hostile camps. Dispossessed Muhkam Singh with his continual machinations to regain the leadership posed a potential threat to the new chief. There is little doubt that the adherents of Churaman and his sons, like Khema,[5] Bhure Singh and Daya Ram[6] of Mendu,[XV]

---

1. Iqbal, 210; *Memoires des Jats,* 16, Qanungo, *Jats,* 60; Bhatnagar, *Jai Singh,* 103.
2. Author's article, 'Badan Singh Ke Kal Main Bharatpur Ka Pradeshik Vistar' (Hindi), *Uplabdhi,* (Samvat 2025), 66.
3. Contra see Sarkar, *Fall,* II, 427.
4. Author's article referred to above.
5. We have no definite information about the doings of Khema during Jai Singh's second seige of Thun. However, we do come across a reference in *Shahnama Munawwar Kalam* (*Shivdas* 103), showing Khema offering presents (two *mohars*) to the Emperor alongwith the imperial grandees just before the Nauroze festival in 1133 A.H. (C. third week of July, 1721). This leads us to infer that this chieftain continued to pretend his loyalty and thereby escaped being chastised by Jai Singh.
6. Bhure Singh and Daya Ram respectively were the son and grandson of Nanda Jat (see *Imad,* 82). It seems that Nanda died at this time for we do not find his name being mentioned any more—leaving Bhure and Daya Ram as his successors at Mendu.

XV. The author mis-takes Mendu for Mudsan, the fort of the successors of Nand Ram Jat of Thenua clan. Suraj Mal crushed the Bhadoria Rajputs of Agra district and the Porach Rajput *taluqdar* of Mendu in Aligarh district. He did not spare even independent Jat *Zamindar* of Mudsan, and evicted him from his fort. See J.N. Sarkar, *Fall,* II, (1991 ed.) p. 266; *Allygurh Statistics,* 239; *S.P.D.,* XXI, 100 and XXVII, 206; *Rajwade,*I, 285, 295.

Chhatar Singh and the chief of Motia (near Fatehpur),[7] were on the look out for re-installing either Muhkam or asserting their own authority or both. Acquisition of booty and protection against the Mughals had been the magic-bond of Churaman and his successor (to increase their following). But since Badan Singh did not mean to plunder,[8] the Jats, used to the ways of Churaman, must have kept themselves aloof from him. Moreover, there is little to show that solidarity, based upon devotion to a common superior, prevailed even among those who had all through supported him. In fact, all the chieftains kept their own band of troops[9] and were determined to preserve as far as possible their separate existence. Consequently, power and wealth lay dispersed among various Jat headmen.[10] Then again, some system of administration had also to be evolved, if Badan Singh aimed at establishing an independent state. Churaman, with all his worth, had done little in this direction. Finally, in order to buttress his image, he had also to repel the likely impression[11] that he was Jai Singh's parasite or worthless weakling.[12]

Thus, the task of Badan Singh was onerous indeed. But gifted as he was with bravery, perseverance, "unrivalled wisdom and cunning"[13] he rose equal to it. Internal consolidation and territorial expansion being out of scope of this study, we may analyse only the relevant facts for a

---

Mendu is situated 20 miles south, Hathras, 22 miles south of Aligarh, both on N. Rly. and Mudsan lies 7 miles west of Hathras. For correct situation of these places, see, J.M. Siddiqi, *Aligarh District: A Historical Survey*, 110, 113 f.n. 4, 207, f.n. 6, 210 f.n. 7, 211 f.n. 6.

Jagbir Singh informs that Raja of Mudsan shifted to Sasni about 12 miles east of Mudsan. Suraj Mal put Mendu under the control of Daya Ram/ Baran Singh of Hathras. After the death of Maharaja Suraj Mal his successor Jawahar Singh handed over Mudsan again to Raja of Sasni, who returned back to his old fort. Jagbir Singh, *The Jat Rulers of Upper Doad*, p.128 also 9. For the detailed history of the successors of Nand Ram called Nanda Jat of Thenua clan and the description of their *garhis*—Mudsan, Hathras, Sasni, Beswan and Tochigarh etc. See Jagbir Singh's said book. I am familiar with all these places.—Editor.

7. This can be clearly inferred from his intimacy with the rebel, Khema Jat. See *Tawarikh-i-Hunud*, 21a-21b.
8. Infra, f.n. 22-32 of this chapter.
9. *Ajaib*, 122; cf. *Tawarikh-i-Hunud*, 15a.
10. *Memoires des Jats*, 17.
11. Badan Singh's apprehensions have come true in the belief of some modern scholars like Sarkar who states (*Fall*, II, 428) him to have been "raised from the dust" by Jai Singh. This is, for the most part, untenable. Whatever the measure of Jai Singh's assistance, a personage who led the rival group against redoubted Churaman and Muhkam Singh can hardly be deemed to be so low lying.
12. *Memoires des Jat*, 16-17.
13. *Tawarikh-i-Hunud*, 14b; *Dirgh Nagar Varnan*, 3-4; *Ras Peeushnidhi* and *Madhav Vinod* in Somnath-3-4, 318; cf. *Memoires des Jats*, 16.

proper appreciation of his role in the imperial affairs. To begin with, his political ideology, (endorsed by his able successor, Suraj Mal as well) was that the Jat power could be "integrated" and thus made stronger under only one leader.[14] More precisely, conscious of the need of a unified political system, Badan Singh wanted to transform his princely insignia into the "reality of a sovereign power".[15] This presupposed his reducing different Jat headmen to submission, after seizing their estates and wealth. But any such endeavour had to be reconciled to their deep-rooted democratic and individualistic temper. Added to it, was the fear of the possible Mughal opposition.

Badan Singh, therefore, began cautiously, combining coercion with conciliation, force with appeasement and princely grandeur with humility. He raised a well equipped force consisting of infantry and cavalry.[16] In place of Thun, Sogar and Sinsini[17] destroyed earlier, he began building new forts at Deeg and Kumbher, the foundation of the former having been laid by Jai Singh.[18]

With a view to enhancing his power and position, he almost like Tudor Henry VII of England, contracted political marriages in the families of the leading chieftains such as those of Kama and Sahar[19] and possibly of Salempur, Hodal, Bachhamadi and Pathena.[20] He, however, meted out a different treatment to those who did not submit even after persuasion. The hardcore followers of Churaman and Muhkam Singh largely fell in this category. Their independent existence and pro-Muhkam predilections, besides hindering expansion and stability also constituted a serious threat to his own existence. Further, having had a taste of predatory life in the past, they apparently still persisted with it. There is little room for suspicion that it were these rapacious chieftains, as also the local malefactors who perpetrated all that loot which Wendel

14. *Memoires des Jats*, 29.
15. Sarkar, *Fall*, II, 428-429; Also Qanungo, *Jats*, 60.
16. *Memoires des Jats*, 17.
17. Badan Singh was Jai Singh's favourite and an accomplice at the time. Hence, Wendel (*Memoires des Jats*, 19) seems to be mistaken in supposing that Sinsini, the paternal place of the Sinsiniwara ruling chiefs and currently in the possession of Badan Singh himself, was also destroyed.
18. *Tawarikh-i-Hunud*, 19a; *Sujan*, 217 and 219; *Memoires des Jats*, 19 and 27; Also *Dirgh*, 1-2.
19. *Tawarikh-i-Hunud*, 19a, 20a; Qanungo, *Jats*, 61, Sarkar, *Fall*, II, 432.
20. Badan Singh had many Queens and of his several sons only Suraj Mal had six (almost all of them married during the life time of Badan Singh). It is not possible to state how many of these were received in marriage, we keeping the above object in view. The places cited above were owned by those chiefs, who, are told, had married their daughters with Suraj Mal. Vide *Tawarikh-i-Hunud*, 22a-22b, 26b; *Pathena Raso*, quoted by Ganga Singh, *op.cit.*, 100; *Memoires des Jats*, 63, cf. *TAH*. 23a.

mistakenly imputes exclusively to Badan Singh. He asserts that amidst the administrative disorder, following Sayyid's usurpation of power, Badan Singh roamed with impunity, depopulating villages, demolishing houses, gardens, mosques, tombs, statues etc., lifting girders, stones, lime in a word everything deemed useful for building purposes. The armed Jat robbers, in bands of two to three hundred, carrying axes and torches and blowing trumpets, pounded on the houses of the wealthiest.[21] At another place, Badan Singh is charged with deputing a part of his force in robbing the countryside, the road to Delhi and the outskirts of Agra. Wendel's obsession with Badan Singh seems to be getting out of hands, when he makes that chief surpass even notorious Churaman in what he calls—cruelty and robbery, arguing that his bands were more numerous, more daring and better sustained and consequently they wrought widespread and irredemiable havoc.[22]

This allegation is mostly distorted and seems to be based on hearsay. That the Jat leader grabbed booty[23] and confiscated wealth and estates of his enemies, is undeniable. But wanton and unparalleled pillage and robbery looks incredible in case of a man who himself even at the risk of his life, had opposed it and other nefarious trends in the days of Churaman and Muhkam Singh. In juxtaposing the case of the Sayyids here, Wendel appears to place the alleged havoc in the first few years of the reign of Muhammad Shah which mostly coincided, with the activities of Muhkam Singh. However, true in the context of a later period, at least during these days Badan Singh just did not have all the means of Churaman to be believed to have outclassed the latter in armed strength, which Wendel links with plunder. In fact, Father Wendel is himself contradictory in his statements. Here he talks of Badan Singh's armed superiority while at the other place he acknowledges that he started keeping infantry only "gradually".[24]

Similarly, on the one hand he accuses Badan Singh and his men of cruelty, while on the other he concedes "sweet, humble and submissive" manners of that leader, which were "so contrary to those of others".[25] It is, therefore, risky to accept Wendel with approbation[26] when he himself is not quite sure of what he makes us believe.

---

21. *Memoires des Jats,* 20.
22. *Memoires des Jats,* 17; Also *Tawarikh-i-Hunud*, 4b.
23. Once Badan Singh himself admitted it by implication. See *Sujan*, 217.
24. *Memoires des Jats, 17.*
25. *Memoires des Jats, 16.*
26. Thus Sarkar, *Fall*, II, 429, 430—431. It is significant that K.R. Qanungo has not taken the slightest note of Wendel's version.

Fortunately, we also have contemporary evidence to disprove Wendel's notion. Testifying Badan Singh's repugnance to predatory life, *Iqbalnama* emphatically states that he:

"Sowed the seeds of happiness and made the plant of virtues green. He acted in a way contrary to the habits and practices of his predecessors ... who had been accustomed to ... plunder ... (and) ... who practised theft and robberies as highwaymen."[27]

A later authority (Shah Nawaz Khan), though one of the most relentless critics of the Jats, also corroborates it, saying that the Jats under Badan Singh gave up their marauding practices.[28] It is also significant that the Polish historian who took note of loot by some other Jat chiefs, is absolutely silent about Badan Singh. Further, if Badan Singh really indulged in highway robbery, the normal traffic on the roads was bound to be suspended, a fact which even Wendel has not suggested about, much less to prove. On the contrary, we learn from an eye witness that Suraj Mal during the reign of his father ensured continual flow of traffic on the highways passing through the Jat sphere of influence.[29] Likewise, the other contemporary authorities (*Tawarikh-i-Ahmad Shahi* and *Tarikh-i-Alamgir Sani*) testify that Badan Singh's principality had been an extremely safe place, where in face of the external dangers, the terror-stricken people of the Capital fled for shelter and the Jats not only protected them but also treated them well.[30] If Badan Singh had really let loose the reign of loot and terror, one wonders how did the numerous refugees willingly chose to throw themselves inextricably within a notorious robber's den. The fact is that probably nowhere in contemporary Hindustan wealth and honour of the people was as safe as it was in the reign of Badan Singh and Suraj Mal, where, as is to be noticed, on several occasions, the multitudes in their dire distress flocked to. This needs no stress that they were inspired with the humane outlook of the ruler concerned and the measure of peace and order that he was able to enforce in his realm. This confidence was not generated overnight nor the political stability achieved accidentally. Both were the gradual offshoots of the benign attitude and policies that Badan Singh and his regent Suraj Mal had adopted at the very start. Thus, apart from the positive written proof, the circumstantial evidence is also there to confute Wendel's notion regarding Badan Singh. Loot and robbery was never his policy nor was he in any way personally

27. *Iqbal*, 210.
28. *M.U.*, I, 441.
29. *Sujan*, 10.
30. *Tawarikh-i-Alamgir Sani*, Anon. (R.S.L. Sitamau Ms.), 166; TAH, 33a.

associated with it.[31] At best the only thing relevant in Wendel's version may be that during the traditional phase of his leadership, Badan Singh did not possess sufficient strength to control plundering by the local malefactors[32] and other chieftains and hence for the time being he was obliged to get on with them.

In the light of contemporary evidence, the only point that looks relevant in Wendel's version is the occasional outburst of loot and lawlessness in the countryside of Agra. Much of the turbulence was engineered by the rapacious chieftains like Khema Jat, whom, Fransoo calls, "a notorrious robber.[33] In sticking to their familiar ways, they not only gratified their lust for money but apparently also attempted to sabotage the plans of their enemy, Badan Singh.

That Jat leader could have hardly remained for long, a silent spectator of their pernicious activities. He proceeded to deal with them as soon as he mustered up adequate strength. Vijay Ram Garasia, the chief of Pathena, being a close associate of Churaman and his sons, had in the past and still opposed Badan Singh. In an attempt to bring the Garasia close to him, he married Suraj Mal with his daughter, Kalyan Kaur (Kalyani).[34] But this conciliatory step failed to mend his ways. Thereupon, he granted Pathena as a *jagir* to Shardul (the son of Ati Ram of Halaina) whom he had earlier won over to his side. Shardul killed Vijay Ram and held Pathena under Badan Singh.[35] Similarly, he got Bhure Singh and Daya Ram of Mendu, subdued (c. 1730) by Suraj Mal.[36, XVI] Then came the turn of yet another strong partisan of Churaman, Thakur Khema Jat of Fatehpur. In 1733, Suraj Mal attacked him and demolished his *garhi* at that place. But Khema was not killed in the action as is commonly believed.[37] He lived on for some time more till Suraj Mal managed his end through Bhunda Ram Jat of Arig (c. 1753).[38] It is said that Badan

---

31. Prof. K.R. Qanungo (*Jats.*, 60 and 62) rightly remarks that "sincerely desirous of promoting the arts of peace". Badan Singh had "no taste for a predatory life" and that he "meant to rule and not plunder ... like his predecessors". Also see Bhatnagar, *Jai Singh*, 103.
32. To cite one instance, on 8th July, 1723, an organised Jat band looted near Nakita, a two storeyed carriage loaded with.cotton bales. *Akhbarat* 15th Shawwal, 5th year of Muhammad Shah's reign.
33. *Tawarikh-i-Hunud*, 20b.
34. That one of the Queens of Suraj Mal bore the name of Kalyani is substantiated by Fransoo, See *Tawarikh-i-Hunud*, 22b.
35. *Pathena Raso*, quoted by Ganga Singh, *op.cit.*, 100-101 also 91.
36. *Sujan*, 6. It, however, does not refer to the names of Bhure Singh and Daya Ram.

XVI. Poet Sudan does not mention these names because Mendu does not belong to them. Mudsan was the stronghold of the successors of Nanda Jat i.e. Bhure Singh and Daya Ram. See for details, Ch. V, f.n. XV.—Editor.

37. U.N. Sharma *Itihas* 325-330; Qanungo, *Jats*, 65-66; Pande, *Bharatpur*, 46.
38. For details see *Tawarikh-i-Hunud*, 20b-21b.

Singh also removed from his way Chhatar Singh, who had been "the right hand" of Churaman.[39] Sometime early in 1730 Suraj Mal crushed the Sikarwar and Gujar miscrents of Bayana and Rupbas. He demolished their fortresses and established his authority over the region. This was formally handed over to Badan Singh on a promise to pay an annual tribute and then the construction of the fort at Wair was taken up. This place was given as a *jagir* to Pratap Singh.[40]

If he could succeed in toppling down such redoubtable chieftains, it was not at all difficult for him to reduce the petty ones to the level of common Jats. By and by he established his hegemony over the area approximating to Agra and Mathura districts. From the status of a *zamindar* he became a small Raja, strong enough to manage his business and inspire awe among his neighbours.[41] He increased his forces as he gained new territories. The construction of new forts also continued side by side. He furnished his strongholds partly with small cannons seized from others but mostly with self-designed large cannons.[42] Hoarding wealth underground was a practice fairly popular among the Jats. Hence, there is sufficient ground to accept the then current belief that Badan Singh had his luck in discovering treasures of Churaman and his other predecessors. This largely enabled him to meet his "immense" expenditure.[43] Meanwhile, Badan Singh also started keeping a harem befitting a King.[44]

Once he became the undisputed strongman in his home, Badan Singh set himself to expanding his possessions and authority, following the general practice of the age.[45] Apart from his own commendable resourcefulness and uncanny wisdom, three other factors that facilitated his bid, were the lethargy and growing imbecility of the Mughals, the good will and patronage of Jai Singh and the invaluable services of Suraj Mal as also of Pratap Singh.[46] Here, we shall take up the last two factors leaving the first one to be discussed in the following chapters.

The relations between Jai Singh and Badan Singh continued to be close till the death of the Rajput ruler in 1743. Several factors obliged the Jat chief to remain friendly to, and keep on courting the favour of

---

39. Ganga Singh *op.cit.*, 99-100.
40. *Sujan*, 118, 222; *Shah*, 2; *Imad*; 84; *Memoires des Jats*, 19; *Ras Peeushnidhi* in Somnath, 4; Qanungo, *Jats*, 61; U.N. Sharma, *Itihas*, 348.
41. *Memoires des Jats*, 17 and 29; Also *Tawarikh-i-Hunud*, 18b; Sarkar, *Fall*, II, 429.
42. *Memoires des Jats*, 17, 27, 29.
43. *Ibid.*, 18.
44. *Memoires des Jats*, 20-21; *Tawarikh-i-Hunud*, 20a.
45. *Memoires des Jats*, 17.
46. Author's article, 'Badan Singh ke Kal main Bharatpur Ka Pradeshik Vistar,. *Uplabdhi.*, 65-66.

the Raja. First, he was grateful to him for his role in his political ascendancy. Second, his intimacy with Jai Singh could serve as a counterpoise to Muhkam Singh's intrigues against him. Third, Jai Singh happened to be one the most influential grandees of the Empire.[47] Therefore, his favour could be helpful in attaining more power and glory in the same way as the Sayyids' help had earlier done in case of Churaman II. Fourth, the intricacies of the contemporary political situation, perhaps, also tended him to the same direction.

Isolation was inexpedient and risky in the politics of his day. None, much less an astute and ambitious Badan Singh, could afford to stand in proud isolation and yet have pretensions for increasing one's power. Even the highest in the land, the court-nobles, the Marathas, the Rajputs etc. sought allies. Finally, Badan Singh knew that until recently the Amber house had been the relentless foe of the neighbouring Jats. As such what he had obtained through its favour could well be endangered by its frown. Here was, then another consideration emphasizing the need for retaining the goodwill of his benefactor.

On his part, Jai Singh had his own reasons to be amiable and helpful to Badan Singh. The sentiments of gratitude moved Jai Singh as well. If he had helped Badan Singh in assuming the leadership, the latter had saved his (the Raja's) very life from the devouring jaws of death, at Thun. Moreover, the Raja could count on the Jat help in need if he remained friendly to them. Further, with his own protege being at the helm of the Jat affairs, Jai Singh's cherished designs of personal hegemony over Agra looked to be atleast indirectly fulfilled. Side by side, the Raja felt that his patronizing the Jat chief would "shed reflected lustre" on his person.[48]

Thus, convinced of the usefulness of Badan Singh as also of his ever remaining grateful to him[49], Jai Singh generally extended him his favours. During his governorship of Agra, Badan Singh and Suraj Mal became "plenipotentiaries" with liberty to do what they wished. The Raja's deputy, (Kirat Singh of Diggi) in fact openly sided with them. Jai Singh connived at the Jats' encroachment upon the imperial territories and turned a deaf ear to the complaints thereon.[50] He also procured for the Jat chief the *rahdari* of the roads between Faridabad, Agra and Jaipur.[51] On the

---

47. Sarkar, *Fall*, I, 242.
48. Sarkar, *Fall*, II, 428.
49. *Memoires des Jats*, 19-20.
50. *Memoires des Jats*, 19-20; *TAH.* 23a; *Sujan*, 36.
51. *TAH.*, 23a; *Memoires des Jats*, 19; *Sujan* 10, 40 (by implication).

occasion of the *Ashwamedh Yagya*, Jai Singh betook and blessed Suraj Mal as his son.[52]

On his part, Badan Singh reciprocated the kind gestures of the Jaipur chief by his humility and submissiveness. Whereas not even once did he appear in the Mughal court, he never missed, so long as his age permitted, going every year to Jaipur to pay his homage to Jai Singh.[53] If *Iqbalnama* is to be believed he hardly took any step without consulting the Rajput Raja.[54] The gallant Jat warriors matched the kindness of Jai Singh by shedding their blood at his and his successor's call. More than once did they rescue the Jaipur rulers from gloomy situations, fighting bravely in their vanguard. Sudan hardly exaggerates when, keeping in mind the *heroic performance* of Suraj Mal in the battle of Gangwana, he says that the Jat "defended Kuram (Jai Singh) by wielding sword in his hand."[55] Apart from this battle, the Jats fought on the side of the Jaipur Rajas in 1740 against Jodhpur, in 1744 against Kota, in 1748 against Madho Singh.[56]

Yet, the amity between the two need not be over-emphasized. Under it lay a dormant feeling of mutual suspicion and jealousy. Two immediate neighbours, having an age old record of socio-political feud,[57] could not have turned forthwith really sincere to their professions of friendship. More so, when their respective ambitions overlapped with regard to the occupation of the Agra province. There is ground to share the then prevailing suspicion that even if Jai Singh did not openly lend his troops to Badan Singh, he did secretly "employ" him to weaken the Mughal authority in the province so that his own dominance might be established there.[58] By implication it meant that he could be the last man to acquiesce in the emergence of an independent and strong Jat State. It is noteworthy here that Jai Singh forbade Badan Singh to construct the scheduled fort on a hill at Paharatal or Bayana lest its strategic site should induce the owner to become independent of Amber.[59] Jai Singh also used his influence to

52. Qanungo, *Jats*, 63; Pande, *Bharatpur*, 34; U.N. Sharma, *Itihas*, 326; J.S. Gahlot, *Rajputane Ka Itihas* (Jodhpur: 1966) 103; Dikshit, *Brijendra Vansh Bhaskar*, 40-41.
53. For this purpose he built a mansion, garden and other houses in the outskirts of Jaipur. The locality was named "Badanpura" after him. *Memoires des Jats*, 27; For a discordant note see Pande, *Bharatpur*, 33.
54. *Iqbal*, 157.
55. *Sujan*, 6.
56. These wards formed the part of the internal affairs of Jaipur and did not directly affect the fortunes of the Mughal Empire. We have left out their details as they do not relate to our subject. Details of these wars may be found in Dr. Ram Pande's *Bharatpur*.
57. Sarkar, *Fall*, II, 423; Also Qanungo, *Jats*, 62.
58. *Memoires des Jats*, 19.
59. Pande *Bharatpur*, 34-35; U.N. Sharma, *Itihas*, 326.

mould the Jat policy to suit his designs, often detrimental to the Jat interests. His attitude during Baji Rao's march through the Jat area (1736) is a case in point.[60]

In ultimate analysis, then, Jai Singh was trying to fulfil his ulterior designs rather than help the Jats. And all along he was expecting Badan Singh to show him servile devotion.[61] This was in an age marked by surging ambitions, his shedding the temptation of personal sway at least over his homeland would have been a miracle indeed. As it was, Badan Singh aspired for an independent principality of his own and as such Jai Singh's ulterior motives—insofar as they pertained to his neighbouring areas—were bound to discomfit him. This coupled with his own expansionist goal possibly lay at the root of his understanding with the Meo rebels, carrying raids to the Jaipur territories. Jai Singh was then compelled to placate the Jat chief by granting him the lands of Sinsini, Thun and Nagar, which yielded rupees 18 lakhs per annum.[62]

Viewed in this light, the gestures of Jai Singh and Badan Singh, like the former blessing Suraj Mal and Badan attending the Jaipur *darbars* and so on appear to have been the part of a clever game calculated to conceal their inner designs. With both nursing conflicting ambitions, and yet keeping a show of cordiality, one wonders if they were not attempting to outwit each other. Amidst the circumstances, it was obviously the outweighing considerations of mutual utility, as also gratitude, that kept them together.

However, the factor which helped Badan Singh most in expansion was the invaluable assistance of his eldest (living) son and the destined successor, Suraj Mal. Born about the beginning of the year 1707,[63] of his Jat wife Rani Deoki of Kama,[64] Suraj Mal showed "signs of boldness with a bit of manner and behaviour" quite early in his youth.[65] Amiable, soft and unostentatious in living, he wore rather a simple dress and spoke his mother-tongue, Braj. He was prudent, shrewd and brave.[66] In an

60. *Infra*, Ch. VI, f.n. 27-29.
61. *Memoires des Jats,* 19-20.
62. *Imad*, 84; *Tarikh-i-Khanzadas* quoted by Pande, *Bharatpur,* 33; *Tarikh-i-Bharatpur,* 4b; Qanungo, *Jats*, 61; U.N. Sharma, *Itihas*, 323.
63. This can be inferred from Suraj Mal's own letter dated March 1757, to Ahmad Shah Abdali in which he wrote about his having "already crossed fifty of the stages (life)" by March 1757. See *Infra,* Xth chapter, f.n. 45.
64. *Tarikh-i-Hunud,* 20a, For a detailed discussion suggesting that Suraj Mal was the real son of Badan Singh, See Appendix B.
65. *Memoires des Jats,* 28.
66. *Imad*, 84; See alos *Tarikh-i-Bharatpur,* 4b; *Memoires des Jats,* 63; *Majma-ul-Akhbar* in Elliot, VIII, 362.

apparent reference to the earlier part of his long career, Ghulam Ali Khan remarks, "in prudence and skill, and ability to manage the revenue and civil affairs, he had no equal among the grandees of Hindustan except Asaf Jah Bahadur (the first Nizam)".[67] He was a good statesman too.[68]

Right from the early seventeen thirties, Suraj Mal helped his father, who seems to have been an loving person. Shortly after, his younger brother, Pratap Singh also became helper.[69] As Badan Sing advanced in years and his sight deteriorated,[70] Suraj Mal's participation in the state affairs increased. Gradually, there arrived a stage when the aging chief found it physically impossible to carry on. He, therefore, willingly entrusted the sole management of his principality to his loving and ablest son and the heir apparent (Suraj Mal) as regent[71] (governor), while he himself chose to lead a quiet life, disturbed only in face of political exigencies requiring his attention as well.[72] Suraj Mal became regent around 1750.[73] More markedly than before, Badan Singh was now only to reign, while Suraj Mal became the *de facto* ruler.

---

67. *Imad*, 84.
68. *Tarikh-i-Bharatpur*, 4b
69. *Memoires des Jats*, 28 and also 27.
70. *Ibid.*, 21; *Majma-ul-Akhbar* in Elliot VIII, 362; cf. *Tarikh-i-Hunud*, 20a.
71. *Memoires des Jats*, 27 and 29; *Tarikh-i-Hunud*, 20a; *Dirgh* 4-6; *Majma-ul-Akhbar* in Elliot, VIII, 362. In absence of no support whatsoever, R. Pande's claim (*Bharatpur*, Introduction, iii) that Suraj Mal led a rival group against Badan Singh, looks to be the sheer figment of imagination. Much to the contrary, *Sujan Charitra* (5) expressly speaks of his affectionate devotion to his father. Even otherwise, the fact that later in spite of his being in a position, he refrained from supplanting his disabled father, itself reveals his filial love and devotion to his father. Also see *Memoires des Jats*, 63.
72. *Badan Singh's anxious deliberations with the state councillors on the eve of the Maratha invasion in 1754, is a case in point.*
73. None of our authorities clearly mention any exact date for it. Wendel and Fransoo, however, leave some clues about it. From Wendel's statement that Suraj Mal (who died in Dec. 1763), guided the destiny of his nation for "more than 20 years" (*Memoires des Jats*, 63), we make out that he would **have** liked to put the required date round about 1740. As for Fransoo **(20a), he** states that Badan Singh died in June 1756, after having lived **"as a blind-man** for 20 years". Thus, he points to 1736 as the commencing **date of** Suraj Mal's regency. Coming to the modern historians, R. Pande (*Bharatpur*, 39) is the only one among them, to have touched this point. He says that by 1734 ended the "reign" (c. rule) of Badan Singh. But once more he quotes no source nor does he acquaint us with his own reasons for that contention. But all the three views fall to the ground at the mere touch of a relevant reference in an exactly contemporary document. It shows (see *infra*, 111-112) Badan Singh personally leading his troops in 1739 in a mood of resistance. It clearly implies that at least till 1739, he possessed sufficient vigour to withstand a fight. As such, the period of decline in his health leading to his retirement must be sought well after 1739 and not before.

With a devoted son and a powerful Raja (Jai Singh) by his side, Badan Singh resumed expansion in right earnest. In the interest of clarity we may list here at one place the main events of the subsequent Jat expansion although they are interspersed with diplomatic history in the succeeding chapters also. Mewat with its local unrest and geographical proximity had attracted Badan Singh, as pointed before. Step by step he obtained footholds here to the anguish of the Jaipur chief in whose *zamindari* it lay. At last Muhammad Shah was obliged to farm out the *parganas* of Khoh, Nagar and Kathumar (in Mewat) to the Jat chief for Rupees 2,40,000 per annum.[74] Taking advantage of it, he further strengthened his position there.[75] In 1738, Suraj Mal subjugated the lands of Farah, OL, Achhnera and their neighbourhood in the Mathura and Agra districts.[76] Nadir's invasion of 1739, while it proved so destructive to the Mughal Empire, eventually led to a sudden and vast expansion of Badan Singh's dominions and fortunes. He acquired control of the neighbourhood of both Delhi and Agra. He made further additions to his dominions wherein he began building new forts.[77]

Once he gained an unassailable footing in the countryside of Agra and Mewat, his eastward expansion across the Yamuna appeares natural. The *mahals* contiguous to his domains were inhabited predominantly by the Jats, who, ever since the days of Aurangzeb, had joined hands with their brethren of Agra and Mathura. The Jats of those areas were not slow in taking advantage of the prevailing situation. Thus, we learn

---

Incidentally, we learn from *Tarikhi-i-Ahmad Shahi* (43b) that Badan Singh was not personally present in the Court when in 1752, the Mughal Emperor conferred upon him the title of *"Mahendra"*. This was too great an occasion for him to have ordinarily missed. Even the fear of treachery which had so long dissuaded him from going to the Court (see *Memoires des Jats*, 26; c. *Sujan*, 55) was now apparently meaningless in the days of the predominance of Suraj Mal's friend, Safdar Jang; the latter in fact was the man who had procured this favour for the Jat chief. And yet Badan Singh remained absent on this unique occasion. This fact assumes significance here.

A probable inference would be that old age as also dissipation (*Memoires des Jats*, 21) had by this time worn him out and this eventually forced him to stay back.

In the light of these facts, the year 1750 seems to be the nearest approximation of Badan Singh asking his son to look after the entrie affairs of his state. cf. *Majma-ul-Akhbar*, in Elliot, VIII, 362.

74. *Sujan*, 6, 40 (by implication); *Ashub*, II, 316 quoted by U.N. Sharma, *Itihas*, 323; Sarkar, *Fall*, II, 434.
75. cf. *Sujan*, 40; *S.P.D.* XXI, 34; *TAH.* 21b; *Siyar*, III, 312 Mewat was brought under the Jat rule only gradually. As is to be seen, Jawahar Singh was busy subjugating it as late as in 1763.
76. Agra Gazetteer, 161; *Muttra Gazeteer*, 198-199; Also see author's article, Badan Singh Ke Kal Main Bharatpur Ka Pradeshik Vistar', *Uplabdhi*, 67.
77. *Memoires des Jats*, 27, 29; Also *Shah*, 2, *Iqbal*, 210.

that a local chief from Mahaban, assuming the name of Wantar Shah(?), raised a force of 5,000 horsemen and stated ravaging the lands. In the 22nd year of reign (1741-42) the said Jat and his men killed Hakim Kazim, the *faujdar* of Firozabad, plundering all his property.[78] About this time Suraj Mal captured the fortress of Mendu. This gave him a suitable opening for expansion in the lower middle Doab. It can be reasonably inferred from *Sujan Charitra* that by Agahan, Samvat 1802 (28th October to 27th November, 1745) the Jats had penetrated into parts of modern Aligarh and Bulandshahar districts.[79]

During the reign of Muhammad Shah, Suraj Mal extended his patronage to his near relation, Balram Jat (of Tewatia gotra) of Ballamgarh. We learn that his father Charandas (son of Chowdhary Gopal Singh) withheld revenue and defied the local Mughal officer, Murtaza Khan (at Faridabad). The latter imprisoned him. But Balram, playing a trick on the Khan, secured his father's release. Thereafter both of them made off to Suraj Mal, and gaining his, as well as the local support, killed that officer.[80] Within a short time Chowdhary Balram carved out a taluka, where he built a mud fort, named Ballamgarh. Emboldened with his success and the powerful backing of Bharatpur, he seized Palwal and Faridabad (which were in the *Jagir* of the Nizam). With the passage of time he became prosperous and fairly strong and assuming the title of "Rai", he started ruling over the usurped lands.[81]

Thus, availing himself of the indolence and imbecility of Muhammad Shah, Badan Singh vastly increased his possessions and authority. By the end of his reign large parts of the *suba* of Agra and some parts of Delhi upto Faridabad, had passed in his or his tribesmen's control.[82] He grew powerful enough "to be ranked among the best in Hindustan" and became convinced of his potentiality to resist an attack.[83] In terms of riches that he had amassed he "vied with the biggest of the Rajas."[84] Thus, the long cherished dream of a Jat State had materialised all but in name.[85]

Notwithstanding, "the start of the fortune of the Jats" was only "half risen" so far. It was in the succeeding and more troubled reign of Ahmad Shah that it rose to the full.[86] Early in his reign Balram Jat,

---

78. *Rustam*, 579.
79. *Sujan*, 60 and 91.
80. *Delhi Gazeteer.*, 213; Also *TAH.*, 23a; *Chahar Gulzar Shujai* in Elliot, VIII, 212.
81. *TAH.*, 22b, 23a and 39a; *Chahar Gulzar Shujai* in Elliot, VIII, 212.
82. *TAH.*, 22b, 23a and 90a; *Memoires des Jats,* 34.
83. *Memoires des Jats,* 33, 27 and 29.
84. *TAH.*, 23a; *Memoires des Jats,* 33.
85. *Hadiqat-ul-Aqalim* by Qazi Murtaza Husain (Lith. Lucknow), 171.
86. *Memoires des Jats,* 31 and 33.

banking upon Suraj's support, renewed lawlessness and thought of occupying more villages around Faridabad. The new Wazir, Safdar Jang, therefore, pledged himself to punish the insurgents.[87] However, his punitive operations virtually ended in his assiduously wooing the friendship of his enemy, Suraj Mal. The latter's alliance with the imperial Wazir, besides heightening his image and status ensured the official recognition of Badan Singh as a Raja (October, 1752). It also expedited the issue of patents for the fiefs earlier ordered to be given to him.[88]

In 1752, Balram, ejecting the local *faujdar*, Faqir Ali, eclipsed the imperial authority in Sikandarabad and Dankaur.[89] In April 1753, his patron, Suraj Mal achieved a greater feat. Having expelled Bahadur Singh Bargujar from his *faujdari* at Aligarh, he wrested from his patrimony Ghasera and placed it under Amar Singh.[90] Shortly after his eldest son, Jawahar Singh annexed some lands across the Yamuna in Doab.[91]

The Jat control over the newly acquired territories passed through vicissitudes in proportion to the fluctuations in the contemporary political situation. Though never eliminated, more than once it was eclipsed in the distant north and east due to the heavy military pressure both from within and without. But once it decreased, the Jat ruler re-established his authority over the affected areas. Thus, in 1753-1754, Imad-ul-Mulk and his Maratha allies superseded the Jat rule in the region stretching from Mathura to the environs of the Capital on one side and to Shikohabad on the other.[92] But following their departure Suraj Mal recovered his outposts and also made new additions.[93] On 27th Sept., 1754 (9th-Zil-Hijja) he despatched from Hodal a contingent under the sons (Kishan Singh and Bishan Singh)[94] of the deceased Balram Jat to capture Palwal (which lay in Imad's *jagir*). The Jats occupied it in

---

87. *TAH.*, 22b; Also *Chahar Gulzar Shujai* in Elliot, VIII, 212; *Memoires des Jats,* 33, however states that Suraj Mal, acting boldly, subjugated "some villages and lands" in front of Delhi.
88. *TAH.*, 25b, 43b, 45a, 52a, 52b; *Sujan*, 54, 56-57, 60-62, 92, 98, 146, 147; *S.P.D.*, II, 15 Also XXI 44, 50; *Memoires des Jats,* 33, 34, 38; *Tawarikh-i-Hunud*, 21b-22a; cf. *TAL.*, 108.
89. *TAH.*, 39a-40a; Also *Shakir*, 71.
90. *Sujan*, 97ff.; *TAH.*, 47a, 52a, 52b, 106b. Also see author's article, 'Ghasera Ke Yudha Ka Aitihasik paryalochan'. *Nagari Pracharini Patrika* (Commemoration Volume, Samvat 2024), 504 ff.
91. *Sujan*, 193.
92. *TAH.*, 89-92b, 94a, 94b, 104b-106a, 107a, 109b, 111a; *Sujan*, 203 ff.
93. *TAH.*, 9; S.P.D., XXVII., 90, *Shah*, 2.
94. The Court history does not here (*TAL.*, 39) mention the names of Balram's sons. But from the fact that Kishan Singh and Bishan Singh were appointed fort commandant and Nazim of Ballamgarh by Suraj Mal (Delhi *Gazetteer*, 213), it may be concluded that it were probably those who led the said force.

a surprise attack, killing the local *qanungo*, Santosh Rai, in retaliation for his earlier instigating Aqibat Mahmud Khan to kill Balram. They also seized the local Qazi. Imad tried in vain to get his *mahals* vacated with the help of Raghunath Rao, then in Delhi. The Jats also recovered Ballamgarh and their *mahals* in Mewat.[95] In the second week of November, 1755, Jawahar Singh attacked Fateh Singh (son of the deceased Bahadur Singh Bargujar) who had earlier regained Ghasira from the Jats with the help of Imad. Giving out that he was going to meet Madho Singh of Jaipur, he issued from his taluka (stretching upto Mewat) and took Fateh Singh by surprise. The latter despairing of his life fled and sought refuge with Kamghar Khan Billoch, the chief of Farrukhnagar and Jawahar reannexed the areas of Ghasera and Garhi Harsaru. Emboldened with their successes, the Jats organised raids upto Sarai Ali Wardi Khan (24 miles from Delhi). The Wazir (Imad) and Prince Ali Gauhar at that time were encamping at Palam. Despite a rumour of their impending attack, they did nothing to expel the usurpers from that region.[96] It is noteworthy that for another eight years Jawahar Singh remained busy subjugating Mewat, which Suraj Mal plann.ed to develop as a separate state to be assigned to his restless and over-ambitious son.[97]

Meanwhile, Suraj Mal had been active on the other side of the Yamuna. It appears that he deputed his men to different quarters of the middle Doab. Thus, a Marathi newsletter refers that Ghasi Ram Rajput encroached upon (c. 1754-55) the Faizpur taluka (in Meerut) of the Rohillas. He occupied and fortified some twenty villages. For want of requisite amunition Antaji Mankeshwar found himself helpless in getting these vacated.[98] On the other side, Suraj Mal captured the country of Kol (Aligarh), Dankaur, Khurja etc. and later sent contingent to reduce Sikandarabad, then under the occupation of the Marathas. The latter evacuated both the fort and the town merely at the bidding of the Jats, who occupied them. They followed up this easy success with overrunning the environs including the *pargana* of Tal Begampur.[99]

A close perusal of the following treaty of Dasna would suggest that most of the above lands possibly formed parts of the *jagirs* formerly (in the reign of Ahmad Shah) assigned though not actually transferred to

---

95. *TAL.*, 39-40, 47.
96. *Ibid.*, 114.
97. *Life of Najib-u-Daulah* (by Sayyid Nur-ud-Din Hasan translated in English by Sarkar in *Indian Historical Quarterly*, 1933 and *Islamic Culture*, 1933, 60b; Also *Memoires des Jats*, 60, 46.
98. *S.P.D.* XXVII., 93. There is some difficulty in identifying this Faizpur. It could .be Faizpur Ninana, a place 5 miles north of Baghpat in Meerut district.
99. *TAL.*, 106.

Suraj Mal and his men. He now pressed his claims by force of arms. However, his recent movements annoyed the Court especially the Wazir and consultations between the latter, the Emperor, Raja Nagar Mal (the Diwan of the *khalisa*) Najib and Damodar Pandit were held daily as to the recovery of the above lands. The Wazir opted for war and ordered Najib to proceed against Suraj Mal. But Nagar Mal pleaded for a negotiated settlement instead. As such, Sujan Singh (his agent) and Meghraj (the Vakil of Najib) entered into negotiations with the Jat Vakil. But Suraj Mal, "proud of his superior prowess" was not in a mood to resign his advantages and showed intransigence. He merely offered to pay Rupees 5 lakhs but outrightly refused to make over his recent acquisitions. This angered the Wazir and he planned a grand punitive expedition. Though it was not undertaken, Najib received fresh orders and on 17th June, 1755, he along with Jeta Gujar and his home auxiliaries moved on to Ghazi-ud-Din Nagar.

On the other side, Suraj Mal, who had been busy subduing the countryside moved forward in a fighting mood upto six to eight miles from Najib's camp. Nagar Mal was, however, all along opposed to war and so persuaded the Wazir to make terms with Suraj Mal. With Ibadullah and Muhammad Ashiq (the confidants of the Wazir) he went to Najib, mediated between him and the Jat prince and thus followed the treaty of Dasna (c. 10th July, 1955). According to it, Suraj Mal was to retain all his *mahals* including that of Kol in the Doab that he had held before the capture of Sikandarabad. The last place was to be vacated. Rupees 26 lakhs was fixed as the perpetual quit rent of all these territories, out of which Rupees 18 lakhs was deducted as cash compensation for the *jagirs* that Javed Khan and Safdar Jang had previously allotted to him but which had not been actually put in his charge. Out of the balance of Rupees 8 lakhs, the Jat Prince paid 2 lakhs and agreed to clear the balance in a year in monthly instalments of Rupees 50 thousand. Following this agreement Suraj Mal pulled back his forces by four to six miles.[100]

Even when he was so busily enagaged in the affairs to his north and east, Suraj Mal did not forget to respond to the frantic call of his tribesman, Rana[101] Bhim Singh Jat, the *zamindar* of Gohad (Chakla

---

100. *TAL.*, 105-109; Also Sarkar, *Fall* II, 438-439; *Nur*, 32b.

101. Murtaza Husain relates that one of the ancestors of Bhim Singh was a brave but one eyed man. He, therefore, went by the nickname of "Kana". He marched under Birbal to Kabul, where he was killed in fighting. In reward for his services, Akbar granted to the Kana's descendants the *zamindari* of Gohad. Murtaza Husain records two current version explaining how the word "Rana" came to be associated with names of the Gohad chiefs. According to the one, the above Kana, while accompanying a royal hunting party, bravely killed a

Gwalior). Having built a fort at that place, this Rana enlarged his possessions[102] and in the process occupied the imperial fort of Gwalior when its commandant preferring him to the waiting Marathas capitulated that fort. This ran contrary to the Maratha ambitions and they besieged Gohad[103] (about June, 1755). Now the local Jats knocked at the doors of their big brethren, the Jats of Bharatpur, for help and Bhim Singh sent his emissary Fateh Singh to Suraj Mal. The latter thus obliged and despatched with Fateh Singh a force of 500 horse and 2,000 foot to Gohad. Encouraged by this support, the Jats initially worsted force of 15,000 Marathas. But with the arrival of reinforcements, the Marathas ultimately overpowered the Jats. Those perished in the fighting included 125 Jat horsemen.[104] It is relevant here to take note of an important reference in a Marathi despatch. Speaking about the Gohad Jats, it, at one place, refers to that they lay "banking upon (the support of) Suraj Mal". This may be taken as a prima facie evidence to prove that as in case of the Jat Rai of Ballamgarh, Suraj Mal all along displayed a patronizing attitude towards the Jat Rana of Gohad as well.[105] This may account for the grateful Rana[106] as also the Rai often marching in person under the Bharatpur banners.

The examples of Ballamgarh and Gohad suggest that Suraj Mal displayed a similar attitude, among others, towards the Jat chieftains of

---

lion. Seeing it the Emperor exclaiming "he is Rana not Kana". Thence forward he and his successors began calling themselves Rana. The other version goes that the Jat chiefs of Gohad hailed from the family of Nusherwan. As such, in order to emphasize their high lineage, they used the word 'Rana' before their names. See *Hadiqat,* 164.

102. As a result of the effort of Bhim Singh and his successors, Gohad grew into one of the three most powerful centres of the Jat rule (the other two being Bharatpur and Patiala) by the time Wendel penned down his account. See *Memoires des Jats*, 4, footnote.

103. *Hadiqat*, 164-165.

104. *S.P.D.* II, 45, XXIX, 60 XXVII, 118, also 113; *Hadiqat*, 165; Also see *S.P.D.*, I, New series, ed. P.M. Joshi (Bombay: 1957), P. 175. Murtaza Husain Bilgrami reproduces a fanciful story that, during the siege of Gohad, Suraj Mal seized and later married a beautiful female relation of Rana Bhim Singh and that he (Suraj Mal) was then killed by Chitra Singh (a future ruler of Gohad, styled Rana Chitra Singh Lokendra Bahadur). On verification, however, he found the whole thing false. *Hadiqat*, 164-165.

105. *S.P.D.*, II 45.

106. *S.P.D.*, XXI, 26; William Irvine's article, 'The Bangash Nawab of Farrukhabad' (in *J.A.S.B.*, 1879), 97.

Bajhor, Kajraura and Karauli[107] as well. Significantly, Sudan also makes a casual hint in this regard.[108]

Coming to the middle Doab and Mewat, unfortunately, full chronological details of Suraj Mal's movements in these regions have not come down to us. Yet, it can be inferred from the scanty and casual references that besides recovering the tracts of Jalesar and Shikohabad, he pushed himself further towards Delhi[109] and improved upon his former position elsewhere too.[110]

The most valuable acquisition that he made during these days was the imperial fort of Alwar in Mewat. Paying Rupees 50 thousand as bribe to its custodian and sending 500 men, Madho Singh of Jaipur had occupied Alwar. When Suraj Mal heard of it, he despatched a strong force of 5,000 under Rup Ram Katari and the siege of the fort was taken up. Soon after Jawahar Singh also joined him. In the ensuing fight there, the Jats easily gained the day and thus wrested the fort from the Rajputs (c. 23rd March, 1756). The Jaipur ruler, though visibly mortified by the reverse, held back as he felt himself powerless in ejecting the Jats.[111] This shows that Suraj Mal annexed Alwar by humbling Rajput occupiers, and not "by composition with its custodian."[112]

---

107. Bajhor and Kajaraura were the Jat baronies. Hindupat Jat and Bharat Singh Jat respectively were their chiefs when Murtaza Husain visited these places. As for Karauli, some parts of this old Rajput State lay under the Jat while some others under the Maratha control at the time of Bilagrami's visit. *Hadiqat,* 165 and 169.

108. *Sujan* (213-214) seems to convey that on the eve of the Maratha invasion (in 1753-54) Badan Singh's territories stretched from Ramgarh (Aligarh) in the North to Kalyanpuri (old name of Karuali) in the south, from Haryana in the west to Etawah (it may be a mistake for Etah) in the east and beyond upto Gopacha (Gwalior or a mountain in that region bearing the same name) and from Nimran (33 miles south-west of Pataudi) in the south-west to beyond Shah-pau (31 miles east of Mathura) in the north-east and Garhmukteshwar in the north-west. As is to be noted the display of rhetoric herein has marred the clarity of this reference. Besides, the geographical locations are also not quite correct. They, in fact, indicate a rightward swing from their actual direction. Likewise, it is difficult to believe that far flung regions like Gwalior and Karauli actually formed the part of the Jat state. Notwithstanding, coming as it does from the pen of the one whose knowledge of the Jats was incomparably fuller and deeper, all that Sudan says cannot be lightly brushed either. It seems reasonable to conclude that as a result of his patronizing attitude Badan Singh exercised appreciable influence over the Jats of those areas, which Sudan, out of enthusiasm, includes within the limits of Bharatpur. It should not be surprising if in those tumultuous days the Jats in general preferably looked for protection and help towards the Raja of Bharatpur, their most powerful and distinguished tribesman.

109. *Shah*, 2; *S.P.D.*, XXVII, 206 and 172.

110. *Memoires des Jats,* 43; Also *Tarikh-i-Bharatpur*, 4b.

111. *S.P.D.*, I, New series, p. 189; Also see *S.P.D.*, XXVII, 128. The Jat capture of Alwar had Shah Waliullah (*Shah*, 2) lamenting that none of the Mughal grandees could muster up courage to prevent Suraj Mal's men from seizing Alwar.

112. Sarkar, *Fall*, II, 438.

Three broad phenomena come to the forefront if we minutely pursue the course of the Jat expansion. First, Badan Singh and Suraj Mal mostly kept their eyes on ethnologically Jat areas. This impression we gather from the fact that once they subjugated the districts and the environs of Aligarh and Bulandshahar, they, instead of moving further to the east, turned to the north along the left of the Yamuna in the direction of Meerut. Second, although they tried to bring maximum lands under their own domination, they were not averse to supporting the submissive Jat chieftains like those of Ballamgarh and Gohad. If this revealed their sturdy commonsense in war and politics—for even if desired, a sudden annexation of all the Jat regions was impossible—this also symbolized their efforts towards establishing a Jat confederacy[113] under their overlordship. Finally, with all their deference to the individualistic temperament of their tribesmen, they were not normally prepared to brook defiance to their authority. The suppression of Muhkam Singh's henchmen before, and the intractable chief of Mursan[114] Bhure Singh later,[XVII] bears it out.

JAT KINGDOM AT THE END OF BADAN SINGH'S REIGN

Coming to the Jat possessions, a little over two months had elapsed since the prized capture of Alwar, when the reign of Badan Singh came to an end. At the time his dominions roughly extended in length from the neighbourhood of Delhi to beyond Agra and in breadth from Mewat and hereditary Bharatpur territories to parts of Meerut, Etah (Jalesar) and Mainpuri (Shikohabad) districts.[115] His state, besides being spacious, was financially well off and militarily very strong. It has been noted how, from the last two stand points, he had come to rival the biggest of the Rajas even before 1750. In the subsequent period also he kept up his preceding tempo. On his death the areas under his dominance were worth an annual revenue of Rupees one crore[116] and there is little room for doubt that with a man of Suraj Mal's administrative ability and skill at the helm of affairs, he did realize almost the same amount if not more.[117] The fact that time and again expectant multitudes flocked to the Jat state for asylum speaks of peace and security being ensured in

113. cf. Qanungo, *Jats*,147.

114. *S.P.D.*, XXI, 100, cf. Sarkar, *Fall*, II, 445.

XVII. In 1761-62, see Sarkar, *Fall*, II, (1991) p. 266 and f.n. XV of Ch. V.—Editor.

115. *Shah*, 2; Khazan-i-Amirah (By Mir Ghulam Ali Khan Bilgrami, Litho edition), 99; *Majm-ul-Akhbar* in Elliot, VIII, 362.

116. *Shah*, 2; *Sujan* (207) refers to that Badan Singh possessed seven crores of cash in his treasury in 1753-54; *Tawarikh-i-Hunud*, 22a; for exaggerated account of the Jat riches see *Dirgh*, 6.

117. *Majma-ul-Akhbar* (in Elliot VIII, 362) is incorrect in stating that the areas under his control yielded "more than two crores".

the Jat State. Respite from the preceding administrative oppression ushered in better conditions of life for the local populace amidst the general chaos and commotion of the period. It paved the way for almost uninterrupted pursuit of agriculture, the mainstay of the hardy Jats, as also trade and commerce, as can be inferred from an eye-witness's account.[118] It would appear that Suraj Mal's was one of the best governed principalities of the period.

As regards the armed strength, the Jat King possessed a regular well equipped and gallant army. It consisted of approximately 30,000 regulars, over and above the garrisons stationed in several forts.[119] It could easily be ranked among the best in Hindustan. The subsequent chapters would show how, on several occasions, it won laurels fighting under one of the best generals of the period.

Besides the army, Suraj Mal also raised a network of fairly strong forts. The notable Jat forts built or repaired during his father's and his own period were those of Bharatpur (1743-1750), Deeg, Kumbher, Wair, Ramgarh (alias Aligarh), Ramghat(?), Khurja, Kishangarh, Nimran, Thun (built on another site), Sinsini, Sonkh, Sogar, Sahar, Kama, Noh etc.[120] Besides emphasizing his splendour, these forts served to strengthen his defences. They were strongly fortified, profusely stored and well-garrisoned. Especially the first four were wonderful creations of the native genius. Their mud ramparts, coated with bricks and rocks were incredibly formidable in dimension, while the ditch around was very wide and dug so deep that water burst up. Yet another rampart, probably the city-wall, surrounded them at a distance of "two or three kos", followed by "*marhalas*" at a distance of one "kos". Apart from their strong garrisons, and big and

---

118. *Sujan* 212-213; Also see *Dirgh*, 1.

119. The lack of genuine evidence, hampers us in giving its exact numerical strength. *Majma-ul-Akhbar* (in Elliot VIII, 362) claims that about this time it stood at 1,00,000. Much to the contrary a Marathi letter (*S.P.D.*, XXI, 105) casually suggests the figure of 20,000. Both these are untenable. If the former is too inflated, the latter is too modest. It may be worthwhile to remember a relevant fact in this regard. We know that Suraj Mal took with himself as many as 15,000 troops, when he moved out to participate in the first Bangash and Civil Wars (*Sujan*, 64, 146). It stands to reason to believe that while doing so he must have left behind at least the same number of troops, if not more, to stand by for the defence of his realm in his absence. This would make a total of 30,000 Jat regulars, over and above those stationed permanently in the forts. This figure looks quite probable in the context of 1756, all the more if we keep in our mind that barely seven years later, it stood at 40,000 strong, apart from the fort garrisons. Vide *Memoires des Jats*, 67.

120. *Sujan*, 212-213; *TAH.*, 109b; *TAL.*, 220; *Memoires des Jats,* 19 and 51; *Tawarikh-i-Hunud*, 20b, 22b; *Ras Peeushnidhi* in Somnath, 6-7; Nur, 32b, 60b; *Imad* 84; Siyar IV, 27-28; (Baldeo Singh, 30, 42 quoted by U.N. Sharma, *Itihas*, 327). The above list does not include those captured from others.

small cannons atop, these strongholds contained immense supplies of food, fodder and ammunitions, "*ban*", lead, and gunpowder, sufficient to last for years together, without requiring any external aid whatsoever. The walls especially of Kumbher and Deeg were literally lined up with cannons atop. All this had rendered these forts quite impregnable.[121] The contemporary authorities have bestowed lavish praise on the marvellous strength of these Jat forts. To quote a few, a eye-witness says that no other places in India contained such enormous provisions as did the Jat forts. He adds that no power in Asia had the capability to capture by assault those impregnable forts.[122] Their builder, Suraj Mal emphasized the same thing by proudly likening them with "Alexander's Rampart".[123] In the eyes of Ghulam Husain nothing short of a complete volume could do justice to the descriptions of the Jat fortifications or the means of their defence.[124]

CHARACTER AND ACHIEVEMENTS OF BADAN SINGH

Braj Raj Badan Singh breathed his last on Wednesday, 9th June, 1756 (Jeth Sudi Ekadshi Samvat 1813).[125] He must have been over 75 at the time of his death.[126] Turning completely blind, he "abondoned the world" and spent his last days in "meditation on God". He kept the revenue of the village Kasawali (in *pargana* Deeg) in his own hands for giving "alms" to the poor and the destitutes.[127] Worship apart, the pleasant memories of his great political achievement-foundation of the Jat State—perhaps, must have lessened the agony of his blindness.

Dignified and amiable in manners, Badan Singh was an astute and shrewd man knowing fully well how to avail himself of his opportunities. Eulogizing his bravery, Fransoo tells us that he was "unrivalled in the

---

121. *TAL.*, 215; *Memoires des Jats,* 27, 39, 40 and 44; *Siyar*, IV, 27-28; *Sujan*, 222; *TAH.*, 109b; *Majma-ul-Akhbar* in Elliot VIII, 361.
122. *Memoirs des Jats,* 40, footnote.
123. Vide his letter to the Abdali *infra*, ch. X, 166, f.n. 45, 166; Also *Memoires des Jats*, 40 footnote 44.
124. *Siyar*, IV, 28.
125. *Tawarikh-i-Hunud,* 20a; Following *Delhi Chronicle* K.R. Qanungo (*Jats*, 64) and other scholars mention 7th June. Though Fransoo is a later authority, in this case he is more dependable than the *Delhi Chronicle* for the simple reason that the date (9th June) given by him is based on the Persian records of the Munshis of the Jat Court.
126. Our sources (*Sujan*, 217 and *Memoires des Jats,* 21) do mention of his old age but do not record the actual age at the time of his death. They do not indicate the date of his birth either. The only clue in the matter is provided by the persistent tradition which tends to place his birth in early sixteen eighties (*supra*, p. 34f). It would show that Badan Singh must have crossed 75 before his death. His son Suraj Mal was about 50 at that time. This also lends weightage to the persistent tradition.
127. *Tawarikh-i-Hunud*, 20a.

art of a soldier" and "possessed much proficiency in (the art of) spearmanship".[128] However, this skill does not quite accord with his general indifference towards military life, as is obvious from his subsequent career as a ruler. Even state affairs were mostly managed by his son, Suraj Mal. Badan Singh's main interest centred round non-military pursuits, namely politics and diplomacy in which he showed himself quite adept.

As a figure in history, Badan Singh's importance rests on his efforts at building up a state out of casual collection of heterogeneous chiefdoms as well as on making his intensely democratic tribesmen conform to the institution of kingship. By the time of the commencement of his leadership, the Jats had no doubt clinched a position for themselves, but it was more shaky than stable. They had attained a reckonable power, but it lacked cohesion and proper direction. It was left to Badan Singh to rectify the prevailing abuses and to lead their people in the right direction.

Expediency and his own sense of grandeur made Badan Singh set his heart upon the institution of kingship. Being a realist, however, he could foresee the likely hazards of precipitating the matter. He, therefore, proceeded with caution showing remarkable patience and sagacity. On the one hand he managed to disarm external opposition[129] and on the other he endeavoured to augment his internal position, suppressing the pretentious while rewarding the faithful. Both ways he gained in stature till he touched the heights as no predecessor of his had ever done.

With kingly power he sought kingly splendour as well. Thus, in order to heighten his image he sought his descent from God Krishna.[130] His court bards linked him on the mother's side with the Rajput dynasty of Karauli.[131] Badan Singh held his Court at the Capital (Deeg) with requisite pomp and

---

128. *Ibid.*, 14b; For hyperbolic description see *Dirgh* 3-4; *Ras Peeushnidhi* and *Madhav Vinod* in Somnath, 3-4, 318.

129. *Memoires des Jats,* 19, 31.

130. *Sujan* 4-5, 211, *Dirgh,* 3; *Ras Peeushnidhi and Madhav Vinod* in Somnath, 3, 318; *Tawarikh-i-Hunud,* 13a.

131. *Memoires des Jats,* 28. Sudan (*Sujan*, 218) mentions about a certain "Bhupat Bhatwar" at the Court. This may refer to one of the Court eulogists, whom Wendel refers to here. Fransoo (*Tawarikh-i-Hunud*, 13a-14a), however, traces his pedigree from the Rajputs of Bayana. According to him the Jats of the Sinsinwara clan to which Badan Singh and the preceeding chieftains belonged are the offsprings of the union of Sobhu Thankur and Devsani. He records that centuries ago Sobhu, for fear of Subuktgin (?) migrated from Bayana to Sinsini, then inhabited by *kalals. Having established friendly relations, he invited all the male kalals* to a drinking feast. When they got intoxicated with wine, the said Thakur treacherously put the whole lot to the sword, but married one of their ladies, Devsani, a worshipper of Shiv. The first born of this marriage was Raja Ram, and thus Sinsinwaras took to worshipping a god named Sinsinkumar, whose temple, an object of common veneration, was established in Sinsini, cf. the local tradition given by Pande, *Bharatpur*, 28.

show.[132] He introduced royal etiquette with the help of Muslim officers employed for the specific purpose. He took a fancy for "Islamic culture and aristocratic training" as is evident among others from the living and education of Jawahar Singh, Pratap Singh and Bahadur Singh.[133] The big harem which he kept was again a princely paraphernalia. It consisted of a prodigious number of 150[134] or according to one estimate about 400 inmates[135] and compared favourably with any other in the country, as is upheld by a contemporary.[136] If it pointed to his passion for women, it, in keeping with the standard of that age, also attested to his yearning for appearing great, glamourous and affluent.[137] To avoid his sense of dignity being suffered he even took to the shedding of his daughters blood.[138] Whether or not Badan Singh had any education we have no means to ascertain, he and his successor extended their patronage to men of letters and artistes. Sudan and Somnath were two such celebrities. Unlike his predecessors, Badan Singh took a keen interest in architecture. Even if we exclude Suraj Mal's work in the field, we find his name being associated with several palaces, tanks, temples and gardens, over which he spent big sums. The fort of Deeg, including its beautiful water palaces and gardens was begun by him. At Kumbher he built many houses, a harem palaces and gardens, was begun by him. At Kumbher he built many houses, a harem palace and a fort.[139] At Kama and Sahar also, he constructed palaces, now in ruins. At Wair, beside the fort he laid out a large garden with a beautiful mansion called "Safed *Mahal*" and reservoirs in the centre called "*Phulbari*". He built a temple at Vrindaban, known as "*Dhir Samir*".[140] All this work, besides gratifying his aesthetic sense, undoubtedly served to emphaize his splendour as well.

Thus, both by his deeds and behaviour Badan Singh tried to emphasize the dignity of his stature. To secure the title of Raja was one of his longings.[141] Though Ajit Singh and Abhai Singh of Jodhpur would

---

132. *Sujan*, 217ff.; *Dirgh*, 3 also 6; *Madhav Vinod* in Somnath, 318; Qanungo, *Jats*, 63.
133. *Imad*, 84; *Ras Peeushnidhi* and *Mahdav Vindo* in Somnath, 4-5, 6-7, 318-320; Qanungo, *Jats*, 63.
134. *Memoires des Jats*, 20, 33.
135. *Tawarikh-i-Hunud*, 19a. Though Fransoo claims that all these 400 were "Ranis as his wives" this figure most likely included concubines as well. Vide *Majma-ul-Akhbar* in Elliot, VIII, 361-362.
136. *Memoires des Jats*, 20.
137. *Ibid.*, 20, 23.
138. Badan Singh put them to death lest the Mughal Emperors should demand them as they did in case of Rajput Princesses. See *Tawarikh-i-Hunud*, 19a; *Memoires des Jats*, 20.
139. *Tawarikh-i-Hunud*, 19a.
140. Growse, *Mathura*, 139; *District Gazetter*, Muttra, 198; Qanungo, *Jats*, 64.
141. Qanungo, *Jats*, 62.

in their letters address him as Raja, he yearned for a formal sanction of the regal title. He appeared to be crazy when in 1730, he urged through his officers (Khizrakhan and Nur Ali Khan) Sarbuland Khan (then at Agra) to address him as Raja instead of as Thakur.[142] The jealousy of Jai Singh and his own hesitation in attending the Mughal Court due partly to his fear of treachery,[143] and partly to his blindness, apparently delayed the realization of his cherished desire till 1752 when Safdar Jang induced the Emperor to make him a Raja with the title of "Mahendra".[144] As a cumulative result of these developments, Badan Singh came to command adequate respect of and authority over his tribesmen. Yet to suppose that they completely or forthwith approved of the institution of kingship would be to ignore the fundamentals of the Jat character. Badan Singh himself had no illusion about it. This may account for the discernible fact that with all he or his son aspired for, they did not cherish the vision of an absolute monarchy of the Mughal type. Instead they discreetly kept themself content with the one of the Afghan type, which suited the character and sentiments of their people better.

To conclude, even though Suraj Mal's contribution is associated with the major portion of Badan Singh's work, the credit of giving a shape to the Jat kingdom should be accorded to Badan Singh. This was his great achievement.[145] Badan Singh outlined the Jat kingdom and Suraj Mal was its first real King.

---

142. Sarbuland Khan was very hardpressed for money following his fight with Abhai Singh. Badan Singh offered to pay him Rupees one lakh but the Khan politely refused the offer and sent a horse and a jewelled sword as a present to Badan Singh with a letter addressing him as Thakur. The Jat chief returned the letter with Rupees, 5,000, requesting the Khan to address him as Raja, a title promised first to Churaman by Husain Ali and then to himself by Jai Singh in 1722, but not fulfilled in either case. Sarbuland Khan pointed out his own limitations in the matter but assured him to plead his case if he (the Khan) regained the Emperor's favour. Thus he sent the letter and money back to Badan Singh. *M.U.*, III, 801, *Khizra,* 122; *Hadiqat*, 381; quoted by Irvine *Later Mughals,* II, 213-214.

143. *Memoires des Jats,* 26-27; Qanungo, *Jats,* 62.

144. *TAH.*, 43b.

145. Author's articles, 'Badan Singh Ke Kal Main Bharatpur Ka Pradeshik Vistar', *Uplabdhi*, 70.

VI

The Jats as the Feudatories of the Empire (1723-1748)

JAT POLICY AND IMPLICATIONS OF THE EMERGENCE OF JAT KINGDOM

It has been noticed in the preceding chapter that gradually by 1756, Suraj Mal extended his hold over large parts of the province of Agra and some parts of Delhi. The area under his control was worth Rupees one crore which amounted to nearly one eighth of the total revenue, but most of it was never paid to the royal exchequer since long.[1] It is apparent that at a time when the Empire had miserably shrunk, the Jat usurpations between the two Capitals (Delhi and Agra) inflicted a big territorial and financial loss upon it. The loss it suffered in terms of prestige was also great, indeed. Side by side, the Jat daring must have also emboldened others to commit aggression. The Jats thus had their share in aggravating the malady of the Empire.[2]

However, it would not be fair to view the Jat expansion as an isolated event. It has to be examined dispassionately in the general context of the Empire as a whole. All repercussions of the Jat encroachments conceded, the pertinent questions remain whether the Emperor retained any effective grip over the Jat areas during the period commencing from 1739, which coincided with the major part of the Jat expansion; could he have staved off other aggrandizing powers in case Badan Singh had kept his hands off; if not, to what extent the Jat aggression by itself inflicted the real as against the ostensible loss upon him.

This leads us to recollect the prevailing situation, which was characterized by the indolence and frivolity of Muhammad Shah, self-aggrandizement and insane jealousy of the nobles, administrative and financial breakdown and military impotence. Shakir's couplet meaning - the house goes desolate if its master behaves like a child[3] -applies with

---

1. *TAH.*, 2b; *Shah*, 2; Sarkar, *Fall*, II, 33.
2. *Memoires des Jats*, 1; Also *Shah*, 2.
3. *Shakir*, 89.

as much aptness to Muhammad Shah and his ministers as to their immediate successors. Inactive and indifferent as ever, even the horrible experience of Nadir's invasion did not make the Emperor any wiser. He failed to appreciate that, to rule, something more was needed than getting sunk in the embrace of the harem beauties or sports and pastime and that it is only the hand armed with the sword that commands fear and authority. This neglect on the part of the ruler was speedily taken advantage of by all his nobles. With a few exceptions, the *faujdars* of every *sarkar* and the *subedars* of every province "refused to pay the revenue on *khalisa* and *jagir* lands". Instead they now merely "sent gifts and presents to the Court."[4] Nay more, some of the imperial governors like Nizam-ul-Mulk, Safdar Jang and Aliwardi Khan set up their semi-independent rule in their respective provinces and thereby encouraged others to defy the Emperor's authority under the cloak of loyalty, so much so that "proud and haughty of every region raised their heads"[5], and "every *zamindar* became a Raja and every Raja a Maharaja."[6]

The *suba* of Agra was very much within the same Empire. Of the *Khalisa parganas* that continued to send revenue even after Nadir's invasion, were a few situated near Agra, which the Jat chief grabbed during the worsening anarchy.[7] But if we keep the general trend in view, it would appear that except the above *parganas* the rest of the areas passing under the Jat control after 1739, must also have ceased to remit revenue. By implication it means that as a result of the Jat expansion as such the real financial loss to the imperial treasury would not have been as much the statistics might lead us to believe. And if some expelled officials happened to pay something casually to it or to offer gifts, similar instances are not altogether wanting in case of the Jat usurpers either.[8] Likewise, the comparative ease with which Suraj Mal expanded himself, suggests that as an upshot of the breakdown of the Emperor's authority, his neighbourhood had been practically reduced to a '*no man's land* and whosoever possessing the requisite strength would have occupied it. That this was partly due to his policies and doings is not as relevant in this context as the manifest impotence of the Mughal government. And weakness invariably invites aggression. Few would deny that irrespective of the Jats, in this state of affairs, the impoverished and crumbling empire would not have succeeded in

---

4. *TAH.*, 2b-3b; *Jauhar-i-Samsam* in Elliot, VIII, 73; *Memoires des Jats,* 29-30.
5. *Jauhar-i-Samsam* in Elliot, VIII, 73; *TAH.* 3a-3b.
6. *Supra*, p. 74; *Rustam Ali* in Elliot, VIII, 60.
7. The remnant were seized by Najib-u-Daulah, Imad and the Rajputs, *TAL.*, 28; *TAH.*, 2b-3a; Sarkar, *Fall*, II, 35.
8. *Infra*, pp. 109, 201ff; *TAL.*, 330.

keeping Agra under its folds, more so in view of the ambitions of Jai Singh as well as the Marathas. Having wrested Malwa, Gujrat and Orissa and overrun Bengal, Bihar and parts of Rajasthan and Agra the encroaching Marathas now threatened to devour the territories in Agra.[9] Supersession of the Mughal authority here thus looked only a question of time and so far as the overall interests of the Empire were concerned it did not matter who the aggressor was.

As it was, seeing the writing on the wall, the calculating Badan Singh, cleverly availed himself of opportunities for expansion and thereby forestalled the rest in the fray. In doing so he conformed to the all-pervading spirit of the age, which he lived in. The Jesuit Father aptly remarks, "none of these two (Suraj Mal and Pratap Singh) could act otherwise", that is, contrary to what he terms, "The maxim of the (whole) country".[10] The irony was that for their own considerations the governor of Agra (Jai Singh) and the imperial Wazir themselves heartened him in his defiant objectives. What part the former and his deputy played we have already noted. As to the Wazir, Qamar-ud-Din, either through suppleness or heavy presents, Badan Singh and Suraj Mal procured his support and he espoused their cause like that of Ali Muhammad Rohilla. If and when any complaints were taken to the Court, the "great advocate of the Jats" (The Wazir) would silence them by "pointing out a lot about what Badan Singh had done (for the sake of the Empire)" and insisting that "it was for the reputation of the Empire to have *zamindars* as powerful as the Jats, who could serve (in future also) well in moments of necessity. Such was the judgement of a minister on such a delicate affair of such consequence, lamented Wendel.[11] The attitude of the Wazir and the goverment had to thank itself directly for propping up the nascent Jat power. Incidentally, the fact that Qamar-u-Din and Jai Singh represented the rival factions at the Court[12] and yet Badan Singh and Suraj Mal succeeded in having their backing simultaneously may give an insight into the working of the initial Jat policy towards the Mughal government. In humouring the rival factions they obviously calculated to ward off possible opposition,[13] although as they struck roots of their own became confident to face any eventuality.[14]

However, harmful to the Empire, Suraj Mal provided the Jat areas with a measure of peace and security from predatory raids and

---

9. Irvine, *Later Mughals*, II, 275.
10. *Memoires des Jats*, 29.
11. *Memoires des Jats*, 19, 31 and 20.
12. It is noteworthy here that both these held opposite views with regard to the Maratha problem.
13. *Shah*, 2.
14. *Memoires des Jats*, 27.

administrative oppression[15] as the irresolute and imbecile Emperors had latterly ceased to guarantee. He accomplished it at a time when the Marathas were repeatedly ravaging the major part of the Empire. Suraj Mal thus appeared to be timely safeguarding his people from possible ruin. This implies that the instincts of self preservation[16] also guided his distinct ambition, which was in no mean measure sustained by the imperial government itself. If contrast has any relevance in sober history, it is manifest in the present context. Comparative fate of the Delhi government and the local people as a whole can be visualized if we suppose that instead of the Bharatpur rulers the ever squeezing and formidable Marathas —who did feel sour about Agra being not under them[17]—had entrenched themselves here and thereby permanently brought their peril so dangerously close to the imperial metropolis.

A new aspect of the Jat policy under Suraj Mal was that unlike his predecessors (excluding ofcourse Badan Singh) he never repudiated in theory the Mughal suzerainty, and remaining always on the side of the Emperor and his ministers, participated in his military operations. This as much reflected the prevailing tactics as his own expediency and conviction. We know that all the ambitious personages of the day including the pillars of the state such as the Nizam, Saadat Khan, Sarbuland Khan, Aliwardi Khan, Najib-ud-Daula and Imad-ul-Mulk either established their own independent rule or usurped the crown lands, and yet they were never tired of calling themselves the loyal servants of the Emperor. Similarly, Suraj Mal, even though he seized extensive areas always styled himself as the old and loyal servant of the Emperor.[18] Such loud professions (on the part of the contemporaries) lacked sincerity. They, in fact, make a depressing reading. However, the only redeeming aspect of the Jat claim was that Suraj Mal showed himself willing to serve faithfully the Emperor[19] in all his ventures, save those endangering his local position. In addition, he, unlike Imad and the Marathas, refrained from outraging the royal dignity and also, like Najib, never did he enter into collusion with an alien foe. That all this he did to procure the formal ratification of his territorial gains is apparent.[20] But that undermeath it also lay an intention for the Empire to survive as a balancing factor in the contemporary political situation, can hardly be denied. Despite all his ambitions, Suraj Mal for one, never desired the extinction of the Mughal authority.[21] All these aspects merit our attention

15. *Supra*, 99-110; Bharatpur, *Jai Singh*, 103.
16. *Memoires des Jats*, 29.
17. Raghunath Rao's letter, *S.P.D.*, II, 84.
18. *Sujan*, 14, 40, 52, 55; *M.U.*, I, 440, 441; *Tarikh-i-Bharatpur*, 4b.
19. Suraj Mal's statement in *Sujan*, 60.
20. Sarkar, *Fall*, II, 431, footnote.
21. *Infra*, 173-174ff.

while assessing the overall implications of the Jat policy and the emergence of the Bharatpur State.

JAT PARTICIPATION IN THE IMPERIAL AFFAIRS

Having surveyed the Jat policy towards the Empire and vice versa, we may now turn to the Jat participation in the imperial affairs. We have already noted that Suraj Mal was assigned the guardianship of the imperial highways between Agra, Delhi and Jaipur and also the lease of a part of Mewat. It appears that Khema Jat was also granted some office befitting his status.[22]

Barring these three instances of a different nature the rest of the references pertaining to the Jats relate to their sharing in several campaigns[23] fought during this period (extending upto 1749).

The first information about Suraj Mal's movements refers to the time of Peshwa Baji Rao's sudden dash upon Delhi (March, 1737). But it is both ambiguous and insufficient. The Marathi letters tell us that Suraj Mal lay emcamped with 5000 troops in Urabag at Agra, probably to join the incoming Saadat Khan and Qamar-u-Din against the Marathas. Though it is not specified, it appears that later he marched in the vanguard of Saadat Khan's army.[24] On the other side, the Peshwa deluding the Mughal forces and passing through the west of Deeg,[25] rushed to Delhi and created panic there. It may be reasonably inferred from *Iqbalnama* that the Maratha movements in general, and the march of Baji Rao in particular, caused deep concern to Suraj Mal and his men.[26] Of late they had their own grievances, against the encroaching

---

22. *Tawarikh-i-Hunud* (20b) claims that Khema was granted the governorship of Agra by the Emperor (presumably Muhammad Shah). Its only basis that it seems to be assigning for the favour is the pleasure of the Emperor over the Jat's skill in killing tigers by wrestling. It is, however, ridiculous to presume that such a dignified office could be conferred on such a trifling ground. Moreover, this is not corroborated by contemporary sources either. Hence, it cannot be regarded as historically accurate. It is likely that Fransoo mistook some inferior office for governorship.
23. Muhammad Khan Bangash, in one of his despatches (Vide letter quoted by Irvine, *Later Mughals*, II, 233-234) covering his campaigns in Bundelkhand during 1727-1728, refers to a certain 'Jat' who joined the Bundelas against him. The Jats and the Marathas have been described by him as the "brethren" of the Bundelas. Which Jats are meant herein, has not been specified. We know that Churaman II had allied with the Bundelas. But we have no information about Suraj Mal ever helping or receiving any aid from Bundelas. Besides an alliance against the Emperor stood opposed to his professed loyalty to him. Suraj Mal was too astute a man to have provocated the Mughals for nothing. He had little interest in the affairs of the far off Bundelkhand. It leaves the impression that the Jats in question were other than under his following. May it be Muhkam Singh, the desperate ally seeker or some other local chieftain that is referred to by Muhammad Bangash.
24. *S.P.D.*, XXX, 196, XV, 20, 29 also see 37, 47, 22.
25. *Rustam*, 529.
26. *Iqbal*, 157.

Marathas. Remaining south of the Chambal till 1732, they later carried their activities across the river upto a few miles from Agra. Their bands roamed along the countryside, fleecing the people and plundering the villages. They imposed arbitrary dues and failing that despoiled "Jatwara" (a name used in the Marathi despatches, to denote the region roughly from Gohad to Chhata), Bhadawar and other places. Thus, we learn from a news report how about 1735 the greedy myriads "ate up supplies to a grain" in Jatwara; impliedly subjecting the local populace to severe hardships.[27] Now with Baji Rao's march through the heart of their territories, the Maratha danger appeared to have been veritably carried to their doors. This naturally generated reaction among the Jats. It cannot be said with certainty, whether or not they stood for renewed concerted move against the Marathas. But Jai Singh, who was in collusion with the invaders,[28] hushed up the Jats and the latter at this stage could not afford to antagonize the Raja for reasons already explained.[29] It is these undercurrents that *Iqbalnama* seems to be alluding to. The Jat reaction, though primarily born of the instinct of self-preservation, tended in the right direction. The interests of the Empire demanded a converted and bold stand against the increasing Maratha danger. This was, however, not forthcoming.[30]

Next, the Jat troops accompanied the Mughal army to Bhopal, where they gave a good account of themselves in an otherwise abortive fight against Baji Rao on December 9, 1737. The Peshwa's march to Delhi had terrified Muhammad Shah and he summoned Nizam-ul-Mulk to the Court and ordered him to expel the Marathas from Malwa and Bundelkhand. Asaf Jah then moved out with an army and the Jats under Pratap Singh also joined him along with several other contingents. The opposite army met at Bhopal. The Nizam, though a renowned and experienced general, displayed over-cautiousness, which proved to be his undoing. Instead of outright attacking the Marathas, he entrenched himself in the neighbourhood of the fort of Bhopal, with the tank on his

---

27. *S.P.D.*, XIV, 52, XV, 4, 8, 10-13, 15, 47, 89.
28. *S.P.D.*, XIV, 47, 31, 39, XV, 89; Raghubir Singh, *Malwa*, 266, 279; Sarkar, *Fall*, I, 257-259; G.H. Khare, "Some New Records on the Maratha-Jaipur Relations", *I.H.R.C.*, XIV (1948); For a discordant note see Satish Chandra, 'Raja Jai Singh Sawai's Contribution to Imperial Politics', Proc. *I.H.C.*, 1948.
29. *Supra*, Ch. V, f.n.s. 47-62.
30. It is interesting to note that side by side, some Jats were busy gratifying their lust for money. Thus, we learn that the Jats of Mitrol, a village between Palwal and Hodal, plundered the baggage of the Amir-Ul-Umra and Muhammad Khan while they were on return march to the Capital. Thereupon the royal troops sacked that village and set it ablaze. *Rustam*, 543; Elliot (VIII, 55) in his translation of Rustam's extracts, mistakenly writes Kodal for Hodal.

back and a '*nallah*' on his front. He thereby allowed himself to be besieged and harassed by the Marathas. On 14th December (3rd Ramzan) he detached the Jats and the Rajputs to move forward and offer a battle to the enemy. Ranoji Scinde and other advanced from the other side and the fight that ensued both sides suffer losses. None could, however, gain any decisive advantage. Twelve days later when the Nizam suddenly turned towards Bhopal, the Marathas fell upon his rear. It was the Jats who bore the brunt of this surprise attack. As they grappled with the advancing Maratha columns, the Mughal artillery opened fire, and the Nizam managed his way to the fort. The Marathas, thereafter, completely invested the fort and at last the Nizam was forced to sign a humiliating peace (of Duraha Sarai, 6th January, 1738), practically ceding Malwa to the Marathas.[31]

Incidentally, the above two events may help in rectifying a lapse, namely that it was 1748 or 1749 that the Jats and the Marathas confronted each other for the first time.[32]

Next, the Jats helped the Mughals against Nadir Shah. Living upto their reputation to oppose foreign invaders, they marched to Karnal (February, 1739) to resist the Persian invader. Both Badan Singh and Suraj Mal advanced upto south of Delhi where they stayed to watch the developments but despatched a contingent which was placed under Rao Kripa Ram, the Vakil of Jai Singh. On the battlefield, the Jats were posted to the right of the Emperor in the division of the Amir-ul-Umra.[33] But the man (Kripa Ram), who was to lead them, was a chicken-hearted fellow and he fled in the face of the relentless fire of the Persian artillery.[34] The cowardly flight of the leader must have demoralized the remaining troops, including the Jats and they apparently followed suit.

Following the crushing defeat and utter humiliation of Muhammad Shah and his surviving grandees, the Capital, now defenceless, experienced the grasping tyranny of the victors of Karnal. Indulging in sack, rape and massacre, they created panic and intense commotion in

---

31. *Sujan*, 5, 212. It is, however, wrong in assigning victory to the Nizam and Pratap Singh. In its passing reference of this event, the only fact is the gallantry displayed by the Jats. *S.P.D.*, XV, 58, 59, XXX, 207, XXII, 368, 369; *Raj*, VI, 117; *Brahmendra Swami Charitra*, 33-36, 116, 134, referred to by Raghubir Singh, *Malwa*, 287-294; Bhatnagar, *Jai Singh*, 155; *M.U.*, (I, 441) seems to suggest that it was Muhkam Singh who sent "one of his relatives" to Bhopal. This is misleading Y. Husain (The First Nizam, 178-181) has somehow overlooked the Jat participation in this battle.
32. Qanungo, *Jats*, 87; Hari Ram Gupta (ed.) *Marathas and Panipat* (Chandigarh, 1961), 45; Pande, *Bharatpur*, 57.
33. Mirza Zaman's Journal, quoted by Fraser, *Nadir Shah*, 81; *Iqbal*, 186, 174.
34. *Iqbal*, 186; Peshwa Baji Rao's letter, *S.P.D.*, XV, 71.

the city. The passages of the Capital were blockaded and the city granaries sealed up by the order of Nadir Shah. As a result, grain became exceedingly dear and scare and famine gripped the city. Not only Delhi but also the villages around upto several miles felt the atrocious touch of the arms of the Persian invaders.[35]

It was during these excesses that the Jat chief, Badan Singh, and his son, Suraj Mal, then encamping in the neighbourhood of Delhi, helped the distressed a lot. An eyewitness tell us, "Thana Rai (?) and Badel Singh Jat, the zamindar of Chitwarh (?)[36] have stationed themselves assisted by the gallant Jats upto Sarai of Bakhtiar Khan while the Chowki of Nadir Shah does not extend beyond the tank of Kishan Das."[37] As S.H. Askari suggests,[38] Badan Singh's encampment with a "gallant" force displayed an attitude of "resistance", even though the above writer does not specify whether or not any engagement occurred between Badan Singh and the roving Qizilbash bands. However, we do have a definite proof of Badan Singh's (and impliedly also of Suraj Mal's) exertions for ameliorating the distress of the victims of Nadir's cruelty. The sad plight of the people of the Capital deeply stirred the feelings of the compassionate Jat. The author of *Iqbalnama I* adds:

> "He (Badan Singh) ordered that whosoever came from those environs, (the Capital) to his side would find refuge and shelter under his protection and none was to interfere with any such body. Consequently, many people stricken with misfortune and having been pillaged, plundered and ruined came and were taken care of and treated kindly with favours, each according to his own condition and circumstances. Many people who had gone to Faridabad to bring grains received protecting guards, which escorted them safely. In this situation a world of people became busy in bringing grains and food (which came under heavy fire from the Persians) from that direction and the rates rose (sic.) from two seers to five and six seers."[39]

---

35. Fraser, *Nadir Shah,* 97-110; Anand Ram Mukhlis, in *Elliot*, VIII, 88-91; *Iqbal*, 203-209; Sarkar in *Later Mughals*, II, 364ff.
36. It is difficult to identify "Chitwarh". There is one place of a similar name called Chitwar, about 4 miles south of Hathras. Same is the case with "Thana Rai" also. It may be a mistake for Suraj Mal who was encamped south of Delhi, wherefrom had passed Babu Rao Malhar as a fugitive from Karnal, *Raj.*, VI, 131.
37. *An Anonymous Journal of Nadir Shah's Transactions in India*, trans. S.H. Askari entitled. '*A Contemporary Correspondence Describing the Events at Delhi at the Time of Nadir Shah's Invasion*; in *Proc. I.H.C.*, X (1947), 366.
38. Askari, *op.cit.*, Introduction, in *Proc. I.H.C.*, (1947), 358.
39. *Iqbal*, 210; *TAL*, 166; On this occasion Rao Bahadur Singh of Kharisa (perhaps Ghasira) played a role nearly similar to that of Badan Singh, *Iqbal*, 197.

It has been noticed in the preceding chapter that by seventeen forties the Jats had grown into a first rate military power. The reputation of Suraj Mal as a skillful commander and his Jats as gallant fighters spread far and wide and "there came repeated solicitations for his sword from the highest in the land."[40] Reference has already been made of their participation in the battle of Gangwana (1741). Next the Bharatpur troops accompanied Muhammad Shah and Safdar Jang in the Rohilla expedition (May, 1745). '*Memoires des Jats*' is the only source referring to the Jat participation in it. But even this does not enlighten us any more beyond speaking of their heroic fight (in that otherwise shameful campaign) and rating that as "the most honoured of all their exploits (until then)". It adds that after the termination of this campaign, the Emperor granted a '*seropa*' to Suraj Mal. This expedition, however, inglorious for the Mughal army, added to the popularity of Suraj Mal and he was now poised for a bigger role.[41, XVIII]

About six months later in Agahan, Samvat 1802 (28th October to 27th November, 1745), Suraj Mal extended help to Fateh Ali (son of Sabit Khan, the governor of Aligarh) against Asad Khan Khanahzad, the agent[42] of Saadat Khan, the fourth Bakshi of Muhammad Shah. Asad Khan with 10,000 men issued from Delhi and subsequently seized parts of the paternal estates of Fateh Ali in Aligarh district. This alarmed Fateh Ali and through his Vakil he supplicated Suraj Mal (then on a hunting excursion at Noh, a place beside the Yamuna) for help. Later Fateh Ali personally met him at Ikhu with the request and discussed the plans for the proposed campaign. It looks almost certain that the possibility of his own local interest being affected by Asad's movements also influenced his decision to espouse the cause of Fateh Ali. The opposite troops met in the neighbourhood of Chandos (16 miles from Aligarh), where, in a swift action Suraj Mal completely routed and killed Asad Khan putting his soldiers to flight. They were given a hot chase upto 7 miles and large booty fell into the hands of the Jat pursuers. Suraj Mal sent Jawahar Singh to Kol and he himself returned to Sahar to meet his father.[43] Incidentally Suraj Mal's fight against Asad Khan was destined to create some trouble for him a few years later.

---

40. Sarkar, *Fall*, II, 434; *Tarikh-i-Bharatpur*, 4b; *Sujan*, 11; *Memoires des Jats*, 30.
41. *Memoires des Jats*, 30-31; Sarkar, *Fall*, II, 434; For details of this expedition see Sarkar, *Fall*, I, 57ff.,
XVIII. also *Sujan*, 16-26; *Bharatpur Gazetteer*, 63.—Editor.
42. Sarkar, *Fall*, I, 309, 341; *Sujan*, the only source to have described this campaign, does not specify the mutual relationship between the two. It, however, suggests Salabat Khan's deep interest in Asad Khan. *Sujan*, 40.
43. *Sujan*, 9-24; Suraj Mal earlier humbled certain Sultan Khan(?) (*Sujan*, 10).

As in Karnal so in Manupur, a Jat contingent served the Mughal army against another foreign invader, Ahmad Shah. Unfortunately, the part played by the Jats in the battle of Manupur (March, 1748) has not been elucidated by Murtaza Husain, the only historian who has cared to mention this significant and hitherto unknown fact.[44]

We may notice here briefly a brilliant feat achieved by the Jats in course of the fraternal feud between Raja Ishwari Singh and Madho Singh, although, being the internal affair of Jaipur, it does not lie within the scope of our subject. Ishwari Singh appealed to Suraj Mal for help when confronted by the hostile and formidable combination of seven confederated States. Responding to his call, Suraj Mal and his 10,000 gallant Jat soldiers fully justified the trust reposed in them. In the battle of Bagru (1st week of August, 1748) Suraj Mal displayed, what K.R. Qanungo calls, "superhuman valour" by defeating the Marathas, under Malharao Holkar, opposed to him, although taking as whole, the campaign ultimately went against the Jaipur Raja.[45]

THE MARATHAS DUN THE JATS FOR TRIBUTE

An interesting feature of this period, not emphasized so far, was the beginning of the Maratha pressure for arbitrary dues on the Jats. The available evidence suggests that right from the seventeen thirties the Marathas visited the Jat country to levy tribute. Failing in that they resorted to their eternal practice of plunder. In 1736, a Maratha Sardar wrote of his resolve to proceed to Bhadawar and the Jatwara for the same, although, he apprehended that "there is little (prospect of collecting) money on way to Delhi across the Chambal."[46] About the same time, Baji Bhimrao unsuccessfully tried to put apparently the Jats of the environs of Gohad under tribute.[47] In time, as the frequency of the Maratha movements in the north increased, the Jats felt added pressure of their extortionate demands. In 1748, Yashwantrao Pawar and Ram Chandra entered the Jatwara to settle the terms with "the Jat".[48] In April next year, another Maratha army issued from Datia and ravaging the countryside and realizing tribute from the Rana of Narwar, it came to the environs of Agra. Suraj Mal sent his Vakil to the Marathas, but at the same time also prepared himself for resistance. Eventually, Damodar Mahadev went to the Jat and made some settlement regarding the money matters.[49]

---

44. *Hadiqat*, 135.
45. *Sujan*, 2nd Jang; Qanungo, *Jats*, 67ff., Sarkar, *Fall*, I, 239ff.
46. *S.P.D.*, XIV, 54, XXX, 196.
47. *Ibid.*, XIV, 52.
48. *Ibid.*, XXVII, 34.
49. *Ibid.*, XXVII, 42, 43, 44, 46, 53, 54; *S.P.D.* New Series, I, 103.

VII

The Rising Importance of the Jats in the Imperial Affairs (I) (1749-1753)

Marching merely as auxiliaries in the Mughal army till the end of Muhammad Shah's reign, the Jats in the reign of Ahmad Shah came to play a bold and varied role in the imperial affairs. Incapable and imbecile, the new Emperor, Ahmad Shah, spent his days in debauchery and childish acts. He entrusted all his functions to an intriguing and corrupt eunuch, Javed Khan, who was equally ignorant of state affairs. The Queen mother, Udham Bai, lacked capacity and sense but cherished high ambitions. At a time when the treasury was empty and the soldiers daily rioted for their long overdue salary, she squandered big sums of money in celebrating her birthdays.[1] Verily had the Mughal Empire become "a child's game".[2] There being no master to be feared, the nobles and *zamindars* grabbed what they could.[3] Dismemberment going space, the term 'Empire' looked a misnomer. It had degenerated virtually into a petty tribal chiefdom, with no force of its own except that maintained by the top nobles. The new Wazir, Safdar Jang, tried to put the Empire into gear. But the Turani nobility throughout conspired against him and the Emperor himself deprived him of his confidence and pursued the ruinous policy of playing one group against the other. These exigencies obliged Safdar Jang to devise means on the one hand to weaken his opponents and on the other to seek powerful allies.[4]

These cross-currents of the situation provided the Jats unique opportunities to increase greatly their fortunes as well as to emphasize their status in the contemporary politics.[5] They continued to profess

1. *TAH.*, 13b-15a, 21a, 25a, 28b, 46b, 85b and 86a; 108; Sarkar, *Fall*, I, 328ff.
2. *Shah*, 2
3. Sarkar, *Fall*, I, 343, 339, 344-345, 461.
4. For details see, Srivastava, *Oudh*, 130ff., Vide also Mirza Ali Azhahar, *A History of the Freedom Movement* (Karachi: 1957), I, 215.
5. *Memoires des Jats*, 31-33.

loyalty and yet they did not lag behind others in territorial acquisitions. In addition, they made it clear that they were not prepared to brook interference in their affairs. We shall now take up these developments.

SAFDAR JANG'S FIRST EXPEDITION AGAINST THE JATS

Whereas Muhammad Shah generally pursued a policy of conciliation, his successor initially adopted a punitive attitude towards Suraj Mal and his men. His Wazir and the Mir Bakhshi took field against the Jats and though the Bakhshi had left Delhi slightly earlier,[6] it was the Wazir who confronted them first. Towards the middle of November, 1749 (Zil-Hijja) 1162 A.H.), Safdar Jang moved out of Delhi, following the refusal of Suraj Mal and his protege, Balram, to vacate Faridabad, which lay in his *jagir.* He soon recovered Faridabad from Balram and then sent messages to Suraj Mal asking him to make over the usurped imperial territories. Suraj Mal, however, was not prepared to resign the advantages that he had endeavoured hard to gain and he began to fortify, Deeg, Kumbher and other forts to measure sword with the Wazir. Meanwhile, he addressed Safdar Jang "sometimes with promises of surrender and sometimes with threats of vengeance". The situation was fluid when the Wazir, hearing the news of the death and defeat of Qaim Khan Bangash (12th November), hastened back to the Capital.[7]

SURAJ MAL DEFEATS THE MIR BAKHSHI

A few weeks later the Mir Bakhshi, Salabat Khan Zulfiqar Jang, who held the governorship of Agra and Ajmer, including the *faujdari* of Narnaul,[8] forced a foolish contest on Suraj Mal. Leaving Delhi in November, 1749 with 15 to 20 thousand men,[9] Salabat was proceeding to Ajmer following an agreement between the Court and Bakht Singh (the chief of Nagor) requiring the Bakhshi to extend armed help to the latter in seizing the *gaddi* of Jodhpur from his nephew and the reigning King Ram Singh. In return Bakht Singh was to assist Salabat Khan in defending Agra and Ajmer against the Maratha interlopers and other local rebels.

---

6. *TAH.*, 21a and 22b. A.L. Srivastava (*Oudh*, 141) says that Safdar Jang and Salabat Khan had entered into a understanding against Suraj Mal.
7. *TAH.*, 22b; *Chahar Gulzar Shujai* in Elliot, VIII, 212-213. Though its date is wrong *Chahar* narrates the episode in some details as against the Court history of the reign, which has obviously intermixed the events of the first with the second expedition of Safdar Jang. Despite being a contemporary work, *Tarikh-i-Ahmad Shahi* at places gives very short and even wrong account of the events. For instance it erroneously asserts (*TAH.*, 27b) that the Jats did not participate in the second Afghan expedition.
8. *TAH.*, 29a and 21a; *Siyar*, III, 311; cf. *Sujan*, 40.
9. *TAH.* 21b is silent about the number. Another contemporary work, *Sujan Charitra*, (38) seemingly puts it at 20,000, while the author of *Siyar* (III, 311) whose uncle was present in the Bakhshi's army, speaks of "about 15000 troops".

Halting at Pataudi for some time, Salabat Khan proceeded, ravaging Mewat, to the fort of Nimrana (33 miles south-west of Pataudi), which he wrested from the Jat garrison on 30th December, 1749. The Bakshi now changed his original plan and decided first to go to Agra and attack the Jats. The reversal dismayed his lieutenants who counselled him that "a quarrel with the Jat was improper" at this stage and it should be thought about only when Bakht Singh had joined them and the Mughal troops had been heartened following their success in the Rajput expedition. But the easy success against an insignificant garrison had inflated the Bakhshi. He disregarded their reasonable advice, recalled his advance camp and set out for Agra. The night halt was made at Sarai Sobhachand.[10]

Meanwhile, Suraj Mal had advanced with his forces to a nearby place, Naugaon. Herefrom he sent his Vakil to the Bakshi, entreating him not to despoil the country (Mewat) as it had been assigned to him (by Muhammad Shah)[11] and he was living as a royal vassal of the Emperor. Salabat Khan, however, arrogantly rejected his petition. Demanding an explanation for killing Asad Khan, he asked Suraj Mal to pay Rupees two crores, vacate the lands of his *jagir* and "join the Emperor". The last demand, in the light of Suraj Mal's former affiliations with the late Qamar-ud-Din, impliedly meant that he (Suraj Mal) should break off relations with his son, Intizam-ud-Daula and his group and join the Mir Bakhshi and his friend, the Wazir instead. In the end the Bakhshi warned Suraj Mal either to accept these terms or be prepared for war.[12]

Suraj Mal accepted the challenge and he swiftly moved with his lieutenants (Gokul Ram, Surati Ram, Balram, Pratap Kachhwaha etc.) the Rana of Gohad, and picked a force of over 6,000 horses (rest he left behind). He divided it into five squadrons to attack and invest the Bakhshi from all sides and he overtook him on the night of 31st December, 1749. Next day (1st January, 1750) at midday his men surrounded and harassed Salabat's troops under Fateh Ali (the same whom Suraj Mal had helped against Asad Khan, 1745) some 3 miles away from the Sarai. Ali Rustam Khan and Hakim Khan and Hakim Khan Kheshgi led re-inforcements two hours before sunset. But the Mughals could not cope with the mounted Jat matchlockmen. Panic gripped the Bakhshi's camp. The Jats fired the volley of muskets causing heavy slaughter. Hakim Khan, the commander of the Bakhshi's right wing, was fighting on an elephant. Har Narain charged his horse upon

---

10. *Siyar*, III, 311-313; *S.P.D.*, XXVII, 58, XXI, 26; *TAH.*, 21b; Sarkar, *Fall*, I, 306-308; cf. *Sujan*, 37-39.
11. cf. *Supra*, Ch. V, f.n.76.
12. *Sujan*, 39f. *TAH.*, 21b, says that Ishawari Singh had called in Suraj Mal's troops.

the elephant and killed the Khan. Ali Rustam who led the vanguard was severely wounded. The Jats achieved a singular victory. They fell upon Salabat Khan's camp and plundered it for four "*gharies*". The Amir-ul-Umra was so much struck with terror that it was only the vigilance of his commanders that prevented his cowardly flight.[13] At last, after two or three days of strict confinement, the helpless Bakhshi sued for terms. He sent his Vakil (probably Fateh Ali) to Suraj Mal, offering to vacate the lands he had just recovered. Jawahar Singh was then sent to the Bakhshi to dictate peace (c. 4th January, 1750) on the following terms : (i) the Bakhshi's men would refrain from cutting the '*Peepal* trees, desecrating the temples or any other object of Hindu worship, (ii) that Suraj Mal would realize Rupees 15 lakhs from the Rajputs as the revenue of Ajmer, by personally sharing in his (Bakhshi's) Rajput expedition, provided that the latter did not proceed beyond Narnaul.[14]

The phenomenal encounter at Sarai Sobhachand marks a glorious stage in the career of Suraj Mal. No other Jat leader had ever before succeeded in humbling the commander-in-chief of the Mughal Empire. The material gains of this success were negligible beyond the recapture of his former possessions in Mewat. It, however, enhanced his prestige and increased his self-confidence as is evidenced by his accepting the onerous task of realizing the revenue of Ajmer. As for the Empire, the defeat of its highest military official revealed once more its rottenness to the core.

The Bakhshi had to lament his own rashness for his utter disgrace. He did not exercise due caution while embarking upon the hazardous expedition. More than one authority testifies that the contest was forced on Suraj Mal and it was "only in his own defence"[15] that he had arisen to confront him. It is noteworthy that despite his being in a position to do so, Suraj Mal refrained from capturing or killing the Amir-ul-Umra. Instead he expressed his regrets over his "impertinence" and assured him of his loyalty as well.[16] Undoubtedly, this humility demonstrated his practical wisdom. He attempted to assuage the wounded pride of the Bakhshi, now that his immediate object had been attained. At the same time, it symbolizes his chivalrous magnanimity towards the fallan foe. His extending of asylum later on to his arch enemy, the Wazir, Imad, furnishes another similar example.

It can be inferred from *Siyar* that after the contest Salabat Khan and Suraj Mal marched to Narnaul, where Bakht Singh came to know of the

---

13. *Siyar*, III, 313f; *Sujan*; 41-51; *S.P.D.*, XXI, 26; XXVII, 58; *TAH.*, 21b.
14. *Siyar*, III, 314-315; *Sujan*, 51f.
15. *Siyar*, III, 314; *S.P.D.*, XXVII, 58, *Sujan*, 40.
16. *Sujan*, 52; *Siyar*, III, 314.

Bakhshi's recent understanding with Suraj Mal. His prospects in Marwar now appeared to be adversely affected by it. He, therefore, prevailed upon the Bakhshi to revert to the original plan, namely to march to Ajmer in his company. This offended Suraj Mal and he personally left his camp, leaving 5,000 horses under Jawahar Singh. His protege, the Rana of Gohad, followed him, leaving 200 horses under Fateh Singh.[17]

Whatever the justifications, it was perhaps a tactical lapse on the part of Salabat Khan to discard Suraj Mal in preference to Bakht Singh. It is true that both of them were largely inspired by their selfish motives. But the question was one of their relative merit, Salabat could not judge that Suraj Mal—whose superior prowess he had the occasion to taste just then - was unquestionably better to deliver the goods than the one (Bakht Singh) who himself depended upon his (the Bakhshi's) might. As it was, Salabat Khan returned a ruined man, wrapped in disgrace and bankruptcy, neither gaining victory nor money in his Rajput campaign.[18] With this also ended the last attempt to retrieve the Mughal fortunes in Rajasthan.

SAFDAR JANG'S SECOND EXPEDITION AGAINST THE JATS: JULY, 1750

About six months later, Safdar Jang who had returned to the Capital after settling affairs at Farrukhabad, once more marched against Balram Jat. Balram had meanwhile shown more daring. His men attacked and expelled the Wazir's outpost at Shamspur near Delhi. Safdar Jang on receiving this news detached a fresh force but the miscreants refused to bow down and showed readiness for fight. Thereupon, he marched in person and spent the night near Shamspur. Here he received the news of the fomidable Pathan uprising. This distracted him once more and he became inclined to a patch up with Jats. On the other side, Balram, getting confounded by the Wazir's arrival, had become eager for terms. A Maratha Vakil, who mediated between the two, brought Balram with his wrists bound together to the presence of the Wazir at Khizrabad (July, 1750). Safdar Jang pardoned him on his promising to become his adherent and thereby implicitly sanctioned his illegal acquisitions. The Wazir then hastened back to Delhi.[19]

---

17. *Siyar*, III, 315; *Sujan* (52) gives an interesting information here that after this campaign Suraj Mal celebrated his marriage at Mathura; *S.P.D.*, XXI, 25, 26 also 34.
18. cf. Sarkar's comments (*Fall*, I, 357). His (Salabat Khan) *subahdari* of Agra and Ajmer yielded him no revenue, thanks to his fatuous policy of antagonizing the Jats, who alone could have kept that region in order. For details of Rajput expedition see *Fall*, I, 310ff.
19. Delhi Chronicle (R.S.L. script of Sir J.N. Sarkar's abridged trans.); *TAH.*, 22b-23a; Qanungo, *Jats,* 80; Srivastava, *Oudh*, 147f.; cf. *Memoires des Jats*, 33.

ALLIANCE BETWEEN THE WAZIR AND SURAJ MAL

We learn from the despatch of the Peshwa's agent that when the Wazir was yet to leave Delhi for the Bangash country, "the Jat" (Suraj Mal) in response to the former's invitation, came to the neighbourhood of Delhi. The Wazir despatched one of his officials to receive him. Then he himself followed and had a friendly parley with Suraj Mal at the tank of Krishna Das, near Khizrabad. Bidding farewell to Suraj Mal, the Nawab Wazir then returned to the Capital.[20]

The details of what both of these talked about are not known to us. It is, however, clear that the above parley tied them in an alliance of friendship.[21] The spectacle of the imperial Wazir favouring Suraj Mal with a personal visit was indeed a unique and unprecedented honour done to any Jat leader by the highest dignitary of the realm. It demonstrated the growing importance of the Bharatpur family in the political arena of the day. Side by side it also pointed to the compulsions of the Wazir already explained, which made him go more than half way to placate the redoubted Jat. On his part, the astute Suraj Mal obviously deemed it advantageous to come to terms and court the good-will of the Wazir. The recognition of mutual merit and the prospect of reciprocal gains thus fastened the Nawab and Suraj Mal with each other in 1750. More precisely they rather renewed and made stronger the relationship of the days of their respective uncles, Saadat Khan and Rup Singh.[22]

SURAJ MAL AND THE FIRST AFGHAN EXPEDITION

Safdar Jang was worried over the recrudescence of the Afghan rebellion. He, therefore, planned an expedition and accordingly set out from Delhi (25th July, 1750). On his way he received the upsetting news of the defeat and death of his deputy, Nawal Rai. Realizing the gravity of the situation, he resolved to muster up additional troops and he sounded, among others,[23] the Jats also. He sent letters to Suraj Mal (then at Sahar), urging his immediate help.[24]

---

20. *S.P.D.*, II, 15. The date printed on this letter refers to December, 1749, which does not seem to be correct. By placing the above event after the second Ballamgarh expedition, Prof. Srivastava (*Oudh* 147) also doubts the printed date. *Memoires des Jats,* 33 confirms that "interview", but wrongly states that immediately after that Suraj Mal went to the Court.
21. *Amirah*, 80; *Memoires des Jats,* 33; Imad, 73, 85 and 94.
22. *Sujan*, 54 and 60.
23. *D.C.*; *TAH.*, 25b-26a; *S.P.D.*, II, 14a; *Siyar*, III, 292; *Imad*, 74; *Shakir*, 63; Srivastava, *Oudh*, 156.
24. *Sujan*, 54f.

Accordingly, Suraj Mal came to Kol to join the Wazir (c. end of July, 1750).[25] According to *Sujan Charitra*, the Wazir sent one of his officials[26] to greet the priced ally. When Suraj Mal went to pay his respects, the Wazir displayed utmost friendliness, "clasping" Suraj Mal and taking his hands into his own while talking over the new problem. Suraj Mal emphasized the need of calling in more help such as from Himmat Singh of Bhadawar. The Wazir then paid him a return visit.

Suraj Mal greeted him submitting, "We *zamindars* feel honoured by your visit." In course of consultations Safdar Jang urged his host to support him wholeheartedly. Assuring him of it, Suraj Mal called in troops making the number to 15,000.[27] From Kol the Wazir marched to Marahara (beginning of August) where he halted for one month, awaiting fresh arrivals. At last his muster fully made up (about 70,000 men), Safdar Jang resumed his march and finally encamped near Ram Chatauni. On the other side, Ahmad Khan Bangash assisted by 20,000 of his own men and 10,000 Rohillas stood to oppose the enemy.[28] According to *Sujan Charitra*, Ahmad Khan sent his Vakil to Suraj Mal, to persuade him not to fight against him. But the latter refused to budge from his alliance with the Wazir.[29]

At last the fighting commenced at 9 A.M. on 13th September, 1750. Safdar Jang with most of his troops stood in the centre, while Suraj Mal commanded at the Wazir's right, nearest to the van and Ismail Khan to his left. On the other side, Ahmad Bangash, divided his troops into two parts; the first one consisting of 10,000 was deputed under Rustam Khan Afridi against the enemy, while the other under his own command was kept in hiding for a surprise attack. An interesting story goes that Rustam Khan offered to the Bangash chief that soldier (*i.e.* himself) should fight the soldier (*i.e.* Suraj Mal) and the Nawab (*i.e.* Ahmad Khan) should fight the Nawab (*i.e.* Safdar Jang).[30]

---

25. *Ibid.*, 56; *TAH.*, 25b; *S.P.D.*, II, 23; *Amirat,* 80; *Memoires des Jats*, 34; *Hadiqat*, 174; *Gulistan*, 37; *Gul-i-Rahmat* (Litho. Agra, 1836), 56.
26. *Sujan* (56) mentions the name of Ismail in this connection. This is wrong. The fact is that he joined Safdar Jang later at Marahara. The man in question must have been other than Ismail.
27. *Sujan*, 56-64. Among the notable Sardars accompanying Suraj Mal were, Balram of Ballamgarh, Balram, Gokul Ram, Mohan Ram, Surati Ram, Mansa Ram, Kripa Ram, Pratap Kachhwaha, Har Nagar Misur, Samar Singh Chandel, Chain Singh and Tilak Singh Tomar. *Gulistan* (37) *Gul* (56) and probably following these Irvine (*Bangash Nawabs of Farrukhabad, J.A.S.B,* 1878-79, 67) stretch the number of the Jat army to 30,000. It is wrong.
28. Srivastava, *Oudh*, 155-157.
29. *Sujan*, 69-70.
30. Irvine's *Bangash Nawabs*, 71.

The fight began with the advance of the Pathans and the boom of cannons from both sides. Suraj Mal and Ismail Khan moved forward to confront Rustam Khan. Balram Jat (of Ballamgarh) captured and implanted his guns upon a rising ground lying between the two armies. The Jat guns opened murderous fire upon the Pathans and at first repulsed them. But soon Rustam Khan with 7,000 men moved forward to reinforce his men and eventually succeeded in wresting that ground alongwith the guns atop. Balram and his Jats fought most vigorously but they were outnumbered and suffered heavy losses. Chain Singh, Sahib Ram and Tilak Singh Tomar were among those who perished there. At this Suraj Mal immediately sent his maternal uncle, Sukh Ram to reinforce Balram, instructing him to use arrows and firelocks instead of swords and he himself moved forward, assisted by Ismail Khan and Himmat Khan in a semi-circular form and discharging matchlocks and arrows pounced upon the Pathans. Rustam Khan and his men fought most gallantly. But they could not cope with the enemy. Rustam Khan was killed along with six to seven thousand Pathans. On the opposite side, three to four thousand Jats perished in the process. Suraj Mal vigorously pursued the surviving enemies a long way in the direction of Aliganj and grabbed a rich booty.[31] He thus scored a complete triumph in his theatre of war.[32]

But what Suraj Mal achieved, his master (in his own quarter) could not. This eventually changed the complexion of the campaign and spoiled the fruits of his personal exertions. We have little interest in the details of Safdar Jang's personal encounter with Ahmad Khan. Suffice it to remember that as a tactical move to boost the morale of his men, Ahmad Bangash publicized the rumour that Rustam had won the day and imprisoned Suraj Mal and his colleagues. In the circumstances, they would become the scoff of the Afridis if they failed to accomplish the same against the enemy pitted against, that is, the Wazir.[33] The Afghans now made a determined rush upon the Wazir, who, by detaching reinforcements to the pursuers, had dangerously weakened his position. To make matters worse, the generals placed in the vanguard, such as Rao Bahadur Singh, Mir Baqa, Kamghar Khan Billoch and Sher Jang (most of whom were in treacherous collusion with the enemy) fled from the battle-field. The Afghans, taking fullest advantage of Safdar's helplessness, attacked him from two sides. A severe bullet shot drowned the Wazir in

31. Qanungo, (*Jats*, 81) thinks that Suraj Mal occupied Farrukhabad.

32. For Suraj Mal's part see *Sujan*, 72-90; *Siyar*, III, 295; *Imad*, 74; *Hadiqat*, 171 and 174; *TAH.*, 26b; *Amirat*, 80-81; *S.P.D.*, II, 23, 21 also 20; *Gulistan* 38f.; *Gul*, 57f; *Memoires des Jats*, 34; Irvine, *Bangash Nawabs*, 71, 72 and 84; also *Shakir*, 63-64.

33. *Imad*, 73; *Gulistan*, 38; Gul, 58; Irvine, *Bangash Nawabs*, 72.

his *houda.* Completely beaten, he was somehow led out of the field into safety at Marahara enroute to Delhi.[34]

When the triumphant Suraj Mal returned from the chase of the Afridis he heard of Safdar Jang's defeat and flight. He stayed for a while at the grove of '*Palash*' trees. Understandably this caused anxiety to Ahmad Bangash and he forbade his men to move towards the Jats. Suraj Mal himself was equally anxious about the Afghan movements. Hence, he left the field and spending the night on the bank of the river Kali, he went back to his home.[35]

JATS AND THE COURT POLITICS BETWEEN THE TWO AFGHAN EXPEDITIONS

Misfortune never comes alone. The defeat at Ram Chatauni eventually plunged Safdar Jang into a triangle of troubles. Besides involving him in deep disgrace and inevitable mental agony, this, in its wake, created a potential danger for the security of his dominions, now defenceless. His victorious enemies overran and occupied their considerable parts, making a bid for the rest. To make matters worse, this also provided a golden opportunity to his Court adversaries. Javed Khan, Udham Bai and Intizam, with the connivance of the Emperor, devised schemes for attaching his property and mansion and also for overthrowing him from the Wizarat in favour of the old claiment, Intizam-ud-Daula.[36]

The available evidence shows that amidst this deep predicament his thoughts turned hopefully to his trusted and powerful ally, Suraj Mal. *Memoires des Jats* states that "after giving him the honour of putting him (Suraj Mal) among his children, he (Safdar Jang) sent him off (promised) many more licences for land (*jagirs*)" and granted him "other similar favours" to fasten Suraj Mal "more strongly and to assure himself of his assistance" on a foreseeable occasion.[37] *Memoires* is a later work, but the points emphasized by it find their endorsement in others including the contemporary sources, as well.[38]

Even after giving due allowance to the element of political cleverness on the part of the Wazir, there remains much in what we have seen above to suggest his increasing dependence upon Suraj Mal for his enterprises and in the same proportion Suraj Mal's share in the political transactions of the day.

---

34. For details see Srivastava, *Oudh*, 160-162.
35. *Sujan*, 91. It claims that in a momentary flush of anger Suraj Mal thought of re-attacking the Pathans. Also *Gulistan*, 39; Irvine, *Bangash Nawabs*, 75.
36. For details see Srivastava, *Oudh*, 163-164.
37. *Memoires des Jats*, 34.
38. *TAL*, 108; (for assignment of the jagirs only); *Tawarikh-i-Hunud* 21b-22a; Also *Siyar*. 92.

However, as Safdar Jang strengthened his alliance of friendship with Suraj Mal, his Court opponents conspired to undermine it in a like manner. The intriguing Javed Khan used Suraj Mal's ambitious son, Jawahar Singh (restless over what he thought the long governance of his father) as his tool for the purpose. He summoned Jawahar Singh and presented him to the Emperor. Jawahar was granted the title of "Rai" and other "favours"[39] which usually were shown to "most honoured people" and befittingly should have been conferred on his father or the reigning grand-father instead. Having been "filled up with highest hopes", Jawahar Singh was presently dismissed till it was planned when and how to exploit him to weaken the strength of his father and in a corresponding degree that of Safdar Jang, who was the ultimate object of this game.[40] In a way this incident was the precursor of Javed's promptings to Balram Jat, two years later.[41]

THE JATS AND THE SECOND AFGHAN EXPEDITION

But Javed Khan could not cash this tendentious favour to the lucky Jat as presently he himself climbed down for a bribe of Rupees 70 lakhs and thus got Safdar Jang pardoned and re-installed on the Wizarat. Safdar Jang now seriously planned for avenging his defeat, the thoughts of which had kept him occupied ever since his return. Ismail Beg, Raja Lakshmi Narain, Raja Nagar Mal and Suraj Mal and others were called in and after consulations to acquire the Maratha help as well was decided upon. Safdar Jang promised to pay Rupees twenty five thousand (or thirty five thousand) and rupees fifteen thousand a day for the Maratha and the Jat armies respectively. Necessary preparations having been made, the Wazir resumed his march. On reaching Agra, he detached 20,000 Marathas against Shadil Khan (the Bangash governor of Kol and Jalesar) while the rest of the army, including the Jats, marched towards Farrukhabad. The Maratha contingent overpowered and put to flight Shadil Khan's small force at Qadirganj (c. 20th March, 1751).[42]

---

39. *Memoires des Jats*, 34; *Sujan*, 5. It adds that Ahmad Shah granted him the right of *Naubat* also. Whether or not any *mansab* was given to Jawahar Singh on that occasion has not been specified by the above sources. We, however, learn from *Delhi Chronicle* that Jawahar Singh retained one of 3000 *zat* and 2500 horse when shortly afterwards (March, 1751) it was raised to 4000 *zat* and 3500 horse.
40. *Memoires des Jats*, 34-35.
41. *TAH.*, 39a ff.
42. *Siyar*, III, 304-305; *Amirat*, 83; *Sujan*, 92; *S.P.D.*, II, 32, XXVI, 176; *Majma-ul-Akhbar* in Elliot VIII, 362; Irvine *Bangash Nawabs*, 83 and 86; Srivastava, *Oudh*, 176, 179-180; *Ibratnama* by Khair-ud-Din Muhammad Allahabadi (My own extract Micro Film copy from Br. Mus. Or. 1932), 15a. *TAH.* 27b is wrong in its assertion that Safdar Jang did not take the Jats with him that time.

On hearing about it, Ahmad Bangash raised the siege of Allahabad, rushed to his Capital and entrenched himself at Fatehgarh. Here he worsted a Maratha contingent under Gangadhar Tantia. Meanwhile, Safdar Jang accompanied by the Marathas and the Jats reached the spot and besieged Fatehgarh from three sides except the east. Daily skirmishes took place at the fort but with no decisive gain to either side. When the siege had dragged on for over a month Sadulla Khan with his Rohilla re-inforcement of 12,000 came to the riverside (Ganga) opposite Fatehgarh. Herefrom he sent a message to Ahmad Bangash boasting that next day he would bring in the heads of Safdar Jang, Suraj Mal and the Maratha generals.

His approach caused some anxiety to the Wazir and he called Suraj Mal, Malharrao Holkar and Jayappa Scinde for consultation. The decision taken was that Sadulla Khan be prevented from effecting a junction with the Bangash troops across the river. Accordingly, the Marathas under Khanderao and Tantia and the Jats under Jawahar Singh and Rana Bhim Singh (of Gohad) moved forward and crossing the river at Singirampur, they attacked Sadulla Khan's van under Bahadur Khan. The latter fought bravely but could not cope with the Marathas charging him from one side and the Jats from the other. Ultimately he was defeated and killed. Ten to twelve thousand Afghans were either slain or wounded (April, 1751). Bahadur Khan's rout changed the complexion of the campaign. Sadulla, now growing fearful, fled to Amla. Hearing of his flight, Mahmud Khan Bangash also lost heart and hurried across the river to his father at Fatehgarh. Jawahar Singh might have intercepted him effectively but for the objection of Bhim Singh of Gohad who was friendly to the Bangash family. Meanwhile, the Marathas and the Jats, who now commanded the northern side of the Ganga, set ablaze Sadulla Khan's camp. Already disheartened, now the sight of its high flames completely unnerved Ahmad Bangash and the fort garrison. During the same night he left the fort and fled across the Ganga towards Amla. With the Marathas and the Jats pursuing the fugitives closely, their flight while crossing the river at Shikarpur presented a pathetic sight. Many of them either fell to the enemy or were drowned in the river. Next morning (19th April) Fatehgarh was occupied by the victors. Hereafter, the approaching rains brought a lull in the fighting and Safdar Jang went to Lucknow. But the Marathas remained busy ravaging the Afghan country and in the process they amassed huge plunder.[43]

---

43. *Siyar*, III, 305-307; *Shakir*, 84; *Sujan*, 93-95 (Hereafter it ignores the course of operations in Rohilkhand. May be its author accompanied most of the Jats back home following the suspension of the campaign (cf. Qanungo, Jats, 83). Suraj Mal, however, stayed on till the end); Irvine, *Bangash Nawabs*, 87-100 (His figures putting Jats at 40,000 seems over stretched); Srivastava, *Oudh*-180-185.

After the rains Safdar Jang came back and in November, 1751 commenced the desultory and drawn-out warfare in Rohilkhand. Barring sporadic rebuffs, the imperialists on the whole kept pressure on and the allied Afghans were pushed into the Tarai of the Kamayun Hills. The Wazir and his allies encamped within six miles of the Afghan entrenchment at Chilkea. Skirmishes and artillery duel between the opponents continued but without any decisive results. The difficult terrains, the inaccessible forests, the stream of water around the Afghan encampment and the increasing indifference of the Marathas - the biggest partners - towards an enterprise now that promised little booty, hindered the imperialists. Both the Holkar and Suraj Mal attempted in vain to discover a way of entrance into the Afghan positions. Meanwhile, the Wazir was getting impatient. He expressed his disapproval of the allies not being able to advance during the past two months. At last the valiant Rajender Giri Gosain came forward to attack the enemy entrenchments (under Najib Khan and others). But Jayappa treacherously passed on his plans to Ahmad Bangash and this largely contributed to the Gosain's subsequent defeat. Meanwhile, the news of the coming of the Abdali worried the Emperor (at Delhi) and he ordered the Wazir to make peace with the Pathans and repair the Capital. Safdar Jang himself had no other alternative. So he terminated the war now in progress for over a year and made peace with the Afghans (April, 1752). Thereafter, he proceeded to Lucknow to restore administration there and the Marathas to Qannauj, while Suraj Mal apparently went back to his home.[44]

Thus ended the expedition in favour of Safdar Jang. His overall gains were, however, more apparent than real. Both his allies earned him good success in its first place but none of them proved so effective in the concluding one. Specially at Chilkea even the Maratha hordes failed to accomplish anything. They, in fact, played double game and manipulated the expedition in such a way as to emerge the real gainers,[45] whereas Safdar Jang achieved little more than a hollow gratification of humbling his enemies. Success at Chilkea eluded Suraj Mal as well, but he served his master faithfully throughout in proportion to his available strength.[46]

---

44. Irvine, *Bangash Nawabs,* 108-122; Srivastava, *Oudh*, 185-189. The following sources describe the above event without tracing the role of the Jats. *TAH*. 27b-28b; *Imad*, 86ff.; *Gulistan*, 40-44; *Gul*, 62-66; *Shakir*, 64; *Hadiqat*, 175.
45. Srivastava, *Oudh*, 190.
46. *Siyar*, IV, 29; *Majma-ul-Akhbar* in Elliot, VIII, 362; Dow's assertion (*The History of Hindustan*, II, 322) that instead of helping, Suraj Mal frustrated the Wazir, is baseless.

VIII

The Rising Importance of the Jats in the Imperial Affairs (II)

JATS AND THE COURT DEVELOPMENT : 1752-1753

In December 1751, Ahmad Shah Abdali led his third invasion into the Panjab to press his demand for tribute from the four *mahals* ceded to him in 1750. The news of his capture of Lahore (reaching Delhi on 13th March, 1752) created intense panic in the Capital and a lot of frightened inhabitants fled for safety to Mathura and other places in the dominions of Suraj Mal, considered "Extremely Safe".[1] Amidst these circumstances, Ahmad Shah sent express summons to the Wazir, asking him to bring with him the Marathas (then at Qannauj) at any price. Accordingly, Safdar Jang entered into a subsidiary defensive alliance with the Marathas, among others on the following terms: (i) in lieu of Rupees 50 lakhs the Peshwa was to defend the Empire against the Abdali and the local rebels and to recover and handover the royal lands to the Emperor. (ii) The Peshwa was to be given the governorship of Agra (including the *faujdari* of Mathura) and Ajmer (including the *faujdari* of Narnaul).[2]

This pact, (paving the way for the Maratha expansion) particularly its second article, caused concern to the ambitious Suraj Mal, who since long had his eyes over the province of Agra. Madho Singh and Bakht Singh also resented the pact. Hence, adds Antaji, all the three went to the Wazir, expressed their resentment over the grant of Agra and Ajmer to the Peshwa and offered to bear the expenses of the proposed expedition to push the Marathas back to the south.[3] Though the Wazir himself had such a scheme in his mind,[4] it was not translated into practice. As for

1. *TAH.*, 33a, 37b.
2. For details see *Rajwade*, I, 1; Also see *TAH.* 33a and 34a.
3. *S.P.D.*, XXI, 50 and 57.
4. *Shakir*, 65; *S.P.D.*, XXI, 44.

Suraj Mal's objection, he had to content with the *faujdari* of Mathura, which he got through the Wazir, later on (c. end of October, 1752).[5]

Earlier, on his return to Delhi (25th April) Safdar Jang discovered to his bitter annoyance that he was Wazir in name only and that all his powers and privileges had passed into the hands of Javed Khan. The latter, in fact, had all along been his arch enemy, conspiring to frustrate his objectives, weaken his strength, turn the Emperor against him and dislodge him from the Wizarat unless bribed heavily. Among other hostile acts, he had got Salabat Khan (also a Shia like the Wazir), Safdar Jang's strongest ally, dismissed from the post of the Mir Bakhshi and Ghazi-ud-Din Firoz Jang, the pillar of the Turani party, appointed instead.[6] Now he tried to wean away Balram Jat (of Ballamgarh) from Safdar Jang, an attempt reminiscent of his tendentious favour to Suraj Mal's son (Jawahar Singh) earlier.

BALRAM'S AFFAIR AND THE MURDER OF JAVED

This incidence runs as follows: On 2nd July, 1752 (1st Ramzan, 1165 A.H.), when the Wazir was moving to his mansion in Delhi from his camp across the Yamuna, Nawab Javed Bahadur sat down in the Anguribag (which lay on the Wazir's way) expecting the Wazir to pay him respects. But Safdar Jang went straight without caring for the eunuch. This highly offended Javed and he immediately called Balram (then in Delhi),[7] gave him a *khilat*, appointed him *faujdar*, of Sikandarabad and ordered him to expel forcibly the lawful holder of that post, Qamar Ali. He also instigated Balram to foment as much trouble there as possible.

Balram, who was a man with little scruples, executed heartily the task assigned to him. On reaching Sikandarabad, he asked Qamar Ali to vacate the city since the *faujdari* now lay with him. When Qamar Ali insisted on being shown the order, Balram attacked him and killing his son put him to flight. The Jat occupied the district and plundered everything that he could lay his hands upon. He dug up the floors of the houses and tortured the local traders to extort money. The Wazir and Javed were both present in the Court, when this horrifying tale was reported the same night. Safdar Jang asked his opponent:

> What is the matter? If Balu has been appointed by you as the new *faujdar* of the place, why is he plundering and killing the people there? If he is acting against your wishes, I am going there and would bring him a prisoner.

---

5. *TAH.*, 45a. Antaji writes in one of his despatches (*S.P.D.*, XXI, 44) that the Wazir attempted to get the *suba* of Agra assigned to Suraj Mal and Madho Singh.
6. Sarkar, *Fall*, I, 364, 368-369.
7. Balram must have been in touch with Javed for some time which accounted for his prompt ready availability. It is significant to note that we do not find Balu being referred to in the context of the 2nd Afghan expedition. It may show that this time he stayed back.

Javed evaded the answer but offered that he would punish the Jat himself. Next day, Javed sent an insignificant force under his *jamadar*, Narsingh Rai, apparently instructing him not to fight the Jat. Safdar Jang also despatched Rajender Giri Gosain against Balram. But Narsingh passed on to him the news of Gosain's coming and allowed him to escape with all his loot to Dankaur (15 miles due east of Ballamgarh), in the eunuch's Jagir. Meanwhile, Rajender Giri arrived and though a skirmish followed, he safely managed his way to Ballamgarh. Thus ended the show of a campaign against the incited plunderer of the Emperor's privy purse estate. Balram's victims begged for justice but in vain.[8] Safdar Jang sent for Balram. On being inquired, he plainly told that whatever excesses he had committed, he did "at the instance of Nawab Bahadur. Hearing it, the Nawab's (Javed's) head hung down in repentance and he (Javed) begged pardon for his mischievous role."[9]

The above details suggest that Javed Khan was playing a very clever game. By seducing a section of the Jats he calculated to decrease, however small in size, the ranks of the Wazir and if the desired did not take place, to artfully defame his rival, as the patron of the atrocious plunderers of the Emperor's privy purse estate.

Balram's affair turned Safdar Jang mad with rage and he resolved to remove from his way his greatest hurdle, Javed. In a momentary flush of anger, the Emperor himself sent him a word to that effect.[10] Safdar Jang now called his "steadfast ally", Suraj Mal, ostensibly for consultation on political matters but really to crush possible opposition jointly. Suraj Mal responded and leading his force encamped at *Kalkappahari* (c. third week of August, 1752). An agent of Madho Singh and Balram (of Ballamgarh) joined him there with their respective forces. Javed grew curious about the purpose of their coming as in the past they (impliedly Suraj Mal's son, Jawahar Singh and Balram Jat)[11]

---

8. *TAH.*, 38a, 39a-40a; *Shakir*, 71.
9. *Shakir*, 71. It, however, confusedly mentions the name of Suraj Mal in place of Balram.
10. *Imad*, 91; *Amira*, 85; *Bayan-i-Waqai in Elliot*, VIII, 133.
11. *TAH.*, 40a-40b. The word "Inha" (these) occurring in this passage of this work has to be interpreted carefully. Whatever impression it might leave outwardly, it cannot properly incorporate the name of Suraj Mal personally. This may be inferred from one simple fact that ever since their alliance, the Wazir never remained out of Delhi without Suraj Mal not accompanying him. But same was not the case with Balu and the former's own disgruntled son, Jawahar Singh. We know that both of them had been the recipients of Javed's favour and significantly both had not regularly marched under the banners of Safdar Jang, Jawahar keeping back in his first while Balram in his second Afghan expedition. It is thus clear that the Jats implied herein were actually Balram and Jawahar and that it were these, one time beneficiaries rather than Suraj

used to court his patronage. He wished that on this occasion also they should meet him first and discuss their affairs. However, due to the presence of the Wazir in the Capital no way could be found for the intended separate meeting. It was then settled that Javed should go to the Wazir's mansion and there the two together should meet Suraj Mal and others on 27th August, 1752 (27th Shawwal). In the morning on the date fixed, Safdar Jang sent Ismail Khan to call Suraj Mal, instructing him to intimate Javed of Suraj Mal's coming and also request him to come and hold talks with Suraj Mal at his residence. Soon after Javed arrived followed by Suraj Mal in the afternoon and discussions between the three were held. In the evening the Wazir led rival (Javed) to an inner apartment where after a brief talk he was done to death by the Mughal soldiers. The news of this murder occasioned great commotion but no hostile movements. The rumour spread that the Wazir had also killed Suraj Mal. Thereupon, the infuriated Jat troops mobbed his mansion and it was only when Suraj Mal in person came out and sat for a while before them that their fears were dispelled.[12]

However imperative it might have looked to Safdar Jang, the treacherous assassination of Javed produced results contrary to his expectations. It antagonised the Royal family, alienated the nobility and aroused misgivings on all sides. The Emperor, always prone to depending upon others, now extended his confidence to the Wazir's more capable and dangerour Turani opponents, Intizam and Imad, the new Mir Bakhshi. A concerted and more powerful opposition thus came into existence which ultimately led to the Wazir's overthrow.[13] Javed's removal, however, enabled Safdar Jang to exercise for the first time the full authority and privileges of the Wazir. Apart from what he himself grasped, in the next few months he promoted the interests of his adherents to the exclusion of his adversaries. Suraj Mal had all along stood by him. As an expression of his gratitude thereof, the Wazir, on

---

Mal, who, along with other favours also got (on paper) the fiefs mentioned in *TAL*, 108. And yet if the name of Suraj Mal is referred to at both the places (i.e. in *TAL*. and *TAH*. in the present context) it is probably because of the fact that in the Jat affairs of this period, it was generally his transcending name that ultimately counted for every thing. Its greatest proof is that even during the life time of the reigning King, Badan Singh, we find nearly all the Jat transactions being carried in the name of Suraj Mal.

12. *TAH*., 40b-41a; *Bayan-i-Waqai* in *Elliot*, VIII, 133; *Shakir*, 71; *Ahwal*, 119; *Tarikh-i-Muzaffari*, Elliot VIII 317; *S.P.D.*, XXI, 54, 50; *Imad*, 91; *Ibrat*, 15a; *Memoires des Jats*, 35-36, devotes full two pages on Javed and his murder. yet it is silent on Balu's affairs (in fact at no place the name of this Balram occurs in this Ms.) and Suraj Mal's presence during this deed. Also see Srivastava, *Oudh*, 207f; cf. Sarkar, *Fall*, I, 372.
13. For details, Srivastava, *Oudh*, 210ff.

20th October, 1752 (11th Zil-Hijja, 1165 A.H.) presented his ally and friend to the Emperor, who conferred on Badan Singh (then at Bharatpur) the title of "*Mahendra*" and thereby made him a Raja and on Suraj Mal that of "*Kumar Bahadur Brijendra*".[14] Without specifying the time Wendel claims that Ahmad Shah gave him (Suraj Mal) the title of "*Jaswant Singh*" ("Josand Sing"), which amounted to his being recognized as a Raja and also the right of beating drums but this privilege ceased to operate within "12 kos" of the residence of the Emperor.[15] A few days later Suraj Mal was also appointed *faujdar* of Mathura, which according to the pact with the Marathas, was to remain with the Peshwa. This placed into his hands the governorship of most of the territory on both sides of the Yamuna in the *suba* of Agra, for an annual contribution.[16] All these favours were in addition to an earlier (March, 1751) conferment of the mansab of 3,000 *zat* 2,000 horse upon Suraj Mal, the title of 'Rao' upon his son Ratan Singh and the *mansab* of 1,000 *zat*, 1,000 horse upon his next son, Jawahar Singh - in addition to Jawahar's former rank - making him in all a holder of 4,000 *zat*, 3,500 horse.[17]

This honour marked a momentous stage in both the Jat Wazir relations and the evolution and growth of the Bharatpur State. Though it possessed the basic prerequisites, its head still lacked regal title and authority officially sanctioned by the Mughal Emperor. This was now made good by the grant of the regal title to Badan Singh, which amounted to the Emperor's recognition of the Jat State. Now Badan Singh could legally claim a rank among the Princes of Hindustan. Wendel concludes that now the head of the Jats was created a Raja by the Great Mughal himself as Jai Singh and other Rajas were. It is from here that "the era" of their political ascendancy should be traced.[18]

The Jat Prince had every reason to be thankful to the gracious Wazir. He presently went to his home[19] but after a short while he returned to

---

14. *TAH.*, 43b. J.N. Sarkar (*Fall*, II, 435) and following him R. Pande (*Bharatpur*, 53, 47) reads Suraj Mal's title as "Rajendra". This does not seem to be correct. The way the first letter of desired word "*Brijendra*" is written in the above MS. it looks to us "*Brijendra*" rather than "*Rajendra*". That its author did not mean "Rajendra" becomes clear from the different style in which he writes the first letter of word "Rajendra" (*TAH.* 449) while mentioning the name of the famous Rajendra Giri Gosain. So significantly, "*Brijendra*" also agrees with *Nur-ud-Din's* (*Nur.* 33a) mention of Raja Suraj Mal's title as "Maharaja *Brijendra* Bahadur" and Somnath's (*Brijendra Vinod*, Kashi Nagari Pracharini Sabha, 212) "*Shriman Maharaj Brijendra, Shri Sujan Singh*".
15. *Memoires des Jats*, 33; cf. *Tarikh-i-Bharatpur*, 4b; cf. TAL's (158) reference about Suraj Mal beating drums.
16. *TAH.* 45a; *Memoires des Jats*, 33.
17. *Waqa i-Shah Alam Sani*, 70, quoted by Qanungo, *Jats*, 83-84.
18. *Memoires des Jats*, 33-34; Sarkar, *Fall*, II, 435.
19. *TAH.*, 45a.

the Capital and remained with Safdar Jang[20] till he moved against Rao Bahadur Singh of Ghasira, the *faujdar* of *chakla* Kol (Aligrah). We shall now turn to this event.

SURAJ MAL'S CAMPAIGN AGAINST BAHADUR SINGH

It seems that a feud over land and other things existed between Suraj Mal and Rao Bahadur Singh Bargujar.[21] The Wazir himself was angry with Rao probably over his treacherous collusion with Ahmad Bangash during his first Bangash expedition.[22] The Bargujar presently joined the camp of Malharrao Holkar and the Jat Vakil justified the attack almost solely on this ground.[23] Thus, the Wazir and Suraj Mal both dissatisfied, the former reportedly induced the Emperor to sanction the expedition under Suraj Mal.[24]

About the first week of February, 1753,[25] Suraj Mal moved out and halted for some time at Samogar near the Yamuna in order to call up sufficient troops from his State. Since Bahadur Singh was at Kol, Suraj Mal, with a picked force of 4,000 horsemen, marched to that place, leaving the rest of his foces at Samogar. Realizing the weakness of his position at Kol, Bahadur Singh avoided confrontation with the Jats there and managed his way to his stronghold of Ghasira. This was a spacious and fairly strong fort, containing sufficient quantities of artillery and munition and a garrison of 8,000. In addition, a rainwater pool stretching upto its southern and western ramparts provided it safety from those two sides. Meanwhile, as Rao fled, Suraj Mal occupied Kol and leaving a contingent there, hotly pursued him along his circuitous route upto Ghasira which he attacked from the north and the east.[26]

Rao, at the head of 5,000 matchlockmen and about 800 horse, came out of the eastern gate and offered battle to the Jats under the personal command of Suraj Mal. Rao fought most gallantly but was wounded and forced back. But on the northern side the Jats under Jawahar Singh, sustained heavy losses as a result of the gunfire from the fort. Suraj Mal

---

20. *Sujan*, 97-98; *S.P.D.*, XXVII, 68, XXI, 54.
21. *Sujan*, 118; Also see author's article, 'Ghasira Ke Yudha Ka Aitihasik Paryalochan, *Nagari Pracharini Patrika*. Samvat 2024, 510-511. The story also goes that the Meenas of Ghasira stole away some camels belonging to Suraj Mal. But on being asked Rao returned neither the camels nor the culprits, which provoked the Jat Prince further.
22. Rao later deserted the Wazir's vanguard amidst the crucial moments of the battle. See Chapter VII, First Afghan expedition at second last page.
23. *Sujan*, 119 also 214.
24. *Ibid.*, 97-98, also 119.
25. *TAH.* 47a. This is the only other source to refer to this campaign but its account is very brief. Therefore, we have generally followed detailed description of *Sujan Charitra*, whose author, unlike that of the former, was obviously present on the spot.
26. *Sujan*, 98-103; *TAH.*, 47a.

ordered the impetuous Jawahar to dig up the trenches first and then resume the fight. But the next fortnight's desultory struggle brought no decisive results. Suraj Mal then closely inspected the southern and the western approaches to the fort. Discovering some dried up pockets along there, he shifted himself to the western side and sent Jawahar to the southern side and thus completely besieged Ghasira. Cannonade continued and a number of Jats fell victims daily. Yet in time the complete investment and the accompanying fight reduced the besieged to severe straits and they forced an unwilling Rao to send his envoy, Zalim Singh, to settle peace with Suraj Mal. The latter demanded Rupees 10 lakhs in cash and all the arms and munition of the fort as a precondition for raising the siege. Rao did not really mean to fulfil the exorbitant demands and yet he could not afford a total rejection either. He, therefore, practiced evasive tactics.

His dissimulation infuriated Suraj Mal and he resolved to get rid of Rao and capture Ghasira. The siege was pressed more vigorously. On 23rd April, 1753, (6th *Krishna Paksha in Vaishakh*) the valiant Jats under Paim Singh, Prithvi Singh, Raja Ram and Sayyid Mir Panah pushed forward, and despite the murderous gunfire, Ram and Sayyid Mir Panah pushed forward, and despite the murderous gunfire, succeeded in climbing up the fortwalls and opening the gates. Heavy was the carnage that the Jats suffered at Ghasira. Fifteen thousand of them perished but not before hopelessly thinning the enemy ranks as well. Yet Rao's forces could be destroyed but not his will. He went to the other fort, put his family to the sword, then rushed out with a hundred survivors and engaged Sheo Singh in a fierce combat. A bullet shot pierced through him, yet he bravely stood his ground till he was beheaded (along with a lone survivor) by Dalla Mev. Suraj Mal, thus, won a sanguinary contest. It was here at Ghasira that he received most pressing call for help, couched in rather flattering words, from the Wazir. He, therefore, left for Delhi, posting a Jat garrison under Amar Singh at Ghasira.[27]

THE JATS AND THE CIVIL WAR

Suraj Mal spent the night (30th April, 1752) at Faridabad. On 1st May (27th Jamadi II, 1166 A.H.) with a force of 15,000 horse and foot he joined his old friend and patron at his camp at Khizrabad (6 miles south of Delhi), having been earlier received by his son and then Mir

---

27. *Sujan*, 103-140, 146; *TAH*, 50b, 52a-52b, 106b; Also author's article, Ghasira Ke Yudha Ka Aitihasik Paryalochan' *Nagari Pracharini Patrika*, (2024), 505-512; For the Wazir's call only *Memoires des Jats*, 37; *Tawarikh-i-Hunud*, 21b; *Shakir*, 73; *Siyar*, III, 332; *Tarikh-i-Muzaffari in Elliot*, VIII, 320; *Hadiqat*, 136.

Atish, Shuja-ud-Daula.[28] Next day, the Wazir went to the nearby Jat camp and held consultations with Suraj Mal.[29] Safdar Jang's fortune was in the ascendant when Suraj Mal had left for Ghasira, but much had happened in the meantime to put it slowly but steadily on a downward scale. Due to his own indiscretion as well as the ingenuity of his adversaries Safdar Jang lost control over the palace and the Capital and he was obliged to leave his Delhi residence (March, 1753). He was still in a fairly commanding position but gradually he lost that advantage by his indecision and inactivity primarily due to his waiting for "obtaining assistance from Suraj Mal", then entangled at Ghasira.[30] Nevertheless, "Every day that passed told against him and in favour of his enemies." However, with each day passing, the strength of Safdar Jang dwindled and that of his opponents increased. While he was incurring huge expenses in feeding an inactive camp, his enemies, especially Imad-ul-Mulk with his added resources (amounting to Rs. 2,70,00,000), energetic leadership and great cunning in exploiting religious feelings, not only raised a strong army of his own but also gradually seduced a big number (totalling 23,000 men) of Safdar Jang's men. Apart from the hired Maratha[31] and Rohilla allies,[32] quite a number of other partisan chiefs (Rajput, Gujar and Billochi) later joined the steadily increasing enemy ranks. Added to these odds was Safdar Jang's own lack of good generalship.[33] It was against this background that Suraj Mal was to fight under his banners during the coming war.

To resume, three days after the coming of Suraj Mal, the ex-Mir Bakhshi, Salabat Khan, joined the Wazir. Taunting him with the charge of cowardice, he incited the wavering Safdar Jang to launch a vigorous offensive. Suraj Mal supported him. Next day Safdar Jang haughtily demanded the expulsion of Intizam and Imad, failing which he threatened the Emperor to attack their houses and the imperial fort itself. The Emperor responded by dismissing Shuaj-ud-Daula and ordering the completion of the trenches on the river edge. Though forbidding an open attack, Safdar Jang now ordered Suraj Mal and Rajendra Giri Gosain to

---

28. *TAH.* 52a, 52b; *Sujan*, 146; *Memoires des Jats*, 37, wrongly mentions about 8 to 10 thousand *Jats* being under him; *Bayan-i-Waqai in Elliot*, VIII, 134; *Shakir* 73; *Siyar*, III, 332; Also see *Hadiqat*, 136 and 171.
29. *Sujan*, 146-147.
30. *Bayan-i-Waqai in Elliot*, VIII, 135, 134; *Aftabnuma*, 357; *Ahwal*, 119.
31. *Imad* sent his Vakil, Mahbub Ram to call Melharrao Holkar from Aurangabad but Suraj Mal's men interrupted him on his way (near Palwal). *TAH.*, 50b.
32. Suraj Mal advised Safdar Jang to intercept the incoming Najib with 15,000 Rohillas. But Safdar Jang's efforts in this direction did not bear fruits. *Nur*, 8b-9a.
33. For details of Safdar's lapses and difficulties see Srivastava, *Oudh*, 223ff; Sarkar, *Fall*, I, 471ff.

attack and plunder old Delhi, especially the grain market. If *Sujan Charitra* is to be relied upon, Suraj Mal had earlier tried to dissuade him from this, pleading that it would leave an indelible stigma over the Wazir's (as also his own) forehead.[34] Safdar Jang, however, calculated that in consideration of the interests of the city populace the Emperor would not carry matters to extremes and would ultimately bend down. Therefore, he stuck to his decision of "political" loot as a device which was short of the greater horrors of a mighty assault.[35]

Consequently, the Jats, the Nagas and the Wazir Qizelbash's soldiers commenced the sack of Delhi on 9th May, 1753. *Bayan-i-Waqai* adds that Salabat Khan also engaged himself in robbing and plundering the old city.[36] The plunderers looted the eastern part of the city near Lal Darwaza and the innocent victims, largely poor and middle class people, destitute of their property, were driven to take shelter elsewhere. Next morning, Sayyidwara, Panchkoi, Abdullah Nagar, Tarkaganj and the areas around Bijal mosque were ravaged. The plunderers maltreated and mercilessly sacked the multitudes, demolished their houses and rendered Churnia and Wakilpura "lampless". Every day, the Jats and Qizilbashes appeared in one or the other part of old Delhi. Great consternation prevailed in the city. Terror stricken victims scampered through and sought refuge in the new city, carrying with them whatever was possible. In about a week's time the old city was completely ravaged and destroyed.

The ferocity of the Jats long outlived their misdeed in the memory of the local people under the name of "Jat gardi". Whatever the circumstances and order (issued to them), the cruelty which they perpetrated deserves severe condemnation as has been done by most of the authorities.[37] What a misfortune of the Indian Capital! Within short span of merely two decades (1739-1761) "it fell a victim to nine gardis". It was sacked in all seven times by the two invading Emperors, Nadir Shah and Ahmad Abdali, eight times by Najib-ud-Daula, eight times by the different Maratha stalwarts, four times at the behest of the Wazir Imad-ul-Mulk and once each by Jeta Gujar and Bahadur Khan Billoch.[38] As if it were not enough, in the meantime the Jats in company with others added one more number to this already long list of Delhi's sack.

---

34. *Sujan*, 147-148.
35. Srivastava, *Oudh*, 230 and 232; According to Shah Walliullah (*Shah*, 2) then residing in Delhi, Safdar Jang himself indulged in the loot.
36. *Bayan-i-Waqai in Elliot*, VIII, 135; 136-137; *Shah* 2.
37. *TAH.*, 53b-55a; *Sujan*, 149-165 (hyperbolic account); *Bayan-i-Waqai in Elliot*, VIII, 136-137; *Shah*, 2; *Imad*, 96; *Shakir*, 74; *Memoires des Jats*, 38; *Siyar*, III 334; D.C.; *Aftabnuma*, 359; *Ahwal*, 119; *Tarikh-i-Muzaffari*, in Elliot, VIII, 320; *Tawarikh-i-Hunud*, 21b.
38. Gupta, *Panipat*, 321ff.

One wonders if it were the same Suraj Mal and his Jats who, on several occasions both before and after 1753 (with the lone exception in 1757), providing refuge to scores of thousands of the same Delhi populace, protected them from the rapacious cruelty of others, who earned a name for letting live in their midst "helpless, afflicted and indigent people"[39] and who were to spend lakhs of Rupees in just one instance, looking after thousands of refugees from Panipat.

This outrage broke all relations between the Emperor and Safdar Jang. He dismissed the latter from the Wizarat and appointed Intizam-ud-Daulah as Wazir instead. The property and houses of the ex-Wazir's followers and all those suspected of having sympathies with him, were plundered. The Emperor sent letters to different *zamindars* and chiefs asking them to join him against Safdar Jang.[40] The Emperor and Safdar Jang's opponents attempted to wean away Suraj Mal, sometimes with promises of high honour and sometimes with threats of vengeance. But the faithful Jat treated both "with equal scorn".[41]

On the other side, in retaliation for his dismissal, Safdar Jang enthroned a rival Emperor, entitled, Akbar Adil Shah, making himself his Wazir and Salabat the Mir Bakhshi. Suraj Mal concurred with the move.[42] Amidst daily skirmishes Safdar Jang wrested Kohtila of Firoz Shah (3 miles south of new Delhi) from the hands of the imperialists (night of 17th May). Ismail Khan mounted guns on it and opened fire. Some shots fell inside the fort, but the Jats in the royal service stood their ground. This enthused other Mughal gunners and they charged guns, placed at Lal Darwaza, causing some damage to Kohtila. Ismail now pushed forward his trenches and in order to capture Intizam's house, he laid out a mine which he fired on 5th June. At this time the Jats and Gosains rushed at the enemy and their victory appeared in sight when Najib and others enforced the imperialists and they pushed them back. Thereupon, 5,000 Jat mounted matchlockmen and Qizilbashes advanced to restore the fight, while the imperialists sent yet another succour under Hafiz Bakhtawar, Sadal Khan and others to Najib. The fight was long and bloody but remained indecisive. The artillery duel continued all night but about 4 a.m. Ismail evacuated Kohitila, which was occupied by the imperialists. They now opened fire on Safdar Jang's tents, which forced him to move southwards towards Tal Katora (4 miles from the city).[43]

---

39. *Mirat*, 893.
40. Srivastava, *Oudh*, 231-232.
41. Qanungo. *Jats*, 85; *Memoires des Jats*, 38 footnote.
42. *TAH.*, 54b; *Sujan*, 148, 149; *Bayan-i-Waqai in Elliot*, VIII, 135.
43. *TAH.*, 55b-57b; *Bayan-i-Waqai in Elliot*, VIII, 138; *Nur*, 9a-9b, 10b-11b.

The Jats and Qizilbashes, however, led sporadic attacks daily on this or that part of the city but the imperialists would rush in and restore the outposts. In the evening of 12th June, an action took place at Idgah in which many Jat soldiers and some of their officers were slain. Yahya Khan Mir Munshi, who was posted there, had relations with Suraj Mal. He was, therefore, arrested and his property was confiscated.[44]

On 14th June, Safdar Jang suffered a stunning blow in the death of his valiant commander Rajendra Giri Gosain at the battle of Tal Katora. Early on that day, the Gosain, Ismail Khan and the Jats under Surati Ram Gour attacked all the enemy trenches. The Jats and the Qizilbashes, bearing the brunt of this charge, inflicted heavy losses upon the opposite Bandakhashi and Maratha troops. Their victory appeared in sight when Imad-ul-Mulk rushed in with reignforcements and after a great battle he repulsed the enemy. Amidst the shower of the muskets Rajendra Giri and Surati Ram were wounded. The former succumbed to his wounds next day. The death of this brave monk so much shocked Safdar Jang that for full 10 days he remained completely inactive.[45]

Safdar Jang had as good as lost the contest by now. His falling morale and general indifference depleted his following further. Even his high officials and near relatives, like Sher Jang, crossed over, while the strength of the imperialists, as a result of the desertions from his side and fresh arrivals, swelled to 1,00,000 men. With the master lying heart-broken, and his strength badly reduced, and the jubilant enemy getting additions everyday, the utter hopelessness of Safdar Jang's cause could not have remained a secret to Suraj Mal. And he was too practical a man to invite ruin. Therefore, he became anxious for honourable peace, even though he neither crossed over nor drew back from Safdar's side. He sent his agents (end of June) to the Wazir, Intizam, to negotiate pardon and peace but on the condition that he be left in possession of all his territories. The Wazir responded and sent his man to settle peace with Suraj Mal. At the same time the Emperor prompted Raja Devi Dutta to send Ram Nath to Suraj Mal. He spent the night at the Jat camp and then came back with the Jat chief's petitions addressed to the Emperor. However, in the ensuing discussion, Imad-ul-Mulk, who stood for a fight to the end, opposed the matter and thus the peace move fell for the present.[46]

Meanwhile, desultory warfare continued. A fierce battle occurred on 1st July in which artillery played the leading role. One of the Jat

---

44. *TAH.*, 58a.
45. *TAH.*, 58b-59a; *Sujan*, 172-173; D.C.; *Gulistan*, 49; *Gul*, 73.
46. *TAH* , 60a-60b; Srivastava, *Oudh*, 236.

Bakhshi's, Gokul Ram, was furious as his brother, Suratı Ram, had been wounded in the preceding encounter. He, therefore, directed a determined assault in junction with the Nagas, and worsted his enemies, putting many of them to flight. But in the process he was fatally struck with a ball. "Continue the pursuit", was the dying wish of the gallant Jat commander. Yet shocked as the Jats were by this tragedy, they could not carry their advantage of its logical conclusion. Victory thus eluded Safdar Jang once again.[47]

Suraj Mal advised Safdar Jang to withdraw further south as a strategic move to draw out the enemy in the open, away from the safe refuge of the city and the fort. Safdar Jang agreed and moved to Chirgh-i-Dilli and then on 16th July to Tilpat (12 miles south of Delhi). As they retreated, Imad moved forward upto Khizrabad. The imperialists sacked the adjoining areas, dragging away money, property and women. On 25th July, the Jats under Jawahar Singh, Balram and Raja Gujar attacked the Rohillas, then besieging the fortress of Garhi Maidan. A long and fierce fight ensued wherein the rival combatants displayed their characteristic cool and defiant valour. Ultimately, the Jats emerged victorious. They routed the Rohillas and put them to flight, capturing all their guns and arms. Despite being in an overall position gaining this defeat "highly contorted Imad with anger." The very next day he went to Delhi and appealed to the Emperor to take command in person, so that matters could be expedited. But, Ahmad Shah refused it on the advice of the Wazir.[48]

A few days later Suraj Mal entrenched himself between Badarpur and Sarai Bakhtawar Khan. On 30th July (29th Ramzan), his troops appeared near the Badarpur canal, skirmished with the imperialists and then retired. After a lull, on 19th August (19th Shawwal) the Jats, the Qizilbashes and the Nagas issued forth and fierce though scattered, fighting occurred at several points between Tughlaqabad and the Yamuna, in which the Jats and the Rohillas signalized themselves. At one place, a Jat contingent under Sheo Singh grappled with the Marathas. Initially, the former gained the upper hand, but Sheo Singh received a spear thrust in his thigh. Soon the Marathas rallied forth and the Jats were repulsed. Next morning, Safdar Jang left Faridabad and in the next few days fell back south of Ballamgarh. All this while, Imad kept on pushing forward, and reaching north of Faridabad, decided to remove the thorn, the fort of Ballamgarh. Meanwhile, some auxiliaries, and the imperial artillerymen clamouring for their arrears of salary drew back from their posts. At this Safdar Jang reassembled his men and

47. *Sujan*, 174-176; *TAH.*, 60a-61b; Srivastava, *Oudh*, 237.
48. *TAH.*, 66a, 64a; *Sujan*, 176-181; cf. *Bayan-i-Waqai in Elliot*, VIII, 139.

launched an attack, but in vain. On 7th and 8th September, 5 to 6 thousand Jats readvanced upto Faridabad. They completely cut off the enemy supplies through their intermittent attacks, though in the process they lost one of their Sardars, Muhkam Singh. This turn in the situation "despaired" Imad and he again appealed to the Emperor for help but with no better results than before. Thinking that he alone could not crush his enemies, Imad sought help from the Holkar and Scinde (then in south), promising them one crore of Rupees, over and above the governorship of Awadh and Allahabad assured to the Marathas earlier.[49]

Meanwhile, the Wazir and the Emperor, dreading Imad's capability and his rapidly growing prestige, became eager for peace. Hence, on the one hand they wrote to Madho Singh to come and help to establish peace, while on the other once more readily responded to Suraj Mal's renewed overtures. The very day when Imad met the Emperor (12th September), Suraj Mal contacted the Wazir, promising to pay a few lakhs of Rupees for making peace. On 14th September, Intizam sent his Vakil Lutfulla Beg to Suraj Mal and the two together met Safdar Jang. Meanwhile, taking advantage of the helplessness of hard core Imad, the forces of Suraj Mal and Safdar Jang, proceeding forward, attacked and defeated the imperialists at Sarai Bakhtawar Khan, Badarpur and a few other places. About a week later, Safdar Jang's troops attacked the royal trenches of Bakhtawar Khan from the south, while the Jats (who had been sent upto Badarpur to escort back Lutfullah Beg along with Safdar Jang's envoys, Raja Lakshmi Narain, Raja Jugal Kishore and others) from the north. A fierce fight raged all night till the Bikaner and Maratha (under Antaji) reinforced Bakhtawar Khan and the assailants were driven back. This treacherous attack justifiably bewildered the Emperor and his courtiers. Die hard elements got an opportunity and peace talks were cut short once more (22nd September - 24th Zi-Qad), despite the all out efforts of the Wazir.[50]

On 29th September (1st Zil-Hijja) was fought the last notable battle of the series at the tank of Faridabad. Safdar Jang and Suraj Mal decided to launch a vigorous offensive on the imperialists before fresh troops under Imad could reach them. Keeping Jawahar Singh (who had just re-joined his father) in the rear, both these moved on and amdist cannonade, overpowered the right wing of the royal trenches, killing many Marathas. However, Hafiz Bakhtawar, Abu Turab and others led successive re-inforcements to restore the struggle. In the end came Imad and Najib with yet another reinforcement. Displaying exemplary

---

49. *TAH.*, 67a-67b, 69b-71b; *Sujan*, 181-193; D.C., Srivastava, *Oudh*, 239.
50. *TAH.*, 72b-74b; *D.C.*

courage on this occasion, Imad drove his elephant amidst his enemies and then after a severe contest, in which both sides suffered heavily, he succeeded in worsting the Jats. Ismail Khan and Sada Ram (a Jat general) were among those wounded. Imad pushing his enemies further south, occupied Najesar and opened fire on nearby Ballamgarh while Najib occupied Sihi and along with the Marathas he plundered the Jat populace.[51]

A few days later, Madho Singh arrived as per the Emperor's orders. By now every one except Imad, had become positively keen to end the war. Apart from the huge expenditure in the futile contest the possibility of Imad's junction with the Marathas increasingly worried the Wazir, the Emperor, Safdar Jang as also Suraj Mal. The latter had tried to make peace through the Wazir but had failed due to the opposition of Imad. Now about the middle of October, he opened direct negotiations with Imad through Najib. Imad now relented and directed Najib and Bahadur Khan Billoch and Ajit Singh to negotiate with Suraj Mal and Balram Jat, at a place midway between Ballamgarh and the royal trenches. Suraj Mal wanted status quo *per ante* to be maintained, namely, that he be allowed to retain his present dominions and Safdar Jang the governorship of Allahabad and Awadh. He also offered to pay a few lakhs of Rupees as tribute. To these propositions Imad did not agree. Instead he asked Suraj Mal to surrender all the *mahals* over and above those originally belonging to his father. In case of Safdar Jang he replied that in place of the above two provinces (which actually he wanted to keep for himself) Ahmadabad, Gujrat could be given to him. The Bakhshi added that peace could be made only if he paid a big sum as tribute and indemnity, failing that war would continue. Excessive severity of Imad's demands thus disrupted the negotiations once again.[52]

However, Imad had to retrace his steps very soon due to the underhand policy of his rival, the Wazir (backed by the Emperor). The Emperor's plan of making terms behind his (Bakshi's) back, leaked out. This upset the Bakshi, who, wished to take the credit himself and he opened a dialogue with Suraj Mal. But Intizam stole a march on him. He arranged that the Emperor should go to Madho Singh's camp and there conclude peace with Suraj Mal. Accordingly on 25th October (27th Zil-Hijja) Ahmad Shah, later joined by Intizam, went to Khizrabad. After offering his own customary presents, on behalf of Suraj Mal, Madho Singh presented 9 *asharfis* to the Emperor and requested him to pardon that chief. The Jat Vakil, offering 1 *mohar*, appealed for the same. The Emperor accepted the presents, pardoned

---

51. *TAH.*, 75b-76a; *Sujan* (193-201) wrongly assigns victory to Suraj Mal in this contest; *D.C*; *Akhbarat*, 25th September, Peshwa Daftar Poona (in *R.S.L.* Vo. XXIX, part II, p. 73) incorrectly asserts that Ballamgarh fell to the imperialists.
52. *TAH.*, 78a-78b.

Suraj Mal and returned to Delhi. The Wazir "greatly rejoiced" that the peace (with Suraj Mal) was not made by Imad. From his camp (near Ballamgarh) Suraj Mal went to the camp of Madho Singh. There he met and presented *asharfis* to the Wazir who was waiting there by previous arrangement. The Wazir later left but Suraj Mal and Aqibat Mahmud (the agent of Imad) stayed on in the Raja's camp for that night and the next five days.[53] There is every reason to believe that Suraj Mal shared in the efforts for securing an honourable pardon for his old friend, Safdar Jang as well.[54] On 1st November (4th Muharram), Suraj Mal returned to his camp having earlier paid a visit to the Emperor.[55] Peace with Safdar Jang was also made (7th November) in the same secret way.

J.N. Sarkar seems to be a little ungenerous in his estimate to the Jats' part in the Civil War, from the viewpoint of Safdar Jang. He says that the sack of Delhi by the Jats "alienated the people of the Capital and its environs" from Safdar Jang and that "the faithful Jat allies" .. failed to turn a single field" in Safdar Jang's favour.[56] We have already examined the sack of Delhi in all its aspects. As regards the latter issue, the Jat triumph in the battle of Garhi Maidan seems to have escaped his attention. To cite one more example, the Jats beat the imperialists in the campaign of 1st July, but it was the chance killing of their Bakhshi in the last moment that deprived them of a clear victory. All the same, their performance in this as also in most other fields does not endorse the underlying purport of the above view, if we only keep in mind the kind of master and the circumstances under whom the Jats had to fight. Valour and courage the Jats never lacked, but they could not make up the deficiency in numbers. Safdar Jang's advantage of 15,000 Jats was nearly neutralized the day (early in June) Najib with 15,000 and Jeta Gujar with another 2,000 joined the opposite side. And then it was Safdar Jang with his poor or at best average generalship, accompanied by his subsequent despondency and unending desertions (totalling 23,000), that was pitted against the gallant and shrewd captain Imad with his big numbers (83,000 over and above 17,000 mentioned). In the context, it would be futile to expect a miracle from Suraj Mal and his men. As seen above, in more than one campaign the Jats gained initial advantage but a stream of reinforcements followed eventually turning the scales against them. But

---

53. *TAH.*, 81b-83a; S.P.D. XXVII 83; *Rajwade*, I, 17; cf. *Sujan*, 201; *Memoires des Jats*, and *Tawarikh-i-Hunud*, though dealing exclusively with the *Jats*, has inexplicably avoided all the details of Suraj Mal's part in the Civil War.
54. Francklin (*Shah-Aulum*, 3) says that Intizam pursuaded the Emperor to accept "the mediation of the Jauts in favour of Mansur Ali". Also see Sharma, *Jaipur*, 176; Qanungo, *Jats*, 86.
55. *TAH.*, 83a-83b.
56. Sarkar, *Fall*, I, 152.

for Suraj Mal what would have been the ultimate fate of the lone Safdar Jang with his inalienable handicaps is not difficult to visualize. This negative measure in itself may sufficiently reveal the real importance of Suraj Mal's arms to Safdar Jang, even though that chief positively failed in serving his ally to victory. It is true that after the war had been in progress for sometime, Suraj Mal desired peace, but only in a gloomy situation and even then not at the cost of his friend. Safdar Jang's relatives and top officials deserted him in his distress but Suraj Mal faithfully stood by him and while carrying on negotiations (with Imad), he did not forget to do his worth to safeguard the interests of his ally as well.[57]

Parting company with each other must have saddened the hearts of the old friends (Safdar Jang and Suraj Mal), who had done so much for each other in the past. While bidding farewell (c. 17th November, at Mathura), Safdar Jang gave a splendid '*khilat*' to Suraj Mal and the latter provided his "great friend" (grand Ami) the ex-Wazir with the accessories -- "horses, camels, carriages, and other similarities in great quantity" -- for his homeward march.[58]

Suraj Mal had usurped the royal territories and also opposed both the imperial Wazir and the Mir Bakhshi but never before had he waged a war against the Emperor as he did while helping the former Wazir. This was a new development and ran contrary to his usual show of loyalty to the Mughal throne. Rebellion is always a rebellion. Yet it is worthwhile to keep in mind that the struggle of Safdar Jang, and impliedly of Suraj Mal also, was really against Intizam and Imad and only ostensibly against the Emperor. Safdar Jang had said, "my enemies are Intizam and Imad and my business is with them". The Emperor, who was neither "his own master" nor "acted according to his own judgement", was merely a cipher. In setting himself to crush the Emperor's rebels, Imad outwardly showed himself to be the most obedient servant. But reality took only a few months to dawn upon the Emperor (as also the new Wazir) and then he himself sought to pardon and preserve his rebels as a means to counteract his Bakhshi. It is interesting to note here that even in their rebellion, Safdar Jang and Suraj Mal did not go beyond what we have already narrated, but Imad, while posing loyalty, was destined to put two sovereigns to death. Whatever be the technical nuances, the fact is that the same Emperor and the then Wazir had begun to draw close to the rebels and vice versa, even before their rebellion ended.

57. K.R. Qanungo (*Jats*, 86) observes, "The Jat Rajah refused to sheathe his sword unless the Emperor restored the vice royalties of *Oudh* and Allahabad.. to Safdar Jang."

58. *Memoires des Jats*, 38-39; Herein it contradicts the baseless rumour then afloat that the Jats captured treasures of the discomfited Safdar Jang. It is, however, likely as *Tawarikh-i-Hunud*, 21b would suggest that Safdar Jang resigned to Suraj Mal booty captured during the war, as a means to defray the expenses of the Jat contingent.

IX

The Jats in the Vortex of Hostile Forces (I) (1753-1757)

Prince Suraj Mal's alliance of friendship with Safdar Jang was not an unmixed blessing. If it contributed to his fortunes and status, it also entangled him in the precarious court politics. Moreover, his wealth tempted the greedy, while his strength caused resentment to the ambitious and the aggrieved alike. All this coupled with his persisting ambitions worked to implicate him in tremendous trouble and yet, with his political sagacity, grim determination and courage he steered clear of it, baffling all his enemies. We shall now take up these developments.

IMAD-MARATHA ATTACK ON THE JATS (NOVEMBER 1753-MAY 1754): ITS CAUSES

The Civil War, particularly its closing stages contained the seeds of portentous developments. Hardly two weeks had elapsed since its formal termination when Khandoji Holkar came to Delhi (21st November) at the order of his father (who hearing about peace himself went to Jaipur) "to join the Bakhshi in his campaign against Suraj Mal"[1] and the next week, operations were resumed against the Jats.

It is clear that the Bakhshi was furious at Suraj Mal and his men for their help to Safdar Jang.[2] However, this alone cannot fully explain his attack on them. There were other deeper factors involved in it which have not been taken notice of. We have seen how the Wazir in league with Suraj Mal had in the last minute deprived him of the credit of settling peace. The decisive military triumph and the diplomatic success were both denied to him. Moreover, he could never relish Suraj Mal drifting close to his arch rival, the Wazir, as became evident during the closing stages of the Civil War. The Wazir and the Bakhshi knew that

1. *TAH*, 88a, 94a; Sardesai, *Marathas*, II, 390-391.
2. *Shakir* 76; *Siyar*, III, 335; Dow, *Hindostan* II, 323; *Francklin*, 3; Qanungo, *Jats*, 86; *Tarikh-i-Majaffari* (in Elliot, VIII, 321) says that Imad wanted to punish Suraj Mal for the part he had taken with Safdar Jang in plundering Delhi.

Suraj Mal was then the only person capable of containing the latter (the Bakhshi).[3] Hence, the Wazir befriended and supported him (along with Safdar Jang),[4] while the Bakhshi was out to destory him. The Wazir scrupulously avoided annoying the Jat Prince. The way he refused to entertain the entreaties to regain Ghasira by his (the Jat's) enemy's son, Fateh Singh, fully bears it out.[5] The Wazir all through wished Suraj Mal's power to remain intact as a bulwark against Imad's ambitions and was, therefore, opposed to the Jat war[6] (As we shall see, the news of the Jats discomfiture grieved him). Imad smelt it but he calculated otherwise. The powerful Marathas were already on his side, and now only Suraj Mal remained to be "extirpated"[7] to clear his way to exclusive power, if possible to the very Mughal throne.[8]

Side by side, the proposed Jat campaign could also help to solve the appalling financial crisis. The treasury was empty and the starving soldiery persistently rioted to get their dues cleared.[9] The Jats had usurped the Crown lands and Imad's own jagir of Faridabad. As such, he intended to get them vacated, realize rents and impose large tribute on the prosperous Jat state and thereby make payments to the soldiers. Imad devised a novel plan. He readily entertained the pretentions of Muhkam Singh, the inveterate enemy of Suraj Mal. On 11th December, 1753, Muhkam Singh supplicated (through Aqibat Mahamud) Imad's favour to regain his patrimony. On 24th, he went to Imad's residence from his camp at Khizrabad. Imad found this man most suitable to his designs against Suraj Mal and he lent him his support.[10] He insisted on the Emperor to accompany him, suppress the Jats south of Delhi and collect the rents or else restore Muhkam to his ancestral *zamindari* in lieu of Rupees two crores, which that chief was willing to pay. The Emperor at first desired Muhkam Singh to forthwith pay five crores in cash apart from the '*nalbandi* at the rate of seven annas per Rupee.[11] But later he reconciled to two crores.[12] The execution of this plan was as difficult as its formulation was easy. Yet it enabled Imad and the Marathas to utilize the services of their protege against Suraj Mal.

3. cf. Sarkar, *Fall*, I, 531-532.
4. Srivastava, *Oudh*; 247.
5. *TAH*; 106b. We have no information whether or not he was approached for help by the more desperate Muhkam Singh as well but in case he was, he must have been turned away.
6. *TAH.*, 106b.
7. *Ibid.*, 106b; *Mirat*, 763.
8. *TAH.*, 95b, 108b; *Siyar*, III, 335.
9. *TAH.*, 87a, 88a-b, 102b-103b, 105a, 107a, 110a, 113b.
10. *TAH.*, 94b, 98b.
11. *Ibid.*, 102b-103a.
12. *Ibid.*, 131b, also 103b.

Liquidating the State debts by dispossessing the Jat usurpers and realizing dues from them was a commendable proposition, if Imad had only the pious intention to serve the Empire. The fact that he himself misappropriated the proceeds from the *khalisa* and *sarf-i-khas* and even the amount (15 lakhs) given to him (by the Emperor) for paying the soldiers and yet incited them to daily riots against the Emperor and the Wazir,[13] shows that while emphasizing the ill effects of the Jats acquisitions, he was merely invoking a legal ground to settle a personal score with Suraj Mal. We have no proof that Imad displayed the same ardour in restitution of lands under the other aggressors. It seems that the Emperor saw through the game and whatever his outward posture, inwardly on the advice of the Wazir, he kept back[14] from Imad during the Jat war as he had done during the Civil war also.

Yet despite all his grievances, Imad with his crippled resources alone might not have dared challenge the might of the Jats but for the arrival and concurrence of his Maratha allies. Prone to lending their sword to any higher bidder, the Marathas had added incentive to serve Imad, whom they found to be a man of their own liking.[15] They had, however, their own designs against Suraj Mal. To plunder rich lands and extort money from others had been a perennial feature of their policy. As such the growing riches and general prosperity of the Jat state naturally formed a big attraction for, what a contemporary calls, these "professional spoilers".[16] To their insatiable greed was added the provocation offered to them by Suraj Mal.[17] We know that more than once had the Bharatpur contingents joined the imperial banners in a bid to oppose their advance. Only a couple of months back Suraj Mal, in concert with the Rajputs, had attempted to form a joint front against them, offering to bear his share of expenses of the war to drive them out from the north.[18] Again, in November, 1753 he entered into an understanding with the visiting Jaipur ruler, against them.[19] Obviously, this anti-Maratha policy of the Jats deeply annoyed them, even though this in itself was the logical corollary of their (Maratha's) own doings. Malharrao Holkar's sarcastic remark before the Jat envoy, (Rup RamKatari) that he had come (against the Jats) partly at his own

13. *TAH.*, 103a-104b, 110a-110b, 113b, 120a.
14. cf. *TAH*, 133a, 92a, 92b.
15. *Ibid.*, 88a, 93a, 94a, 98a.
16. cf. *Memoires des Jats,* 39.
17. Contra see Qanungo, *Jats*, 39.
18. See Ch. VIII, f.n.3.
19. From Delhi Madho Singh alongwith Jawahar Singh went to Kama (17th November) wherefrom Badan Singh led him to Deeg. Having discussed the Maratha problem with Suraj Mal, he went to Jaipur. *Sujan* 202-203; *TAH.*, 89h; Sarkar, *Fall*, I, 519; Contra see, *Memoires des Jats*, 48.

bidding and partly at that of the Emperor (impliedly Imad)[20] fully bears it out. Suraj Mal had already attained much power and if he was not crushed right now he might prove dangerous later on, so the Marathas seem to have argued.

This apart, the importunities of Muhkam Singh also tended the Marathas to the same end. Hardly been in touch with the Marathas since at least 1753,[21] he entered the service and won the favour of Malhar Holkar.[22] In 1753, a Maratha Sardar requested the Peshwa to send him and his brother Zul Qaran a consolatory letter asking them to meet the Marathas when they came to the Jat country and then their "problems would be solved".[23] Yet another contributory factor of the Maratha attack as Malhar Holkar gave it out,[24] was their anger over Suraj Mal's killing of Rao Bahadur Singh Bargujar of Ghasira.

Thus, in the light of the above analysis, it becomes clear that irrespective of Imad, the Marathas themselves would have brought sooner or later their force to bear upon the Jats. Fortunately, they had in their master, the Bakhshi, a man also determined to wreck his vengeance upon the same people. The operations against the Jats were thus undertaken by Imad and the Marathas after "perfect concord",[25] as is also borne out by the statement of Khandoji mentioned in the beginning.

From a close perusal of the line of their campaign it would appear that Imad and his allies attempted to catch hold of Suraj Mal from two sides, Imad and Khandoji attacking from the less guarded north, while the main Maratha army from the west. In going to Jaipur, first Ragunathrao not only meant to collect dues from the Rajputs but also to separate Madho Singh from Suraj Mal. Till his arrival Imad and Khandoji were to attack the northern possessions of Suraj Mal, who for fear of the Maratha hordes being in his rear was not supposed to spare sufficient troops for their defence. Annihilation of the Jat power could not have been better planned.[26]

---

20. *Sujan*, 214.
21. *S.P.D.* XXX, 134.
22. *Tawarikh-i-Hunud*, 19b.
23. *S.P.D.* XXVII, 83.
24. *Sujan*, 214
25. *Amira*, 51; *Akhbar-i-Muhabat* in Elliot, VIII, 384; *Tarikh-i-Muzaffari* (in Elliot, VIII, 321), goes to the extent of saying that Imad was "urged on by the Marathas" to attack Suraj Mal. G.S. Sardesai (*Marathas*, II, 390-391) says that the Holkar sent Khandoji and Gangadhar Tatya to Imad to "arrange plans for the (Jat) campaign". Having reached Delhi they "decided to (immediately) conduct a war"; *Ibrat*, 15b.
26. Imad-Maratha-Jat war which began in November, 1753 and continued till May 1754 was one long event. It would be improper to study campaigns at Mewat or Aligarh in isolation from those at Deeg or Kumbher. For the former as much formed the part of Bharatpur State as the latter did.

In the last week of November 1753,[27] Suraj Mal despatched his agent, Rup Ram Katari, to the Maratha camp at Jaipur to know their real intentions and strength and if possible to negotiate an honourable settlement. Malher Holkar demanded two crores, but the envoy offered him merely four lakhs. The Holkar rejected it and when he repeated his threat to destroy the Jats, the envoy quipped, "you cannot assault the Jat forts even with the help of four lakh men".[28] When the talks were still going on, Rup Ram informed Suraj Mal about the Maratha determination "to force a war" adding that he should, therefore, duly prepare himself.[29] Accordingly Raja Badan Singh called his courtiers for consultation at Deeg. All of them preferred an honourable war to an ignominious surrender. Preparations for war were taken up with added vigour. Assisted by his brave compatriots, Suraj Mal provided strong defence to the main forts of Deeg, Bharatpur, Kumbher and Wair because ultimately the fate of the Jats was to be decided there.[30]

ATTACK ON THE NORTH AND EAST

The departure of the Jat Vakil to Jaipur almost coincided with the commencement of Imad-Maratha offensive in Mewat. On 26th November, 1753 (29th Muharram, 1167 A.H.), Imad sent his chief agent, Aqibat Mahmud Khan, with 500 Badakhshi and 20000 Maratha soldiers to reconquer Faridabad, which was in his *Jagir* but had been in Balram's occupation for some time. On being demanded revenue and tribute, Balram became ready for a fight. Imad then sent 700 additional troops and 30 pieces of high artillery and rockets. After some resistance Balram decided to submit. Hence, he met Aqibat, presented him *asharfis* and promised to clear the dues.[31] Aqibat sent his men to Suraj Mal also demanding the *peshkash* due from him but that chief, "pround of his beg forces", ignored him. At the same time, Aqibat found the peasants at Palwal evasive in paying the revenue. They pretended that Balram might demand it again. Santosh Rai, the *Qanungo* of the place (Who on account of his expulsion by Balram has become his mortal foe) asked Aqibat that unless he killed Balram he would fail to recapture the district. A *thanahdar* despatched by him to Fatehpur was expelled by the local peasants who stood by Balram.

---

27. *Sujan* (203-204) does not give the date. But since it puts Balram's murder (29th November, 1753) just "a few days" after Rup Ram's departure, we infer that the latter left early in the last week of November.
28. For details see *Sujan* 203-204, 206-207, 215, 226; Sarkar, *Fall*, I, 520; Following *Bakhar*, a later source Qanungo (*Jats*, 88) and Pande (*Bharatpur*, 58) make a doubtful assertion that Malhar demanded one crore while Rup Ram promised 40 lakhs and that Suraj Mal haughtily sent cannon-balls and gun powder to the Marathas.
29. *Sujan*, 206.
30. For details see *Sujan*, 217ff.; Also *Memoires des Jats*, 39.
31. *TAH*, 89a-90a.

On 29th November (2nd Safar), Aqibat, therefore, returned to a plain at Ballamgarh and sent for Balram. He arrived along with his one or two sons, his *diwan* and 250 *sawars* and foot.[32]

The authorities differ regarding the manner of Balram's murder. The Court historian says that Aqibat insisted on Balram to pay the promised tribute, saying that Imad had made the peace for him (although it was incorrect) and that Imad was reproaching him for the delay in collections. Balram replied that he had not brought "the money in his pocket" which he had promised to give only after collecting the rent and that if he (Aqibat) wanted to wrest this tract he would have to fight for that. Aqibat got displeased over this reply and heated arguments followed. When Balram put his hand to his sword, the Badakhshis under Aftab Khan fell upon him and killing him along with his son, the *diwan* and nine others, losing two of their colleagues in the process.[33] *Sujan Charitra* on the other hand says that Aqibat sent his agent to Balram, taking most solemn oaths to lull his suspicion. When the Jat arrived Aqibat spoke "sweet words" but the assassins, hiding close by, fell upon and cut the heads of Balram and his sons.[34] Whatever the truth, both these sources agree that Balram's family, fled to Suraj Mal. Aqibat then got hold of the fort along with its artillery, treasures and other goods. The name of Ballamgarh was changed to Nizamgarh and the head of Balu was ordered to be exposed on a pillar near Faridabad, so that it might serve as a deterrent to other rebels. The news of the fall of Balram and his fort made the Wazir "unhappy".[35]

Getting the news of the death of Balram, Suraj Mal sent a message to Jawahar Singh, then at Deeg, to call up troops and proceed towards Barsana apparently to watch the enemy movements.[36] Meanwhile, heartened by his success, Aqibat stiffened his offensive. Early in December, he plundered the villages of Mitraul and Hathin (12 miles south west of Palwal). The villagers stoutly resisted him all day long but evacuated their places in the night. Then he raided other villages around Palwal. On 20th December, he went to Delhi at Imad's call. On 27th December (1st Rabi I) he despatched Gangadhar and Sukh Ram towards Faridabad and he himself followed the same day, taking Khandoji with all his troops, to resume operation against the Jats. But the situation there had changed during his absence. Taking advantage

---

32. *Ibid*, 90b-91b.
33. *TAH.*, 91b.
34. *Sujan*, 204.
35. *TAH.*, 91b-92b, 106b; Also *Sujan* 205; Dow, *Hindostan*, II, 324.
36. *Sujan*, 205.

of the soldiers' defiance of the *jamadar*, whom Aqibat had left behind, the Jats recaptured Garhi Hathin and other places. Unable to cope with the situation, Aqibat and the Marathas requested Imad to come in person and so he rushed from Delhi to Ballamgarh, without waiting for the reticent Emperor to accompany him.[37]

According to their mutual understanding, Khandoji and Imad put simultaneous pressure on the Jats along both sides of the Yamuna, while Suraj Mal apprehending the onrush of the Maratha myriads any day, was not in a position to reinforce his struggling tribesmen. Making Hodal his base, Khandoji, towards the close of December, 1753 ravaged and occupied various Jat '*garhis*' including Garhi Hathin, Jorgarhi (?) and Panah Garhi. He moved on to Nandgaon and Barsana which Jawahar Singh had evacuated earlier. On the other side, the Marathas uprooted the Jat outpost at Shikohabad.[38] Fateh Ali Khan (whom Suraj Mal had saved against Asad Khan in 1745) with 10 thousand men occupied Kol following its evacuation by the Jat garrison.[39] These successes enthused Aqibat Mahmud. On 5th January, 1754 (10th Rabi I, 1167 A.H.), he surprised the Jat village of Ghangaula under one of the brothers of Balram. Aqibat despoiled the village, killed the Jat, imprisoned 6 others and established his own outpost there.[40]

On 8th January (13th Rabi I), Imad with Aqibat moved on from Ballamgarh to Palwal, while he sent Muhkam Singh to Khandoji at Hodal. Imad granted a splenddid khilat to Suraj Mal's sworn enemy, Fateh Singh appointed him to his father's estate with orders to plunder, kill and imprison the Jats around.[41] About the middle of the month, Imad sent Aqibat, Muhkam Singh and Fateh Singh with 5 to 6 thousand troops towards Narnaul and Rewari in Mewat and Saifullah Khan, Zahid Beg and others with big numbers towards Kol, Sikandarabad and Jalesar. Thus, extensive Jat areas on both sides of the river fell into his hands. On 3rd February (9th Rabi II), it was learnt that the Maratha forces, having expelled the Jat officials, were busy subduing the country around Mathura and Agra. Khandoji was made '*hakim*' there.[42] Multitudes of evacuees out of terror fled from those areas and sought shelter with the Jat Raja.[43]

---

37. *TAH.*, 93b, 94b, 97a, 102a, 104b-105a.
38. *TAH.*, 105a, 105b; cf. *Sujan* 215-217.
39. *TAH.*, 105b-106a.
40. *TAH.*, 106a.
41. *Ibid.*, 106a-106b.
42. *Ibid.*, 107a, 108b, 111a also 109a-109b. On this occasion Imad misappropriated Rupees 50,000 realized by Aqibat from *Sarf-i-Khas mahal* (Rewari and others).
43. *Memoires des Jats,* 40; Also *Sujan*, 223; cf. *TAH.* 107a.

THE SIEGE OF THE JAT FORTS

Amidst these reverses poured into the heart of the Jat country the huge Maratha army under Raghunathrao on 16th January, 1754.[44] Khandoji, Har Govind Natani (of Jaipur) and Imad also joined it to swell the number to formidable 80,000 men, consisting of the "best troops" then in the country.[45] Suraj Mal however, remained undeterred,[46] even though his numerical strength fell short of the enemies. As suggested above, his foes had devised a clever scheme against him but still cleverer was the one matured by the sagacious Jat veteran, which enabled him to withstand successfully "the hoppers of the Deccan"[47] for full four months. Having known the aggressive designs of the Marathas as early as November, Suraj Mal wisely refrained from moving out to confront Imad-Khandoji combine (in the north and east, as there was dual risk in it; the heart of his kingdom could have been surprised likewise and he himself could have been caught between two fires. His strategy was commensurate with his means. He apparently wished to draw his enemies in front of his forts, which formed his main strength, in the same way as the formidable number did that of his foes. He, therefore, employed the short time at his disposal in stockpiling provisions and fortifying his forts to confront such a massive threat. Elaborate arrangements for the defence of the Capital, Deeg, were made under the personal guidance of the King, Badan Singh, his Minister Gaj Singh and Jawahar Singh. It was well fortified and provided with guards on all its ten gates and five *marhalas.* The prodigious number of evacuees and foragers were camped in the dense jungles adjoining the fort of Bharatpur and the ramparts with bastions hurriedly put up there. The defence of this fort was entrusted to the Diwan Chain Singh and that of the fort of Wair to Bahadur Singh.[48] Suraj Mal personally decided to stay at Kumher, which until then was an "ordinary fort".[49] This decision reflects the commendable shrewdness of the great Jat general. Now Kumbher, besides being midway between Deeg and Bharatpur was situated in the centre of a great "sandy plain with no spring of fresh water."[50] In selecting it he obviously wished to keep

---

44. *S.P.D.*, XVII, 79 (Raghunathrao encamped on 16th January at Nagar; from 17th to 19th at Jalukhar (both the places near Deeg); from 20th January to 27th Febrary at Pingora (near Kumbher); from 28th February to 22nd May at the plain before Kumbher; *S.P.D.* XXI, 60; *TAH*; 109b; *Memoires des Jats,* 39; *Mirat*, 763; *Amira*, 51; *Siyar*, III, 335; *Sujan*, 224-225 (announcing their coming only); *Tarikh-i-Muzaffari* in Elliot, VIII, 321.
45. *Memoires des Jats,* 39; *Sujan* (2206) and *Tarikh-i-Muzaffari* (in Elliot, VIII, 321) put the *Marathas* at 60,000.
46. *Memoires des Jats,* 39.
47. *Memoires des Jats,* 43.
48. *Sujan*, 217ff; *Memoires des Jats,* 39, For a discordant note see *TAH.*, 109b.
50. *Ibid.*, 39.

himself free to fall upon from behind on either side, in case the enemies, considering their greater importance, concentrated on Deeg or Bharatpur. And if in view of his presence here, they converged on Kumher, (which he presumably wished and the Marathas did it also) there remained the scope for harassing the enemies on both sides, Deeg and Bharatpur, while their encampment on a sandy and waterless plain would have fully exposed them to the fort artillery as also to nature's fury in the coming hot months.

And yet, considering the overwhelming strength of the combined opponents he would not take any chances at Kumbher either. Incredible though it might sound, it was during the preceding two months that the Jats advanced the "fortifications" in such a way that Kumbher became bigger than before."[51] The provisions stocked there were in such abundance that no other fort in India could rival it. Its formidable ramparts were literally lined up with small and big pieces of artillery.[52] A few long-range heavy cannons placed atop were such as would not permit enemy to come any where near the walls, thus rendering effective investment, even by the Maratha swarms, impossible. As it was, he made the enemy exert mainly on the place of his choice and with what results is narrated below:

> Soon after their arrival the Marathas made an onrush on the forts only to be driven back by the gunfire. Later, Suraj Mal came out and a sanguinary battle ensued, in which both sides had big numbers killed or wounded. Then according to his strategy, he retired to Kumbher, which becoming the main target was besieged along with Deeg and other places by the Marathas.[53] Thus commenced the siege which dragged on for four months. But the impregnability of the forts proved to be the undoing of the Marathas. Their best exertions remained absolutely ineffective for want of suitable cannons. With their huge numbers they, however, succeeded in devastating the countrysides.[54]

Tawarikh-i-Hunud records an interesting incident that Malharrao Holkar, in an apparent attempt to assuage the feelings of Muhkam Singh, ploughed the site (of the demolished fort) of Thun with elephants and

---

51. *Ibid.*, 40.
52. *Ibid*, 40 including its footnote.
53. *TAH*; 109b; *S.P.D.* XXI, 60; *Memoires des Jats,* 40; *Amira*, 51; *Siyar*, III, 315; *Chahar Gulzar Shujai* and *Tarikh-i-Muzaffari* in Elliot-VIII, 208, 321; *Mirat* 763; Scott, *Dekkan*, II, 229.
54. *S.P.D.* (XXI, 60) wrongly says that Suraj Mal "Plundered the whole city in Kumbher". *TAH.*, 110a; *Memoires des Jats,* 40; *Mirat*, 763; *Chahar Gulzar Shujai* in Elliot, VIII, 209.

sowed there "pearls instead of grain". Thereafter he "fought great battle with the Jat forces posted at the fort of Deeg."[55]

In Jamadi I (24th February to 25th March), Imad-ul-Mulk, followed by Aqibat Mahmud, came from Mathura to Kumher at the call of the Holkar. He also put up "daily exertions" to make an assault on the fort, but in vain.[56] Meanwhile, the Holkar had been unsuccessfully trying through Imad to get the big size guns from the Imperial arsenal at Delhi and Agra. The Wazir was, however, opposed to Suraj Mal's suppression by Imad and his allies for reasons already explained. He, therefore, prevailed upon the Emperor not only to refuse the guns but to write secret letters to the Jat Prince, assuring that the Mir Bakhshi was fighting against his (the Emperor's) will. A few of these letters were apparently intercepted by Imad and the Holkar. Imad now sent Aqibat to terrorize the Emperor into yielding the guns but to no avail.[57] The Marathas, however, were not wholly dependent on the imperial arsenal. Early in March, Naro Shankar was ordered to bring 4 big guns, gunpowder and lead in sufficient quantity from Jhansi to Kumbher.[58] Similarly, Muzaffar Khan was also reported to be dragging in some places from Malwa.[59] But even these pieces, if and when brought, failed to create an impression on the fort walls.

Meanwhile, a tragedy befell the Marathas. One day (middle of March) Khandoji (earlier summoned from Hodal) riding a *palaki* was inspecting his advance trenches[60] at Gangarsauli (4 miles north of Kumher), when the fort artillery opened fire and he was killed by a chance *zamburak* shot. The tragic sight of the corpse of Khandoji overwhelmed Malhar Holkar with grief. The incident touched the heart of Suraj Mal also. He sent "the mourning robes" to the bereaved Holkar and expressed his profound condolences, forgetting the deep hostility of the Holkars. However, in spite of this gesture, the death of his lone son enraged the Holkar and he swore "to extirpate" the killers of Khandoji. The siege was pushed on more vigorously than before.[61] The

55. *Tawarikh-i-Hunud*, 19b. In employing elephants and pearls, the Holkar seemingly meant to purify and honour the former chief's seat, which we know, had been desecrated by Jai Singh's ploughing it with asses.

56. *TAH.*, 114a.

57. *Ibid.*, 109b-110a, 114b, 120a, 131b, 133a; *S.P.D.* XXI 60; XXI 60; *Shakir*, 76; *Amira*, 51; *Memoires des Jats,* 41-42; *Siyar*, III, 335-336; *Tarikh-i-Muzaffari*, in *Elliot* VIII, 321; *Mirat* (763), assigning different reasons says that the Emperor wrote to Imad to desist from war; cf. Dow, *Hindostan*, II, 324-325.

58. *S.P.D.* XXVII, 81also 134.

59. *S.P.D.* XXI, 59.

60. There is a shrine containing the marbel statue of Khandoji in Gangarsauli, suggesting that he was killed there.

61. *TAH.*, 117a-117b; 121b, *S.P.D.* XXI, 59; *Memoires des Jats*, 41; *Tawarikh-i-Hunud,* 19b; *Chah Gulzar Shujai* and *Tarikh-i-Muzaffari* in *Elliot* VIII, 209, 321; Also *Francklin*, 3.

indomitable defenders replied with making frequent sorties and forays. Thus, they created diversion for the besiegers and prevented them from stiffening the siege. They put in "untiring labour" in repairing occasional damage to the fortwalls by the enemy artillery. Wendel adds that a breach made in the day was so soon and so well filled up the following night that it was difficult to discover the marks next day.[62]

Yet, on the basis of Bhau Bakhar it is said that the destruction of Suraj Mal now appeared only a matter of days; that Rani Hansia encouraged his despondent husband; and that Jayappa Scinde's eagerly sought favour contributed in rescuing Suraj Mal from his impending doom.[63] It is likely that the Jats came in touch with the Scinde whose estrangement with the Holkar was well-known. But the rest of the version seems to be over-drawn. The forts, which in point of their strength evoked the lavish praise of all the contemporaries and which fifty years later were to baffle the mighty British for two long years, were not going to succumb to the Holkar's wrath only. Suraj Mal was a courageous man, he retained his habitual calm and poise even in most desperate situations. In the present case, Kumher, to use his own words, was "almost impregnable" and it contained provisions sufficient to last "more than a year". All this militates against his supposed increasing despair. The fact, as borne out by the contemporary sources, is that despite the enemy "deluge" the Jats made persistent forays and thus kept the enemy in "great alarm". There was no night when their raids were not sure, just as no day passed by when the enemy convoys were not attacked. Backed by the fort artillery they hovered round "as if there was no enemy in the environment or capable of harming them at all."[64] The Marathi letters and the court history generally support this defiant spirit of the defenders. Thus, we learn that Naro Shankar had to seek safety in flight before a Jat force from Deeg.[65] Another letter alludes to an encounter having taken place between the Marathas and the Jat foraying party from Deeg. The latter, however, disappeared when Dattaji arrived on the spot.[66] On the night of Ist April, 1754 (7th Jamadi II), Suraj Mal interviewed the Jaipur general, Natani, outside the fort of Kumher. Thereafter a Jat artillery force came out and attacked the enemy trenches in the plain. The battle was even with casualties on both sides.[67] Again,

62. *Memoires des Jats*, 40.
63. Qanungo, *Jats*, 89-91. *Tawarikh-i-Hunud*, 19b and *Chahar Gulzar Shujai* (in Elliot, VIII, 209) make us believe that the death of Khandoji despaired of the Marathas instead. This is also misleading.
64. *Memoires des Jats*, 40 also footnote, 41.
65. *S.P.D.*, XXVII, 96.
66. *S.P.D.*, II, 38.
67. *TAH.*, 121b; The Maratha doubt that Natani was in a secret collusion with the Jats (See *S.P.D.*, XXVII, 94) does not appear baseless in the light of the above event.

on 30th April, a Jat squadron surprised Shivdeo, killing 41 Maratha soldiers and wresting his total sum of Rupees 29,500.[68] Earlier (c. late in March) a Jat force from Wair under Bahadur Singh, fell upon a Maratha detachment and grabbed "a lot of money" along with a few (two or three) distinguished Maratha ladies of the Holkar's family. Malhar justly felt humiliated at this boldness. Suraj Mal was, however, courteous enough to send the ladies back honourably.[69] These sporadic instances suffice to belie the fancied despair of Suraj Mal and his imminent destruction.

All the same, there was certainly no reason for Suraj Mal being complacent either. By far the most formidable foes in their myriads were waging war against him. His countryside, already ravaged by them still lay at their mercy. Besides, the daily skirmishes were causing him recurring losses, whereas in the ultimate analysis he "did not expect anything from this war."[70] Finally, Imad's persistent efforts to secure the big cannons must also have made him anxious for its early termination. He, therefore, wrote to the Wazir and the Emperor, submitting that if Imad in league with the Marathas succeeded in his designs, it would turn his head and he would cast his eyes upon the throne itself and ruin the Empire as well as the Wizarat. He suggested to them to move out of the Capital and, forming a joint front of the Rajputs and Safdar Jang, drive out the common oppressors, the Marathas, from northern India. He was himself to join the proposed front, once he became free from the Maratha menace.[71] This proposition, no doubt, reflected his cleverness to get rid of his immediate problems. But side by side this also agreed with the stand that he had taken just two years before. It appears that he also wrote to his old friend, Safdar Jang. This was probably the reason why Raghunathrao, in an obvious attempt to discourage the Nawab, sent him the false information of his victory over Suraj Mal.[72]

Meanwhile, Imad and the Marathas themselves had become "fed up" with, and 'felt ashamed" over, undertaking a war which even after all their efforts, had failed to turn in their favour. It had already incurred them huge expenses and all the procurable supplies in the environs. In addition, their encampment in the open, sandy plain of Kumbher, with the burning sun on their head and the scarcity of water, food and fodder in their immediate neighbourhood, had reduced them to dire straits,[73]

---

68. *S.P.D.*, XXVII, 81 also 94.
69. *Memoires des Jats*, 41.
70. *Memoires des Jats*, 40.
71. *Siyar*, III, 336; *Akhbar-i-Muhabbat* in Elliot, VIII, 384; Scot, *Dekkan*, II, 229; *Ibrat*, 15b; Also *Tarikh-i-Muzaffari*, in *Elliot*, VIII, 321; Srivastava, *Oudh*, 248; Qanungo, *Jats*, 92-93; cf. *Amira*, 51.
72. *Rajwade*, I, 35.
73. *Memoires des Jats*, 40-41.

while the impregnability of the enemy forts and the tenacity of their proud defenders ridiculed them even now as before. Besides, the rainy season was close by, which would have rendered military operations impossible in the coming months. It was in this background of helplessness ignored by the scholars that the besiegers also got smell of the proposed counter-offensive. This naturally made them anxious to extricate themselves from the elusive war. At length peace was made on or just before 18th May, 1754. Harnath Singh Jat participated in the negotiations with the Bakhshi. It was settled that Suraj Mal would pay Rupees 30 lakhs to the Marathas over the above Rupees two crores, which had been previously imposed by Imad as tribute due from the Jat to the Emperor but was now to be paid to Imad and the Marathas instead. Rup Ram furnished a written bond to the Marathas to pay 30,00,001 in instalments in three years.[74]

With his cool undaunted courage, masterly defensive strategy and sagacious diplomacy, Suraj Mal succeeded in thwarting the designs of a formidable combination of 80,000 men. This fetched him "high reputation" all over India.[75] The revengeful Imad and the extortionate Marathas had left no stone unturned to wipe out his existence, but they utterly failed in their avowed objective. The extortionate hostility displayed by them ran deep into the Jat bosom and duly influenced the Jat policy towards them, both in the succeeding days and also during Panipat.

The Jat war continued to be an important issue in the Court politics. The Wazir and the Emperor, dreading Imad, themselves thought along the lines of Suraj Mal. The Wazir had written secret letters to Safdar Jang, Suraj Mal and Madho Singh, inviting their help against the Marathas. He arranged that the Emperor should go out of Delhi to Kol and there effecting a junction with Safdar Jang (who had come upto Mehdighat), move on to Agra. Suraj Mal and the Rajput Kings were to join there and then anti-Maratha campaign was to be commenced.[76] But formulating the scheme was different from its execution. The Emperor with most shabby equipment moved out of Capital and roamed about Sikandarabad. On the other side, on 18th May, Imad left Kumher and

---

74. *TAH.*, 128a, also 131b; *S.P.D.*, XXVII, 81, XXI, 60; Also *Memoires des Jats,* 42; *Ibrat*, 15b; *TAL.*, 9 cf. *Amira*, 52; *Siyar*, III, 338; *Tarikh-i-Muzaffari* in *Elliot,* VIII, 322; Qanungo, *Jats*, 96 speaks of Rs. 60 lakhs to be paid to the Marathas which is not correct.
75. *Memoires des Jats,* 42, 43.
76. *TAH.*, 133a, 125b, 126b; *Tarikh-i-Muzaffari* in *Elliot*, VIII, 321; Scott, *Dekkan*, II, 229; *Memoires des Jats,* 42, 43; Srivastava, *Oudh*, 248-249; cf. *S.P.D.* XXI, 60; *Amira*, 51.

encamped at Mathura. On 23rd, Raghunathrao followed him and he remained at Mathura till 25th. The same night his vanguard under the Holkar moved towards Sikandarabad and subsequent developments there (26th May) dashed all hopes of the formation of the proposed coalition. Suraj Mal, or for that matter no other sounded potentate, was responsible[77] for whatever befell the cowardly Emperor and the Wazir at Sikandarabad. A week later at Delhi, Imad usurped the Wizarat and replaced Ahmad Shah with his creature, Alamgir II.[78]

SURAJ MAL AND THE IMPERIAL WIZARAT

Suraj Mal's policy following Imad-Maratha invasion centred round three broad objectives, namely to recover' his former possessions and grab his share of fresh territories amidst worst anarchy; to see an amicable candidate assume the Wizarat; and to get the common oppressors, the Marathas, expelled from the north. The first of these has already been narrated in the V Chapter and hence needs no repetition. We shall discuss the last two here.

The developments at the imperial Capital evoked lively interest of all the ambitious personages of the day because their trend made or marred their respective fortunes. In case of the Jats, their association with the powerful elements at the Court had been an important condition of their rise and growth ever since the days of Churaman II. Munim Khan, Zulfiqar Khan, Khan-i-Dauran, the Sayyid brothers, Qamar-ud-Din, Javed Khan, Safdar Jang and Intizam-ud-Daula had in one way or the other been helpful in the growth of the Jat fortunes. Generally serving as a shield, these dignitaries procured them royal favours and also legalization (in case of Badan Singh) of their usurpations. It is true that by the middle of the century the imperial ministers (except Safdar Jang) had been reduced to shadowy phantoms, and now they themselves (Safdar Jang, Intizam and later Imad) looked for help to the redoubtable Jat Prince. Nonetheless, they, especially the Wazir, still commanded a reckonable prestige and authority. However, with the replacement of Intizam by his ruthless foe, Imad, Suraj Mal for the first time confronted a hostile Court at Delhi. As we shall see, Imad's Maratha props, especially Malhar Holkar also bore deep grudge against him. This set-up ran contrary to his aspirations. He seems to have calculated that friendly Wazir might serve as a convenient instrument to imparting legality to his enterprises and also add to his prestige. Hence, he wished to have a person of his liking at the helm of affairs at Delhi.

---

77. Qanungo, *Jats*, 94-95; *Oudh*, 249.
78. For details of the above developments, see *TAH.*, 125b till the end; Also *S.P.D.*, XXVII.

First, he explored if his trusted well wisher Intizam could be propped up to counterbalance Imad. On 22nd October, 1754 his envoy, Rup Ram, met and held discussions with the Holkar's *diwan*, Gangadhar, at Jaisinghpura (Delhi). Both these contended that Ballamgarh should be retained under Suraj Mal as before and Intizam be allowed to wait on the Emperor but on the condition that Imad's men in the fort be replaced by those loyal to the Emperor. But the domineering Imad never wanted the Emperor to slip out of his hands. He, therefore, rejected the proposition, left Jaisinghpura and went to Raghunathrao. The latter had become convinced by now that the prospects of money would not improve under Intizam and Imad thus retained the Wizarat.[79]

A few months later, a much more capable aspirant approached a willing Jat Prince. Shuja, the son and successor of his friend Safdar Jang, longed for the imperial Chancellorship. Taking advantage of Imad's predicament at Panipat,[80] Shuja sent his emissary Ali Quli Khan Daghastani to his hereditary friend Suraj Mal and Ahmad Bangash to solicit their help in superseding Imad on Wizarat.[81] Suraj Mal relished this proposal and readily agreed to back Shuja against his enemy. Ali Quli also contacted Saif-ud-Din Muhammad Khan and Kishan Chand Sud also at the Capital. The Emperor also approved of the plot as a means to get rid of the tyrannical Imad.[82] The requisite forces were set in order to effect a change which in the circumstances might have proved better both for the Empire as well as Suraj Mal.[83] However, the imprudent delay in execution by Shuja, the key figure in the conspiracy, gave Imad an opportunity to assert himself. He rushed back to Delhi (May, 1755) and at once suppressed the local accomplices. The conspiracy was thus nipped in the bud.

Next, he endeavoured to wreck vengeance on the main accomplice, Suraj Mal and a big punitive expedition against him was planned. Although it could not materialize, in the name of the Emperor, he sent Najib (17th June, 1755-7th Ramzam) ostensibly to disgorge Suraj Mal from his recent annexations in the Doab, but really to express his fury over his complicity with Shuja. The powerful Jat who "completely disregarded the forces of the Wazir and the Rohilla" moved forward in a fighting posture.[84] But in the meantime Raja Nagar Mal who did not

---

79. *TAL.*, 47-48; Sarkar, *Fall*, II, 40ff.
80. For details see *TAL.* 81ff.
81. *Ibid.*, 101.
82. *Ibid.*, Also A.L. Srivastava, *Shuja-ud-Daulah* (Agra; 1961) I, 20.
83. cf. Qanungo, *Jats*, 109.
84. *TAL*, 105.

desire a confrontation intervened and carried through his efforts for peace. It was signed at Dasna (10th July, 1755), on terms already narrated before.[85] Imad, who meant to punish his enemy, had to legalize, instead, most of his territorial acquisitions. But Suraj Mal was still unreconciled. A Marathi despatch of the following month reads:

> The Wazir and the Jat are not able to adjust themselves. The Jat is intimidating but the Wazir does not have the strength (to cope with Suraj Mal).[86]

Shuja had too great a fascination for the exalted office to have given up hopes after the present rebuff. There is little room for doubt that he remained in touch with his 'steadfast ally", Suraj Mal. Yet, he (Shuja) would not display the requisite initiative, courage or strength of will and the shrewd Suraj Mal, with all his interests, would not involve himself inextricably in the circumstances. On his part, Imad was prepared to go to any length to retain the Wizarat. He first intended to wean away Suraj Mal and then tried "to play off" Shuja against the Bangash. He got the Viceroyalty of Allahabad transferred from Shuja to Ahmad Bangash (July, 1756). This worried Shuja and he marched towards Farrukhabad to prevent the Bangash from going to Allahabad. About October, 1756, the rumour was afloat the Raja Suraj Mal[87] and Shuja had formed a coalition, and that uprooting the Bangash they intended to fight the Wazir. This perplexed him along with his advisers, Nagar Mal and Najib. Nagar Mal tried to arrange for Suraj Mal's meeting with the Wazir, while Najib prevailed upon the Wazir to get Allahabad restored to Shuja. The latter now gave up his intention to press the matter. With Shuja virtually drawing back, the move to replace Imad fizzled out once again. The Wazir, however, remained anxious about the movements of Suraj Mal.[88]

SURAJ MAL ON THE IMPERIAL PROBLEMS; TILPAT TALKS

Meanwhile, the rumour of the coming of the Abdali to Delhi vexed the Wazir all the more. Unable to do anything himself and disillusioned from others, the fearstricken Imad at last turned for help to his old, though powerful, enemy Suraj Mal. But thanks to his persistent hostility placating the Jat was not easy. He, therefore, sought the services of Raja Nagar Mal as pointed above. The Raja sent his envoy Sujan Brahman to Bharatpur to persuade Suraj Mal to meet the Wazir. The Jat Raja

---

85. See Chapter V; Also *TAL.* 105-109.
86. *S.P.D.* II, 48.
87. He ascended the throne after his father's death on 9th June, 1756; *Tawarikh-i-Hunud*, 20a-20b.
88. *TAL.* (Pers Ms.), 157-158; *Shuja*, 22-24.

consented and arrived at Tilpat, probably in the first week of November, 1756. Najib went to see him followed by Nagar Mal (c. 11th November-17th Safar) who stayed on in the Jat camp for negotiations on the Wazir's behalf. Mehdi Quli Khan, a confidant of the Wazir, was present all along there.

Sounding a different note, the Jat Raja spoke:

> We *zamindars* live on with the Emperor's help. At this juncture the army of the Dekhani Marathas has penetrated these parts (the northern India) and is plundering the houses of the *ryots*. Ravaging and devastating the *talukas* of (all) the *zamindars*, big and small, it has spread rebellion, disturbance and uneasiness. And (amidst the situation) all the Rajas namely of Jodhpur, Merta, Jaipur and of other places (including that of Bharatpur) have decided to bar its arrival to this (northern) side of the Narmada and (also) to expel them (the Marathas) from those places under their occupation and (thus) to restore the royal territories to the Emperor we ourselves should also disgorge all the (usurped) *mahals* over and above of old *zamindaries*. Acceding to these propositions the Wazir-ul-Mumalik should also support and help us and, marching towards Akbarabad, should endeavour to liberate Malwa and Gujrat from the grip of the Marathas.

Having thus safeguarded their homes, the Jat went on, the combined forces should then turn to the Panjab to expel the Abdali as had been done in 1748.[89]

This piece of advice reveals the political sagacity and realistic grasp of the Jat statesman. He regarded both the Marathas and the Abdali as the potential sources of trouble. But of the two he gave priority to the tackling of the Maratha problem.[90] Little doubt, his approach was basically governed by his personal experience. Their recent invasion apart, the extortionate Marathas had been dunning him for dues and ravaging the Jat areas, whereas he had yet to feel the horrors of the Abdali. But similar was the experience of most of thc other potentates also. The Abdali did not threaten the whole of Hindustan[91] as was the case with the Marathas. The latter had inflicted by far the heaviest blow to the decaying Empire by bringing its major part either in their direct political rule or under their economic subordination. Their hordes frequently visited the plains of the north not for promoting the imperial, Hindu or truly speaking,

89. *TAL.*, 157-158; Sarkar, *Fall* II, 84.
90. Contra see, Qanungo, *Jats*, 115.
91. See Indu Banga's article, "Ahmad Shah Abadali's designs over the Panjab", Proc. *I.H.C.*, 1968; Ganda Singh, *Ahmad Shah Durrani*, (Bombay: 1959), 260-261.

even the Maratha cause, but for squeezing money from all.[92] If the regular, though illegal, tribute was not forthcoming these spoliators invariably took to their familiar practice of indiscriminate loot and creating desolation.[93] In the process they incurred the indelible hatred and animosity of all.

In 1752, the Marathas undertook the responsibility to fight and banish the Abdali. Yet they themselves did not exert fully, while their exclusive responsibility for the imperial defences, tampered with whatever initiative was there in others to strive for the same. The example of February, 1752 illustrates it when the nobles and different potentates (including the Jat) kept back, submitting to the Emperor that as he had given them (the Marathas) Agra and Ajmer and the *chauth* of all the 24 provinces and placed all the authority in their hands, "Ask them what should be done now".[94] It is significant to note that in 1748, the same potentates had joined the royal army against the Abdali. But this was generally wanting after the pact with the Marathas.

Under the pretext of serving the Empire the Marathas aspired for an exclusive authority over Hindustan.[95] Yet they hardly cared for its fate. Nor, with their divided and mutually jealous leadership, to say the least about their general policy, were they capable of delivering any good to the ruled;[96] "They (the Marathas) have despoiled and devastated the whole of Hindustan", is the comment of the Court historian on their expansion."[97]

Little wonder, therefore, that Suraj Mal advocated that "the best defence of the Empire"[98] was first to expel the perpetual and common oppressors from the north by a joint front under the Mughal Emperor. Then the task of expelling the Afghan interloper from the Panjab was to be undertaken, according to his bold plan. And in the light of the result of the battle of Manupur, the success with the joint endeavours was not impossible.

Suraj Mal's proposition also reflects his general attitude towards the tottering Empire. At the outset it must be conceded that he, for one, could never have wished its restoration to its former vigour and strength, as it was sure to wipe out his own existence. But at the same time, he by no means desired its extinction either.[99] By his emphasis on a bold front

---

92. Gupta, *Panipat*, 255-256, 121; Sarkar, *Fall*, II, 226, 190; *Francklin*, 5.
93. What fate befell the people in general can be understood in the confession of a prominent Maratha Sardar. He writes, "I burnt (devastated) the country upto wherever my hand could reach," *S.P.D.*, XXI, 79.
94. *S.P.D.*, XXI, 79.
95. Srivastava, *Shuja*, 38.
96. Gupta, *Panipat*, 121; *Freedom Movement* (M. Husain), I, Introduction, 29.
97. *TAL.*, 380.
98. Sarkar, *Fall*, II, 84.
99. Contra See Dow, *Hindostan*, II, 339.

against the Marathas and the Abdali; especially by his reported offer to part with the recent usurpations (provided others did the same) he wished to impart the Empire "a new lease of life".[100] He seems to have argued that if the deterioration went its way, not only the Empire would perish but in the ultimate analysis various potentates would also suffer heavily amidst the resulting political vacuum and anarchy. It was to ward off this common danger that he stood for the above re-adjustments. What he contemplated was the inception of a confederacy, with the Mughal Emperor as its supreme head and a co-ordinating link between the semi independent ruling chiefs.[101] It was certainly not an ideal situation from the Emperor's viewpoint. But what is ideal is not always practical. Things (during the preceding decades) had reached a stage, where putting them back (to the former stage) was an impossible task. It was better to live on with reckonable authority than with no authority at all. Suraj Mal's plan, thus, offered a sensible and realistic solution to the complex political problems of the day.[102] What is all the more noticeable is its patriotic and national touch. It envisaged a political regeneration with the united efforts of the sons of the soil and not with the help of the Abdali, who being a foreigner could have no instinctive attachment to this land.

But Imad-ul-Mulk did not desire to curb the Marathas, upon whom depended his Wizarat. Hence he disregarded Suraj Mal's wise propositions. "Getting disgusted" he went back home leaving the Wazir to his fate. One cannot miss the note of disappointment in the words of the Court Historian,"... and Suraj Mal could not serve the Empire."[103]

RELATIONS WITH THE MARATHAS

Though the Tilpat talks reveal the real state the Jat-Maratha relations, we may pause here to discuss them in some detail. Wendel claims that some time after the siege of the Jat forts, the Marathas entered into an "agreement" with Suraj Mal under which the latter agreed not to oppose their "enterprises", nor to obstruct their frequent march of their forces through northern India. In return, the Marathas permitted him to occupy much of the lands in the "government of Agra", then under Maratha "disposal".[104] However, no contemporary Persian or Maratha source

---

100. Qanungo, *Jats*, 116.
101. *Ibid*, 116-117.
102. Cf. Sarkar, *Fall*, II, 84.
103. *TAL.*, 158; G. Singh (*Durrani*, 170-171) rightly doubts the veracity of *Tazkirah-i-Imad*, (quoted by him) that Najib's meeting with Suraj Mal was partly responsible for his rift with the Wazir. For we know that rift, nay enmity, already existed between the two. Also makes a doubtful assertion that Suraj Mal asked Jawahar Singh to remain near the Capital, "ready for emergency".
104. *Memoires des Jats*, 44.

speaks of this agreement. The Court history merely contains a reference that on 29th September, 1754 (11th Zil-Hijja, 1167 H.), Raghunathrao declined to join Imad in an attack on Suraj Mal (who had recaptured Palwal two days ago), saying that he had "made peace with Suraj Mal" and he would not deviate from their promise to the Jats.[105] But this cannot be confused with the alleged pact, on which that historian is completely silent. At best, it may suggest Raghunathrao's disinclination to get re-entangled in an elusive Jat war or his avarice to get the promised tribute from Suraj Mal which could have been jeopardised in the event of open hostility. The fact that he assured Imad to warn Suraj Mal to vacate his *mahals*,[106] disagrees with the spirit of the said agreement. The Marathas had taken pains to retain the governorship of Agra,[107] which they wanted to hold with full administrative and financial control.[108] Hence, the view that they gifted away the same *suba* looks highly doubtful especially in the situation of 1754. The fact is that Raghunathrao himself resented the Jat occupation of the Agra province.[109] Further, we have positive evidence to show that at least upto 1757, if not beyond, Malhar Holkar nursed the designs to fight Suraj Mal to the better end[110] and he was the man who controlled the Maratha affairs in the north. This all the more reduces the chances of the supposed friendly understanding. Finally, had there been anything like that, it must have been specifically mentioned in the Marathi despatches. But we do not find in them even the slightest hint about it. Thus, it is unsafe to accept Wendel's testimony about the Jat-Maratha "agreement" of 1754.[111] If at all there occurred anything of that sort, it must not have been more than the routine expression for amity (on the part of Raghunathrao and Suraj Mal) which usually marks the termination of a war, while rancour and enmity lie concealed in the opponent's hearts.

It was this enmity which continued to characterize the Jat-Maratha relations, till the Abdali returned after his fourth invasion. Barely two months after the peace with the Jats, Purshottam Mahadev wrote (July 1754):

> Shri Pant and *Subahdar* (Raghunathrao and Malhar respectively) are in Delhi. The Jat remains to be crushed after settling the matters here (at Delhi).[112]

---

105. *TAL*, 39-40.
106. *Ibid.*, 40.
107. *S.P.D.* XXI, 57, 44.
108. *Ibid.*, XXVII, 158.
109. cf. the tone of Raghunathrao's letter, *S.P.D.* II, 84.
110. *S.P.D.*, II, 80.
111. Contra see Sarkar, *Fall*, II, 437-438; Gupta, *Panipat*, 48. Qanungo (*Jats*, 96) rightly ignores Wendel's 'agreement', but he thinks that Malhar and Imad tried to win over Suraj Mal.
112. *S.P.D.* XXI, 60.

Purshottam was the political agent of the Peshwa at the Court. His statement, therefore, may be taken to reflect the official Maratha policy of wrecking vengeance on the Jats. We have seen how in 1755, the Marathas under Vithal Shivdev attacked Bhim Singh Jat of Gohad, who was the protege of Suraj Mal and to whose help the latter had sent his troops as well.[113] Next, on 27th December, 1756, the Marathas wrested the district of Jalesar from the Jats.[114]

On the other side, Suraj Mal himself persisted with the anti-Maratha policy. After Jayappa's murder in July, 1755, Bijay Singh of Marwar endeavoured to form a powerful front consisting of various chiefs including Suraj Mal to banish the Marathas from the north. He offered to bear the expences and appealed to the Emperor to lead the joint command. The talk was in the air that the Emperor, taking Suraj Mal, Madho Singh, the Wazir and the Rohillas, would fall upon Dattaji Scinde at Marwar.[115] However, even the open offer failed to arouse the impotent Court of Delhi and nothing substantial was done in this direction. As Suraj Mal was personally involved at the time in his northern affairs, he sent his son with 10,000 men against Antaji, who was leading a succour of 10,000 (including the Jat retainers from Gohad) to Dattaji. The Jats and the Jaipur Bakhshi tried to impede Antaji's march while he was crossing the river Mar, near Karauli. Antaji was then forced to make a detour through the hills,[116] and he eventually succeeded in joining the Maratha forces. We have no information about the subsequent Jat movements. Incidentally, during this later phase of the Maratha-Bijay Singh conflict, the former dunned Suraj Mal for dues amounting to Rupees seven lakhs.[117] In November, 1756, how Suraj Mal strongly advocated 'the drive-out-Maratha' policy, has already been seen above.

JAWAHAR SINGH'S REBELLION AGAINST RAJA SURAJ MAL

Before taking up the Abdali's Jat invasion, we may briefly notice a preceding internal Jat crisis. Raja Badan Singh died on 9th June, 1756 (Jeth Sudi Ekadasi Samvat, 1813). De facto ruler for long, Suraj Mal now ascended the throne[118] with the title of Maharaja Brijendra Bahadur.[119] It

---

113. *S.P.D.*, II, 45 XXIX, 60, XXVII, 113, 118.
114. *S.P.D.* XXVII, 206.
115. *Ibid*, 119, XXI, 73, II, 48; cf. M.L. Sharma, *Jaipur*, 177.
116. *Ibid*, II, 54-56, also 52 XXI, 79, 70. Antaji, a habitual boaster, however, claimed (*S.P.D.*, II, 56) that he frightened Suraj Mal and occupied his country.
117. *S.P.D* XXI, 80.
118. *Tawarikh-i-Hunud*, 20a-20b it, however, does not refer to Jawahar's rebellion, while *Memoires des Jats* (45ff., 63) does not specify the date of his coronation. In all likelihood, Suraj Mal ascended the throne after Badan Singh's death and the revolt of Jawahar occurred after that.
119. This can be inferred from *Nur.* 33a and *Brijenda Vinod,* 212.

seems that shortly afterwards Jawahar Singh raised the standard of rebellion against his father, which rocked the Jat State, apparently till his departure for Tilpat (i.e. till the first week of November, 1756).

Born with boundless courage, and a habitual delight in fighting, this "Young absalom" (Jawahar Singh) was an impetuous, extravagant and extremely ambitious man. His expenditure over his Court and train, exceeded the decent allowance fixed for him by his father and he insisted on for more. Suraj Mal strongly disapproved of his ways. But his frequent remonstrances, more and more aggravated the mind of Jawahar Singh. Already at a young age he had begun to nourish high ambitions. We have noted that, in 1751 Javed Khan, attempted to play off dissatisfied Jawahar against his father. Suraj Mal tried to satisfy him by making him the governor of Deeg. But it whetted his appetite for more. Of later, a few sycophants, who resented the growing influence of Balram and Surati Ram, veered round him and poisoned his ears against the two officials. Suraj Mal reprimanded his problem-son for having been swayed by his advisers, who, being dangerous, should be dismissed instead. But all was in vain.

Partly on his own and partly at the instigation of his evil flatterers, Jawahar Singh prepared for revolt and took position at the fort of Deeg. Persuasion having failed, Suraj Mal had no other way left except to personally besiege his son. In order to expedite the matter, he threatened the families of Jawahar's supporters with dire consequences. The rebel Prince came out and a fierce fight with the state forces raged under the walls of the fort. His followers were driven back but not the undaunted youth. He rushed into the thickest of the fight but was incapacitated with three severe wounds from sword, spear and bullet. Suraj Mal, who would rather see Deeg lost than his son dead, ran immediately to snatch him away from those, who inspite of his shouts, hastened to kill the fallen Prince. Jawahar Singh survived but due to his wounds his right arm became weak and one leg lame.[120] Suraj Mal now seriously thought of entrusting Mewat as a small estate to his ambitious son.[121, XIX]

---

120. *Memoires des Jats*, 44-47, also see 83-84, it, however, presents a highly exaggerated picture of Suraj Mal's personal simplicity. The popular belief, recorded herein, that Jawahar contained the "bill" to the buried treasures of the late King and that Suraj Mal pressed the severely wounded son, to surrender it, also looks incredible, not only in the light of the positive evidence to the contrary (see *Tawarikh-i-Hunud*, 20a) but also common sense.

121. *Memoires des Jats*, 46; Also see *Nur.*, 60b.

XIX. For assessment of early life of Jawahar Singh, see Rajpal Singh, *Rise of the Jat Power*, Annexure, III, 243-250 and Upendra Nath Sharma, *Brijendra Bahadur Suraj Mal Jat*, 95, 147, 344 f.n., 148, 151, 152, 159, 167-8, 182, 185, 201-2, 210, 216, 221-226, 245, 251, 286, 287, 309-313, 341-51, 443-461, 478.—Editor.

X

The Jats in the Vortex of Hostile Forces (II)

AHMAD SHAH ABDALI'S JAT EXPEDITION

Hardly had Suraj Mal got relief from the internal crisis, when the Abdali invaded India, (December, 1756). Partly on his own and partly at the supplications of Mughalani Begam, Najib and others,[1] Ahmad Shah Abdali swooped down on the imperil Capital (January, 1757) without meeting any effective resistance on his way. The invaders methodically sacked, tortured and outraged the populace of the Capital. Alamgir was deposed, Imad imprisoned and the Wizarat conferred upon Intizam on his promising to give two crores to the Shah. To escape the Afghan havoc, about half the population of the city flocked to popular refuge, the Jat dominions. However, unlike their earlier behaviour, the Jats this time added to the misery of the refugees by extorting money from them at every post from Badarpur to Mathura. Yet, such a heavy influx continued that getting accommodation became difficult at Mathura. Thefts became frequent.[2]

The threatening march of the invader within the striking distance of his dominions obviously created an unprecedented situation for Suraj Mal.[3] It needed to be talked with great caution, foresight and courage. Earlier on 19th December, Imad (who had earlier rejected Suraj Mal's plan of the imperial defence) had written and sought help from him, the Marathas and Shuja.[4] The element of compulsion was apparent in the entreaties of Imad. Suraj Mal suspected that once the danger was over, he would attempt his (the Jats's) destruction with the help of his Maratha allies whose designs he (Suraj Mal) equally feared.[5] Hence, he wisely

---

1. For details see G. Singh, *Durrani*, 148ff; Also *Nur.*, 14b; Francklin (*Shah Aulum*, 4-5) is wrong in asserting that Mansur Ali Khan (who died much earlier) and Suraj Mal also invited the Shah.
2. *TAL* 166-167 and 236; *D.C.*; *S.P.D.*, XXI, 96, XXVII, 144 is wrong in saying that the Wazir took shelter with Suraj Mal; Also Sarkar, *Fall* II, III, 88.
3. cf. *Rajwade*, I, 54; *Memoires des Jats,* 47.
4. *D.C.*; cf. *S.P.D.*, XXI, 96.
5. *S.P.D.*, XXI, 100, 101.

refused to feed milk to such a dangerous viper. On the contrary he wished to utilize the opportunity to get rid of the mischief monger. Towards the end of January, 1757, he sent his envoy to the Abdali, professing submission and joined Najib, Nagar Mal and others in petitioning the Abdali, professing submission and common enemy Imad, "the son of Malharrao and the sworn brother of the Dada Sahib (Raghunathrao)" and detain him, (Imad) "beyond Attock". In return the signatories promised to give Rupees fifty lakhs as tribute to the Shah.[6]

The Marathas suspected Suraj Mal's hand also in the Shah's transfer of the Wizarat from Imad to Intizam. A report reads that Intizam and Suraj Mal were at the root of Imad's overthrow. "Khan-i-Khana became the Wazir. The (existing) Wazir was imprisoned and (thus) the influence of the Jat increased". It was also believed that Intizam, Suraj Mal and Shuja agreed to raise Rupees one and half crores from their own and the Capital's resources as a price for the Abdali's return. Thereafter, they would jointly chastise the common oppressors, the Marathas.[7] Whatever be the truth, the Marathas were convinced of Suraj Mal's mischief and they resented his conduct on the occasion. The talk was loud in their circles that after expelling the Abdali, they should settle their score with Suraj Mal.[8]

On his part, the Abdali refused to be satisfied with the Jat King's submission in absentia. Early in February, 1757, he wrote to Suraj Mal ordering him to disgorge his acquisitions, pay money, attend his Court personally.[9] The Abdali's perfidy was apparent from the fate of Imad hence the clever Jat would not wait on the invader, nor seek cowardly safety by giving him money or surrendering his lands. And yet precipitating clash with the Durrani swarms would have also been a foolhardy act on his part. The Mughal Emperor and his grandees lay prostrate before the Durrani whereas the treacherous Najib had crossed over, swelling the invader's ranks to about one lakh.[10] He rightly told Antaji at Mathura:

> The Padshah of Iran has captured the Empire of India with only fifty thousand troops. None has fired a bullet at him and not one (man) has sacrificed his life (in resisting him). What then can I do (alone)?[11]

---

6. *S.P.D.*, XXI, 96; Also Ghulam Husain Samin's narrative (trans. by W. Irvine in *Indian Antiquary*, 1907), 46. He is, however, wrong in placing Suraj Mal's petition after Imad's marriage with Umda Begam i.e. on 21st February.
7. *S.P.D.*, XXVII, 166, XXI, 100.
8. See the Peshwa's letter in *S.P.D.*, II, 80; *S.P.D.*, XXI, 100, XXVII, 166.
9. *S.P.D.*, XXI, 99; Also *Samin*, 46.
10. Vide Gupta, *Panipat*, 85; A Marathi report (*S.P.D.*, XXI, 101) hardly exaggerated that all that the Indian Rohillas the Pathans possessed was to be treated "as belonging to the Abdali".
11. *S.P.D.*, XXI, 99.

Amidst the circumstances the Jat Raja resorted to the dilatory tactics. Sometime after 4th February, he despatched his Vakil, ostensibly to discuss terms and bribe the Afghan Court but really to gain time to explore the possibility of an effective allied front against the invader and failing that to organise his defences in the meantime.[12] The Rajput and the notable Muslim potentates being either reluctant or helpless,[13] only the Marathas remained whom Suraj Mal looked forward to help in his adversity. With them also rested the responsibility to expel the Abdali. Accordingly, in November 1756, the Peshwa sent Raghunathrao and Malharrao at the head of an army to Delhi.[14]

Had they so desired, they could have easily reached in time to confront the invader. But they loitered on their way (Indore and then Rajasthan), despite the most pressing and persistent appeals by their subordinates on the spot. One of these (Antaji) wrote that at the moment, as Suraj Mal was neither paying money nor serving the Abdali, the Marathas could join him. But in case his (the Jat's) patience wore out and he joined the invader, "what safety do we (the Marathas) have?"[15] This shows that the Maratha sardars then in the north were not less eager for the Jat help than Suraj Mal was for theirs. Determined to fight the Abdali, Suraj Mal offered to join with his men and money provided the Maratha army arrived there.[16] But Raghunathrao kept back. In the circumstances, Suraj Mal sent his son to make a bid to defend his northern possessions, while he set himself to strengthening his defences in the centre of his realm, which was most likely to be the object of the Afghan fury.[17]

Meanwhile, Ahmad Shah insisted on Suraj Mal to return some eminent personages, like Nagar Mal (at Kumher), Bal Govind Sahukar, and the Khan-i-Saman, who had taken shelter with him. But the Jat King courageously refused saying, "How can I send Raja Nagar Mal and others, who have sought asylum with me?"[18] Obviously the Jat Raja was made of a stuff different from that of the carpetknights whom the Abdali had so far come into contact with. This was too much for the ferocious Abdali. So far no native Prince had dared disobey him, this pround Jat had

---

12. *S.P.D.*, XXI, 99.
13. The Jaipur and Jodhpur rulers expressed their allegiance to the Shah. See *S.P.D.*, XXI, 101, 105; G. Singh, *Durrani*, 242. The Bangash chief also courted his favour. Shuja, was pinned down in his affairs. See Srivastava, *Shuja*, 31, cf. *S.P.D.*, XXI, 105.
14. Sardesai, *Marathas*, II, 405.
15. *S.P.D.*, XXI, 105 also 100, 101, 110. The writer of the last letter went to the extent of saying that if Raghunathrao and Holkar were late in coming the Marathas would become a laughing stock for the Jats and the Rohillas.
16. *S.P.D.*, XXI, 99*S.P.D.*, XXI, 99, 101; Also see *Rajwade*, I, 54.
17. *TAL.*, (Pers. Ms), 200; *S.P.D.*, XXI, 96, II, 80; *Samin*, 48.
18. *Samin*, quoted by Ganda Singh, *Durrani*, 172; *S.P.D.*, XXI, 96; *TAL.*, (Pers. Ms.) 236.

mostly defied his authority.[19] The Abdali now resolved to march in person against the Jat Raja and he sent a foraging party to Faridabad. Jawahar Singh, who was then at Ballamgarh, took 5 to 6 thousand men, fell upon and routed it, slaying some 60 men and capturing 150 horses. This exasperated the Durrani and he ordered Abdus Samad Khan to go out in the night, lie in ambush, despatch 100 *sawars* to draw out the Jats from their hiding place, and then annihilate them. Abdus Samad literally followed his master. Jawahar Singh narrowly missed falling a victim to the Afghan stratagem. He escaped to Ballamgarh, but a number of his men were killed. The Afghans then attacked and pillaged several Jat villages, killing as many inhabitants as they could. They returned to Faridabad taking the booty and 500 severed heads.[20]

On 22nd February, Ahmad Shah Abdali left Delhi and, moving slowly, came to Faridabad on 26th. At first he ignored nearby Ballamgarh, declaring that his objects were Deeg and Kumher. But the insistence of Imad and the presence of Jawahar Singh there made him change his plans. He personally invested Ballamgarh, despatching (c. 27th February) his vanguard of 20,000 under Jahan Khan and another 20,000 under Najib,[21] with the instructions:

> Move into the boundaries of the accursed Jat, and in every town and district held by him slay and plunder. The city of Mathura is a holy place of the Hindus....let it be put entirely to the edge of the sword. To the best of your power leave nothing in the Kingdom and country. Upto Akbarabad leave not a single place standing.

Lest the Afghans should fail to execute the command literally he also issued a general order:

> To plunder and slay at every place they reached. Any booty they acquired was made a free gift to them. Any person cutting off and bringing in heads of the infidels should throw them down before the tent of the chief minister, wherewith to build a high tower. An account would be drawn up and five Rupees per head would be paid them from government funds.[22]

ASSAULT ON BALLAMGARH: (3RD MARCH)

It was one of the weakest Jat fortifications. The swivel pieces and muskets formed the only fire of this fort against the fire mortars of the Durrani. Besides, Jawahar Singh, who had just returned after having

---

19. Francklin, *Shah Aulum*, 6.
20. *Samin*, 48-49; *TAH.*, 195.
21. *TAL.*, 192 ff.; *Samin*, 58, 48-51; Also *Amira*, 53 and 99; *Memoires des Jats*, 47; *Siyar*, III, 350; *Ibrat*, 17a, 16b; Gupta, *Panipat*, 85 and 105.
22. *Samin*, 51.

been defeated at Chaumuha, must not have been able to muster up fresh strength. He was unable to hold for long against the enemy fire and he along with the Maratha sardars (Antaji and Shamsher Bahadur) escaped in the darkness of the night (3rd March) dressing as Qizilbashes. The Afghans broke open the gates of the fort and put the remainder to sword. Imad searched in vain corpses after corpses to trace Jawahar Singh. The invaders grabbed 12,000 Rupees, silver and copper utensils, gift idols, 14 horses, 11 camels, grain and clothes in large quantity. The Abdali stayed on for two more days and ordered general massacre and plunder. The environs of Faridabad were desolated and the terror stricken survivors fled elsewhere for safety.[23]

Then the Abdali himself proceeded southwards dealing death and destruction all round. An eye-witness giving its minute details says that the Afghans moved on in slow paces (one march never exceeded five 'kos' i.e. ten miles) after which one day's halt was made:

> It was midnight when the camp followers went out to attack....one horsemen mounted a horse and took ten to twenty others, each attached to the tail of the horse preceding it,...when it was one watch after sunrise I saw them come back. Every horseman had loaded up all his horses with the plundered property and atop of it rode the girl captives and the slaves. The severed heads were tied up in rugs....and placed on the heads of the captive....The severed heads....were ...(then) entered in the register and then built up into heaps and pillars....It was an extra-ordinary display....Wherever your glance fell nothing else was to be perceived but severed heads...Daily did this manner of slaughter and plundering proceed. And at night the shrieks of the women capitives, who were being ravished deafened the ears....These things went on all the way to the city of Akbarabad nor was any part of the country spared.[24]

BATTLE OF CHAUMUHA (28TH FEBRUARY)

Earlier the strong Afghan vanguard, reaching nearer Mathura, planned to fall upon that unfortified city. But 10,000 Jats under Jawahar Singh stood firm on the way to lay down their lives for the defence of that sacred place. A fierce and long battle commenced between the opponents on 28th February at Chaumuha (8 miles to the north). The Jats displayed their traditional valour and courage. But the odds against

---

23. *Samin*, 56, 58-59; *TAL.*, 198; *D.C.*; *S.P.D.*, XXI, 108, also; Also *Amira*, 99; *Siyar*, III, 352; Francklin, 6-7.
24. *Samin*, 55 and 60; G. Singh, *Durrani*, 176 footnote. This is untenable in the light of the eye-witness evidence to the contrary.

them were overwhelming. They had to cope with the superior generalship of Jahan Khan, who commanded a bigger force. After nine hours of grim fighting, the Jat resistance broke up and 10 to 12 thousand perished on the two sides taken together. Those wounded were "beyond count". The Mughal Emperor expressed his pleasure when he got his news through the two messengers, who were rewarded Rupees 300 each.[25] Suraj Mal suspected that the Afghans might turn to Bharatpur, Deeg and Kumbher. Therefore, he "remained stationed there, prepared for war."[26]

BLOOD BATH AT MATHURA

Stamping "bleeding marks of their inhumanity",[27] the Afghans wrought greater havoc upon the innocent non-combatants of Mathura and its holy environs. Their only crime was their money and belief in a different religion. Early in the morning of 1st March, Jahan Khan and Najib pounced upon the people of the place. They were indiscriminately massacred, ravished and plundered. The Holi, though celebrated only two days ago, was now replayed not with colour but with the blood of the Hindus. The houses were pulled down in search of money and then put to flames. The places of Hindu-worship were desecrated, the temples demolished, idols broken and kicked on the streets like "polo-balls". The Afghan plunderers did not spare even their own co-religionists. Dissatisfied with the organised loot, Jahan Khan imposed Rupees one lakh upon the remnant of the city populace. He departed the same night to carry out his mission elsewhere. But this by no means relieved the people of their misfortune. Najib, the "infernal guide" of the "devilish"[28] Durrani, stayed on for three days to inflict further brutalities on them. He plundered much wealth and carried off many beautiful women as captives. The ladies who could seek refuge into the deep waters of the Yamuna or the wells were fortunate. But those who survived suffered " a fate worse than death". Their modesty was cruelly outraged by the Afghan soldiers. Samin thus records what he saw a fortnight later:

> Every where in lane and Bazar lay the headless trunks of the slain; and the whole city was burning. The water (of the Yamuna) flowing past was of a yellowish colour as if polluted by blood. The man (a Muslim jeweller) said, for several days following the general slaughter the water flowed of a bloodred colour. Now fourteen days have elapsed and the colour of the water has turned yellow.

---

25. *TAL*; 190-200; *Nur*, 15b; cf. *Rajwade*, I, 63; *S.P.D.*, XXI, 107; Sarkar, *Fall*, II, 118.
26. *TAL.*, 200; Also *Memoires des Jats*, 47.
27. *Memoires des Jats*, 47.
28. Gupta, *Panipat*, 85; Also *S.P.D.*, XXI, 144, 176; G. Singh, *Durrani*, 177; cf. Najib's cow-slaughter at Barari Ghat in 1757. *Nur*, 17a-17b.

The Hindu hermits were butchered in their huts. "In each hut lay a servered head with the head of a dead cow applied to its mouth and tied to it with a rope round its neck." A Muslim jeweller informed Samin that the Afghans daily appeared to dig the already dismantled houses in search of the buried treasures.[29]

SACK OF VRINDABAN (C. 6TH MARCH)

Woeful was the tale of the countryside as well. The Afghans perpetrated rape, rapine and unmitigated bloodshed all round. About 6th March the people of Vrindaban, another sacred place, were put to the sword and their property was plundered by Jahan Khan and Najib. Our informer relates:

> Where ever you gazed you beheld heaps of slain; you could only pick your way with difficulty owing to the quantity of bodies lying about and the amount of blood split. At one place we reached, we saw about two hundred dead children lying in a heap...The stench and feter and effluvium in the air were such that it was painful to open your mouth or even draw a breath.[30]

BLOODY ENCOUNTER WITH THE NAGAS OF GOKUL (16TH MARCH)

Ahmad Shah Abdali was slowly coming pillaging and killing the people and desolating the rural areas. He divided his forces into groups of 50 soliders each for the purposes of combing the adjacent areas. Halting at Shergarh, Hasanpur, Nadinah, and other places he arrived near Mathura on 15th March, 1757 and encamped at closeby Mahaban. On the 16th, the greedy invader directed a contingent to loot Gokul (two miles away from his camp). But 4,000 martial naga Sanyasis of that place were determined, to defend their religious shrines. In a fierce action 2,000 Nagas fell but not before killing an equal number of the Afghan soldiers. Yet, none of the two sides would yield, Jugal Kishore, an agent of the Bengal governor, was present in the Abdali's camp. He pointed out the futility of fighting the Sanyasis as they possessed no money. The Abdali, therefore, recalled his troops[31] and Gokul became an exception to the all round Afghan devastation. Incidentally, this episode disclosed that the Abdali's cupidity outweighed his religious fanaticism. About this time Sarwar Khan had gone to sack Dhawalpuri.[32]

---

29. *TAL*; 199, 215, *Samin*, 60 and 62; *Nur*, 15b; *D.C.; S.P.D.* (New Series) I, 198; *S.P.D.*, XXI, 107, 108, II, 71, XXVII, 152., *Rajwade*, I, 63; *Amira*, 99; *Memoires des Jats*, 47; *Siyar*, III, 352; Sarkar, *Fall*, II, 118-120; cf. *Shah Alam Nama* (Bib. Ind. New Series No. 1324), 28; *Tarikh-i-Ahmad* (Sultan-ul-Matabe: 1266 A.H.) 9.
30. *Samin*, 60 and 62; Also see *S.P.D.*, II, 71.
31. *Samin*, 60-62; *Raj*. I, 63; Also *TAL.*, 215; D.C.
32. *S.P.D.*, XXI, 111, 112.

SACK AND MASSACRE AT AGRA (21ST MARCH)

About 20th March, Jahan Khan and Najib were recalled from their "commission of raid and slaughter" and directed:

> To move on to Akbarabad where there were many wealthy men, who are the subject of the Jat. These must be either slain or made captives and all their property seized.[33]

Obviously the Abdali's thirst for money had not quenched even after two months of incessant plundering. With 15,000 men, Jahan Khan reached Agra on the morning of 21st March. In order to avoid the horrible fate of lakhs of innocent people, some prominent bankers of the city waited on the general and promised to pay Rupees 5 lakhs. But what he desired was not their empty promises but money which was not easy for them to manage immediately. Jahan Khan lost his patience, more so because the general loot of the former Capital held out better prospects. So he entered and plundered the city, carrying out a general slaughter as far as the Nila Gumbaj. His hectic efforts to take the fort were, however, thwarted by the garrison. While Jahan Khan was still at Agra, his master "suddently" sent to him (23rd March) an urgent message, calling him back to Mahaban. He, therefore, left Agra with the plundered booty along with one lakh of Rupees out of the promised ransom and joined the Abdali on 24th March.[34]

CAUSES OF THE ABDALI'S RETURN

Ahmad Shah kept his "intentions secret" and three days later[35] he suddenly resumed his homeward journey, without making an effort to fulfil his avowed objective of capturing Deeg and Kumbher. The outbreak of sickness in his camp was one of its important reasons. The misdeeds of the Afghans had at last begun recoiling upon their heads. The water of the Yamuna, which they used, reached them after getting polluted at the upstream places (such as Vrindaban and Mathura) which they had converted into "slaughter houses".[36] Consequently, cholera broke out, which took a toll of 150 men daily.[37] However, the pestilence as a factor in his abrupt return should be studied in its proper setting. There is ground to suppose that much of the heat of cholera had receded by the

---

33. *Samin*, 63; Sarkar, *Fall*, II, 122 says that the Abdali's plan was to proceed from Agra as his base and to caputre the Jat forts to extract large tribute from Suraj Mal.
34 *TAL.*, 222, 215; *Samin*, 65; *S.P.D.*, (New Series) I, 198; *Rajwade*, I. 63; *S.P.D.*, XXVII, 146, 152, 155, XXI, 111 also 108, 118 and II, 71; *Memoires des Jats*, 47; G. Singh, *Durrani*, 179-180.
35. *TAL.*, 206; Gupta, *Panipat*, 89.
36. Sarkar, *Fall*, II, 125.
37. *Samin*, 64-65.

time he returned from the Jat country. The exorbitant price of tamarind 100 Rupees per seer, suggests its extensive use. Since the drink made of it was beneficial,[38] it must have prevented infection and also remedied the surviving petients. This apart, we learn that the Afghan soldiers went back on foot as their chargers were required to carry the booty. They even left their artillery behind to spare their draught cattle to do the same job.[39] By implication it means that the Abdali's army was nearly cured. Otherwise the soldiers suffering from diarrhoea and vomitting could not have moved at all, leave alone undertaking long and strenuous homeward journey. One of the two things was bound to be correct, either sickness had ceased to be serious or the patients were also abandoned like the camp baggage, about which we have no information. Finally, the Maratha sardars such as Antaji Bapu, Hingne and Shamsher Bahadur (who were in the Jat country all this while) have not taken notice, of the dreadfulness of the pestilence as the cause of the Abdali's return,[40] even though they had every reason to rejoice over nature's retribution against their foes. All this would show that whatever its form in the beginning, the threat of cholera had more or less been overcome in a short time. Hence, the pestilence, however important, was not the sole cause of the Abdali's sudden return as is commonly believed.[41]

The trend of the events warrants the inference that the Jat's "threatening demeanour"[42] and the Abdali's fear of the Jat forts coupled with the coming of the Maratha army in the adjacent Jaipur State[43] also contributed to his retreat without even having a look at his targets, Deeg and Kumbher. The Abdali had sent repeated messages for tribute to Suraj Mal at Kumbher but he negotiated[44] merely to gain time. Through his diplomatic tact, he on the one hand impressed upon the Abdali the impregnability of his forts, while on the other he held out to him veiled threats. As described below, his professed humbleness was ironically worded and smacked more of stinging taunt than pleasing humility.

Surprising Vrindaban a second time when the Abdali reached Shergarh, he sent to the Jat a letter (through Jugal Kishore) and an officer in another bid to extract money from Suraj Mal. In case of non-

---

38. *Ibid.*, 65.
39. *S.P.D.*, II, 71.
40. Naro Shankar (*S.P.D.*, XXVII, 146) does mention at one place that the summer did not suit the Durranis. But this cannot be stretched to account for the fury of the epidemic.
41. Qanungo, *Jats*, 105; Sarkar, *Fall,* II, 125-126; G. Singh, *Durrani*, 180-181.
42. Sardesai, *Marathas,* II, 405.
43. *S.P.D.*, XXVII, 155.
44. *S.P.D.*, XXVII, 146 says that at one stage Suraj Mal gave out to pay twenty lakhs; *Shah Alam Nama*, 28 and K.R. Qanungo, *Jats*, 106 relying on later sources carry this to incredible figure of fifty lakhs and one crores respectively.

compliance, the invader threatened to destroy him along with his forts. Suraj Mal wrote back in sarcastic though polished language:

> I have no important position and power in the empire of Hindustan. I am one of the *zamindars* living in the desert and on account of my worthlessness not one of the Emperors of the age thought it worthy of him to interfere with my affairs. Now that a powerful Emperor like Your Majesty, determined on meeting and opposing me face to face in the field of battle, would draw his armies against this insignificant person, that action alone would be discreditable to the dignity and greatness of the Shah and would help in the elevation of my position and would be a matter of pride for my humble self. The world would say that the Emperor of Iran and Turan had, out of extreme fear, marched his armies upon a penniless nomad. These words alone would be a matter of great shame for Your Majesty....Moreover, the ultimate result is not altogether free from uncertainty. If with all this power and equipage, you succeed in destroying a weakling like myself, what credit will there be gained? ...But if by divine decree, which is not known to anyone, the affair takes a different turn (i.e. Ahmad Shah is forced to embrace defeat)... all this power and predominance brought about by Your Majesty .... during a period of eleven year will vanish in a moment.
>
> ....As to the threatening and violent order issued for the slaughter and devastation of myself, warriors have no fear on that score. It is well-known that no intelligent man has any faith in this transient life. As for myself, I have already crossed fifty of the stages (of life) and know nothing about the remaining. There shall be no greater blessing than that I should drink the draught (or martyrdom)....in the field of battle with valiant soldiers and leave my name and that of my ancestors, on the pages of (the book of) the age to be remembered that a powerless peasant breathed equality with such a great and powerful emperor as had reduced mighty Kings to subjection and that he fell fighting. And the same virtuous intention lies at the heart of my faithful followers and companions. Even I wish to make up my mind to attend at the threshold of your....Court, the honour of my friends does not permit me. Under such circumstances, if Your Majesty .... forgive me .... and turn your attention to expeditions of greater importance, no harm shall come to your dignity and glory.

The truth about the three forts belonging to (me) the object of your wrath, which have been regarded by Your Majesty's chiefs as (weak as) spider's web, shall be tested only after an actual contest. God willing, they shall be (as invincible as) Alexander's Rampart.[45]

A later authority, summing up the Jat-Durrani negotiations, remarks that the Jat Raja did not leave Kumbher and prepared himself for war. He told the envoys of the Abdali:

> You have not conquered India as yet. If you have taken hold of an inexperienced child (Imad) who held Delhi, what is there (to be pround of)? If you have any pretentions, why this delay (in attacking me)? ..... I have spent large sums of money on this fort. The Shah can be kind to me by fighting with me as that the world may remember in future that a Badshah came from Vilayat and conquered Delhi, but was helpless against an insignificant *zamindar*.[46]

This was perhaps the mightiest challenge, couched in biting sarcasm, to his prowess and authority that Ahmad Shah Abdali even faced in India. Yet he dared not accept it. The argument that 'the terrible loss of life' and the 'daily increasing heat' prevented him from doing it,[47] does not look convincing. Even if we concede the continued severity of the pestilence, the total loss according to the authentic figure of daily deaths would not have exceeded a thousand or so by the time of his departure. And this cannot be termed "Terrible" in the context of such a big army. As for the heat of the summer, it is to be remembered that it was merely the beginning (March) and the climax was still far away. Then again, we know that in 1760 the same Abdali had chosen to brave one full Indian summer with all its scorching heat. Positive evidence suggests that it was the impregnability of he Jat forts accompanied by the threatening postures of their owner, which deterred the Abdali from moving against the forts. Emphasizing that the task of their reduction was "beyond human comprehension" the *Tarikh-i-Alamgir Sani* says, "Since Ahmad Shah calculated that it would take him years to reduce these strong forts, he thought it better to keep off his hands from this expedition." What is more, the Court history accords precedence to this fact over the Afghan sickness as the primary factor obliging the Abdali to return.[48] *Jam-i-Jahan Numa* confirms it when it says, "(Getting) Fearful of the strength of the Jat forts the Shah went back...."[49] Suraj Mal's tact and boldness had borne fruits. The fear of what the

---

45. *Tazkirah-i-Imad-ul-Mulk*, 243-245 quoted by G. Singh, *Durrani*, 181-183.
46. *Jam-i Jahan Numa*, quoted by G. Singh, *Durrani*, 183.
47. G. Singh, *Durrani*, 183.
48. *TAL.*, 215.
49. *Jam i-Jahan Numa*, quoted in *Durrani*, 183; Also see Sardesai, *Marathas*, II,405.

Abdali regarded "spider's web" - Deeg, Kumbher and Bharatpur, had worked up in his mind.

Apart from the Jat ruler's postures the Maratha army also arrived in close by Jaipur and carrying back his immense spoils safely became a source of anxiety to the Shah.[50] It was believed that he "sought an assurance from Suraj Mal not to deceive him (surprise him in his rear) until (he reached) Delhi."[51] On the other side, the Jat envoys in order to be sure that the Shah definitely left for Afghanistan, accompanied him (upto the suburbs of Delhi) alternating their master's stubbornness with the gestures for giving tribute. But when his intentions became certain, the fast camel riders broke the news to Suraj Mal and he dismissed the Abdali's negotiators without paying "a single Kauri" out of the settled tribute of seven lakhs, (five lakhs to the Shah and another two to his Wazir) the first half of which was to be paid at Delhi, while the remaining one at the Shah's next halt.[52]

UNDERLYING CAUSES OF THE SHAH'S EXPEDITION

A close perusal of the Afghan doings gives us an insight into the underlying causes of their Jat expedition, which have not been fully appreciated so far. K.R. Qanungo appears to suggest that the Abdali's attack on "refractory" Suraj Mal was the part of his assumed political duty as the occupier of Delhi's throne.[53] This is untenable. On the other side, Sarkar and Ganda Singh refer to the Jat Raja's noncompliance of the Shah's command to pay tribute, to wait on him, and to surrender recent usurpations and certain refugees as the factors neccesitating this expedition.[54] But even these do not cover every aspect of the issue, in the proper perspective.

All these matters, except tribute, were more in the nature of provocations and as such were the immediate rather than the basic causes. Grabbing the Jat wealth was the primary reason of the Afghan expedition. Confronted with poor resources at home, squeezing money from this country was a perennial objective of the Abdali's doings in

50. Gupta, *Panipat*, 88 and 89; cf. *S.P.D.*, XXI, 119, XXVII, 146, 155; *Amira*, 100.
51. *S.P.D.*, II, 72. It was supposed that Suraj Mal was pursuing the Shah with his men. See *S.P.D.*, XXI, 116.
52. *S.P.D.*, XXI, 111, II, 72, XXVII, 155; cf. *Memoires des Jats*, 48; Relying upon Bhau Bakhar Professor Qanungo (*Jats*, 106-107) puts the settled tribute at 10 lakhs although at another place (*Jats*, 144) he speaks of 5 lakhs. G. Singh (*Durrani*, 183-184), apparently following Qanungo, also mentions 10 lakhs; *TAL.*, 215 says that since Suraj Mal had not at all been compelled he did not accept to pay any tribute whatsoever.
53. Qanungo, *Jats*, 98.
54. Sarkar, *Fall*, II, 115 and 114; G. Singh, *Durrani*, 172.

India.[55] Only his recent loot of Delhi (it could not escape plunder for the second time after Jat war) showed that like that of the Marathas his own greed for money was insatiable. A contemporary, therefore, correctly anticipated:

> He (Suraj Mal) possesses enormous wealth. The foremost enemy of the Hindus (the Abdali) shall never leave him unfleeced.[56]

Apart from the Bharatpur treasures, the rich Jat country also held out an irresistible temptation to the avaricious invader. He, therefore, resorted to a systematic and exhaustive plunder of the extensive Jat areas as it promised him great return.

This expedition was also intended to be a "*jihad*" against the Jat "infidels" as was put by the Bangash envoy (in the Abdali's camp).[57] The Afghans indulged in large scale killing of the civilians including their infants - which smacked of a genocide. In addition, they completely destroyed their habitat and the objects of their religious veneration. This incidentally differentiated the Afghan rapacity from that of the Marathas. The Abdali was not averse to exploiting religion for political ends. Notwithstanding, he was not a fanatic[58] noSr being a foreigner he could have sufficient grounds to be so ruthless towards the local populace (overwhelmingly Jats). And yet they were subjected to such a terrible persecution in course of his expedition.

To a great extent its secret may be traced to the operation of a strong anti-Jat-Maratha- Sikh movement under the leadership of Shah Waliullah of Delhi. Its ultimate aim was to revitalize Islam along its earlier traditions and through it retain Hindustan under the effective Muslim hegemony. This was to be fulfilled through Najib (whom Shah Waliullah encouraged and advised) and the real Islamic soldiers imbued with the spirit of "Jihad".[59] The expansionist Jats were regarded as the mightiest thorn[60] as they were the first supplant the Mughal authority under the very walls of the Capital. Shah Waliullah stressed that

---

55. Sardesai, *Marathas*, II, 372; Gupta, *Panipat*, 68-69, 164; cf. G. Singh., *Durrani*, 261.
56. *S.P.D.*, XXI, 100; Scott (*Dekkan*, II, 233) says that unsatisfied with the wealth of the capital, Ahmad Shah marched against the Jat Raja.
57. *Samin*, 62.
58. On his own he generally displayed a restrained zeal in the religious matters. See G. Singh, *Durrani*, 339-341. It is noteworthy here that once informed that the recluses possessed no wealth he recalled his men from Gokul without destroying the religious shrines there.
59. K.A. Nizami in *Shah*, Introduction and also in *Freedom Movement*, I, 512 ff; Gupta, *Panipat*, 118. Formerly, Shah Waliulla centred his hopes (*Shah*, 31) on Firoz Jung. While inspiring Najib, he also tried to make the Wazir, Imad, mend his ways. *Shah*, 28-30, 33 also 26.
60. Nizami, in *Freedom Movement*, I, 552.

subjugating them "ensures both religious and material gains."[61] He reminded Najib that the Emperor, nobles and people as a whole would have no peace till the above three harsh groups were "extirpated".[62]

Shah Sahib being such an influential figure of his age,[63] his 'root out the Jat' advice must have left its impress upon the leading personages especially Najib, who himself sought his guidance and inspiration on different matters including those concerning the Jats.[64] And the same Najib was the guide of the Abdali in the Indian affairs and as such as believed to be "at the root of all absurdities."[65] What a havoc he and Jahan Khan wrought at, has already been seen before.

The letter which Shah Waliullah wrote (c. February 1757)[66] to Ahmad Shah Abdali offered immediate and added inducement to that Emperor to be all the more rigorous upon the Jat people. Dwelling briefly upon the socio-political conditions and the nature of the Jat-Maratha danger, the reputed theologian described the pitiable plight of the Muslims vis-a-vis the Hindu in India. He says:

> All control of Machinery of government is in the hands of the Hindus...All wealth and prosperity is piled up in their (Hindus) houses, while poverty and misery is threatening the Muslims.

If the situation was allowed to drift "even the name of Islam would not remain anywhere". He further informed him about the persecution of the Muslims by Suraj Mal at Bayana and in the Jat Kingdom saying,

---

61. *Shah*, 1 also see 7-9, 20, 34, 35 and 39.
62. *Ibid.*, 7.
63. Even the Mughal Emperors (Ahmad Shah and Alamgir II) the Wazir (Imad) and other leading nobles (such as Firoz Jang and Najib) and the Queens (such as Udham Bai and Zinat Mahal) deemed it a privilege to visit and consult Shah Sahib. *Shah*, 3-11, 20, 26, 28, 30-34; Also *Muqadma*, 20ff.
64. It can be easily inferred from Shah Sahib's letters to Najib. *Shah*, 4-10.
65. *S.P.D.* XXVII, 144; Raja Keshv Rao (*S.P.D.* XXI, 176) burst forth, "This wicked (Najib) indulged in slaughter at Mathura". Also Sarkar, *Fall,* II, 92.
66. *Shah*, 2. Like almost all of his other letters the present one also contains no date. K.A. Nizami (*Freedom Movement*, I, 531f.) and following him H.R. Gupta (*Panipat*, 121) seemingly suggest that this letter (i.e. 2nd one) was written sometime after October, 1758, in any case not in 1757. However, two references occurring herein disagree with their suggested date. At one place Shah Waliullah writes 'a year is passing now" when Suraj Mal captures Alwar. See. *S.P.D.*, XXVII, 128; *S.P.D.*, (New Series) I, 189 as the Jats capture that fort about 23rd March, 1756 the Shah's letter can at most be placed upto 23rd March, 1757 and not in October, 1758 or beyond. Besides, it is noteworthy that he appeals to the Abdali not to return like Nadir, without crushing the Jats and the Marathas, and yet he does not make even the slightest hint about the Abdali's present devastating Jat expedition. This, when juxtaposed with the reference about Alwar, unmistakably shows that the present letter written before the commencement of the Abdali's Jat expedition *i.e.* sometime before 22nd February, 1757.

"None has the power to restore the Azan and Salat there (in the Jat Kingdom)."[67] The reputed scholar saint appealed to the Abdali not to return like Nadir, without chastising the Marathas and the Jats. Making the most earnest appeals to his religious sentiment, he reminded him that being the most powerful Muslim King, it was his bounden duty to crush the Marathas and the Jats and thus rescue his brethren (the Muslims of India) from "the clutches of the non-Muslims." Apart from him, Alamgir II (who cherished the ideals of his great namesake) and his nobles also made entreaties to the invader to stay on and crush the Marathas and the Jats.[68]

All this could not but produce the inevitable reaction in the mind of the invader, although it must be borne in mind that the great saint was opposed to the molestation of the innocent people, whether Muslims or Hindus.[69] As the Marathas[70] were outside the striking distance, Ahmad Shah, already having his eyes on the Jat wealth and also provocated by Suraj Mal's persisting defiance, finally resolved to bear his full weight upon that ruler. Various circumstances thus combined to work up his fury and one mighty assault on the Jats appeared to be promising him several rewards; his Indian admirers would be pleased, religious glory[71] attained and Suraj Mal's provocations avenged. All along he stood to collect rich spoils and tribute.

CONSEQUENCES OF SHAH'S EXPEDITION

The consequences were indeed terrible. Enough has been said above to repeat again the harrowing tale of sack, slaughter and sacrilege. In the Afghan doings Samin visualized the spectacle "of the day of Last Judgement."[72] The villages from Delhi to Agra were completely desolated and ruined.[73] "Not a man" was left in any hamlet and not even "two seers of grain and fodder" could be found in the areas traversed by the atrocious Afghans.[74] The marks of this man-made "catastrophe" were too visible even 11 years later, when the Jesuit Father thus wrote:

---

67. However, Suraj Mal's generally liberal policy towards the Muslims warrants a different inference. See Chapter XIV, f.n. 9-11.
68. *S.P.D.*, XXVII, 152; cf. *Samin*, 49.
69. cf. *Shah*, 6.
70. According to *Samin* (51) Ahmad Shah on this occasion expressed his resolve to pursue and remove the name of the Marathas from Hindustan. Significantly, the Marathas also suspected that he would march on to Malwa from Agra. *S.P.D.*, XXVII, 166.
71. Having seen the work of Najib and Jahan Khan around Mathura and at other places, Ahmad Shah gave vent to his desire to be remembered as the hero who gave "to Islam peace from the oppression of the infidel (Suraj Mal)..." *Samin*, 63.
72. *Samin*, 60; K.R. Qanungo, comments (*Jats*, 100); "This was not a war but a scalp gathering expedition on a big scale."
73. *TAL.*, 215; Also *S.P.D.*, XXI, 108; *Ibrat*, 17a.
74. S.P.D., XXI, 99, 111

> (The Brij) was totally set on fire and bloodshed by the barbarity of the Durranis, joined by the Rohillas....(and) the environs of Agra and that city itself were desolated more than ever. We see even at this hour (i.e. 1768) the sad marks of it.[75]

The Afghans practically sucked dry the areas within the reach of their hands and they collected immense spoils. As pointed before, the Abdali had to abandon his artillery (later captured by Suraj Mal) and order his soldiers to return on foot to enable his draught-cattle and the chargers to carry the booty. Horses, camels and even donkeys were seized from others for the same purpose.[76] A considerable portion of the spoils requiring such enormous size of conveyance was obviously grabbed from the Jat areas. According to one report booty worth 25 lakhs of Rupees was carried from the city of Mathura alone.[77] And this was the case when nothing but gold and silver was retained by the plunderers. The rest, however, they did not forget to destroy[78] there and at other places.

Though, it is not possible to endorse Naro Shankar's optimism about the Abdali's rout,[79] it is almost certain that had Reghunathrao arrived and joined Suraj Mal, people would have been spared of much of his atrocities. He, however, kept back inspite of the fact that with him and his men lay the responsibility to resist the Abdali. The streams of blood flowed down the streets of Brij and its shrines continued to be desecrated but no Maratha (or for that matter no Rajput) was stirred to action, although it is argued that the Marathas claimed tribute in return for the promise of protection as also liberating and maintaining the sanctity of the holy places.[80] In explaining their conduct, we need not over-emphasize their lack of sufficient sources.[81] It is noteworthy that not long afterwards they despatched 20,000 men to Agra (May 1757—Ed.) for extracting tribute.[82] And no other man but one of their own commanders (Antaji) testified to Suraj Mal's readiness to fight the Abdali, if only the same number of the Marathas could reach on the spot to combine with them.[83] This leads us to infer that a secret pleasure over

75. *Memoires des Jats*, 47.
76. *S.P.D.*, II, 71 and 72.
77. *Rajwade*, I, 63. Booty worth 12 crores of Rupees was grabbed from different places and 30,000 horses, camels, etc. were needed to carry it away. Numerous ladies were also forcibly taken to Afghanistan. Vide Raghubir Singh in *Brij*, 189.
78. *Samin*, 60.
79. *S.P.D.*, XXVII, 146.
80. J.N. Sarkar, (*Fall*, II 189-190) believes that in view of the above factor, the task was impossible for Raghunathrao. However, G.S. Sardesai (*Marathas*, II, 404) and H.R. Gupta (*Panipat*, 106) do not share his views.
82. Chapter XI, f.n. 11
83. *S.P.D.*, XXI, 105.

the distress of their foe (Suraj Mal) and lack of bold initiative on their part also conditioned their movements. Their keeping away from moments of peril was bound to affect Suraj Mal's policy during the Panipat (in 1761), although the Maratha indifference in itself was appreciably due to his own anti-Maratha policy so far.

The Afghan devastation of its parts was sure to adversely affect the resources of the Jat State. All the same, its military strength and the rich treasury mostly remained unaffected.[84] With all his legions, the Abdali failed, like the Maratha hordes three years before, to annihilate Suraj Mal or his main forts. In addition, he could not get "a single Kauri" by way of tribute. The valiant and shrewd Jat Raja, thus, singlehanded [85] tided over yet another, this being the most formidable storm when the Mughal Emperor and his Courtiers....lay overwhelmed by it.[86] Not merely that he emerged as the "strongest" and "richest" potentate in the north.[87]

---

84. cf. *Memoires des Jats,* 48.
85. Facts of sober history belie T.S. Shejwalkar's rather chauvinistic claim (*Panipat*: 1761, Poona, 1946m 48) that Antaji (with his negligible force) served as a shield for Suraj Mal's dominions and his forts. The truth is rather the other way round. Repulsed by the Afghans, he and other Maratha Sardars hid themselves in the Jat states for safety and they left it only after the Shah's departure.
86. G. Singh, *Durrani*, 344; Also Sardesai, *Marathas*, II, 405.
87. *Rajwade*, I, 71; Also *Tawarikh-i-Hunud,* 22a.

XI
The Phase of Cautious Disentanglement (I) (1753–1760)

The period of four years, preceding the fateful contest at Panipat, was characterized in an added degree by the interplay of mutually hostile forces, unscrupulous diplomacy, unsteady policies and mean intrigues. Hardly did anyone cherish a broad vision. The politicians of the day evolved and forsook policies to suit their selfish and narrow interests. Without caring for the Empire or the Emperor who had ceased to be the master of even his own person. Chaos and anarchy grew apace. It was during this period that the Afghans (new entrants into the fray) and the Marathas came to be locked in a deadly rivalry for the mastery of Delhi's Empire. This in turn, threatened to engulf nearly the whole of Hindustan.

This was especially true in case of the Jat State. It was "nearest the danger zone" and enjoyed "the fatal reputation of being excessively rich."[1] Both the contenders were convinced of the partisan value of the Jat Raja. Yet, the irony was that both of them coveted his riches as before. In addition, the Marathas resented his occupation of the suba of Agra,[2] while the indigenous pro-Abdali elements (the forces of political Islam and Najib) desired his people's outright extinction. Besides, the present and the subsequent Emperors made no secret of their anger towards him. His sworn enemy, Najib was now the real master of Delhi's government. The Rohilla chief on his own, was not powerful enough to cope with his resources and strength. But he had the unflinching support of the mighty Durrani, whose own exasperation in view of his recent failure in crushing the defiant Jat can be easily understood. Thus, it is apparent that probably no other leading Prince, even not Shuja-was simultaneously and to this degree exposed to the dual Afghan-Maratha danger. At least none else had to face their fullblooded invasions. Yet, as things stood,

---

1. Sarkar, *Fall*, II, 441.
2. See Raghunathrao's letter, November, 1757, *S.P.D.*, II, 84, XXVII, 158, XXI, 168.

there was little likelihood of Suraj Mal getting any external assistance—a situation for which he had partly to thank his own lukewarm policy[3] as well as his expansionist designs, which cut the line of the Rajput ambition in the north[4] while that of the Bangashes, Marathas and the Rohillas in the adjacent Doab.

The complex situation, however, brought forth the best in Suraj Mal. He displayed "marvellous sagacity", perseverance and "diplomatic shrewdness" in tackling it (Statesmanship requires exercise of caution and restraint). He re-adjusted his policy in the light of the exigencies of the situation and leaned towards cautious tactics and restrained political enthusiasm amidst the Afghan-Maratha tussle. Yet, he did not forego his opportunities all this while. The result, as would be seen, was more gratifying than ever before. In the end, whereas every other Indian power in the fray got "more or less ruined", Bharatpur grew to be the strongest power in the whole of India.[5]

The Jat Raja's immediate concern following the return of the Abdali, was to re-establish those outposts along both sides of the Yamuna which his men had to relinquish in face of the Afghan myriads. He got hold of the imperial fort of Agra as well.[6] Some sporadic references indicate that in keeping with the general practice (including that the top Mughal officials like Najib),[7] he made significant addition to his former possessions. His Jats stole a march over the Marathas by capturing (July, 1757) almost all the *khalisa parganas* of the district of Rewari.[8] Ethnically Jat areas had an added attraction for him. About May, 1758, with a force of 5000, he was busy settling the tract around Meerut.[9] Shortly afterwards he returned and encamped at Palwal.[10]

JAT-MARATHA RAPPROCHEMENT: c. JUNE 1757

About the middle of May, 1757, Raghunathrao sent a force of 20,000 under his chief agent Sakharam Bapu, with Vithal Shivdev, Gangadhar

---

3. For instance, we know that he had not fully helped the Rajputs in their struggle against the Scindes (1755), even though he was a strong advocate of the drive-out-the-Maratha policy.
4. Rival ambitions (in 1756) over Alwar is a case in point.
5. *Memoires des Jats,* 54, 49; Sarkar, *Fall*, II, 441, 442.
6. *TAL.*, 222-223; Sarkar, *Fall*, II, 136, 138, 159; cf. *S.P.D.*, XXVII, 172.
7. "Being most unscrupulous" Najib appropriated even the proceeds of the Princes' estates in the Main Doab country, treating the Mughal Emperor more disparagingly than even Imad. The Emperor, Alamgir, II, wrote, "I am a prisoner in the hands of this Rohilla". *Nur.* 15b-16a; Gupta, *Panipat*, 106.
8. *S.P.D.*, XXVII, 193.
9. *Ibid.*, 226.
10. *TAL.*, 333.

Tatya and Antaji, in the direction of Agra. Reaching the taluka of Wair, they demanded the old dues from the Jat Raja. Vithal Shivdev, the deputy of the Holkar in the governorship of Agra, and the Jat plenipotentiary Rup Ram Kataria began negotiations on 27th May at Bhusawar (a nearby place). The Maratha deputy insisted on the full administrative and financial control of the *suba*. Eventually, a "friendly settlement" was effected between the two sides under which the Jat King was allowed to retain his annexations, including the fort of Agra, on the condition of his paying the instalments of the outstanding tribute of 1754.[11]

This settlement marked a turning point in the Jat–Maratha relations. Their respective compulsions forced them for compromise. It may be recollected that the recent coalition under the Abdali was hostile towards both the Jats and the Marathas. Though the latter escaped its brunt in 1757, their (Maratha's) clash with it looked certain in the circumstances. Even now their fortunes had not remained unaffected as a result of its operation. Their "bitterest enemy" Najib became supreme at Delhi in place of their tool Imad (who had temporarily gone over to the Abdali). This ran contrary to their ambition of dominating the Mughal government. Besides, their authority in the Doab had also been eclipsed by the Durrani supported expedition (Apirl-May, 1757) under the two Mughal Princes and Imad to recover the Doab and Awadh.[12] The Jat outposts (in the Doab) also being threatened, this project itself contributed to bring Suraj Mal, the Marathas as also Shuja, together.[13] In the prevailing situation, crushing Najib and restoring their authority at Delhi and in the doab were the immediate targets of the Marathas. Subjugating the Panjab and leading an expedition to Bihar and Bengal for collecting money were their subsequent plans.[14] Amidst these compulsions the Marathas, though inwardly prejudiced, refrained from an inopportune and uncertain clash with the Jat King. The Peshwa's letter (July, 1757) referred to above, unmasks the Maratha policy which must have been maturing for sometime. He advised Raghunathrao that despite his mischief this year, Suraj Mal should be befriended. Further, in spite of the malice between the Holkar and Suraj Mal, the former should desist from a fight with the Jat Raja." As far as possible (the Marathas should) avoid a conflict with the Jat this year", concluded the Peshwa.[15]

---

11. *Ibid*, 236; *S.P.D.*, XXVII, 158, II, 79, 80, XXI, 148; Sarkar, *Fall*, II, 159; cf. *Raj*, I, 136.
12. For details of this abortive expedition see Sarkar, *Fall* II 130ff.
13. *S.P.D.*, XXVII, 152; Sarkar, *Fall*, II, 9; cf. *S.P.D.*, II, 74.
14. For details see *S.P.D.*, II, 80, *Rajwade*, I, 136; Gupta Panipat 93.
15. *S.P.D.*, II, 80.

Little wonder, therefore, that the Marathas tried to make friends with Suraj Mal. Instead of downright cash, they kept content with his empty promise for payment (which in the light of his general evasion in the past was as good as not made at all). In addition, they respected the Jat annexations, as they did not wish to leave an estranged Suraj Mal in the rear while undertaking their distant enterprises.[16] It is clear that with all their superior strength, the Marathas could not have accomplished both things at one and the same time to prevent the Jat expansion under their very feet and yet to spare their troops to realize their new ambitions and effectively confront the Abdali and his henchmen.

On his part, the Jat King himself wished to avoid further desolation of his principality now at the hands of the Marathas.[17] Even otherwise it would be foolish to open a fresh front (with the Marathas) when the potential Afghan danger already lurked about. This apart, the difference between the recent Afghan atrocities and the present Maratha gestures was too distinct to have been missed by him. Hence, the pressure of the circumstances and the incomparably greater threat from the mightier and common foe drew the former adversaries together. It is then to the middle of 1757 rather than to 1754,[18] that the Jat-Maratha accord should correctly be traced. Yet, the compulsions which brought about this accord constituted its weakness as well. Underhand dealings and suspicions on both sides still lingered on, though, on a much reduced scale.

SURAJ MAL AND ALI GAUHAR - IMAD TUSSLE: SURAJ MAL'S PATCH UP WITH IMAD

Three months afterwards (September, 1757) the Marathas and Imad (who had again won the former to his side) expelled their common enemy, Najib, from Delhi with the connivance of the Emperor.[19] It is said that the Jats also co-operated with them.[20] The change of the real masters at Delhi, however, brought no change in the general conditions. Undisputed power was the sole concern of the triumphant Wazir, Imad, and he attempted to weed out possible rivals from the Capital. From May 1757 to March 1758 the heir-apparent, Mirza Abdullah (entitled, Ali Gauhar and Sah Alam) had been energetically trying to recover his *jagirs* in the Rewari-Rohtak districts. But the Wazir got him recalled and, treacherously planning for his arrest, attacked him in May, 1758.

---

16. cf. Sarkar, *Fall*, II, 136.
17. *TAL.*, 236.
18. Contra see, Sarkar, *Fall*, II, 437-438; Gupta, *Panipat*, 48; Qanungo, *Jats*, 96.
19. For details, see Sarkar, *Fall*, II, 140ff.
20. *Muharbat*, 10; K.A. Nizami in *Shah*, Introduction, 43.

The prince was, however, fortunate to escape to Vithal Shivdev's camp. Therefrom he again went to his *jagir* in the company of that Sardar (last week of May).[21]

Raja Suraj Mal despatched his son, Ratan Singh, to wait on the Prince at Pataudi. On his father's behalf the Jat Prince presented 101 *asharfis* to Ali Gauhar along with Rupees 2,000, 1 elephant, 7 horses and 5 clothrolls as tribute besides the vast quantities of foodstuffs and other provisions loaded on camels and carts.[22] Apparently, this was a well calculated diplomatic move on the part of the shrewd Jat to turn Imad-Ali Gauhar tussle to his own advantage. By his gestures he tried on the one hand to allure the wandering heir-apparent to his side, while on the other to overawe Imad into seeking terms with him. What was Ali Gauhar's reaction we do not know. But Imad was "greatly perplexed" by the Jat support to his rival.[23] He had earlier (30th March, 1758) put under surveillance his another rival, Intizam following the interception of his letters soliciting help from the Jat and Rohilla chiefs.[24] But Ali Gauhar was beyond his reach and appeared to have the powerful backing of the Jat Raja as well. The Wazir now resorted to cajoling the Jat Raja, whom he had relentlessly opposed since October, 1753.

On 2nd June, 1758 (25th Ramzan, 1171 A.H.), he summoned the old mediator, Nagar Mal (who was intimate to the Jat Raja) and asked him to persuade the latter not to espouse Ali Gauhar's cause. Taking formal sanction from the helpless Alamgir II, the Wazir despatched his envoy on 3rd June (26 Ramzan), with a six piece robe of honour and a studded head-dress for his old enemy (Suraj Mal). It was obviously this development that the astute Jat had been aiming at. The same day Nagar Mal conveyed the Wazir's appeal to the Jat King at his camp at Palwal. The negotiations between them continued for three days. On 6th June (29th Ramzan), Nagar Mal went back accompanied by Nahar Singh (another son of Suraj Mal) and acquainted the Wazir with the Raja's response. Nahar Singh stayed at Khizrabad.[25]

The prolonged negotiations followed by Nahar Singh's visit to Delhi and the subsequent events suggest that Ali Gauhar's case channelized the Palwal talks to the basic issue, namely, the Jat–Wazir relations and that their outstanding differences were sorted out. As one of its first indications, Suraj Mal refrained from extending any help to Ali Gauhar, which Imad

21. For details of Ali Gauhar's activities see Sarkar, *Fall*, II, 161ff.
22. *TAL.*, 330.
23. *Ibid.*, 330.
24. *S.P.D.*, XXVII, 226; Also Sarkar, *Fall*, II, 164.
25. *TAL.*, 332-333; Antaji (*S.P.D.*, XXI, 160) imputes unfounded motives to Nagar Mal's mission.

had apprehended earlier. It is believed that later (c. August, 1758), he positively declined to help redress that Prince's cause.[26] *Tarikh-i-Alamgir Sani* records a hitherto unnoticed incident in this regard. It tells us that to thwart Ali Gauhar's plans of subjugating Bihar and Bengal, Imad got another Prince, Hidayat Bakhsh, appointed (February, 1759) the governor of Bihar and Ali Gauhar declared a rebel. In doing so, the arch schemer solely counted upon Suraj Mal's "big forces". His plan was that Hidayat Bakhsh should first proceed to Agra, enlist the Jat support and then march towards Bihar. But in the meantime (March), came the news of Suraj Mal's departure for Jaipur. This disappointed the Wazir. "What (he had) thought and what happened", remarked the Court historian.[27]

For our purpose the above plan is not as important as the light it throws on the Jat-Wazir relations in February-March, 1759. It indicates to what extent the Wazir had come to bank upon the Jat strength even though he did not yet part with the Marathas either. However, Dattaji Scinde's[28] aggressiveness drifted him closer to the Jat Raja. The process reached its culmination a year later (on or before 9th January, 1760), when Imad, disenchanted with the Maratha alliance, repaired for safety against the Abdali to the Jat Court, where he had already sent (November, 1759) his family and belongings. What an irony: As Wendel puts it, Imad now stood suppliant before the same Suraj Mal and his forts to annihilate which "not long ago he had armed the whole of Hindustan". Suraj Mal showed all respect and attention due to the dignity of the Wazir and lodged him in his best palace at Bharatpur. Political expediency and characteristic generosity alike guided him in extending patronage to the imperial Wazir. This heightened his image.[29] Yet Imad, besides being the Chancellor, was also a notorious regicide. Hence, giving asylum to such a man could not but provide an additional rallying point to his opponents. As a consequence of the Wazir-Jat combine, Shah Alam became apprehensive about his political future. Imad was his mortal enemy and Suraj Mal had latterly been siding with him. He suspected Imad with the help of Suraj Mal would raise some one else to the throne (evidently, he had not heard of Imad's prior enthronment of Shah Jahan II on 30th November, 1759) and he appealed to the Abdali to grant him the Crown of Delhi.[30]

---

26. Francklin, *The History of the Reign of Shah Aulum*, London (1798), 9-10.
27. *TAL.*, 380.
28. For the Scinde's aggressiveness towards the Wazir see Sarkar, *Fall*, II, 199-202.
29. *Memoires des Jats*, 49-50, 63; *Imad*, 111; *Rajwade*, I, 143, 144; *S.P.D.*, XXI, 176; *Mirat* 892, 905-906; *Shakir*, 100; *Nur*. 27b; *Siyar*, III, 375-376; *Ibrat*, 21a; *Gulistan*, 58; *Gul.*, 83; *Majmaul-Akhbar*, in Elliot, VIII, 363; *Muharbat*, 10f.; Francklin. *The History of the Reign of Shah Aulum*, London (1798), 15.
30. *Murasalat-i-Ahmad Shah Durrani*, 21, Quoted by G. Singh, *Durrani*, 232-233.

JATS AND THE AFGHAN MARATHA STRUGGLE

We may now briefly notice the relevant Maratha doings. After the return of Raghunathrao (May, 1758) another army under Dattaji Scinde came to the north (December, 1758). Dattaji made an unsuccessful bid to arrest Najib. This precipitated a war which culminated in the Maratha siege of Sukkartal (July-December, 1759).[31] Najib defended himself brilliantly but in the name of religion and Afghans race, he repeatedly appealed to his master, the Abdali for help. The siege was still on when Dattaji received the news of the coming of the Abdali. In face of heavy odds, he solicited help among others from the Jat King also. Consequently, the latter despatched a contingent of 5,000 under Rup Ram Kataria. It joined the Scinde on 8th November, 1759, at Sukkartal.[32]

Several considerations influenced the decision of the Jat Raja. Of all, the most important was the singleness of purpose. Whereas Malharrao—described as "the chief destroyer of Hindustan" by a contemporary[33]—althrough shielded his adopted son, Najib[34], Dattaji was required to altogether crush that "treacherous" supporter of the Abdali[35]. Suraj Mal also held a similar view, so that the Abdali's "prospects of any assistance from the traitors within "might be finished.[36] Besides this broad issue, the atrocities perpetrated by the Rohilla chief in 1757, and his rival ambitions over the Jat areas in the Doab (such as Meerut), must have also prompted the Jat Raja to make a common cause with the Marathas against the common enemy. Moreover, as against the Holkar, the Scindes were agreeable to the Jats for their (especially Jayappa's) gestures during the siege of Kumbher. Dattaji replaced the Holkar and he reversed the policy of his predecessor. Herein lay possibly another factor affecting the Jat decisions.[37]

At Sukkartal the brave Rohilla showed no signs of giving up and the Abdali, having undone the Maratha gains in the Panjab, was threatening Dattaji in the rear. At last on 8th December, Dattaji raised the futile siege. He entrusted (c. 20th December, 1759) his family, heavy baggage, and the disabled camp followers to the care of the Jats to be escorted to

---

31. For this siege and other non-Jat affairs see *Rajwade*, I, 140-145; *S.P.D.*, XXIX, 56, XXI, 176; *D.C; Nur.* 19b-20b, 22b-26b; *Siyar*, III, 371ff.
32. *Rajwade*, I, 143, 147; K.R. Qanungo, *Jats*, 112 does not take note of the Scinde's invitation to Suraj Mal. According to him Jat troops went to Delhi and not to Sukkartal.
33. *Memoires des Jats*, 41, footnote.
34. cf. Raghunathrao's statement, quoted by Sardesai, *Marathas*, II, 417.
35. See the Peshwa's letter quoted by Sarkar, *Fall*, II, 232-233.
36. Qanungo, *Jats*, 109.
37. cf. *Ibid.*, 112; Also Sarkar, *Fall*, II, 199-200.

Delhi[38] while he set himself to arrest the foreigner's advance. But the fate had decreed otherwise. After two engagements, the first at Tarori (24th December) and the second near the Yamuna (29th), he was forced to retreat to Delhi. Herefrom he sent off (c. 4th January, 1760) his own and his officers' families and the heavy equipage towards Rewari (in the Jat country) in charge of Rup Ram Kataria.[39] On 9th January, 1760, Dattaji was killed fighting heroically against the Abdali at Barari Ghat.[40] A virtual hide and seek then commenced between the Afghans and the dispirited Marathas, which ended only with the rout of the Holkar's men (4th March) at Sikandarabad. The same day Malhar and Gangadhar fled to Agra and Mathura respectively. Rup Ram Kataria also returned with them. Jahan Khan pursued the vanquished upto the bank of the Yamuna opposite Mathura. They sought safety in the Jat State or Etawah. The back of the Maratha's resistance to the invader's combination was thus broken.[41]

In his distress the Holkar swallowed his old enmity with Suraj Mal. As is evident from his own letter (3rd February, 1760), he had begun to realize how helpful his redoubted foe could be in the changed circumstances.[42] He now took steps to defreeze his relations with him. From Agra he made off in the direction of Bharatpur. When he reached some 30 miles from that place, Suraj Mal, who seems to have been nearby, met him (before 12th March). The solemn assurances of friendship, sworn to on the 'Bel' leaves and the Ganga water, followed. As a proof of amity, the elderly Maratha stalwart gave robes of honour to the Jat, while the latter offered full protection to his erstwhile opponent and his men.[43]

---

38. *Rajwade*, I, 147; cf. *S.P.D.*, II, 110.
39. Meanwhile numerous people, both the Hindus and the Muslims, had fled to the "safest" heaven of refuge, the Jat state. *Memoires des Jats,* 49; *S.P.D.*, XXI, 176; *Rajwade*, I, 143, 144, 150; *Mirat*, 892-893; *Nur*. 27b.
40. For details of Dattaji's battles with the Abdali see Gupta, *Panipat*, 126ff.
41. For details see *S.P.D.*, XXI, 182-185, 188, II, 120, 121; *Rajwade*, I, 178, VI, 403; *D.C.*; *Nur*. 31a-31b; *Shakir*, 100; *Siyar*, III, 380-381; *Shah Alam Nama*, 123; *Muharbat*, 11.
42. *S.P.D.* II, 117, Also *Raj*. I, 164. The version of *Amira* (102-103); *Siyar* (III, 380); *Tarikh-i-Ibrahim Khan* (in Elliot, VIII, 272); Scott (*Dekkan*, II, 239) and following *Siyar* of Qanungo (*Jats*, 118) that after Barari Ghat the Holkar unsuccessfully importuned the Jat Raja to jointly move against the Abdali cannot be accepted in view of the Holkar's own omission of the supposed incident. No Marathi despatch or the Jat histories refer to it.
43. *S.P.D.*, II, 121; Gupta, *Panipat*, 132; G. Singh, *Durrani* 243. Completely ingorning the utter helplessness of the Holkar at the moment, *Shejwalkar* (*Panipat*, 49) forwards a strange argument that Suraj Mal joined the Holkar and Scinde simply because they had become weak after their defeat at the Abdali's hands.

AHMAD SHAH AND SURAJ MAL IN 1760

The Abdali had been enquiring about the movements of the Wazir and Suraj Mal and the latter's relations with Najib.[44] After routing Dattaji, he turned his attention to Suraj Mal who had collaborated with the former. On 14th January, he came to Khizrabad and wrote to him and the other Hindu and Muslim chiefs, ordering them to pay tribute, present themselves in his court and join him against the Marathas. But the addressees had no faith either in the perfidious Abdali or in the exacting Marathas. On his part, the Jat King cleverly refused to comply with the Abdali's demands unless he substantiated his claims by an effective and lawful possession of the sovereignty of Hindustan. The Abdali was incensed at this renewed defiance. Meanwhile, Najib also instigated him again to lead an expedition and "destroy" the Jat. Hence partly to punish him and partly to pin him down and thus prevent his possible junction with the Maratha fugitives, he set out for the second time against Suraj Mal. On 27th January, he left Khizrabad, marched into the Jat State and via Shergarh came to Deeg on 6th February. Next day he invested that fort. But a few days' experience revealed to him the magnitude of his task and he left that place in the pursuit of Malharrao, then advancing northwards.[45] He later defeated him as noted above.

Meanwhile, Najib entreated his master to stay on and crush his enemies. For the Abdalis encampment he suggested Ramgarh (Aligarh), which belonged to his enemy, the Jat Raja. Accordingly on 5th March the Abdali arrived at and besieged that place. Ramgarh was a strong and well provided for fort and was deemed capable to hold out for long. But the Afghan occupation of the intervening land upto the Yamuna cut off its garrison from outlying Bharatpur (60 miles). The fort commandant, Durjan Sal grew disheartened and after 19 days he surrendered that place, half of which was plundered by the new occupants. The sudden and unexpected fall of this fort, coupled with the loss of his possessions east of the Yamuna, worried Suraj Mal. As confrontation with the Afghan combination was out of question, he chose to amuse the Abdali by opening negotiations. The Abdali, however, saw through the game and he demanded Rupees 45 lakhs.[46]

---

44. *S.P.D.*, II, 106.
45. *D.C.; S.P.D.*, XXI, 186, 187, II, 118; *Mirat*, 906; Also *Memoires des Jats*, 51; *Francklin*, 15; *Muharbat*, 12; G. Singh, *Durrani*, 233-234; Gupta, *Panipat*, 138. T.S. Shejwalkar (*Panipat* 30) follows imagination rather than facts in asserting that Malhar's tactics "saved" the Jat and Rajput Princes. He somehow ignores that the Abdali did not intend to destroy the Rajputs, with whom he had been on intimate terms (See S.H. Askari,Durrani-Rajput Negotiations 1759-1761) in *Proc. I.H.C.* (1945), 258-269, and that his mere whirlwind march was not going to penetrate the Jat defences.
46. *Nur.* 31b-32b; D.C.; *Memoires des Jats*, 51-52; *Mirat* 906; *Imad* 117; *Gulistan*,

RIVAL ATTEMPTS TO WIN OVER THE JATS

As the shadow of the prospective Afghan-Maratha conflict lengthened, the entire political atmosphere became surcharged with intense and intriguing diplomacy. Pressures and persuasions, threats and allurements and religious excitement, all were brought into full play by the contenders to win over the allies. The Jats occupied a conspicuous position among the northern powers. We learn from a letter of Shah Alam II that some personages, including the imperial Diwan of Crown-lands impressed upon the Abdali the relative strength of the Jat Raja by terming him as "the key to India". This estimate may not be correct in its entirety in the situation of 1760. But it could not be dismissed as a mere "fabrication" either, as the helpless Shah Alam did in his defeatist grudge against the protector of his mortal enemy, Imad.[47] We know that as early as 1757, he had come to be regarded as the strongest and richest ruler in the north.[48] The Nawab of Awadh no doubt possessed the death-defying band of the Nagas and Qizilbashes. But in point of cool obstinate valour, Suraj Mal's Jats were inferior to none. And so far as the generalship was concerned, Shuja compared poorly with the Jat veteran Ghulam Husain adds:

> There were no troops in India that could pretend to face them (mounted matchlockman trained by Suraj Mal himself) in the field.[49]

Moreover, Suraj Mal also possessed, as Shuja did not, at least 4 fairly spacious, best provisioned (both in terms of munition as well as food and fodder) and the then strongest forts, whose strength was such that no power in the whole of the Asian continent was deemed capable of capturing them.[50] These forts could serve as bases for operations as well as refuge in adverse moments. Besides, for reasons of invisible tribal ties, the outlook of their chief spokesman (Jat Raja) could not but condition the friendship or enmity (towards a particular contender) of the entire warlike Jat populace spread distantly around the Capital, which was, as it turned to be, the likely fighting zone. The general disposition of the non-combatants, even though directly meaningless, was sure to affect the flow of supplies, which had a significance of its own in a marathon contest. Thus, from the viewpoint of the military utility Suraj Mal had a definite edge over Shuja as well—a fact which

---

47. *Murasilat-i-Ahmad Shah Durrani*, 21, quoted by G. Singh *Durrani*, 232-233.
48. *Rajwade*, I, 71.
49. *Siyar*, IV, 28. Even if this remark is taken to refer to the post-Panipat period of that Raja's life, it should be borne in mind that this excellence could not have been achieved overnight.
50. *Supra*, 102. Also *Memoires des Jats*, 39-40; *TAL.*, 200, 215.

has not been emphasized so far.[51] The fact that both the opponent (the Abdali and the Marathas) appeared to be taking greater pains in wooing Shuja than Suraj Mal cannot mislead us, if only we keep in mind their respective positions in the setting of 1760. It would appear that Suraj Mal was already more involved than Shuja in the Afghan-Maratha rivalry when both sides intensified hunt for allies. Ever since the siege of Sukkartal (i.e. since November, 1759), his contingents had been associated with one of the two rivals (the Marathas). In addition, he at the time had given shelter to most of the Maratha fugitives against their Afghan enemies. As such there could be no mistaking about his leanings towards the one as against the other rival. To the corresponding degree the intensity of the efforts to win him over was bound to be lessened; from the side of the Marathas because of their basic confidence, while from the side of the Afghans because of their proportionate pessimism. As against Suraj Mal, Shuja's case was evenly open. Having silently gone back from Sukkartal, he had scrupulously avoided taking sides in the subsequent struggle. His impartial postures thus held out equal chance for both the suitors. This possibly formed the secret of their showing more efforts in his than Suraj Mal's case.

And yet Suraj Mal's adhesion, failing that his neutrality was "coveted" by both the contenders.[52] Ahmad Shah had displayed wanton tyranny in 1757 and only recently he had attacked him (February, 1760). As such he stood only a remote chance of an alliance with the Jat Raja[53] and though he instructed his envoy to persuade him to join his side, he mainly concentrated upon securing the Jat neutrality. In addition, he tried to realize a big amount of money from Suraj Mal. With these objectives he despatched Hafiz Rahmat on 16th May to Mathura to negotiate with the Jat as also the Marathas. The Rohilla Sardar proceeded to Bharatpur accompanied by Suraj Mal and Gangadhar Yashwant. Suraj Mal acted as the middleman in the Maratha negotiations with the Afghan envoy but they produced no results. In his own case, as he was unwilling to adhere to the invader, he simply prolonged the discussions to gain time. At length when Bhau arrived (8th June), the Rohilla was dismissed without achieving anything at all.[54]

---

51. Contra see Srivastava, *Shuja*, 76f; Sarkar, *Fall*, II, 274ff. H.R. Gupta (*Panipat*, 137), however, acknowledges "Almost equally important was Raja Suraj Mal, the richest and strongest Hindu ruler in northern India."
52. Gupta, *Panipat*, 137; Qanungo, *Jats*, 138-139.
53. cf. Gupta, *Panipat*, 137.
54. See *D.C.*; *S.P.D.* II, 127, 124; Shakir, 100; *Tarikh-i-Hussaini* quoted by Qanungo, *Jats*, 119 also cf. 139; Sarkar, *Fall*, II, 246-247, 274; Gupta, *Panipat*, 138; Shejwalkar, *Panipat*, 36; cf. *Mirat*, 906; *Gulistan*, 59; *Gul.* 84; *Muharbat*, 12; For a detailed discussion about Ahmad Shah's inability to subdue Suraj Mal see *Memoires des Jats*,, 55-56.

It is noteworthy to examine here the inner working of Suraj Mal's mind in the present context. We know that he was the only Indian Raja to have so heavily suffered at the hands of both the extortionate Afghans as well as the greedy Marathas. Both of them now sought his alliance or neutrality only to fry their pan. The shrewd Jat Raja could easily realize that their (especially Marathas') soft postures accrued from their pressing needs and once they were over, the victor would not hesitate to swing back to the old ways. Raja Keshavrao aptly observed (10th March, 1760) that Suraj Mal and others feared the Marathas on one side while Ahmad Shah on the other.[55] Choice between the two was thus difficult indeed. Yet, in the circumstances it had to be made and[56] Suraj Mal, discarding the Abdali, leaned towards the Marathas as the lesser of the two evils.

Varied considerations seem to have influenced his thinking. At the outset it may be recollected that he hailed from a proud stock, which had opposed to its might almost every foreign invader including Ahmad Shah himself (at Manupur). A treacherous collusion with the Shah by an illustrious son of that stock thus stood against its national characteristic. Suraj Mal had once emphasized it, in his letter to Ahmad Shah Abdali (1957).[57] The weightier factor, however, was his own interest. We know that Ahmad Shah was the prop of the internal anti-Jat forces. Shah Waliullah, who along with Najib, was the "chief agent" in bringing about the battle of Panipat,[58] deemed annihilation of the Jats as a step towards the revival of Islam and the Muslim political hegemony.[59] However, the Marathas had no such avowed objective before them. At any rate there was no scope for the religious considerations to the material differences between the two. Moreover, Suraj Mal could not have easily forgotten the bitter memories of the Abdali's gruesome sack and slaughter (in 1757), which outclassed all the grasping tyranny of the Marathas put together. These factors weighed with the Jat Raja and he turned down the Abdali's "overtures for alliance"[60], both in January, 1760 as also afterwards.

Meanwhile, the Marathas made efforts to win him over to their side. We learn from a despatch that Suraj Mal agreed to depute 10,000 men to fight anywhere in the Marathas van provided they desisted from creating "disturbance" in his country and dunning him for tribute. The acceptance

---

55. *S.P.D.*, XXI, 187 also 188, cf. 186; *Memoires des Jats,* 52, 51; Also see *Rajwade*, I, 71.
56. Qanungo, *Jats* 108.
57. *Supra*, see ch. X, f.ns. 45,46.
58. K.A. Nizami in Shah, *Muqadmah,* 42 also in Freedom Movement, I, 532.
59. *Supra*, ch. X, f.ns. 57-68.
60. G. Singh, *Durrani*, 243; cf. Qanungo, *Jats,* 115-116.

of these conditions amounted to abandoning their age-old practices. Yet, so keen were the Marathas to retain his support that they acceded to these demands.[61] It is noteworthy that when Bhau entered the Jat domains on 8th June, 1760, he forbade his soldiers on fear of strictest punishment to harass the Jats or molest their territories.[62] In response, the Jat ruler supplied the hard pressed Maratha hordes with huge quantities of food-stuffs and other requirements, which sufficed them for over a month.[63]

JATS JOIN BHAU

Right from the start the Maratha commander attempted to win over allies. He wrote, though in vain, to the various Hindu and Muslim chiefs, seeking their help in banishing the invader.[64] The Sarva Khap Panchayat of the upper Doab, however, responded to his call.[65]

From his camp south of the Bangaga river (20 miles south of Agra) Bhau wrote to Suraj Mal entreating him to expeditiously unite with his forces. The Raja, however, suspected treachery and hence hesitated to visit the Maratha camp till the Holkar and the Scinde furnished personal oaths and solemn assurances concerning his safety. On 30th June, 1760, the Holkar conducted the Jat King (at the head of 8 to 10 thousand troops) and Imad to Bhau. Bhau, in person, advanced two miles to honourably welcome his only as also an important ally (Suraj Mal). The renewed pledges followed, Bhau taking the Yamuna's water in his hands as a solemn proof of his alliance with the Jat Raja. The Wazir held a conference with Bhau through the mediation of Suraj Mal.[66]

---

61. *S.P.D.*, XXI, 190. By way of its date, this letter merely refers to 19th Muharram, and not to the particular year. The mention of the name of Badan Singh along with that of Suraj Mal, herein would show that the above negotiations occurred in the former's lifetime *i.e.* before 9th June, 1756. But the fact that the Marathas continued to press Suraj Mal for money even after that date, goes against it. From the tone of the letter as well as Bhau's conduct, respecting the Jat conditions, it seems that the Bhau's arrival *i.e.* before 8th June, 1760 rather than after it, as *S.P.D.*'s, editor G.S. Sardesai guesses. The incorporation of Badan Singh's name appears here due to the slip of its writer.
62. *S.P.D.*, II, 126; Also *Rajwade*, I, 199; contra see Dow, *Hindustan*, II, 339.
63. Sarkar, *Fall*, II, 243-244; *Memoires des Jats*, 53.
64. *Rajwade*, I, 174; *S.P.D.*, XXIX 41; Shejwalkar, *Panipat*, 37.
65. We are told that subsequently the above Panchayat at its meeting held at Sisauli under the Presidentship of Danat Rai, decided to despatch a milita under the command of Chowdhary Sheo Lal Jat of village Shoram (Muzaffarnagar) to the help of the Maratthas. Vide Bhau's letter, *Muzaffarnagar Records*, Kanha Ram, 19.
66. *Purandare*, I, 387; *S.P.D.* II, 127; *Amira*, 103; *Siyar*, III, 382-383; *Tarikh-i-Ibrahim Khan* in Elliot, VIII, 274-275; *Imad*, 121, 272; Scott, *Dekkan*, II, 240; Also *Memoires des Jats.*, 53; *Mirat*, 907; *Nur*, 32b; Qanungo, *Jats*, 123-124 and 132; Dow (*Hindustan*, II, 339) is wrong in claiming that 50,000 Jats joined the Marathas, Francklin, *The History of the Reign of Shah Aulum*. London (1798), 18.

When asked for his advice, Suraj Mal emphasized "caution and reflection in conducting the war" against a mighty and clever enemy like the Abdali. He proposed that the ladies, the heavy equipage, big guns and such other things, which were of little use in the present struggle, should be despatched to Jhansi, Gwalior or any one of his "four iron like forts". The line of supplies should be kept safe and open. The provisions, he ensured, could be procured from the Jat country. The Jat veteran disapproved of pitched contest. Instead, he stressed that unencumbered cavalry should constantly engage the enemy in irregular warfare. In other words the allies should stick to their traditional and tested guerilla system. The astute Jat went on that strong detachments should be sent towards, the Afghan homelands. This would not only cut off the enemies supplies but also create a diversion and thus force his Indian allies to desert the Abdali. Perplexed by this strategem as also by the rainy season, the invader would go back and his Afghan henchmen would be brought to their knees, so calculated the Jat Raja. Malharrao Holkar, by far the most experienced Maratha general, concurred with this sagacious advice. However, young Bhau despite being a complete stranger to the north and its people, preferred the new mode of warfare, namely, to engage the enemy in pitched contest through infantry tactics. He, therefore, slighted this wise counsel. Both Suraj Mal and the Holkar felt disgusted at his attitude. Though differences over the plan of campaign did not lead to open rift, some coolness arose between Suraj Mal and Bhau and whatever enthusiasm the former had developed for the Maratha side was affected at the very beginning.[67]

The facade of unity was however, maintained between the two. Bhau accompanied by Suraj Mal inspected the Yamuna near Agra on 14th July, 1760. Finding it unfordable, the earlier plan to cross the river and then effect a junction with Govind Ballal was now dropped. Two to three thousand reckless Jat soldiers still crossed the flooding Yamuna, but no Maratha ventured the same and the Jats were cut off from the rest of the armies. Bhau now decided to capture the Capital and he moved on to Mathura on 16th July. He asked the Jat Raja to help him in "conquering and settling" Delhi.[68] From Mathura he detached a strong force to Delhi

---

67. *Imad*, 273-276. However, its assertion that Bhau humiliated Suraj Mal at Agra does not appear to be correct for the simple reason that in view of his pressing needs he could not afford to alienate his only ally at that stage. Qanungo, *Jats*, 125ff; *Tarikh-i-Ibrahim Khan* (in Elliot, VIII, 275) claims that Bhau on his own endorsed the Jat plan but eventually discarded at the behest of Vishwasrao. This is incorrect. Gupta, *Panipat*, 153; Also Sarkar, *Fall*, II, 256, footnote; For a discordant note see Shejwalkar, *Panipat*, 42f.

68. *Rajwade*, I, 217, 217a, 216 also 204, 205 and 215; Shejwalkar, Panipat, 43.

under the Holkar and Scinde guided by Suraj Mal and the Wazir. The city was captured and soon (22nd July, 1760) it passed into the hands of the Wazir. The Fort was then put to siege. This was defended, though, inadequately by Yaqub Ali Khan, a relation of the Afghan Wazir. On getting the promise of safe exit he evacuated and handed over the fort on 1st August, 1760.[69] Ali Muhammad Khan who wrote only about a year later, adds that the disheartened commandant (Yaqub Ali Khan) decided to make peace and came out to take "a strong pledge", through the Wazir and Suraj Mal. The latter's order got established inside the fort. Bhau "had farfetched ideas in his mind.... He did away with the (Jat) *bandobast* and appointed his own men there". The Wazir (backed by the Jat Raja) represented to the Maratha commander that as he himself was capable of protecting the fort, he (Bhau) should remove his own men. But Bhau was keen for personal control of the Capital and he spurned this appeal.[70]

In order to win Shuja over to his side, Bhau had been in touch with that chief, promising him the Wizarat.[71] On the other side, he had apparently also assured the current holder of that office, Imad, of his re-installation at Delhi.[72] Otherwise, the Wazir would not have confederated and marched with the Marathas upto Delhi. Bhau, however, concealed from his allies his secret promises to Shuja.[73] It was only on 1st August, 1760 that the reality dawned them (Jat King and Imad). On that day, Shuja who was encamped across the Yamuna sent a letter to Bhau through Devi Dutta. Referring to the Maratha proposal, he pointed out that if among others hc (Shuja) was recognised the Wazir and the Marathas agreed to return to the Deccan, he would persuade the Abdali to go back.

SURAJ MAL'S WITHDRAWAL FROM BHAU'S CAMP

This embassy could not remain a secret. The thought of his prospective overthrow "displeased" power hungry Imad and his patron and both of them marched away to their camp at Tughlaqabad the same day. *Delhi Chronicle* adds that next day (*i.e.* 2nd August) the Marathas "rode out to remove (their) anger."[74] This entry (in the above work) has been mainly relied upon by J.N. Sarkar and H.R. Gupta to establish that Suraj Mal

69. *Rajwade*, I, 222-224, 226; D.C.; *S.P.D.*, XXVII, 258; *Nur*, 33a-33b; *Mirat*, 907; *Imad*, 275; *Memoires des Jats*, 53; *Amira*, 103-104; *Siyar*, III, 383-384; *Shah Alam Nama*, 171-172; *Mirat-i-Aftabnuma, 370; Ahwal*, 124; *Muharbat*, 12.
70. *Mirat*, 907; Also see *Purandare*, I, 389 (suggesting his desire to retain personal control).
71. For details see Srivastava, *Shuja*, 78-80.
72. *Shah-Alam Nama*, 171; Also *Mirat*, 907; G. Singh, *Durrani*, 244, footnote; cf. Qanungo, *Jats*, 130.
73. Gupta, *Panipat*, 156.
74. *D.C.*

abandoned the Marathas on 2nd or 3rd August.[75] That right now he finally departed to Ballamgarh has not been specified even by the above authority. The above scholars supplement their version with such sources[76] (including *S.P.D.,* XXI, 190, *S.P.D.,* XXVII 258) which do not specifically place the Jat return under any of the suggested dates. On the contrary, certain hints in most of them suggest a later date, but this discrepancy has been somehow left un-explained.

The available sources need to be critically examined to ascertain the account and date of Suraj Mal's withdrawal. At the outset it is to be noted that overhwelming evidence of the nearly contemporary as well as important later works, the *Sakhas* and strong local tradition link his presence with such well-known events, which occurred after 2nd or 3rd August. Of the scores of the Marathi newsletters, only one (written from Bhau's camp) refers to Suraj Mal's departure, though only briefly and a little ambiguously too. It tells us that Suraj Mal and Imad got annoyed with, and left the Marathas and Mahipatrao Chitnis, Gangoba Tatya and Ramji Anand "have gone to bring them back". It merely refers to September, 1760, but contains no exact date of that month. Significantly, it does speak of Naro Shankar having been appointed the governor of Delhi[77]—an event which took place on 12th August, 1760.[78] We have another fragmentary letter, written about 16th October, 1760, from Bhau's camp near Kunjpura. It makes the significant disclosure that Suraj Mal then was at Ballamgarh and that the Bharatpur troops under the command of his son(?) were shortly due to join Bhau. This letter also expresses the Maratha conviction, "The Jat is ours" and that there was no fear of supplies being obstructed on the Agra Mathura route.[79]

An entry of 24th September (1760), in *Delhi Chronicle,* whose contents are supported by *Mirat-i-Ahmadi* (a work written only eight months after Panipat) throws a good deal of light on our present issue. We are told that in order to assure themselves that Suraj Mal would not rejoin the Marathas, Ahmad Shah Abdali and Shuja sent robes of honour for that chief (at Ballamgarh) and sought intended assurances.[80] These

---

75. Suraj Mal left according to H.R. Gupta (*Panipat*, 156) on 2nd while according to J.N. Sarkar (*Fall*, II, 255) on 3rd August, 1760.
76. Of all the authorities quoted by these scholars, only *Tarikh-i-Muzaffari* (wr. in 1800) is not acessible to us. We, however, presume that had it contained their dates, K.R. Qanungo, who has used it, must have referred to it while contradicting (*Jats*, 138) *Delhi Chronicle*. He, however, follows Bhau Bakhar to place the Jat departure somewhere between 25th September to 25th October. This is equally doubtful.
77. *S.P.D.*, XXVII, 258.
78. Sarkar, *Fall*, II, 266-267
79. *Rajwade*, I, 259.
80. *D.C.*; *Mirat*, 908; Also Gupta, *Panipat*, 138-139.

references belie *Bhau Bakhar's* claim that Suraj Mal left Bhau just before Bhau's departure for Kunjpura[81] (*i.e.* in October, 1760) and also that of a popular Sakha which even makes the Jat go up to Kunjpura.[82] In addition, they make an important hint about the period that had intervened since the Jat's return. Apparently, the above gesture of the Abdali emanated from his apprehension lest the Maratha efforts to placate the Jat should bear fruit. That it was not totally unfounded is borne out by Bhau's letter of 18th September. Therein he assures Govind Ballal that he could seek assistance from the Jat contingent (at Shikohabad) for threatening the homelands of the Abdali's Afghan allies.[83] We know that Suraj Mal had returned annoyed. And Bhau could express such a conviction which suggests a comparative improvement in his relations with Suraj Mal around the middle of September. This leaves an impression that a reasonable period had elapsed since the Jat withdrawl which enabled the Marathas to re-open dialogue with the displeased Suraj Mal and that too in a manner as to cause concern to the Abdali. This, in turn, leads us to look further back, more appropriately to August, 1760, for the intended date, as is also suggested by a number of important sources.

Mir Ghulam Ali Azad (who wrote roughly two years later) relied upon the testimony of the Maratha negotiator with Shuja, who, being in the same camp, had the unique opportunity to know the actual facts. He places the Jat withdrawal after Bhau-Shuja negotiations and the appointment of Naro Shankar to the Capital's governorship (*i.e.* 12th August, 1760).[84] *Tarikh-i-Ibrahim Khan*[85] and *Siyar* accept this in toto, though the latter attributes the Jat departure primarily to that chief's shock over Bhau's removal of the silver ceiling of the Diwan-i-Khas (6th August).[86] So far as we are able to infer, the well-circumstanced eye-witness, Kashi Raj[87] and *Mirat-i-Ahmadi*[88] also place that event impliedly well after the ceiling episode. Ghulam Ali, whose informant was Rao Radha Kishan, a trusted follower of the Jat Raja says that the latter left following Bhau's exorbitant demand for money and his suspicious watch over the Jat Raja.[89] As regards Shah Alam Nama,

81. Qanungo, *Jats*, 132.
82. The Sakha sung by Imaduddin and Party of Haryana. Its type script was sent to me by ex-M.P. Shri Jagdeo Singh Sidhanti of Delhi.
83. *Rajwade*, I, 244; also see its Introduction (by V.K. Rajwade).
84. *Amira*, 105.
85. *Tarikh-i-Ibrahim Khan* in Elliot, VIII, 277-278.
86. *Siyar*, III, 385.
87. Kashi Raj as referred to by Duff. *History of the Mahrathas* (Oxford press: 1921), I, 520 footnote; also Owen, *The Fall of the Mogul Empire*, 247.
88. *Mirat*, 908.
89. *Imad*, 276.

although it does not connect the Jat alienation with any specific event, it all the same tends to put it quite a few days after the capture of the Delhi fort.[90] *Memoires des Jats* also supports the inference that can be drawn from the above analysis. According to it, Suraj Mal came back when Bhau first thought (c. 17th August 1760)[91] of proceeding northward (apparently to Kunjpura).[92] All that the *Bakhar* and persistent tradition suggest is not correct but both these also agree with Suraj Mal still being with Bhau at that time. Thus, varied, weighty and overwhelming evidence leads us to place Suraj Mal's withdrawal from the Maratha camp sometime in the middle of August, 1760 rather than under the alleged date of the *Delhi Chronicle*.[XX]

---

90. *Shah Alam Nama*, 173.
91. The First clear mention of Bhau's resolve to go to Kunjpura is found in a letter of 2nd September, 1760. See *Rajwade*, I, 237. It is implied that the plan had been maturing in his mind for some time. Significantly we find him ordering Govind Ballal as early as 17th August, 1760, to send immediately 500 bullocks, which were needed for dragging the baggage, See *Raj*wade, I, 231. This would show that Bhau began to toy with Kunjpura project right from this time.
92. *Memoires des Jats*, 53; *Tawarika-i-Hunud* silently sidetracks the Panipat days.
XX. Rajpal Singh puts 20th August, 1760 for withdrawl on the evidence of *Scindhias of Gwalior*, II, letter no. 297 dated 20th August 1760, p. 217; also see Gupta, *Panipat*, 161-162 and *Mirat-A-Ahmadi*, 908, cited in *Rise of the Jat Power*, 127, 151, f.n. 209.—Editor.

XII

The Phase of Cautious Disentanglement (II)

CAUSES OF THE WITHDRAWAL OF SURAJ MAL FROM BHAU'S CAMP

The date having been examined, we may now turn to another controversial issue namely Suraj Mal's withdrawal from Bhau's camp. Some scholars[1] attribute this incident predominantly to Bhau's indiscreet insolence to the Jat King. On the other side some Maratha historians,[2] while absolving the Maratha chief, blame Suraj Mal's selfishness alone. But all these historians have mostly relied upon the Maratha sources, generally ignoring the other relevant ones.[3] The account thus prepared has been neither complete nor convincing. No doubt some other scholars[4] have considered a large number of sources but even they have left out relevant information on the subject. Moreover, as the focus of their attention was on a different subject, they have either dismissed the present one summarily or have treated it in a general manner.

At the outset we would like to emphasize the danger involved in singling out any particular factor. The Jat withdrawal was the result of the joint operation of varied factors, some immediate, while others of an abiding nature. We shall discuss them accordingly.

We have noted that even after his assurances, Bhau refused at Delhi to retain on the Wizarat and made secret overtures to Shuja. This played an important role in Imad-Suraj separation from that chief. This duplicity and breach of faith was followed by the appointment of Naro Shankar and Baloji Palhande as the governor of Delhi and the custodian of the fort respectively. This arrangement had nothing to do with the Wizarat. But

---

1. Duff, *A History of the Mahrattas,* I, 520; Owen, *The Fall of the Mogul Empire,* 247; Qanungo, *Jats,* 133ff.
2. Shejwalkar, *Panipat*, 48-49; Sardesai, *Marathas,* II, 435.
3. Duff has taken note of a few Persian histories like *Siyar*, while Owen mainly follows the account of the Maratha Brahmin Kashi Raj. K.R. Qanungo's narrative (*Jats*., 136) is a "free translation" of *Bhau Bakhar.* Likewise, Shejwalkar and Sardesai also depend upon the Marathi sources only.
4. Sarkar, *Fall,* II, 255-257; Gupta, *Panipat,* 156; G. Singh, *Durrani,* 243f.

in the ultimate analysis, the fact of Bhau picking up his own subordinates for these key posts reflected his ambition to brook nobody else's authority over the capital and the imperial affairs.[5] It is said that Bhau remained obstinate even after the entreaties of the Jat, Holkar and Scinde to restore Imad.[6] The latter's hopes of regaining power were thus completely shattered. There were some other factors as well which affected Suraj Mal's decision but in his protege's case this camouflage alone enraged him beyond limits and estranged him forthwith from Bhau. In the realm of intrigues Imad had few equals. Imad now threw in all his weight to detach his Jat patron also.[7]

Accepting *Bhau Sahibanchi Kafiyat* with approbation, some scholars uncritically maintain that Suraj Mal yearned for being and demanded to be made "keeper" of the Capital. But Bhau declined it, which was the predominant or according to one scholar[8] the exclusive cause of his return. Suraj Mal's ambitions conceded, a critical perusal of evidence and the circumstances, however, do not warrant this claim. It is to be borne in mind that besides the *Kafiyat,* we have a wide range of evidence in Persian, French and Marathi (other than the above source) but nowhere do we find any confirmation of this view. Its total omission in contemporary Marathi correspondence is inexplicably strange and extremely significant also. On the Jat side, Wendel has also nothing to suggest, much less to prove it. *Bhau Bakhar*[9] and the persistent Jat tradition so sensitive about the transactions of the Panipat days, do not allude to it either.

Besides, the inherent logic of the events also goes against this notion. It is difficult to justify on practical grounds Suraj Mal's duality of policy and efforts; his pleading for both the Wizarat of Imad as well as his own guardianship of Delhi. The maximum that the second alternative could hold out would have been automatically guaranteed to him by Imad's defacto Wizart. To be the patron of a subservient Wazir was in itself

---

5. *Purandare*, I, 389; Bhau's doings gave rise to wild apprehension that he intended to enthrone Viswasrao on Delhi's throne. See Duff, *op.cit.* 519; *Muharbat*, 12.
6. *Bahu Bakhar* quoted by Qanungo, *Jats*, 130.
7. Dow, *Hindostan*, II, 340; Gupta, *Panipat*, 156; Raghubir Singh (in Brij, 190) says that Suraj Mal became angry and left the Marathas following the Maratha-Afghan peace negotiations.
8. Sardesai, *Marathas*, II, 435. We presume that this is his revised view on this issue. In *Panipat Prakaran*, (quoted by Qanungo, *Jats*, 136-37) he also included the refusl to send the Maratha families to Gwalior, to re-instate Imad and the removal of the silver ceiling, among the causes, of the Jat defection; Shejwalkar, *Panipat*, 43 and 49
9. If it were otherwise, K.R. Qanungo, who wholly bases this part of his account on *Bhau Bakhar*, must have pointed out accordingly.

most flattering to his honour[10] and also conducive to his personal interests. The fact that he backed Imad's case now and continued to do so even afterwards, looks conclusive. One of the two seems to be incorrect: either Suraj Mal did not stand for his protege's chancellorship, or he did not demand the wardenship of the capital. Thus, in the absence of its corroboration by the weightier sources, extant tradition and implied probabilities, the above view cannot be accepted, much less the assertion that his failure in getting the wardenship was the only cause of his departure.

Apparently, all his calculations were essentially linked with the defacto re-installation of Imad as the Wazir. Destitute of his own resources, the Wazir was then a pensioner of and wholly dependent on the Jat Raja.[11] Little wonder, therefore, that Suraj Mal perceived in Imad's re-installation a good opportunity to promote his selfish interests. The traditional Jat policy to earn the favour of Delhi's Wazir appeared to be reaching its culmination. But Bhau's refusal now not only threatened his calculations but also his plighted words to Imad.[12] This could not but annoy the Jat chief.

Evidence in Persian and Marathi emphasizes (in varying degrees) Bhau's removal of the silver ceiling of the *Diwan-i-Khas* as another factor in displeasing Suraj Mal further. *Mirat-i-Ahmad* refers to the Maratha vandalism in general and the stripping of the ceiling in particular as one of the two main factors which made Suraj Mal "writhe with discontent".[13] *Siyar* is most emphatic on the point. According to it, this episode shocked him most and he left the Marathas.[14] In spirit, Bhau Bakhar and the local tradition also agree with it. The former adds that by offering to pay 5 lakhs he tried to dissuade a too needy Bhau from disfiguring that place as that would bring them "no credit but only odium of disloyalty". But Bhau hoping to get more, disregarded him and stripped off the ceiling. This infuriated him and he said to Bhau, "You have destroyed (the sanctity) the throne while I am present here and thereby brought odium upon me (as well). Whenever I make any request on any affair you disregard and reject it."[15] That partly this utterance was a piece of Suraj Mal's political rehtoric can hardly be denied. But as the shrewdest diplomat and statesman of the time,[16] he

10. *Memoires des Jats,* 50.
11. *Ibid.*, 49-50; *Mirat* (908) puts it, that the Wazir "had strength because of *Suraj Mal*".
12. Qanungo, *Jats,* 133.
13. *Mirat,* 908.
14. *Siyar,* III, 385.
15. *Bhau Bakhar,* quoted by Qanungo, *Jats,* 131f.
16. Gupta, *Panipat,* 144, 153; Also Sarkar, *Fall,* II, 257.

could easily foresee the likely hazards of such an impolitic act[17] and hence his strong objection to it. As it was, Bhau could no doubt secure 9 lakhs of Rupees from the ceiling, but politically it proved harmful. It gave his enemies a genuine ground to exploit the situation.[18]

The persisting discord over the military strategy and Bhau's final rejection of Suraj Mal's war plan was another and a very important cause of the latter's departure. Difference had crept in at the very beginning, dampening Suraj Mal's enthusiasm in the process. Suraj Mal made one more attempt at Delhi when he advised Bhau:

> to make Delhi (now that he had advanced upto and captured that place) the siege of war (base) and not to advance too much in the country guarded by such a powerful enemy, (the Abdali and his allies). Thus, (while remaining in Delhi), the Maratha-Jat army could be furnished with whatever it needed from the (nearby) Jat provinces and Delhi could in any case serve as a retreat. But this "wise" counsel met the same fate as did his preceding one.[19]

It can be reasonably inferred that he tendered this advice when Bhau first thought of proceeding to Kunjpura (c. middle of August, 1760).[20] Not that whatever Bhau thought was useless, but on practical grounds the soundness of Suraj Mal's counsel could not be easily challenged. Whereas Bhau was a complete stranger to north Indian conditions and the adversaries pitted against, the Jat veteran was very well familiar with them. In fact the latter had as much personal experience of north Indian warfare as was then the total age of the Maratha commander. Suraj Mal's suggestion to exercise due caution in facing a consummate general like the Abdali and to keep encumbrances, immobile artillery[21] and a huge number of non-combatants[22] away was militarily correct. The stress on the last three was intended on the one hand to impart extreme mobility to the fighting force, while on the other to reduce greatly was feeding expenses of the camp. Suraj Mal preferred swift

---

17. cf. Sarkar, *Fall*, II, 442.
18. *S.P.D.*, XXVII, 257; Shejwalkar, *Panipat*, 46.
19. *Memoires des Jats,* 53; Also *Bhau Bakhar* referred to by Qanungo, *Jats*, 132. The tradition generally supports it. A Sakha, recited to me by the Jogis of a village near Chhaprauli (Meerut) adds that a war council was convened near the Purana Qila where the Sarva Khap Panchayat levies agreed to follow the leadership of Suraj Mal.
20. *Supra*, ch. XI f.ns. 81-92.
21. Once planted, the big cannons (some were so heavy that 200 bullocks were required to drag them) could not be adjusted with the movements of the army. At Panipat they could do nothing except make harmless noise. S.P. Sangar, (ed. Gupta), *Panipat,* 252.
22. In Bhau's army this number was eight times that of the acutal fighters. Sarkar, *Fall*, II, 352.

cavalry tactics not because the infantry tactics were bad but because both the Marathas and the Jats excelled in the former. And one cannot ignore the best weapon in one's armoury and yet hope for the best.

Equally sagacious was Suraj Mal's insistence on keeping a firm base at Delhi. Impliedly it meant that the line of communication should not be lengthened and that continuous supplies be vigilantly ensured. The real implications of ignoring it were seen later on. After Bhau's departure from Delhi the Abdali forded the Yamuna, intercepted the Maratha line of communication and in time caught Bhau in "trap" from which he could never come out.[23] That the astute Jat had apprehended such a mishap in case the whole Maratha camp moved northwards neglecting Delhi as a base, is evident from the wording of his above advice. Little wonder, therefore, that this has been extolled almost on all sides. Keene observes that had it been followed the "resistance (to the Abdali) would have been more successful and the whole history of Hindustan far otherwise, than what it has since been."[24]

Bhau, however, differed sharply. He stuck to the entrenched mode of warfare through heavy artillery and foot musketeers of his favourite Gardi without appreciating that this system had yet to be synthetized with the traditional Maratha mode to yield the intended results.[25] An "overwhelming majority" of his lieutenants upon whom largely depended the final outcome, never had recourse to this system. They remained sceptical about it and did not exert heartily on the fateful day at Panipat.[26] What an irony! The Abdali himself wished the Marathas to come to a pitched contest rather than their pursuing their traditional mode of warfare.[27] Moreover, the way Bhau declined to make the Jat forts his base and left Delhi also afterwards carrying all his camp impedimenta and non-combatants and leaving a paltry force of 6,000 at Delhi, leaves the impression that he did not share Suraj Mal's concern about encumbrances or a firm base.[28] What disastrous consequences followed from it, are well known to us.

---

23. Sarkar, *Fall*, II, 283; *S.P.D.*, XXVII, 259; *Nur*. 46b.
24. H.G. Keene, *The Moghul Empire*, (London: 1887), 77-78; *Memoires des Jats*, 53; Sarkar, *Fall*, II, 363, 258; Qanungo *Jats*, 128, 131, 133; Owen *op.cit.*, 242; Gupta, *Panipat*, 151 and 251; Also Shejwalkar, *Panipat*, 48.
25. *Rajwade*, I, 174; Mehra (ed. Gupta), *Panipat*, 214ff.
26. Shejwalkar, *Panipat*, 116f.; cf. Nana Farnvis laments that Bhau "though sufficiently wise on all other occasions seems on this occasion to have lost his wisdom...he abandoned our system of warfare and adopted that of the enemy" quoted by Mehra (ed. Gupta), *Panipat*, 213-214; *Mirat* (918) says "when they (the Marathas) turned from that custom (of their own warfare), they got involved in disgrace and affliction".
27. cf. Shejwalkar, *Panipat*, 107.
28. cf. Sarkar, *Fall*, II, 325, 363; Sangar (ed. Gupta), *Panipat*, 251.

Their differences were not confined to the war strategy alone. They also differed sharply in their respective outlook towards the enemies. The period which witnessed Suraj Mal's departure (middle of August, 1760) also found Bhau's bloated with pride. Apart from other sources Bhau's own correspondance shows that his easy capture of the Indian Capital, turned his head. The fort was occupied on 1st August, 1760, and the very next day he wrote, "..the Afghan allies would leave the Abdali and that Shuja now felt swamped by having joined the invader...My capture of Delhi has broken his (the Abdali's) waist."[29] Same is the tone in which he writes on 21st August, 1760, "My conquest of Delhi has terrified the Abdali and caused a split in his camp."[30] Besides his own buoyancy, Shuja's persistent overtures for peace, flattering reports from his subordinates and the intrigues of some Afghan chiefs (such as Ahmad Bangash, and Sadulla Rohilla) supplicating his favour, increased his pride and insolence.[31] All this confirmed his notions that his enemies were frightened and disunited and they would be thankful to him if only he allowed them a safe passage to their homes. Whatever be the initial anxiety of the Abdali, it was foolish on the part of Bhau to take a grossly exaggerated view of the situation and discover in the peace proposals a proof of hopeless weakness of the Abdali's cause."[32] For all practical purposes, the Abdali's potentiality was the same as before and it called for unusual foresight and discretion. But an inflated Bhau fell a victim to an imprudent optimism. This was a dangerous development in the attitude of a general when the real issue was still hanging in the balance. There is not the slightest evidence to show that Suraj Mal at any stage shared Bhau's far-fetched calculations. Sanguine he never was about the war plan of Bhau (to which he still clung), now his conceit, under-estimation of the enemies and the like left the calculating Jat in no doubt about the final outcome. He discerned that the ultimate fate of the Marathas was not good.[33] Nay he became convinced of their prospective defeat under such a fllippant leadership and made a clear prediction to that effect months in advance of Panipat. This conviction became probably the biggest single factor of his return.

In addition, Bhau directly antagonised the Jat Raja by his offensive disposition in course of the discussion at Delhi, alluded to above. Supposing *Bhau Bakhar* to be the only source to bear it out, T.S. Shejwalkar

---

29. *Rajwade*, I, 224; For Bhau's pride also see *Memoires des Jats*, 52; Mir Dard, who met that chief at Delhi found him "very proud and haughty", quoted by Gupta, *Panipat*, 154, footnote; *Mirat*, 907.
30. *Rajwade*, I, 233.
31. *Ibid.*, 236-237.
32. Sarkar, *Fall*, II, 259-260, 279-280; Gupta, *Panipat*, 155; Also, *Raj*. I, 233; *Mirat*, 911.
33. *Amira*, 105; See, for identical statement, *Tarikh-i-Ibrahim Khan* in Elliot VIII, 277; Also *Memoires des Jats* 53.

completely denies that the Maratha leader ever humiliated or slighted Suraj Mal.[34] But he does not have a single authority to support his thesis, which he builds up upon a dubious interpretation of facts and situations. An exchange of views between the top generals at the one or other's initiative is the most common phenomenon amidst a continuing (military) situation. In that case how a puffed up Bhau—whose habitual harshness the learned historian himself concedes[35]—would have reached to any counter advice, can be easily imagined. Luckily, we have evidence of the French historian (who in 1760 was at Bharatpur) backed by the persisting tradition, to safely conclude that even if Bhau did not call him a mere land holder ("Jat"), he certainly offended him by spurning his counsels at Delhi.[36] The contemporary Marathi despatches indirectly corroborate it by assuming complete silence for some time, Suraj Mal's cup of endurance was now seemingly full to the brim.

The above analysis brings forth one relevant point. If we follow Suraj–Bhau relationship closely, it would appear that at least in August, 1760, the Maratha's interest in the Jat alliance had certainly dwindled and this was the period when the Jat relinquished him—the Maratha side. Its convincing proof is to be found in the marked difference in Bhau's earlier wholesome regard for the Jat Raja as reflected in his prompting a veteran like the Holkar to escort him, his personally advancing two miles to receive his ally honourably, his showing earnestness for the Jat alliance by solemn vows and the like, stand in deep contrast with that chief's subsequent stubborn and disparaging attitude towards Suraj Mal, though differences between them had existed right from the very start. His handling of Imad is also a case in point. Its secret may be discovered in Bhau's differencing assessments of his prospects before and after that date. His earlier "wholesome respect" for the Durrani's might vis-a-vis a realization of his own difficulties and Shuja's decision to join the Abdali vis-a-vis the rejection of his appeal for help by the rest of the powers[37] has increased the significance of the Jat co-operation. He, therefore, found it expedient to be respectful towards his only ally. But upon taking Delhi, Bhau

34. Shejwalkar, *Panipat*, 48-49.

35. *Ibid.*, 129.

36. *Memoires des Jats*, 53; Also 64 footnote; Qanungo, *Jats*, 133; cf. Duff, *Mahrattas*, I, 520; Owen, *Mogul Empire*, 247.

37. Sarkar, *Fall*, II, 258. Though conceding Bhau's pride the insolence after Delhi's capture (*Fall*, II, 258, 259, 260) J.N. Sarkar thinks that Bhau yet realized gravity of his situation even after that event. We, however, presume that he does not mean this statement to refer to the first two weeks of August, with the developments of which we are concerned herewith. Incidentally, the two letters (*S.P.D.*, XXVII, 255, 257) that he cites as his authority for his above observation also refer to different periods, the first letter bears the date of 26th June, while the second that of 15th September.

discovered his adversaries frightened and disunited, and consequently success awaiting him. Once the very object of courting the Jat alliance seemed fulfilled, his interest in it was bound to diminish. Vows made in storm are forgotten in calm. Bhau's overconfidence made him callously indifferent towards Suraj Mal when the latter did not toe his line blindly. This gives new dimensions to the present question.

It is obvious that no astute and self-respecting person of Suraj Mal's stature would have stayed on with Bhau when neither his dignity was safe nor his valid objections, counsels and interests were heeded to and when he had grown so sceptical about the final outcome as well. To pull on in such circumstances might be a compulsion with a subordinate like Malhar (whose views were similar to those of the Jat), but Suraj Mal was neither a subordinate nor a vassal but an ally of once passionately sought for alliance. By right Bhau could not claim allegiance from him. Mutual trust and regard, honest execution of plighted words, and reciprocal adjustments are the life blood of an alliance, but they became increasingly scarce in the present case. For Suraj Mal, the Maratha alliance now looked like a servile submission to Bhau's command. How far this could be acceptable to him can easily be surmised.

Alongside these decisive factors must be duly emphasized the contributory role of Suraj Mal's lack of unstinted zeal for the Maratha cause. Ambitious as Suraj Mal was, he never relished the Maratha expansion in the north. We know that right from the days of the Mughal Emperor Ahmad Shah till his accord with them (in 1757), he had been interested in the formation of anti-Maratha coalition. Though subsequent stress and strains he had ceased to pursue the anti-Maratha policy, he was all along apprehensive of their designs. As related above, he had joined them because he regarded them a lesser evil as compared to the Abdali's confederacy. Then again, having thrown his lot with them, he treacherously kept himself in touch with the opponent's ally, Shuja.[38] This was bound to annoy Bhau in the same way as his (Bhau's) own perfidious overtures with Shuja did Suraj Mal and Imad. Whether or not Bhau actually demanded two crores from him we cannot say[39]—for we find him hesitating to demand money[40]—but he certainly had the reason to suspect such an extortionate demand amidst the changing mood of that chief. Here was, then, another probable reason with him for leaving the Maratha.

All the same, there is insufficient ground to agree with T.S. Shejwalkar here. Conveniently ignoring Bhau's part explained above, he confines his inquisitiveness to what he thinks Suraj Mal's rank

38. Shejwalkar, *Panipat,* 51; Also *Shah Alam Nama,* 173; cf. *Mirat,* 908.
39. *Imad*, 276.
40. *S.P.D.*, XXI, 190.

selfishness and unscrupulous tactics.[41] This estimate is not only grossly exaggerated but one sided too. Harping on Suraj Mal's selfishness alone is to ignore the all pervading spirit of the age that he lived in. Everyone in that age, including the Marathas, shaped his policy and conduct to suit his own interests. It must be borne in mind that the Jat interests were not inextricably involved in the present struggle, which was essentially one for political supremacy between the Afghans and the Marathas. It is claimed that Bhau fought for the motto: "India for Indians".[42] But strangely, no Indians except the Jat responded to his call. In the light of the persistent Maratha conduct, no serious student of their history of the period can fail to conclude that actually the "Indians" meant here were none else than the Marathas themselves. Yet, Suraj Mal accompanied Bhau because he would have relished the defeat of the Abdali's confederacy. However, the current flippancy of Bhau, coupled with his clinging to tactics wrong in his eyes, convinced Suraj Mal of the Maratha defeat instead. Possibly, T.S. Shejwalkar would not have termed him so selfish, had he knowingly sacrificed himself at the altar of the Maratha selfishness. The learned scholar seems to have missed that everybody possesses the instinct to safeguard one's existence against an impending disaster and Suraj Mal was not an exception to it.[43] We know that later on Bhau, finding his own existence endangered, sent the imprint of his palm dipped in saffron to Shuja to save himself. It is another thing that with his unerring sense of perception the shrewd Suraj Mal preconceived the odds (under Bhau's leadership) which the arrogant Bhau realized only when he had been irredeemably entrapped by them. The fact is that thrown as Suraj Mal was between two mile stones (the Afghans and the Marathas), caution had become a necessity for his survival, which should not be unsympathetically characterized as rank selfishness.

In his obvious enthusiasm to make a scapegoat of the Jat Raja, the reputed Maratha historian has silently bypassed the injudicious Maratha policies towards him. That Şuraj Mal himself was opposed to the Maratha advance has already been elucidated. But the Maratha record in this respect was apparently worse. Right from its inception the Maratha policy towards the Jat State was characterized by what J.N. Sarkar aptly terms "the grasping tyranny".[44] In 1754, the Marathas had launched a formidable offensive against the Jat State. Thereafter in 1757 they (the accredited defenders of the Empire against the Abdali) had displayed a culpable indifference when the exterminating Afghan

---

41. Shejwalkar, *Panipat*, 49.
42. *Ibid.*, 123.
43. cf. *Memoires des Jats*, 53
44. Sarkar, *Fall*, II, 256.

legion subjected parts of Suraj Mal's State to sack, slaughter and sacrilege. This apart, the Maratha support to the pretensions of Muhkam Singh and Zul Qaran, the staunch enemies of Suraj Mal, speaks of their subversive designs. Even as friends, the Marathas were not remiss in capitalizing the internal matters of the Jat State. An incident of 1758, when they tried to exploit differences between Suraj Mal and his intractable son, Jawahar Singh,[45] is a case in point, although citing here the example of the Maratha ambition to dispossess the Jats of Aligarh (in 1760)[46] looks doubtful. Such bitter reminiscences largely formed the secret of Suraj Mal's cool enthusiasm for the Maratha cause.

Moved by the above factors Suraj Mal, though visibly disgusted,[47] resolved to part company with Bhau. But retreat from his camp was not easy. Presumably, Suraj Mal's underhand dealings with Shuja and his gradual sending back of his men in advance[48] made Bhau suspicious. Every commander remains watchful against a possible desertion, because apart from causing a depletion in his own ranks, it may lead to a corresponding increase in the enemy's strength. Though Suraj Mal never intended to cross over to the enemy, Bhau suspected it and he tried to keep him under surveillance. Meanwhile, the Holkar helped Suraj Mal and alongwith Imad he decamped at night and went to Ballamgarh.[49] The only potentate who had cared to respond to the Maratha call thus left them. This proved disastrous for their cause.[50]

Bhau raged and fumed as he learned of the Jat retreat. He "swore to leave only the remembrances of the Jats in Hindustan" once he was free

---

45. *S.P.D.*, XXVII, 226.
46. Quoting *Rajwade*, I, 187. J.N. Sarkar (*Fall*, II, 256) concludes it. No doubt the wording of this letter leaves such an impression. But from the other despatches of this period it becomes clear that the Maratha intention to capture Aligarh at present implied their expelling the Abdali (then encamping at that place) with the Jat help. Significantly, one letter clearly speaks of the Maratha plan to "re-establish" their own and the Jat's former outposts in the Doab. See *Rajwade*, I, 251, 261 also see 174, 186, 204 and 205.
47. *Imad*, 108.
48. *Memoires des Jats*, 53.
49. *Mirat-i-Ahmadi* (908) claims that Bhau wanted "to do away with" Suraj Mal and Imad and that the Jat escaped the "death valley" with the help of Shuja, who by discharging cannons controve to produce an opportunity for his escape. This part of its version looks overdrawn. If the reported attempt on his life were correct, he could not have displayed that sympathy and compassion towards the Marathas in general and Bhau's wife in particular, which he did later on; *Memoires des Jats*, 53; Imad, 276; *Bhau Bakhar* (slightly differing in details but generally supported by the tradition) quoted by Qanungo, *Jats*, 134-136; *Tarikh-i-Ibrahim Khan* in Elliot, VIII, 277-278; *Shah Alam Nama*, 173; Merely announcing the departure, *S.P.D.*,XXVII, 258; *Amirah*, 105; *Siyar*, III,385; *Muharbat*, 12.
50. Sarkar, *Fall*, II, 256.

from his engagements.[51] This was, however, not to be, as futility of the peace talks became soon manifest and war appeared to be certain to the Marathas.[52] This cooled down Bhau and he thought of placating the Jat Raja. Sometime in the first half of September, 1760, he sent his secretary Chitnis, the Scinde's secretary, Ramaji Anant and the Holkar's secretary, Gangoba Tatya, to persuade the Jat Raja to rejoin him,[53] failing that to ensure that he did not unite with the Abdali[54] and allowed the line of Maratha communication remain open. As Bhau had been exposed, he appeared to be apologetic in sending an elephant and a khilat to Suraj Mal. He also wrote, appealing to him to block the enemy supplies.[55]

A burnt child dreads the fire. Though Bhau's gestures, breathing a spirit of repentance, seems to have calmed down Suraj Mal's anger and anguish, he did not agree to rejoin him. There is no evidence to show that their (Suraj-Bhau) discord over policy was resolved either. It would appear, however, that the Maratha plenipotentiaries yet importuned his favour, which he gracefully agreed to. Significantly, on 18th September, 1760, we find Bhau assuring Govind Ballal of help from the Jat contingent (of Shikohabad) in his bid to seize the enemy supplies.[56] On the other hand, Suraj Mal allowed the Maratha supplies to pass on freely on the Agra-Mathura route as is evident from a despatch of October from Bhau's camp. The addressee therein was assured that "the Jat is ours".[57] On 4th November, Bhau himself emphasized that Suraj Mal was quite friendly and in no way would he obstruct the Supplies.[58]

Ahmad Shah Abdali, who must have relished the Jat-Maratha split, felt disturbed at the renewed Maratha overtures to Suraj Mal. He had earlier sent through Shuja a letter and a khilat for the Jat Raja at Ballamgarh.[59] In the last week of September, 1760, he re-opened negotiations with him through Shuja, trying to assure himself (the Abdali) that he did not re-join the Marathas. The Abdali sent him a

---

51. *Memoires des Jats*, 53; Also *Bhau Bakhar*, quoted by Qanungo, *Jats*, 136.
52. For instance on 12th September T.S. Purandare wrote (*S.P.D.*, XXVII, 256) "Very likely there will be a war". On 14th Krishnaji Anant emphasized (*S.P.D.*, XXI, 191) the same thing, "but the talks will not take a good turn. A battle alone will decide the matter". On 15th Bapuji Ballal reported (*S.P.D.*, II, 130) "Battle will take place.......there will not be a compromise". The same day Nana Fadnis wrote (*S.P.D.*, II, 131) that Shuja "does not appear to be honest. So the talks will not be fruitful"
53. *S.P.D.*, XXVII, 258.
54. *Mirat*, 908.
55. *Ibid. Shah Alam Nama* (173) claims that finding himself secure Suraj Mal begged forgiveness for his sins from Bhau.
56. *Rajwade*, I, 244, see also Rajwade's Introduction, 82.
57. *Ibid.*, 259.
58. *Ibid.*, 264.
59. *Mirat*, 908.

khilat again (at Ballamgarh). Oaths were exchanged on both sides. Displaying diplomatic suppleness, Suraj Mal held assurances not to join the Marathas,[60] even though he of his own had taken such a decision already and his sympathies remained on the side of his countrymen.

Inspite of such a possibility raised in a fragmentary contemporary despatch (October, 1760), referred to above, we cannot say whether or not Bharatpur troops under any one of the Jat Princes reached and sided with the Marathas at Kunjpura.[61] The Sarva Khap Panchayat militia (17,000 in number?) under Chowdhary Sheo Lal Jat of Shoram, however, did the same. It forded the Yamuna near Issopur, reached Kunjpura, and helped Bhau. The latter is said to have expressed his gratitude for help, while the Chowdhary took oaths on the Yamuna's water to remain with him.[62] The tradition goes that the Doab Jats, eluding the Abdali's patrols in darkness of night, supplied provisions to the Maratha army.[63] The Jats on both sides of the Yamuna still feel proud of their ancestors having helped the Maratha during Panipat days.[64]

SURAJ MAL HELPS THE FUGITIVES FROM PANIPAT

As is well known, the Marathas were later completely routed in the battle of Panipat (14th January, 1761). Some 50,000 to 1,00,000 survivors ran to the Jat State for safety from enemy slaughter. The unfortunate fugitives, afflicted with hunger, continuous marching and terror were harassed by the local populace till they reached the Jat dominions where they received the kindest and most hospitable treatment. Forgetting the Maratha wrong the great Jat ruler extended them every comfort. He provided them with food, clothes, blankets, residence and medical facilities. The illustrious Rani Kishori joined her husband and she was specially charitable to the Brahmans and the ladies. The fugitives were fed freely in Bharatpur generally for a week and then escorted safely to Gwalior after each one of the commoners being provided with a minimum of one seer of flour and one rupee. Thus, the Jat Raja altogether spent as much as 10 lakhs of Rupees in this humanitarian work. Among the fugitives were Bhau's wife, Parbati Bai, and wounded Shamsher Bahadur. The Jat King consoled the heart-broken lady when she came to Deeg and after entertaining her for three days he arranged for her safe return to the south. But despite best medical care, he could not save the life of Shamsher Bahadur, the half brother of the Peshwa.

---

60. *D.C.*
61. *Rajwade*, I, 259.
62. Kanha Ram, 20. This is supported by a sakha i.e., that 22000 panchayat Militia joined Bhau. These lines occur in a ballad sung by the Jogis of Sabange in District Meerut.
63. By implication Nur-ud-Din, (*Nur*, 41a and 40b), verifies its general authenticity.
64. Shejwalkar, *Panipat*, 70.

The great Jat built a mosque and a house over his grave.[65] He also helped the Marathas in searching those suspected to be missing, such as Jankoji Scinde. All have bestowed lavish praise on him for his generous behaviour. Even to this day the Marathas view with deepest gratitude the Jat compassion displayed towards their forefathers on the occasion. An eyewitness comments that had Suraj Mal so desired not a single Maratha could have returned alive to the south to tell the woeful tale of Panipat.[66] What adds to his greatness is the fact that he helped the vanquished knowing well that by doing so he would be giving an added provocation to the victors of Panipat.[67]

DURRANI'S JAT EXPEDITION FIZZLES OUT (MARCH, 1761)

After his resounding triumph, the Abdali occupied Delhi, holding his Court in the *Diwan-i-Khas.* He opened negotiations with Suraj Mal. Raja Nagar Mal, the imperial Diwan (who had repaired to the Jat Court along with his office management), Raja Diler Singh, the *peshkar* of the Wazir and Majlis Rai came to Delhi on behalf of Suraj Mal. Meanwhile, in face of the clamourings of his unpaid soldiery, the Abdali had asked Najib to pay him the price of his extrication from the Maratha danger. However, the crooked Rohilla, trying to make Suraj Mal pay for him, presented that Raja's envoys before the Abdali on the evening of 21st February, 1761. He opened negotiations for the payment of *Peshkash* by the Jat Raja in return for the Durrani's pardon. But Zinat Mahal, who abhorred the patron of her husband's murderer (Imad) opposed them. Instead she pleaded for an outright military action, arguing that the Jat would pay nothing unless reduced by force.[68] In the name of "state and religion" Najib also insisted on that the Afghans should march to Agra and beyond, so that the Maratha survivors, as also the Jats and others, who had occupied those environs, might be dealt with and the tribute be realized.[69] He, apparently, wanted to kill two birds with one stone; to find a way out to meet the Durrani's demand and at the same time to crush his foe, the Jat Raja. It is noteworthy that the exultant Rohilla had broken the news of his victory at Panipat to Suraj Mal in a

---

65. This is situated in Charbagh, in front of the Nakhas Sarai at Bharatpur.
66. *Memoires des Jats,* 53-54; *Nur.* 51b; *Imad,* 312; *S.P.D.*, XXVII, 271, XXIX, 1; *Bayan-o-Waqa,* quoted by Qanungo, Jats, 140-141; *Mirat*, 917; Mehra (ed. Gupta) *Panipat*, 240 Francklin, *Shah Aulum* (23) is misinformed in his statement that Naro Shankar was plundered at the orders of Suraj Mal.
67. Qanungo, *Jats*, 140.
68. *D.C.*; *Shah Alam Nama* 187; *Memoires des Jats,* 54; *S.P.D.*, XXI, 202; *Mirat*, 919; *Nur* 52b; G. Singh, *Durrani*, 263. At this time the "rumours arose" that after Najib's insistence the Abdali agreed to march to Malwa and that Suraj Mal consented to send a contingent. See *Nur*, 52b and 53b.
69. Mirat, 919; Also see *S.P.D.*, XXI, 202.

manner that smacked of his malignant threat to that chief.[70] On his part, Suraj Mal was under no illusion about it. He apprehended that his victorious enemies might come down on him.[71]

The expedition was then planned. On 7th March, 1761 Shah Wali Khan, with Zinat Mahal, Prince Jawan Bakht and Mirza Bagar started for Agra to pressurize the Jat Raja. But the Durrani troops refused to march further towards Mathura. Their protracted stay in India had made them home-sick. Moreover, in the approaching summer they were averse to confronting the tenacious Jats, who were determined to received them "with shot and shell" from their strongholds. The mutinous spirit of his soldiers obliged the Abdali to recall them at once and he set out for his home on 20th March, 1761, getting perhaps nothing from Suraj Mal on this third and the last occasion also.[72] Thus Suraj Mal succeeded in keeping himself solidly erect amidst the general ruin. An eye witness rightly observes that there was none in India of his age capable of achieving the same in the circumstances.[73]

While leaving this country, Ahmad Shah Abdali confirmed Shah Alam as the Emperor, re-appointed Najib as the Mir Bakhshi and Imad as the Wazir, thus frustrating Shuja, whom he had won over by promising the same office. The Abdali instructed Yaqub Ali Khan to carry a *khilat* and the pencase of the Wizarat to Imad in the Jat Kingdom.[74] However, Shah Alam and Zinat Mahal could never tolerate their mortal enemy re-installed at Delhi. Likewise Najib was also opposed to Imad's restoration. He tried to exclude Imad dishonouring the wish of his patron (the Abdali) to live in harmony with him. He harped on the fears of the Royal family saying, that on gaining supremacy at Delhi Imad would "enthrone another Emperor". Eventually, Najib procured the sanad from the heir to come and take charge of the Capital and on 7th April, 1761, he entered Delhi and put on the robes of the Mir Bakhsi, *faujdar* of the *gird* and the regent. He appointed his own men on important posts including the *Qiladari* of the fort. Thus, hardly a fortnight had elapsed since the Abdali's return when Najib manipulated to become the dictator of Delhi, while the Abdali's agent (who left Delhi for Mathura only on 9th April, 1761) had yet to deliver the Wazir's robe to Imad at Mathura.[75]

---

70. *Mirat*, 918.
71. *Memoires des Jats*, 54.
72. D.C., *Memoires des Jats*, 54 also 55-56; *Mirat*, 919-920 (wrong in saying that Shuja and Najib marched upto Suraj Mal). Qanungo (*Jats*, 144) states that Suraj Mal paid one lakh to the Abdali. This seems unlikely, cf. *S.P.D.* XXIX, 23 and 24; Also *G. Singh Durrani*, 263-264 footnote.
73. *Memoires des Jats*, 54.
74. *Nur*. 53b-54b; *S.P.D.*, XXI, 202, II, 103; *Rajwade*, I, 297.
75. *Nur*. 54a-55b; *D.C.*, Sarkar, *Fall*, II, 377 and 380; Also *Rajwade*, I, 297; *Mirat* (920) claims that Zinat Mahal deliberately detained the Abdali's agent at Delhi and raised 5,000 men, posting them in the defence of the Capital against Imad's possible move.

XIII
The Clash of Ambitions : (1761–1763)

The battle of Panipat, though a momentous event, proved unproductive from the viewpoint of the stakes actually involved. It hardly decided anything worth the name. The Maratha power, no doubt, suffered a stunning blow but their loss was neither perennial nor irreparable. Similarly, the Afghan Emperor, despite being triumphant, failed to reap any lasting material advantage. Not long after, he found it increasingly difficult to cope with the surging tide of the ferocious Sikhs in the Punjab. On the other hand, his Indian confederates had now to cope with the mighty Jats in place of the Marathas. As for the Mughal Empire, by no means did Panipat prove a panacea for its appalling ills. On the contrary, the Afghan–Maratha rivalry "caused the complete overthrow of the Mughal monarchy".[1] Shakir laments, "on all sides the Empire is encircled by enemies."[2] They were scrambling madly for its slight remains and aspiring for individual ascendancy. The imperial Capital continued to be without the Emperor and the Wazir, who were at daggers drawn with each other. The Mir Bakhshi, who had grabbed all power in his hands, was strong enough, but he would not "make any sacrifice or run any risk" to bring in and instal on the throne his professed sovereign (an exile in his own dominions). Ironically enough, the Mughal Emperor himself apprehended being put "helplessly within the reach"[3] of his Bakhshi, who was leading the exultant Afghans—the traditional enemies of the Royal Mughals.[4] Side by side, the Rohilla dictator exploited his pre-eminence in the government to aggrandize his own power, carve out a large independent kingdom and weld together and promote his own kinsmen and porteges.[5]

---

1. *Memoires des Jats,* 49.
2. *Shakir*, 115.
3. Sarkar, *Fall*, II, 529-530.
4. *Ibid.*, 530; Also Mirza Ali Azhar in *Freedom Movement*, I, 215.
5. Sarkar, *Fall*, II, 39, 384-386.

A deadly clash was unavoidable when this policy came face to face with a similar bid from another quarter.[6] The post-Panipat period witnessed the heyday of Jat power.[7] With "an indescribable wisdom", marvellous political sagacity and an unrivalled diplomatic resourcefulness, Suraj Mal had steered his way through the stormy days in such a manner as to ensure growing prosperity and unstinted rise of his power "amidst the common decay."[8] He was by now the strongest and the richest ruler in the whole of the Indian sub-continent.[9] Amidst the changing circumstances, the animosity that already existed between him and Najib came to the forefront. Their rivalry forms the central theme of the history of Delhi in the succeeding years.

MATHURA CONGRESS (MIDDLE OF APRIL TO MIDDLE OF JUNE, 1761), SURAJ MAL AND EFFORTS FOR PEACE AND REGULAR IMPERIAL GOVERNMENT

In order to ensure regular payment of tribute from Hindustan and his unmolested hold over the Panjab, Ahmad Shah Abdali wanted to come to terms with the Marathas and impliedly with Suraj Mal. With the same purpose he wished to leave behind an agreed peace among all the potentates and a regular and smoothly functioning government at Delhi.[10] He had, therefore, confirmed Shah Alam as Emperor and appointed Imad as the Wazir and Najib as the Mir Bakhshi. Before his departure he had instructed his envoy, Yaqub Ali Khan, to finalize peace with the Marathas and carry the *khilat*, and *qalamdan* of the Wizarat to Imad, then living as pensioner of Suraj Mal. The Abdali had also written to Imad "to come and enter the city of Delhi declaring him plenipotentiary" on his behalf.[11]

On 9th April, 17611 Yaqub Ali Khan and Bapuji Mahadeo, the Vakil of the Peshwa, started from Delhi for Mathura where Suraj Mal and Imad had already arrived. The Jat King granted audience to the Afghan envoy on 19th April, 1761. Imad received the *qalamdan* and the *khilat*. Suraj Mal, Imad, Yaqub Ali, Bapuji and Gangadhar Tatya held talks between them. The "assemblage" especially Imad, Tatya and Suraj Mal dissuaded Yaqub Ali from going to the Peshwa, saying

---

6. cf. *Ibid.*, 385.
7. *Memoires des Jats,* 49, 63 and 67.
8. *Memoires des Jats,* 54; Also *Siyar*, IV, 27; Gupta, *Panipat*, 44.
9. Sarkar, *Fall*, II, 381, 383, 442.
10. For details of the Abdali's objectives see Sarkar, *Fall*, II,378-380; G. Singh, *Durrani*, 260-263.
11. *Nur.* 53b-54a; *S.P.D.*, XXI, 202; Also *Mirat*, 920.

that there was no need for it and things could be discussed right there.[12] The Vakils of the heir, Jawan Bakht, Najib, Shuja and the par-Rohillas also reached there.[13] Thus, began in the Bharatpur State (Mathura) the congress of the important Indian powers to usher in peace and rehabilitate the normal administration of the country.

The congress was in session for two months;[14] but as could be foreseen, it ultimately proved infructuous. Mutual amity and goodwill were the pre-requisites for restoring normalcy. They were, however, lacking in the leading dignitaries of the day. Jealousy and intense political rivalry marked their mutual relations. Added to it were the personal prejudices which vitiated the atmosphere still further. There was no love lost between Najib and Shah Alam on the one hand and Suraj Mal and Imad on the other. When it came to the question of the Wizarat; Shuja also had reasons to be sore with the Jat Raja, who formed the strength of Imad, and who, if the Marathi despatches are to be relied upon, had been instrumental in procuring the Wizarat for him.[15] Then again, if the rohilla chief, Jawan Bakht, Zinat Mahal, Shuja and others abhorred the Wizarat of Imad-ul-Mulk,[16] there were others who were jealous of Najib and resented his growing influence at Delhi.[17]

The failure of Mathura peace congress has been ascribed by J.N. Sarkar to the alleged designs of Suraj Mal "to seize the actual government of the empire and wrest the neighbouring provinces from the Ruhelas, the Bangash and Shuja in the name of the Emperor but keep them himself under a veil." This made the Awadh and Afghan envoys indignant. "The natural result was that the negotiations broke down...."[18]

This conclusion is apparently based on the Hingne's despatch. Bapu Mahadeo Hingne was an eyewitness and being the Vakil of the Peshwa

---

12. *S.P.D.*, XXI, 202, II, 143 and 146, XXVII, 272, also XXIV, 50, *Rajwade*, I, 228; *D.C.*; *Nur*, 54a; *Mirat*, 920-921; Sarkar, *Fall*, II, 380. It may be noted that the basic points of peace had already been discussed and determined by the Peshwa. He informed his Vakil, Hingne, that he had empowered the Holkar to "conclude the subject" and that all matters should be referred to the Holkar and his decision be accepted. (See Peshwa's letter quoted by Sardesai, *Marathas,* II, 463; Also G. Singh, *Durrani*, 262)-The Holkar's Diwan, Gangadhar was already at Mathura. Hence, there was nothing sinister about the Afghan envoy being detained at Mathura.
13. *S.P.D.*, II, 103, XXVII, 272; cf. *Nur.*, 54b.
14. *Nur*, 55b.
15. *Rajwade*, I, 288 also 297.
16. *Mirat*, 921.
17. The Hingnes reporting from Mathura write (*S.P.D*, II, 103), "It is the desire of all that Ghazi-ud-Din should be installed (at Delh) as before, after eliminating Najib Khan." For the Par Rohillas' jealously towards Najib see *Nur*, 43b; Sarkar, *Fall*, II, 381; See also Abdur Rashid in *Freedom Movement,* I, 317.
18. Sarkar, *Fall*, II, 381.

was a leading participant too in the aforesaid congress. His and others' contemporary reports, therefore, form the most valuable source of information on the trends of the parleys at Mathura, especially when Nur-ud-Din (the servant of Imad) and Wendel (most likely present in the Jat Kingdom) do not throw much light on them. The latter in fact totally ignores the Mathura congress. Yet the Marathi despatches, particularly those of the Hingnes, at places appear vague and confusing. These, therefore, need to be interpreted with care and accepted with caution.

A careful scrutiny of the Hingnes' above despatch would reveal that J.N. Sarkar's interpretation is not wholly correct. The Hingnes despatches contain two most relevant points. The first part which reads, "That the Thakur (Suraj Mal) should have the full control over the *Saltanat* is the intention of all and of the Thakur himself"[19] is a logical continuation of the message from a preceding page of the same despatch but reproduced as a separate one. The subsequent part of the despatch apparently emphasizes another point. It goes on:

"The rest of the matter is that Thakur intends that he[20] should take under a curtain[21] the provinces of the Sarkar, to be released by the Thakur from Ayodhya and Patna and the Rohilla.[22] Therefore, the Vakils of Ayodhya and the Rohilla replied frankly that if (you try to) make us relinquish (our territories) by establishing contact with the Jat,[23] we shall not vacate."[24]

---

19. *S.P.D.*, II, 103. The first sheet of this letter is missing, which usually contains the date, the name of the writer and the addressee and the place wherefrom written. G.S. Sardesai, the Editor of *S.P.D.* volumes assigns this letter to the year 1759. This is not correct. Its contents unmistakably refer to the period of the Mathura congress. Incidentally, we have another letter (written by the Hingne brothers from Mathura on 6th May, 1761, *S.P.D.*, XXI, 202). It is incomplete and abruptly ends with "*Ya go*". On the other hand the fragmentary letter printed as no. 103 in *S.P.D.*, II, begins with "*Shtisahi*". Separately both these expressions are incomplete. But if we unite them, it becomes a meaningful word "*Ya gosti sahi*". As both these documents deal with one and the same theme it is most likely that they combinedly formed the orginal complete letter of the Hingnes, which got separated somehow and printed accordingly. Though Sarkar does not establish an irrevocable connection between them, probably on the basis of similarity of theme, he does conclude that the contents of *S.P.D.*XXI, 202 are completed by *S.P.D.* II, 103. See *Fall*, II, 379, footnote.
20. It can also be interpreted as "You" meaning thereby the Peshwa.
21. The text reads "*Padadyanta*" which means "under a curtain, however, it does not appear to be conveying a wholly cogent sense. May be that the original word in the Modi script, in which these despatches were written was "Padarant" which means "under one's control". The latter reading agrees more with the succeeding sentences in the text which express the indignation of the Vakils of Ayodhya (Shuja) and the Rohilla.
22. Obviously Ayodhya and Patna mean *Shuja*, while Rohilla, *Najib*.
23. Apparently J.N. Sarkar interprets (*Fall*. II, 381) *Jathache Talook Karoon*' as lease to the Jat but "*Talook Karoon*" should more appropriately mean 'establishing contact'.
24. *S.P.D.*, II, 103.

At first sight it would appear from the earlier part of the above extract that Suraj Mal wanted to "wrest" Patna, Ayodhya and other distant provinces, as J.N. Sarkar thinks. But such an inference does not tally with Suraj Mal's characteristic caution, self-control, shrewdness and strong sense of realism in politics—the traits which the above scholar by implication himself concedes.[25] Suraj Mal's career disproves of his entertaining such grandiose schemes. For full three years after Panipat he was the strongest Indian ruler and yet we do not find him embarking upon any distant conquests. As we shall see, after recovering his lost territories, his expansionist course was essentially confined to the adjacent areas only. Wendel supports us when he unequivocally says that he "never wanted to involve himself in wars or anything far away from his province."[26]

The Hingnes' report furnishes another relevant information namely the refusal of the Vakils of Shuja and the Rohillas to vacate the Maratha territories. To what extent this refusal reflects upon Suraj Mal remains to be seen. Incidentally, we come across a number of contemporary news-reports whose contents throw sufficient light on the context in which the above refusal was made. The victorious confederates of the Abdali had availed themselves of the first opportunity, after the Maratha defeat to impinge upon their possessions in the Doab.[27] But the Abdali's return without pressing home the advantage of the victory and the leanings of the Shah Alam towards the Marathas,[28] as probably also the realization that the Marathas were still a force to be reckoned with, induced the above usurpers to reshape their conduct. Najib and Shuja found it expedient to convey to Malhar Holkar that they would evacuate the usurped lands, provided he sent his collectors to take their charge.[29] Presumably not taking these chiefs at their words, the Holkar (the custodian of the Maratha interest, authorized by the Peshwa) sent his Diwan, Gangadhar, to seek the support of the sympathetic and powerful Jat Raja for resettling the *mahals* in the antarvedi.[30] Gangadhar was also to seek the *sanads* of the holy places, Kashi and Prayag, from the Wazir, Imad-ul-Mulk.[31] However, the Tatya's mission, his continued stay with Suraj Mal, followed by their

25. Sarkar, *Fall*, II, 257 and 442.
26. *Memoires des Jats*, 67.
27. For details see Srivastava, *Shuja*, I, 117ff.
28. *S.P.D.*, XXVII, 263; Srivastava, *Shuja*, I, 120.
29. *S.P.D.*, XXVII, 263.
30. *S.P.D.*, XXVII, 268 XXIX, 10,15 also XXI, 202, II, 144.
31. *S.P.D.*, XXVII, 269, 114 (the date printed on this letter is wrong).

joint march into the Doab towards Kol[32] as also the Peshwa's correspondence with the Jat King in course of the Mathura congress,[33] possibly irritated the Vakils of Najib, Shuja and others and at the same time provided them with a ready excuse for not vacating the Maratha Doab.

Viewed in this perspective, it is obvious that what is ascribed to as designs of Suraj Mal over the distant provinces was in reality a convenient pretext of the Vakils concerned for not making over the lands to the Marathas,[34] or at worst their (the Vakils) suspicion of Suraj Mal's attitude. Not that the Jat Raja was not ambitious but the implied purport of the part of the Hingnes' despatch quoted above, may reasonably be appreciated in this light.

The Hingne further refers that Imad-ul-Mulk, with the implied support of his patron, toyed at one stage with the idea of putting up somebody else on the throne.[35] Ali Muhammad Khan goes to the extent of attributing the Jat capture of Agra (the second Capital) to Imad's scheme of enthroning there the pretender, whom Safdar Jang had raised to the throne in 1753.[36] Imad obviously knew that his Wazirship would not be acceptable to the Emperor[37] who, if a Marathi despatch is to be believed, wanted "to do away with" his mortal enemy (Imad).[38] Therefore, the archschemer, Imad, wished to enthrone a new Emperor. On his part, Shah Alam always suspected it and it was to counteract Imad that he enticed Najib close to him.[39]

We are told that Imad broached the scheme to the Abdali's envoy, Yaqub Ali and sought his assistance in the matter. But the latter clearly told him that his business had ended with delivering to him the *khilat* and that without the Shah's orders he could do nothing on his own. Yaqub concluded "you (Imad) may do whatever you think fit (but only) upon your own strength".[40] But Imad had no strength of his own. All that he could count upon was mainly the help of Suraj Mal, and only

32. *Rajwade*, I, 285, 295.
33. *S.P.D.*, XXI, 202 also II, 103
34. Except Shuja to some extent, the Rohillas did not show any inclination to part with the upper Doab. See Srivastava, *Shuja*, I, 120.
35. *S.P.D.*, XXI, 202; *S.P.D.*, II, 103.
36. *Mirat*, 921.
37. cf. *Ibid*, 921
38. *Rajwade*, I, 295.
39. *S.P.D.*, II, 103.
40. *Ibid.*; J.N. Sarkar (*Fall*, II, 381) seems to interpret that Yaqub Ali said this in response to Imad's request for reinstating him at Delhi. But if we read in one continuation the last three lines of *S.P.D.*, XXI, 202 and the first three of *S.P.D.*, II, 103, it would appear that Yaqub's answer refers more to the case of Emperorship than that of his Wazirship.

casually that of the Marathas and the Par-Rohillas. Out of these the last two did not share Imad's aversion to the Emperorship of Shah Alam, though they generally supported his claims for the Wizarat.[41] As for Suraj Mal, he was keenly interested in it (Imad's Wizarat). Now that his protege enjoyed the ready sanction of no less a man than the victor of Panipat, the Jat King visualized to dominate the Mughal government through Imad's de facto installation and side by side to obtain a legal recognition for his ventures.[42] But his association with the hated regicide had justly incensed Shah Alam and Zinat Mahal. Only a short while ago, both these Shah Alam by implication[43] and the queen-mother directly[44]—had exhorted the Durrani to march against the Jat Raja. The latter, therefore, felt annoyed with Shah Alam. All the same, it does not appear that the astute Raja was prepared to take upon himself the infamy of enthroning a rival Emperor.

On the other hand, Imad had found it expedient in the past to replace the Emperor to suit his ends and he wished to do it again. But the fact that the Jat King was the mainstay of his power naturally smacked of the former's ready sanction behind Imad's move, whereas the reality was not so. Agra was captured and yet none was raised to the throne, then or ever after. It appears that Suraj Mal's indifference eventually dejected his protege (Imad). We learn on the authority of the same Hingne that by the middle of June, 1761, (*i.e.* when the parleys were still going on) both had become reconciled to the Emperorship of Shah Alam and they even thought of "making friends" with him.[45] As for Imad's Wizarat, Suraj Mal certainly remained interested in it.[46] But Najib had firmly captured the actual government of Delhi with no intentions to tolerate others. In the circumstances, any attempt to install the Wazir designate would have virtually meant an outright invasion upon Delhi. This, Suraj Mal wisely avoided. Najib guessed it, when he said that if he first occupied the Capital, "the farsighted and temperamentally patient" Suraj Mal would not oust him from there.[47] At length, Yaqub Ali returned from Mathura to Delhi[48] and the Par-Rohillas also went back, without venturing to expel Najib, as the shrewd Rohilla had himself foretold.[49]

---

41. It can be inferred from *Nur-ud-Din* (*Nur*. 43b, 54b) that the par-Rohillas supported Imad's Wazirship. For a discordant note see Sarkar, *Fall*, II, 381.
42. *S.P.D.*, XXI, 202; *S.P.D.*, II, 103; Qanungo, *Jats*, 146.
43. See Shah Alam's letter to the Abdali quoted by G. Singh, *Durrani*, 232-233.
44. *Supra*, Ch. XII, f.n. 68-72.
45. *S.P.D.*, II, 146.
46. *Mirat*, 928.
47. *Nur*, 55a.
48. *S.P.D.*, XXI, 91 and II, 146.
49. *Nur*, 55a.

Thus ended the Mathura congress after protracted deliberations. How it reflected upon the Durrani-Peshwa bilateral relations is not our concern. Its one objective was to institute a regular and mutually agreed administration at Delhi. It could not be attained, however, in so far as the controversy about Imad and Najib lingered on. Ignoring Najib's part, explained above, J.N. Sarkar argues further that the parleys failed mainly because the Jat King and Imad were determined to have no lasting peace with Najib and Abdali, to brush the former aside and to assert their singular authority in the Empire.[50] This argument, however, cuts both ways. Comparatively, the blame of exclusive authority applies more to Najib than to Suraj Mal and Imad. It may be recollected that the Mathura negotiations took place to give effect to the Abdali's plan of running the Mughal government with Najib as Mir Bakhshi and Imad as Wazir. But while Imad had yet to receive the insignia of Wazirship and resume his office, Najib, fanning the existing feud betwen the Wazir designate and Shah Alam, manoeuvred to secure all authority and, thus, stole a march on Imad. The verdict against Suraj Mal and his protege would have indeed appeared convincing had they persisted in their hostility even in face of Najib's willingness to let Imad have his due as Wazir at Delhi. But there is nothing to -prove that he ever wished to accommodate or live in friendly co-operation with the Wazir. If it were otherwise, there was hardly any need for Imad to seek others' help for his installation. He and his patron have been accused of wishing to eliminate Najib and seize power, but the latter had as good as banished Imad once he himself grabbed all power at Delhi. It was this precluding hold of Najib coupled with his persisting hostility to Imad that made some contemporaries exceedingly sceptical about the effectiveness, nay the very prospects of Imad's Wizarat.[51] The doors practically seemed slammed in Imad's face. In the situation, only the resort to arms might have enabled Imad to get his legal due. However disappointed Imad might have been, if Suraj Mal and others refrained from precipitating a clash, they certainly do not deserve a censure on that score. Further, the view that Suraj Mal was intransigent towards Najib is also one-sided. We have contemporary evidence to prove that Najib nursed sleepless malignity towards Suraj Mal and was pre-occupied with the thoughts of uprooting him,[52] while outwardly he made a deceitful show of his desire to come to terms with him. Then again, it should not be forgotten that Suraj Mal alone was not hostile towards the Rohilla chief. The

---

50. Sarkar, *Fall*, II, 380.
51. *Rajwade*, I, 297.
52. *Infra*, ch. XIII, f.n.117.

Marathas, Hafiz Rahmat and others were also opposed to him and they all stood for the Wizarat of Imad as pointed before.

If we are then to assign individual responsibility, Najib perhaps had greater share than others in thwarting the efforts to instal a mutually agreed and regular administration in the realm. By his precluding control of the government, the Rohilla dictator had forestalled the fate of the negotiations at Mathura. As for Suraj Mal, he certainly cherished the ambition to dominate the Empire through the Wazir and he did not intend to submit himself to Najib's dictatorship.[53] The lesser powers also had their hand in the failure of the congress. The crux of the matter is that personal prejudices and rival ambitions had vitiated the thinking of all the powers.[54] Few could rise above their petty interests to view the issues from a broader angle. Thus, even if appearances of cordiality could be kept up, big and crucial problems could not be solved in such an environment.

Suraj Mal did not force a war on the question of Imad's installation, but Najib's policy and conduct in this regard annoyed him and increased friction between them.[55] On the other hand, his (Suraj Mal's) espousal of the claims of Imad annoyed the Nawab of Awadh,[56] who, though betrayed by the Abdali, apparently aspired as ever for the Wizarat of the Empire. This brought Najib and Shuja closer to one another against Suraj Mal and Imad.[57] The Par-Rohillas, however, maintained their contacts with Suraj Mal.[58] The latter so much resented Najib's supremacy in the government that after the Mathura congress he even started thinking (early in August, 1761) in terms of Shuja getting the Wizarat and Imad, the Mir Bakhshiship.[59] The Jat King apparently made a suggestion of this nature to Shah Alam II. The Emperor, however, declined to have any truck with Imad. Instead he desired his outright destruction and reportedly pressed for the surrender of his mortal enemy. Suraj Mal, however, did not agree to it. This incident must have marred the chances of reconciliation and increased bitterness between them (Shah Alam and Suraj Mal).[60]

---

53. *Siyar* (III, 402) says that Suraj Mal was disinclined to submit to Najib unless Shah Alam came to the Capital from Patna.
54. G. Singh, *Durrani*, 282.
55. *Rajwade*, I, 297; cf. *S.P.D.*, XXIX, 10.
56. *Rajwade*, I, 297
57. *Ibid.*
58. *Rajwade*, I, 295.
59. *Ibid.*
60. *Rajwade*, I, 295.

SURAJ-NAJIB PARLEY AT DANKAURGHAT (NOVEMBER, 1761)

While the fate of the Wazirship hung in the balance, there was a move to conduct the Emperor to the Capital. Himself powerless, he was dependent on others for his de facto installation. But none was prepared to help him single-handed. This necessitated a concerted effort. The meeting between Najib and Suraj Mal, the two foremost personages, at Dankaurghat was, in part, the corollary of this move. Taking initiative in the matter, Najib despatched Nagar Mal, the veteran mediator to Kumbher (c. middle of September, 1761) to arrange for a personal interview with Suraj Mal. Three weeks later (7th October, 1761) Raja Diler Singh along with Rup Ram Katari and Mohal Singh, the Jat Vakils, left Delhi to meet Suraj Mal at Dankaur. They stayed there for five days, held consultations with the Jat Raja and then returned to the Capital on the 15th. The following day they met Najib to settle terms. Thereafter, Najib sent two envoys, Raja Chet Ram and Diler Singh to Suraj Mal with a Quran, on which he had taken an oath of sincerity for the Jat Raja. They were to arrange for a meeting nearby between the two chiefs. However, as per his programme, Suraj Mal proceeded to the fair of Govardhan, taking the two envoys with him. On 24th October, Raja Nagar Mal, Yaqub Ali Khan, Abdul Ahad Khan and others, after a talk with Najib, went to the Jat King to arrange for payment to the Abdali, who had threatened to invade if the Indian chiefs did not send him tribute. They were also to persuade Suraj Mal to meet Najib near Delhi after a fortnight, when the latter came back from his scheduled visit to Hissar.[61]

About the end of November 1761, the much awaited meeting between the Rohilla chief and the Jat Raja took place in the latter's camp at Dankaurghat. Their respective armies alighted on the opposite bank of the Yamuna. Against the suggestion of his advisers Najib crossed the river in a small boat with only a few attendants, leaving his troops behind. "Suraj Mal displayed 'great purity of heart towards him."[62] It can be inferred from Hingne's despatch that Najib proposed to the Raja to send his son with him to escort the Emperor.[63] It is reasonable to presume that Suraj Mal took the opportunity to raise the question of Imad's Wazirship. However, nothing came of it. Beyond diluting their mutual antagonism, no useful purpose seems to have been served by this meeting.[64] The occasion did not usher in any genuine understanding

---

61. *S.P.D.*, XXI, 89, 90, XXIX, 24 also 23, II, 108 (The date of this letter, as sugguested by the editor is incorrect); *D.C.*; Sarkar, *Fall*, II, 386, 445-446.
62. *Nur.*, 56a-56b; cf. *S.P.D.*, XXIX, 23.
63. *S.P.D.*, XXI, 89.
64. cf. Sarkar, *Fall*, II, 446.

between them. Nor could a mutually agreed plan be devised for conducting the Emperor to Delhi. The fact is that despite its being talked about, none of the potentates except Shuja made any effort to retrieve the fortunes of Shah Alam.[65] On the other hand, Imad too could not be installed as Wazir due to the persisting opposition, apparently from Najib as also Shah Alam and Suraj Mal wisely refrained from carrying matters to the extreme. As the time rolled by, he seems to have dropped the irredeemable cause of Imad,[66] though he continued to support him otherwise, as before.[67]

POST PANIPAT EXPANSION AND STRIFE BETWEEN SURAJ MAL AND NAJIB (1761-1763)

The Maratha rout in the battle of Panipat, coupled with the disinclination of the victor Ahmad Shah to remain here, created a void in north India, which the different powers, often at variance with one another, rushed to fill up. The big potentates and the dispossessed local chiefs alike fell upon the Maratha possessions in the Doab, Rajputana, Bundelkhand, Malwa and other places.[68] The Jats, the Afghans, the Rajputs, the Bundelas and Shuja all joined the race. The first to profit by were the exultant Rohillas, who, greatly enlarged their possessions.[69] Soon after Panipat, they occupied almost the whole of the Doab. Hafiz Rahmat Khan established his supremacy over the region consisting of Bhogaon, Etawah and Mainpuri; Dunde Khan brought under his rule Moradabad, Shikohabad and the nearby *mahals*; Ahmad Khan Bangash got hold of the territories from Sikandara to Akbarpur and aspired to move further to the east.[70] The foremost Rohilla chief Najib took the lion's share. He grabbed the Mian Doab country, Meerut, Sikandarabad, Dasna, Baghpat and seven Maratha *mahals* and several *parganas* in Haryana like Gohana, Dadari, Rohtak and Hansi-Hissar region and also cast his glances over the Sirhind district.[71] Najib aimed at carving

---

65. *Rajwade*, I, 297; *S.P.D.*, XXIX, 5.
66. By the end of 1761 Shah Alam "felt himself free" to elevate Shuja to the Wazirship. The latter's investiture took place in February, 1762. see Srivastava, *Shuja*, I, 125f.
67. Imad stayed on in the Jat principality. In 1763 he marched with the Jat contingent, sent to help the Bangash chief. After the death of Suraj Mal he accompanied Raja Jawahar Singh in his attack on Delhi. See *Nur*, 58a and 76b.
68. A contemporary remarks (*Memoires des Jats*, 56, footnote):There was not a single *zamindar* in this country (northern India) who did not take the advantage of the opportunity to *fall* on and chase the Marathas everywhere.
For details see *S.P.D.*, XXI, 75, 91, 92, XXIX, 5, 6, 12-15, 20-22, 24, 25, 27 also 36, 40, XXVII, 264, 267-269, 271, 276, II, 7; *Rajwade*, I, 285, 288, 295-297 also 299.
69. *Memoires des Jats*, 56.
70. Srivastava, *Shuja*, I, 117-118.
71. *Nur.*, 55b-56a; *Rajwade*, I, 297; *S.P.D.*, XXI 89, XXIX, 24.

out extensive domains roughly stretching from Rohtak to Hissar and Sirhind districts and from the middle of Doab to the borders of his original *faujdari* of Saharanpur.[72]

The powerful Jat Raja was very ambitious and he could hardly remain a mere spectator amidst this mad scramble for the territories all round. As Wendel puts it, the Jats were "neither less nor more eager" than the Rohillas to turn the situation to their advantage.[73] If not throughout, certainly for sometime after Panipat, Suraj Mal had been keen to control Delhi government through Imad and to supplant Najib, his inveterate foe. Suraj Mal had reasons to be restless about Najib and vice-versa.[74] By an irony of circumstances, they had met each other for the first time as opponents, fighting on opposite sides in the second Bangash expeditions and then again in the Civil war of Delhi. Thereafter, their relations went on deteriorating. Suraj Mal had obviously not forgotten the most atrocious role of the Rohilla leader in 1757 (in course of the Durrani invasion).[75] Then, in 1759, Suraj Mal had sent a contingent against him to help Dattaji (against Najib)[76] and during Panipat displayed his sympathies towards the Marathas. After Panipat, Najib had tried to turn the Durranis arms once more against the Jat. But his plan miscarried because of the abrupt return of the Durrani. In view of all this, little wonder if Suraj Mal regarded as dangerous the consolidation of the Rohilla ascendancy at Delhi.[77]

It has been observed that Suraj Mal wanted to annex the entire Doab.[78] But in the light of his policy examined above[79] and his subsequent conduct too, this assertion appears to be over-drawn. Attempts to wrest the whole Doab would have precipitated a dangerous clash at one and the same time with Najib. Hafiz Rahmat, Dunde Khan, Ahmad Bangash, Shuja, the Marathas, the Bundela and other petty chiefs. Being an intensely practical statesman, it is unlikely that with all his superior power, Suraj Mal, would have liked to array such a host of enemies against him, especially when his relations with Madho Singh, on his back, had definitely become strained[80] and the latter had also entered into a collusion with Najib.[81]

---

72. For details see Sarkar, *Fall*, II, 384-386.
73. *Memoires des Jats,* 56.
74. *Siyar*, IV, 28.
75. *Memoires des Jats,* 61.
76. *Supra*, Ch. XI, f.n. 32.
77. Qanungo, *Jats*, 147.
78. Pande, *Bharatpur,* 77 also Introduction.
79. *Supra*, Ch. XIII, f.n. 26.
80. *Memoires des Jats*, 63.
81. *Rajwade*, I, 295.

Suraj Mal, however, wanted to recover his possessions across the Yamuna and expand them further in the ethnically Jat areas along both sides of that river, stretching upto the Ravi.[82] There is ground to suppose that his brethren in those areas resented the Rohilla domination and those of the Doab and Haryana atleast aspired for a union with Bharatpur. Herein, then, lay an added incentive to the Jat Raja for expansionist activities. At any rate, it is a fact that Najib had established his sway over some areas around Meerut and Sikandarabad which Suraj Mal had formerly brought under his control.[83]

Besides the racial ties, Suraj Mal was interested in the tract to the south and west of Delhi for yet another reason. He wished to assign a separate domain comprising Mewat and part of Haryana to his restless son, Jawahar Singh, while his younger son, Nahar Singh, was to succeed him at Bharatpur. Jawahar Singh had been busy also subduing Mewat for the last ten years.[84] This apart, political geography also dictated inexorably a northward expansion. Not interested in further south, and barred on the west by the Rajputs and on the east by Shuja and the Bangash and the Rohilla sardars it was only towards north that he could expand with comparative ease."[85]

Close to the north of his principality lay "a number of rebels' dens"[86] of the Billoch landlords, approximating to parts of Rohtak, Mahendargarh and Gurgaon districts which form the heart of Haryana and where even to this day the Jats form the largest community. Committing usurpations, the Billochis set up their ownership at several places in the region.[87] The Jat being expansionist, the relations between the two could be anything but friendly. Moreover, the Billoch chiefs entertained the enemies of the Jat State and also fostered the forces of disorder and lawlessness in it. The instances of Fateh Singh Bargujar, whom Kamghar Khan, the former chief of Farrukhanagar, had extended shelter in 1755,[88] and of Sanulba the despicable Meo freebooter, whom Musavi Khan and Asadulla Khan Billoch patronized,[89] are sufficient to illustrate the point. After 1760, Najib extended his blessings and protection to those Billochis against the Jats.[90] Their alliance seems to

---

82. Qanungo, *Jats*, 146, 147.
83. *TAL*, 106; *S.P.D.*, XXVII, 226, *Tawarikh-i-Hunud*, 21b; cf. Sarkar *Fall*, II, 385.
84. *Memoires des Jats*, 46, 60, 62; *Nur.*, 60b.
85. *Memoires des Jats*, 60; *Siyar* 29-30.
86. Sarkar, *Fall*, II, 39.
87. Sarkar, *Fall*, II, 38-39, *Siyar*, IV, 29-30.
88. *TAL.*, 114.
89. *Nur.*, 61a-61b.
90. *S.P.D.*, II, 144; *Rajwade*, I, 297; *Memoires des Jats*, 60 and 61; *Nur*, 56b and 62b.

have been as much of the Billochis' own seeking as that of Najib himself. With his deliverer, Ahmad Shah having gone back and his own resources having been depleted, Najib found himself unable to cope with his adversary Suraj Mal "who was too superior (to him) in everything."[91] In the circumstances, the shrewd Rohilla chief entered into a secret understanding with Madho Singh and Billoch chiefs and thus tried to throw a net of diplomacy around Suraj Mal. In emboldening the Billochis, he seems to have calculated to kill two birds with one stone; to create a diversion for the Raja and also to hinder his efforts for union with the Jats further on by interposing a block. This policy as well as his (Najib's) occupation of the disputable parts in Main Doab contained the seeds of portentous developments. They precipitated a deadly conflict with Suraj Mal.[92]

We may now take up Suraj Mal's military activities during the rest of his career. Remaining quiet during the first few months of 1761, he turned to conquer the imperial fort of Agra (middle of May, 1761). The local garrison had not received its pay for seven years and it met its requirements by disposing off precious vessels of the imperial stores.[93] So hard-pressed it was that it appeared to be entrusting the keys to any highest bidder. We learn from a letter of the Peshwa, that the fort commandant had offered or agreed (c. 1759) to surrender the fort to the Marathas in return for Rupees three lakhs in cash and a *jagir* worth Rupees ten to twenty thousand. However, its takeover was reluctantly shelved for the time being, lest Suraj Mal should feel it.[94]

Finding it opportune, now Suraj Mal despatched a big army (said to be consisting of the incredible figure of 50,000 horses and 1,00,000 foot),[95] under Balram, while he himself stayed on at Mathura. The city and the nearby areas were taken over easily. The first Jat assault on the fort was, however, repulsed by the garrison. The Jats then laid a regular siege, but to capture the impregnable fort by an assault was an uphill task. After plundering the houses under the fort-walls the Jats imprisoned the dependents of the fort garrison, living there. At last, after a siege of less than a month, the fort commandant opened the gates, on being assured Rupees one lakh in cash and five villages for his maintenance. It is estimated that the Jats grabbed

---

91. *Memoires des Jats,* 61. Najib himself acknowledged it, when in a message to his rival he said "I know very well that in all things you have superiority over me" see *Nur.*, 66b.
92. Sarkar, *Fall*, II, 385.
93. *Memoires des Jats,* 57.
94. *S.P.D.*, XXI, 168.
95. *Rajwade*, I, 288.

50 lakhs[96] from the place. Large quantities of stores of artillery, gunpowder, balls, furniture and other articles of the royal wardrobe were taken away. The best of the things were carried to Deeg and Bharatpur. Najib, on getting the intelligence of the Jat designs, had earlier planned to move out with Prince Jawan Bakht and to obstruct the Jats. Musavi Khan and Bahadur Khan Billoch had also joined him with a few thousand troops. However, considering his inferiority in men and munition, he wisely refrained from confronting the far out-numbering army of the enemy. Thus, a Jat became the master of Agra, the first Capital of the Great Mughals.[97]

While the siege of Agra was on, a Jat contingent was detached and sent across the river Yamuna to re-occupy the neighbouring areas.[98] After the termination of the Mathura congress, Suraj Mal himself issued (middle of June, 1761) from Mathura and crossing the Yamuna, went to Kol. He encamped there for a few weeks and recovered his former possessions in that region.[99] Gangadhar Tatya, with his small force, accompanied the Jat Raja and stayed on with him at Kol.[100] The Holkar's Diwan had been trying to reach an agreement with Suraj Mal for active assistance against the Rohillas in recovering the Maratha possessions nearby.[101] But beyond extending his initial diplomatic support to some extent, and this bore some fruits as well,[102] Suraj Mal did nothing more in the direction. Presumably, to counteract Najib's diplomatic move, Suraj Mal was keen to entertain the overtures of the Par-Rohillas who were courting his friendship.[103] Hence, in contravention of his own interests the Jat would not fight the Rohillas for the sake of the Marathas. Gangadhar must have felt dejected at the Jat's attitude when he returned to Indore.[104] Later, in tune with the prevailing trend, the clever Jat even laid his hands upon several Maratha possessions. Though it cannot be said with certainty he is also reported to have made a hint to Raja Madho Singh and Raja Bijay

---

96. Wendel simply mentions 50 lakhs. It is not clear whether it was cash or included valuables as well.
97. *Memoires des Jats* (Fr. Ms.) 57-60; *S.P.D.*, II, 144, XXIX, 5 and 10; *Rajwade*, I, 288 and 297; *Mirat*, 921; *Siyar*, III, 402; *Gul.* 116; *Gulistan*, 83; Sarkar, *Fall*, II, 382, 443-444.
98. *S.P.D.*, II, 144; *Memoires des Jats* (Fr. Ms.) 58.
99. *Rajwade*, I, 285, 295.
100. *Rajwade*, I, 285, 295 and 288.
101. *S.P.D.*, XXIX, 10
102. *S.P.D.*, XXVII, 268.
103. *Rajwade*, I, 295; cf. *Shah*, 9; Also *S.P.D.*, II, 103.
104. *S.P.D.*, XXI, 75 (announcing Gangadhar's departure only).

Singh to move on and wrest Ujjain from the Marathas, where he would combine with them after uprooting the intervening Maratha outposts.[105]

About October, 1761, we find the Jat Raja at Dankaur probably busy settling that region. Meanwhile, his troops annexed Jhajhar and other parganas on the other side of the Yamuna.[106, XXI] It has already been referred to above that Najib initiated negotiations with Suraj Mal.[107] Raja Diler Singh, Rup Ram Katari and Mohan Singh went to the Jat Prince at Dankaur and after holding discussions for five days returned to Delhi on 15th October, 1761. According to the agreement, Jhajhar and other parganas recently acquired, were confirmed to Suraj Mal in return for an annual tribute, for which Raja Nagar Mal stood security. On behalf of Najib, Raja Chet Ram and Raja Diler Singh went to Suraj Mal, taking a Quran on which Najib had pledged his sincerity for the Jat Raja.[108] Later in November, 1761 Najib held an interview with the Jat at Dankaurghat the details of which have already been narrated.[109]

We may pause here to examine two letters of Shah Waliullah of Delhi addressed to the Rohilla chief. The latter had informed the former about his "preparations for Jihad against the Jats" and sought his advice about the policy to be adopted towards the group of Mohammadans who had turned favourable towards the Jat.[110] Shah Waliullah wrote to him:

---

105. *S.P.D.*, XXIX 29. There is some difficulty in exactly co-relating the surviving contents of this mutilated despatch the first sheet of which is missing. Dr. Pande (Bharatpur 77) asserts that Suraj Mal, apparently in 1763, (he does not specify the date) entered into a conspiracy with the Rajput chiefs to expel the Marathas from the north. But at least three of the authorities that he cites do not support him *S.P.D.*, XXI, 50 deals with the events of 1753. Its writer Antaji was no more in this world, whereas *S.P.D.*, XXIX, 29, as already mentioned, is too mutilated to bring forth indisputable meaning. As regards Suraj Mal's letter to some Prem Singh, its date, as Dr. Pande gives, is 1809 V.S., which roughly corresponds to 1751-1752 A.D.). In view of this it is not possible to regard his claim altogether beyond suspicion. Even otherwise, it seems a little improbable that Suraj Mal would have preferred to open a new front in an opposite direction in 1763, when the development near Delhi necessitated his exclusive attention.

106. *S.P.D.*, XXI, 90.

XXI. One Jhajhar is situated few miles away from Dhankaur on Chola-Jewar road on the east side of Yamuna. Suraj Mal 'captured Jhajhar, Dhankaur and other places not far away from the capital.' (See last sentence of f.n. 115 of this chapter itself.) On the other side i.e. west of Yamuna, Jawahar Singh annexed other Jhajhar, Mewat and Rewari Parganas in Haryana. Sarkar, *Fall*, II, (1991), 266-267; U.N. Sharma, *Maharaja Suraj Mal Jat*, 443. Jhajhar is spelt झज्जर in Haryana and झाझर in Uttar Pradesh.—Editor.

107. *Supra*, Ch. XIII, Suraj-Najib Parley at Dhankaurghat (November, 1761).

108. *S.P.D.*, XXI, 90.

109. *Supra*, Ch. XIII, Suraj-Najib Parley at Dhankaurghat (November, 1761).

110. *Shah*, 9.

> The victory over the Jats is invisibly confirmed. You should not entertain any misgivings about that. By the grace of God the moment there is a confrontation this (Jat) tillasm will (also) break like that of the Marathas (a clear reference to Panipat).

He further pacifies Najib not to get disappointed and not to have any apprehension because of the numerical superiority of the enemies or on account of the friendship of a group of Muslims with them, as ultimately the latter would not be able to fight against him.[111] "Their hands would be restrained." Shah Waliullah in his letter also warns Najib not to trust the opponents' prevarications for peace or to listen to such Muslims as might attempt to desist him from his course by harping on the innumerable dangers ahead. Exhorting him to exert fully in his task, Shah Waliullah asks Najib to inform him when he "sets out" Jihad against the Jats so that he may remain busy in offering prayers from the core of his heart from the beginning "till his victory."[112]

Najib sent to his guide and mentor a verbal message requesting him for a "detailed" reply with regard to the points raised about the "predominance" and "refractoriness" of the Jats around Delhi.[113] In a tone similar to the previous one, the great thinker again assured Najib that he has perceived the "extirpation" of the Jat people also in the manner in which the Marathas had already been uprooted and that the Muslims, especially the Rohillas would conquer and occupy the Jat villages and forts. Ultimate success being a foregone conclusion, the task of suppressing the enemies should be undertaken at once. In the concluding part of his letter, Shah Waliullah dwells upon two points. He reminds Najib that fortune fluctuates in war and he should not get "disheartened" over any bad news. Secondly, he cautions him against attaching credence to the peace moves of certain Hindu officers, who apparently were "your and your government's servants" but secretly were "in collusion with" the Jat opponents and as such did not like the Jats "to be uprooted". Shah Waliullah ends with a further note of caution that if Najib entertained their overtures "conquest (of enemy's territory) would be delayed."[114]

---

111. Compare from Najib's own statement in respect of the Rohilla Sardars that they "are my brethren and will not gird up their loins for slaying me". *Nur.*, 54b.
112. *Shah*, 9.
113. *Shah*, 8.
114. *Shah*, 8.

A careful perusal of the contents of these letters makes it clear that both these letters were written after Panipat (c. middle of 1761).[115]

These invaluable documents throw a flood of light on the underhand policy of Najib-ud-Daulah towards the Jats. Though these letters communicate Najib's anxiety about the Jats as intermixed with

---

115. The editor, Professor K.A. Nizami, by identifying (*Shah*, 55 and 81) "the group of Muslims" with Safdar Jang, seems to be placing the date of the letter No. 9 between 1753 (when Safdar Jang and Suraj Mal united for the war in which Najib came to Delhi and fought on the opposite side) and October 1754 (when Safdar Jang died). However, it looks a little difficult to accept this hinted date on the following grounds: (i) Najib is addressed in both the letters as "*Amir-ul-Umra Bahadur*". But during this period he was only a *Panch Hazari* noble and not *Amir-ul-Umra*. He was appointed Mir Bakhshi in February, 1757 and Safdar Jang had died about 2 years and 5 months before this incident. This implies that the letter must have been written after February, 1757 and not before that. (ii) The letter alludes to that no sooner the Jats are faced in a battle than their *tillasm* would also be broken like that of the Marathas (earlier). This is by far the most helping statement in determining the date of this letter. The instance of the Marathas here clearly refers to their debacle at Panipat. Impliedly it means that the letter must belong to post Panipat period *i.e.* after Najib's reappointmetn as Mir Bakhshi by the Abdali. (iii) The apprehensions of Najib arising from the stronger position of the Jats are quite apparent from the text. This is also indicative of the post Panipat state of affairs, wherein the Jats were stronger than any other power including Najib. (iv) The theme of the letter also points to Najib's pre-occupation with the Jat problem. That the responsibility of resolving the Jat crisis predominantly rested on Najib is also evident. Both these facts, essentially relate to the post-Panipat days, when on the one hand Najib became the dictator of Delhi and on the other, by virtue of his presence in the Capital was brought face to face with the Jat Raja. The above clarifications may suffice to show that in all likelihood the present letter dates to post Panipat era. As to the group of Muslims in question it may reasonably be identified with Imad, then living under the patronage of Suraj Mal, and the par-Rohillas like Hafiz Rahmat Khan, who partly due to their grudge against Najib and partly to their self interests gravitated towards the willing Suraj Mal, as expalined in course of narrative above. (Also see *Nur*, 54b also 59a; *Raj*. I. 295). The first evidence of their drifting closer coincides with the timing of Mathura congress. On this basis it can fairly be conjectured that this document was penned down either in May, 1761 or a little later but certainly before the commencement of Najib's efforts to seek terms with Suraj Mal, in October, 1761.

As regards letter No. 8, on a critical perusal, this letter also seems to be referring to the same period as the above one. To give a few points; it speaks of the Marathas having been extirpated once again—an indisputable reference to their Panipat diaster. The Hindu subordiantes under Najib's "administration" described to be in league with Suraj Mal appear to be the imperial Diwan, Raja Nagar Mal (cf. *TAL*. 108). Raja Diler Singh, who had served as *Peshkar* to the Wazir, Imad (see *Mirat*, 920) and Raja Chet Singh etc. We have seen above, that all the three were employed to carry on negotiations between Suraj Mal and Najib, while the first two had lived, over a year (1760) at the Jat Court. Besides, the reference to the 'Jat predominance' towards Delhi, may easily be identified with the Jat capture of Jhajhar, Dankaur and other places, not far away from the Capital.

that of Shah Waluillah, there remains much to unfold that chief's fierce animosity towards them. One letter especially connects his fury with the Jat encroachment. But this fact cannot be stretched beyond a limit. We know that Najib had instigated the Abdali (February, 1761) against the Jat chief even when the latter lay inactive in his capital. It would appear that Najib's attitude as revealed in these letters was essentially linked with his basic and old policy towards the Jats. Najib's intimation to Shah Waliullah about his preparations for '*Jihad* against Suraj Mal when read along with Shah Waliullah's desire that he should intimate when he undertook the Jat compaign, reveals that Najib was determined on ruining the Jat Raja. Not that Suraj Mal was not inimical to or worried about Najib, but in his case we do not possess such a weighty and exactly contemporary evidence to show that he too, on his part, nursed such a deadly malignity. The statements in later works such as *Gul-i-Rahmat,*[116] indicting Suraj Mal alone, are obviously biased and half-truths only. Shah Waliullah's letter unmistakably shows that had his resources permitted, Najib would have jumped at the first opportunity to annihilate Suraj Mal. What deterred him from such a course was apparently the superior power of the Jats, strengthened further, in Najib's view by the 'friendship' of the Muslims, impliedly the Par-Rohillas and others. Viewed in this light, it may not be incorrect to say that his efforts for terms with the Jats were not intended to secure honest peace but were born of his own weakness and consequent doubt about his ultimate success. They were a mere pretext to gain time and to conceal his evil intentions, as is impliedly conceded by the author of *Siyar.*[117]

To resume the thread of our narrative, though clear evidence specifying the time of his subsequent annexations is not forthcoming, Suraj Mal seems to have the following two years (1762 and 1763).[118] Jawahar Singh was busy to the west of the Yamuna in Mewat and Haryana, while Nahar Singh[119] was active to the east of that river in the middle Doab. Having captured the countryside of Rewari, the Jats under Jawahar Singh carried their outposts to Sarai Basant and Sambhal (20 miles from Delhi). Their villages stretched upto 12 miles from the

116. *Gul.*, 116.
117. *Siyar* (IV, 28) while criticizing Suraj Mal also for his "ambitions", "restless" and aggressive conduct does remark that Najib "was uneasy at his (Suraj Mal's) power and his character and that he (Najib) concealed his inquietude thereon".
118. cf. *Shah*, 34.
119. *Memoires des Jats*, (Fr. Ms.), 62 (by implication); Qanungo, *Jats*, 148.

Capital and were "administered by the Jats".[120] On the other side, the Jats gradually seized the major part of the modern Bulandshahar and part of Meerut districts upto the Ganga, in addition to their earlier acquisitions in the district of Aligarh, Agra and portions of Etah (Jalesar[121] etc., which previously formed part of the Jat Kingdom).[122]

By the year 1763, the Jat power under Suraj Mal had reached such glorious heights, as had never been attained before or after.[123, XXII] Owner of a spacious Kingdom, of the richest and overflowing treasury,[124] and of the most formidable and gallant troops unrivalled in contemporary India,[125] as Suraj Mal was, little wonder that needy persons like Mir Qasim of Bengal, turned their eyes for help to him.[126] But the shrewd Jat Raja, with his usual restraint, would not get himself involved in the affairs of such distant regions. He, however, did send, presumably on request a contingent of 2,000 under Kripa Ram Purohit early in 1763[127] to the help of the nearby Nawab of Farrukhabad and other Afghans against the veiled threats of Shuja-ud-Daulah. Incidentally, this episode would show the continued association between the Jat Raja and Imad (who had accompanied the above Jat force) on the one hand and the

120. *Nur.*, 60b-61a; Prof. Qanungo (*Jats,* 148-149) says that besides Rewari and Garhi Harsaru, Rohtak was also captured by the Jats about this time. Following him Dr. Pande (*Bharatpur* 78) also says this, but he does not cite any authority in his support. As to Garhi Harsaru proper, it was captured long before in November, 1755 (See *TAL.*, 1114). We have no information when it ceased to remain under the Jats. As for Rohtak, it does not appear to have been occupied by the Jats. If it were so Najib must have included this also, while complaining to Suraj Mal about his "having desolated some villages belonging to him". See *Nur.*, 67a.

121. *S.P.D.*, XXVII, 206.

122. *Memoires des Jats,* (Fr. Ms.), 56 and 57.

123. *Memoires des Jats,* (Fr. Ms.), 49 and 67.

XXII. The estimate of the Jat power at the time of Maharaja Suraj Mal's death in 1763, is very correct. But the author has not studied the period 'after' 1763. Therefore it is uncalled for to include it. The glorious heritage of Maharaja Suraj Mal under Jawahar Singh (1764-1768) was not only well maintained but also the power and prestige of the Jats was enhanced both areawise and efficient military and in political affairs also. See Rajpal Singh, *Rise of the Jat Power*, Chapter VI; Upendra Nath Sharma, *Maharaja Jawahar Singh Aur Uttradhikari*, Ch. I-VI.—Editor.

124. *Ibid*, 64ff. especially 66.

125. *Nur.* 66b; *Siyar* IV, 28.

126. N.L. Chatterji, *Mir Qasim* (Allahabad, 1935) 254—255; Prof A.L. Srivastava (*Shuja*, I, 145), however, disagrees with Prof. N.L. Chatterji. Incidentally, a Marathi despatch of 1764 shows (*S.P.D.*, XXIX, 73) that the Nawabs of Bengal kept in touch certainly with Raja Jawahar Singh. That the former did say in case of Jawahar's immediate predecessor (Suraj Mal) also, does not appear unlikely.

127. *Nur.*, 58a.

Bangash and Rohilla sardars on the other,[128] as also Suraj Mal's strained relations with the Nawab of Awadh.

THE JAT ATTACK ON FARRUKH NAGAR

Towards the end of 1763, arose a quarrel between the Jats and the Billochis. The expansionist ambitions of the former and the latter's unfriendly policy towards the Jats (before and after Panipat)[129] formed the general background of this event. But what precipitated the conflict was the tendentious patronage of Musavi Khan, the chief of the Billochis, to the subverters of law and order in the Jat principality. Mewat was infested with gangs of robbers. Jawahar Singh dealt with them sternly, but robbery seemed to be in their nature and partly because of the encouragement and protection they received from the Billoch barons, and they would not give up their activities. One of these hated highway robbers was Sanulba who, with a gang of ten horsemen, carried out regular depredations upto Deeg, the centre of the Jat principality, or otherwise upto Hodal and Barsana. A constant source of oppression to all, this most notorious outlaw defied Jawahar Singh by slipping into the Billoch territory. The gangster resided in the fortalice of Tauru with Asadulah Khan Billoch, who used to take a share in his booty. Jawahar Singh told his father that unless subdued, the Billochis would not expel Sanulba and other outlaws willingly. Apparently, to avoid hostilities, Suraj Mal at first asked the Billochis "to drive Sanulba out." But they refused "to lose such a profitable agent in crime", and so the Jat Prince moved against them. Taj Muhammad Khan of Bahadurgarh and other Billoch barons rallied to the support of Musavi Khan. In the ensuing encounter, Jawahar Singh, after an initial advantage, was eventually repulsed. This reverse exasperated him and, informing his father about his firm resolve to crush the Billochis, he marched on a second time.

Najib-ud-Daulah, "the patron of the harbourers of these robbers" objected to Jawahar Singh's action but Suraj Mal pleaded his helplessness about his son's determination. He, however, added that the Billochis deserved to be chastised as they sheltered such highway robbers as Sanulba. Suraj Mal himself moved on with a strong force of 20,000 cavalry, big infantry and a part of artillery to re-inforce his son and laid siege to the strong fort of Farrukhnagar in October, 1763. Now Musavi Khan was confronted by a perilous situation. His own resources were much too inferior to that of Suraj Mal's and Taj Muhammad also did

128. cf. Najib's statement (*Nur*, 59a), "The Jat army also is allied to the Afghans (the Bangash and Par-Rohilla chiefs)"

129. *Supra*, Ch. V, f.n. 95-96; ch. XIII, f.n. 47.

not turn up this time to his help. Entreaties for help were made to Najib, who was lying indisposed at Najibabad. The Jat artillery breached the walls of the fort. At last getting desperate, despaired Musavi Khan came out and met Suraj Mal and offered to hand over the fort to him, provided he promised him a safe exit along with his kith and kin. As messages were being exchanged, Suraj Mal must have learnt of Najib's march towards "the scene of war" and the latent purpose behind it. In order to avoid being attacked in his rear, he seems to have been keen to wind up the matter soon and hence extended promises of safety to Musavi Khan (according to Wendel on oath of the Ganga's water). But next day when Musavi Khan and his dependents went to him, Suraj Mal, violating his promises, put them in confinement and later sent them as prisoners to the jails at Bharatpur. Thus, after a siege of two months, the fort of Farrukhnagar, along with all its effects came in the Jat possession (about 12th December, 1763). Nemesis was, however, not slow in taking revenge.[130]

FIGHT BETWEEN SURAJ MAL AND NAJIB (DECEMBER, 1763)

The Billoch incident, in turn, precipitated a clash between Suraj Mal and Najib-ud-Daullah, both of whom "looked with an evil eye at each other like two men inclined to come to blows together on the first occasion."[131] To all intents and purposes, Najib had sent out, from Najibabad with a view to giving succour to the Billochis, following their frantic call for "aid" against Suraj Mal.[132] It stands to reason to believe that they must have been bewildered at the dramatic suddenness of the events. His allies had succumbed to the Jat stratagem only two days before he could reach Delhi (14th December, 1763).[133] Well might have Najib willed to chastise the Jat for uprooting his proteges, but he was constrained by his marked inferiority in resources as also by prolonged indisposition. He, therefore, found it expedient to seek refuge in diplomatic suppleness and "dissimulation", contriving to postpone the issue till some favourable opportunity,[134] may be as Professor Qanungo convincingly argues,[135] his getting assistance from his old protector Ahmad Shah Abdali. On the other hand, Suraj Mal wished to come to a reckoning with him at once now that the revealing fact of his (Najib's)

130. *Nur.*, 60a-64b (best and fullest account); *Memoires des Jats* (Fr. Ms.) 60; *D.C.*; *Siyar*, IV, 30; Sarkar, *Fall*, II, 447-449; cf. Shah Waliullah's letter to Taj Muhammad Khan Billoch, *Shah*, 34.

131. *Siyar,* IV, 28.

132. *Nur.*, 63a-63b.

133. Sarkar, *Fall*, II, 449.

134. *Memoires des Jats* (Fr. Ms.), 61.

135. Qanungo, *Jats*, 150; cf. Najib's entreaties in 1764 to the Abdali for protection against Raja Jawahar Singh, Sarkar, *Fall*, II, 460.

march fanned bitter anger and hatred in him towards the Rohillas.[136] And yet he too tried to conceal his designs. Both Najib and Suraj Mal were skilled in the art of diplomatic guile as is evinced by their counter messages on this occasion. They form one of the finest examples of diplomatic guile. Thus, a message from Najib to Suraj Mal stated:

> You are a great captain and between you and me there is a perfect friendship. These Billochis were my dependents and you have treated them so oppressively and never considered my feelings in the matter. What kind of courtesy is this?......Let what is past be past. You may retain the fort....(but) you ought to release them (the Billoch captives)[137] out of regard for me.

Suraj Mal replied:

> Between you and me there is agreement and alliance. These men are enemies....Now is it proper for you to exert yourself for the release of my enemies and argue in the matter? It was unbecoming of you to march from Najibabad to Delhi. It became known (to all) that you had come on an expedition against me.....If this campaign had not by this time come to an end, you would have joined Musavi (Sic.) Khan (against me). You had been contemplating such action. Then the alliance between you and me was broken and breach of faith took place on your part. Do not have any expectation of good from me.[138]

Najib, dreading the tremendous strength of his foe, attempted to placate him more than once. But Suraj Mal was so much annoyed with his conduct that all his efforts proved to be of no avail.[139] Meanwhile, the

---

136. *Memoires des Jats* (Fr. Ms.) 61; Qanungo, *Jats*, 149-150; Sarkar, *Fall*, II, 450.

137. Musavi Khan and others obtained their liberty from the jails of Bharatpur latter (1766) on the occasion of the birth of a son (Kheri Singh)[XXIII] to Ratan Singh (son of Suraj Mal). See *Memoires des Jats* (Fr. Ms.), 61

XXIII. The name of Ratan Singh's son is Kehri Singh not Kheri Singh, for which Dr. Dwivedi cites Wendel's source where only 'nephew of Jawahar Singh' is written. Qanungo (2003 ed. p. 106) gives the name of this nephew as Kheri Singh which is possibly a misprint for Kehri Singh due to foreigners and Persian pronounciation for 'K' as 'Kh'. C.P. C., II, letter 1499, 1st August 1769, spelt it Kehar Singh and C.P.C. II, letter 1389; Dastur Kaumwar, VII, p. 325 names him Keshar Singh. But most of the sources agree on Kehri Singh. For details see U.N. Sharma, *Maharaja Jawahar Singh Aur Uttradhikari*, p. 196, f.n. 1-3.—Editor.

138. *Nur.*, 64b-65a, Also see Bihari Lal in *Islamic Culture*, X, 654.

139. *Memoires des Jats* (Fr. Ms.) 61; *Siyar*, IV, 30. It says that Suraj Mal demanded the *faujdari* of the "*Gird*" (district around the Capital). *Bayan-i-Waqa* (quoted by Qanungo, *Jats*, 150 footnote) claims that he even asked Najib to leave Delhi and cede Main Doab and that Najib offered to give Sikandara[XXIV] and other parganas, but Suraj Mal was not satisfied with it.

XXIV. This Sinkandara is not of Agra. It is Sikandarabad *Pargana* in Bulandshahr district of U.P. in the said *Gird* around Delhi. Najib has captured it from the Jats after Panipat. See Ch. XIII, f.n. 83.—Editor.

news of the arrival on the bank of the Ganga of a body of Afghans under Najib's father-in-law, Dunde Khan, further angered the Jat Raja.[140] The mediators sent by Rohilla chief—Yaqub Ali Khan, his servant Karamullah and others—failed to pacify him. He told them:

> Cleansing (of heart) is impossible now. He has come from Najibabad solely in pride of his troops of clansmen. It is, therefore, necessary for me to see this army once.[141]

The couriers came back disgusted to Najib on the fifth day *i.e.* 23rd December, 1763.[142] Suraj Mal, leaving Jawahar Singh with a strong garrison at Farrukhnagar, crossed the Yamuna south of Delhi and stayed on the west bank of the river Hindan (a tributary of the Yamuna). His detachments plundered and burnt the villages in the neighbourhood of Ghaziabad. Thereafter the Jats returned south of Delhi. The Rohilla chief, on getting this news, marched out of Delhi with his forces and stood in the garden of Khizrabad within four miles of the Jat troops. But he repaired to the city without engaging them in a battle. Meanwhile, Suraj Mal, detaching his baggage, again crossed Yamuna and encamped on the other side.[143] Making a last minute desperate bid, Najib sent his agents (Karamullah, Sagar Mal Khatri, Yaqub Ali and others) with a present of two pieces of beautiful Multan Chintz and a message to Suraj Mal. The message stated:

> What is past is past. I know very well that in all things you have superiority over me. You have excellent musketeers, mounted on good horses. Strong forts are in your possession, no other Raja of Hindustan, in these days, is so well equipped as you. Therefore, it is not that I am fighting you, but you are wantonly displaying violence.... You ought now to go back.

This appeal too failed to calm down the exasperated Jat Raja who sent a challenging reply to it. While departing, Yaqub Ali requested him not to resolve upon any action until his return the following day (*i.e.* 25th December, 1763). Suraj Mal, however, replied that if he had the same mission he had better not come at all. Obviously, the more the Rohilla turned diplomatically soft, the more daring the Jat became. Little could he realize that his end was drawing close (the following evening). Yaqub Ali still stood for negotiations. But Karamullah, visibly offended, suggested nothing but immediate war, and the Rohilla leader justly getting angry, approved of it.[144]

---

140. *Nur.*, 66a; (completed by) Bihari Lal in *Islamic Culture* X, 654.
141. *Nur.*, 66a; *Siyar,* IV, 30-31.
142. *D.C.*
143. *Nur.*, 66a-66b; *Memoires des Jats* (Fr. Ms.), 61.
144. *Nur.*, 66b-67b; *Siyar*, IV, 30, 31; also Bihari Lal in *Islamic Culture,* X, 654.

The die was now cast. Najib-ud-Daulah, taking Gulab Singh Gujar, Sayyid Muhammad Khan Billoch (Siyyidu), Afzal Khan, Sultan Khan, Zaibita Khan and all his troops, less than 10,000 in number, crossed the Yamuna two hours before dawn and took post on the west bank of the Hindan, 10 miles south-east of Delhi. Suraj Mal, with his army of at least 25,000 strong and heavy artillery, pulled up opposite to them. Several small engagements occurred in which the Jats displayed their superiority. Cannonading was also resorted to between the two sides which lasted till 3 p.m. Thereafter, Suraj Mal tried to surround his foes from three sides, deploying 5,000 men to Najib's rear. About sunset (the same day *i.e.* Sunday, 25th December, 1763),[145] Suraj Mal, while watching the movements of the troops with a small retinue, was killed by Siyyidu and his men who most probably lay in ambush for him.[146] As usually happens in such cases, the leaderless Jats, overwhelmed with shock decamped the same night (25th-26th December, 1763), thereby conceding to Najib-ud-Daulah "a victory which no one had expected." The Jesuit observer aptly says that Najib and his men "were victorious without knowing it."[147]

Fate, thus, cut short at a comparatively early age (nearly 57 years),[148] the illustrious and still rising career of "the eye and shining taper"[149] and the Jat "Plato"[150], Maharaja Brijendra Bahadur Sujan Singh,[151] popularly called Thakur Suraj Mal.

---

145. *Delhi Chronicle* assigns 25th December, 1763 as the date of the death of Suraj Mal. A later authority, Fransoo (*Tawarikh-i-Hunud*, 22a) however, says that the Raja was killed on Paush Badi 12th, Samvat, 1820 (31st December, 1763). Fransoo is no doubt an important authority of Jat history. But in this case we cannot give him precedence over the author of *Delhi Chronicle* for the simple reason that its author most likely present in nearby Delhi recorded the event only two days after its occurence (i.e. on Tuesday).

146. For a detailed discussion about the circumstances of Suraj Mal's death see Appendix D.

147. *Memoires des Jats* (Fr. Ms.) 63; *Siyar*, IV, 29 and 33; *Majma-ul-Akhbar*, in Elliot, VIII, 363; Scott, *Dekkan*, II, 246.

148. This calculation is based on his own confession stating to "have already crossed fifty" by March, 1757. See his letter to the Abdali, *Supra*, ch. X, f.n.45. The testimony of Wendel (*Memoires des Jats*, 63) followed by the modern scholars, that he was about 55 at his death is not correct.

149. *Siyar*, IV, 27.

150. *Imad* (Pers. Ms.), 84.

151. *Nur.*, 33a; *Brijendra Vinod* (Hindi Ms.) 212; cf. *TAH.*, (Pers. Ms.) 43b.

XIV
The Jat Kingdom at its Zenith

If Badan Singh laid the foundation of a Jat State, Suraj Mal consolidated it first as Regent and later on as a King, by his sheer resourcefulness, perseverance and strength of character. He rose to be the greatest Raja in the whole of contemporary India[1] possessing not only a spacious Kingdom but also the richest overflowing treasury and the strongest army.

The Jats under him rose to the heights of playing an important role in the history of the Mughal Empire. The imperial Wazir, Safdar Jang, sought his friendship and Imad-ul-Mulk craved for his patronage. And the history of the Panipat battle, perhaps, would have been different if Bhau had not sidetracked his advice. The renowned diplomat Najib-ul-Daulah also desired to come to terms with him. The Jat King had no pretensions for ruling over the distant provinces even though he possessed the requisite strength. Excepting 1757, the Jat principality always turned out to be a safe and ready haven of refuge for the "helpless, afflicted and indigent" lot.[2]

Improving upon his father (who kept aside the revenue of a village to be distributed among the beggars) Suraj Mal is said to have set up a charity department with Somnath Chaturvedi as its head.[3] In this light Wendel's claim,[4] accepted uncritically by Professor Jadunath Sarkar,[5] that Suraj Mal had a "base" incorrigible lust for other's property, that he employed robbers for a regular hunt for money and that his miserliness made his family and troops languish in poverty, seems to be unfounded. Far from supporting Wendel, Nur-ud-Din (who being the servant of Imad

---

1. *Siyar*, IV, 27; Also *Sujan*, 200; cf. *Dirgh* (Hindi Ms.), 5-6; *Madhav Vinod* in *Somnath*, 318.
2. *Mirat*, 893.
3. Ganga Singh (*op.cit.*, 264) gives this information (charity department), although, he cites no authority in his support. We have, however, an eyewitness's evidence testifying to Suraj Mal giving charities. See *Dirgh* (Hindi Ms.), 6 and 7.
4. *Memoires des Jats*, (Fr. Ms.), 44, 46 and 63.
5. Sarkar, *Fall*, II, 454-455.

must also have had the occasion to study the character of Suraj Mal) testifies to how sternly the Jat ruler dealt with the robbers in his realm. As described above he went to the extent of declaring a war on those who harboured them. Unless they were sure about the safety of their wealth and honour one wonders how the traders and others of the different communities willingly chose to migrate to and settle down in the Jat Kingdom,[6] if it was governed by an employer of the dacoits. Likewise, some lapses apart, no farsighted, resourceful and ambitious leader would risk the emergence of a rebellious spirit among his troops by languishing them in poverty (by deliberately withholding payment of their salary) for years together.

Shah Waliullah depicts him as a fanatic and blames him for persecuting Islam and prohibiting "*azan* and *salat*" throughout the length and breadth of his domain.[7] Though true to some extent in the case of his successor,[8] this view seems to be largely overdrawn and unjust in the case of Suraj Mal. By temperament, he was incapable of such a fanatic conduct. A great centre of Hindu worship, Brij, especially Mathura, had suffered repeated persecution, including the one (1757) in the lifetime of Suraj Mal. Yet, in spite of the deep pangs that this incident caused in his heart, Suraj Mal, even when at the height of his power, did not demolish a single mosque in Mathura and had to bear Bhau's stinging remarks on that score.[9] Far from being vindictive, Suraj Mal displayed a great catholicity by constructing a mosque in his own Capital, as pointed out earlier.[10] We do not know if any other Hindu Prince of the time could boast of it. In this context it is noteworthy that Muslims also formed a part of his personal attendants, who stood by their master and laid down their lives for him.[11]

Whether fighting heroically in Muhammad Shah's Rohilla expedition (1745), or leading the Jaipur van at Bagru, (1748) whether worsting the Afridis at Ram Chatauni (1750) or Najib's Rohillas at Garhi Maidan (1753), whether humbling the Mir Bakhshi at Sarai Sobha Chand (1750) or carrying out other minor exploits, Suraj Mal left behind a name for valour and stubborn courage. His successful defence against the Maratha-

---

6. Qanungo, *Jats*, 289; *Dirgh* (Hindi Ms.) 1; cf. *Imad* (Pers. Ms.), 84.
7. *Shah*, 2.
8. Qanungo, *Jats*, 220-221.
9. *Imad* (Pers. Ms.) 120-121.
10. *Supra*, Ch. XII, f.n. 65.
11. See Appendix D. It may not be out of place to note here that his brother Pratap Singh, who initially shared the Jat administration with Suraj Mal (during the reign of Badan Singh) distinctly relished Muslim culture and friendship with the Muslims. See *Imad* (Pers. Ms.), 84.

Imad myriads (1754) as also against the numerous Durranis (1760) displays his consummate generalship. The lone reverse involving him directly, was the one he sustained along with Safdar Jang in the civil war. Had it not been for his sudden death what would have been the ultimate result at the Hindan (1763) is not difficult to visualize in the light of the respective strength and resources of the contestants.

The hardy Jat peasants have always had the making of best warriors in them. No less brave fighters than industrious peasants, the Jat King could avail himself of their services in moments of a big crisis,[12] such as the one presented by the Maratha invasion (1754). All the same, he realized the extreme necessity of a good standing army and took steps to raise it. Though over-whelmingly consisting of the Jats, his army had soldiers of other castes as well.[13] *Siyar* tells us that this great Jat general had personally trained his mounted matchlockmen in a method of his own. He "introduced an exercise of firing at a mark on horse back and then wheeling round in order to load under shelter". By daily practice, they had become:

> so expeditious and dangerous marksmen....that there were no troops in India that could pretend to face them in the field. Nor was it thought possible for any Indian Prince to wage war against such a Prince with any prospect of advantage.[14]

Endowed with a cool calculating vision, a profound sense of foresight and an exemplary shrewdness, Suraj Mal's genius shone forth in the field of diplomacy.[15] He displayed great adroitness in handling men and matters. Amidst the moments of greatest trial, he exhibited a commendable presence of mind and endurance. In an atmosphere of "intrigue and unscrupulous diplomacy, he equally baffled the dissembling Mughal and the cunning Maratha,[16] as also the crafty Abdali and the subtle Rajputs. His was a most precarious position indeed for he stood between the two most formidable and hostile powers, the Abdali on the north and the encroaching Marathas on the South. His

---

12. On such occasions the peasant fighters were paid in the form of meals, consisting of one seer of wheat, some gram and butter. War ended, they returned to their fields, See *Memoires des Jats* (Fr. Ms.), 67 and 83.
13. *Sujan Charitra* contains several passages referring to the non-Jat soldiers in the Bharatpur army. Incidentally, it is interesting to note that the Sarva-Khap militia of the Upper Doab also comprised various non-Jat groups, as can be seen from Kanha Ram's (Hindi Ms.) account.
14. *Siyar*, IV, 28; cf. *Nur*, 66b.
15. Prof. Hari Ram Gupta calls him "the shrewdest diplomat of the time." Vide *Panipat*, 153.
16. Qanungo, *Jats*, 65.

fabulous treasure was the perennial object of their greed, while his expansionist course and independent existence in the neighbourhood justly annoyed both the Mughals and the Rajputs. In addition, the influential forces of Islamic renaissance were also deadly opposed to him. More than once had the Abdali and the Marathas endeavoured to ruin him. Even normally, a potential threat from their side always stared Suraj Mal in his face.

In such circumstances, the survival of the Jat Kingdom itself was a Herculean task. But mainly by his marvellous diplomatic suppleness, 'peculiar' wisdom and heroic fortitude, he not only succeeded in thwarting all his enemies but also in increasing his fortunes in face of successive crises. Wendel says that Suraj Mal had the guts to save himself from the Maratha-Durrani exactions when others were being squeezed, to protect his territory against the redoubted Abdali while a number of powerful grandees could not help draining out their own resources by joining him (the Abdali), to ensure peace amidst the prevailing trouble which had engulfed his neighbours, to strengthen his power while others were losing to disentangle himself from the Marathas whose discomfiture he had clearly foreseen, to turn the Abdali without a recourse and in a word to become more powerful amidst the common decay. The Jesuit Father aptly concludes, "I do not know anyone else in Hindustan who could do the same".[17] That was Suraj Mal, the master diplomat of the period. No doubt, Najib-ud-Daulah also possessed great diplomatic tact and political sagacity.[18] But the main difference between the two lies in the fact that Najib had the powerful patronage of his deliverer, Ahmad Shah Abdali, whereas Suraj Mal solely on his own outwitted both the Abdali and the Marathas at one and the same time. In addition, Suraj Mal guaranteed to his Kingdom a progress which Najib could not.[19]

"Raja Suraj Mal was endowed with all the qualities of a good ruler....and succeeded by his government in vastly increasing his tenantry and treasure."[20] This was predominantly the result of the patient toil of that Raja. By the time of his death the Jat State had grown to 200 miles in length (east-west) and 140 miles in breadth (north-south), covering a part of the *suba* of Delhi and three fourths of that of Agra. One of our authorities tells us:

> Beyond the Jamuna (on the western side) from the gates of Delhi upto the Chambal, there was no government except his own and towards the Ganga the case was almost the same.[21]

---

17. *Memoires des Jats* (Fr. Ms.) 54.
18. *Ibid.*, 67.
19. Contra see Sarkar, *Fa*20. *Tawarikh-i-Hunud* (Pers. Ms.) 20a-20b.
20. *Tawarikh-i-Hunud* (Pers. Ms.) 20a-20b.
21. *Memoires des Jats* (Fr. Ms.) 56; Qanungo, *Jats*, 167.

It roughly corresponded to the districts of Agra, Mathura, Dholpur, Aligarh, Bulandshahar, parts of Mainpuri, Meerut and Rohtak, Gurgaon and Rewari, besides the original principality of Bharatpur.

The Jat King had a vision to appreciate the innate susceptibilities of his Jat brethren. He presumably knew that it was difficult, if not impossible, for them to shed abruptly or wholly their deep-rooted democratic instinct and sentiments of individual and tribal independence. Therefore, he wisely refrained from an abrupt recourse to a despotic system of the Mughal type. Professor Qanungo rightly points out that the Jat government as it stood at Suraj Mal's death still corresponded to a feudal confederacy with the Jat King as the supreme head.[22]

In consequence of his prudence, skill and administrative ability and the measure of protection guaranteed by him, "peaceful" conditions returned to the region under his control after a long period of chaos and anarchy. He attended "so admirably...to the job of a *zamindar* (landlord)", in increasing the value of the country he had subdued, that he "considerably increased his revenues". Simultaneously, he controlled his expenses so well that "for several years" he used to save "at least half" the annual yield of his dominions, despite the big amounts spent on forts, palaces and markets.[23]

We know that in the beginning of his reign his annual revenue amounted to "one crore of rupees".[24] In 1760, it stood at "one and a half crores".[25] It went up still higher and in the succeeding years he realised "175 lakhs" annually, whereas his annual expenditure approximated to 65 lakhs of rupees.[26] According to his reported confession, in 1760 he had about six crores of rupees in his treasury.[27] Hence, Wendel is correct in estimating that at the time of his death he had rupees 10 crores in cash, mostly buried underground. This did not include jewels and other valuables worth a handsome amount. However, according to popular belief the cash in hand with him ranged between 15 to 20 crores.[28]

Trade and commerce also thrived owing to the direct and indirect encouragement offered by the administration, Suraj Mal remitted transit duties throughout his Kingdom. As a result "grain became exceedingly

---

22. Qanungo, *Jats*, 221; For a discordant note see Pande, *Bharatpur*, 82.
23. *Memoires des Jats*, (Fr. Ms.), 57, 67.
24. *Shah*, 2.
25. *Imad*, (Pers. Ms.) 108.
26. *Memoires des Jats* (Fr. Ms.) 67; Sarkar, *Fall*, II, 455.
27. *Imad*, (Pers. Ms.), 108.
28. Wendel grows prolix in discussing the question of the Jat treasures. See *Memoires des Jats*, (Fr. Ms.) 64-67, 86.

cheap".[29] Similar must have been the case with other commodities. If Suraj Mal constructed royal edifices, he did not forget to order the building of markets. If *Imad* is to relied upon, in Deeg and other places, he built thousands of shops[30] to facilitate the traders. Such steps and the peace guaranteed by his benign rule amidst prevailing anarchy attracted the merchants from the outside to the Jat Kingdom as pointed out elsewhere. Wendel hardly exaggerates in saying:

> I admit willingly that the Jats are rich, that if even today there is any treasure in Hindustan, after all the damage caused by Nadir Shah, the Abdali and the Marathas, it is among the Jats.[31]

To huge wealth Suraj Mal added stately magnificence and provided patronage to art and letters. We have for the first time come to know that it was at the instance of Suraj Mal, that Somnath, a poet whom he patronised, wrote a long poem, *Brijendra Vinod*.[32] Later on when Somnath retired to Wair, Pratap Singh, the brother of Suraj Mal, extended to him his patronage.[33] So also did Bahadur Singh, son of Pratap Singh, a little afterwards.[34] Thus, encouragement to literary activity went on side by side with the growth of other arts in Suraj Mal's reign. In fact, Suraj Mal was a great connoisseur of art. Napoleon grabbed the best pieces of art from the conquered places to decorate Paris. Mahmud of Ghazni took away with him the artists themselves to adorn his Capital. In a way Suraj Mal combined both these traits in him. On the one hand, he carried choicest pieces of the Mughal grandeur from Agra to adorn his Court and on the other his wealth and will galvanised the unprovided for architects of the impoverished Court of Delhi to the new home of art. Besides, on his forts Suraj Mal spent crores of rupees embellishing Deeg. Bharatpur, Wair and Kumbher with "enchanting building", ponds and gardens.[35] The author of *Imad* tells us that some of his buildings were so magnificent that the kind of these could not be found "anywhere—not even in Delhi and Agra".[36] Crowning all these was architecturally sumptuous and "superb" palace of Deeg, which had

---

29. *Nur*, 83b.
30. *Imad*, (Pers. Ms.) 84; Also see *Dirgh* (Hindi Ms.), 1.
31. *Memoires des Jats*, (Fr. Ms.), 66.
32. *Brijendra Vinod* (Hindi Ms.), 212.
33. Under Pratap Singh's patronage he wrote the following poems: *Ram Charitra Ratnakar*, *Rama Kala Dhar* and *Ras Peeushnidhi*.
34. At Bahadur Singh's inspiration he translated the Sanskrit Drama, *Malti Madhav* in Hindi entitled *Madhav Vinod*.
35. *Tawarikh-i-Hunud* (Pers. Ms.) 22a, Also see *Dirgh* (Hindi Ms.), 1-2, *Ras Peeushnidhi* in *Somnath*, 6; Qanungo, *Jats*, 287f.
36. Imad (Pers. Ms.) 85.

been planned and constructed by Suraj Mal on such a gorgeous scale that the work on it did not end even by 1768. A widely travelled eye-witness testifies:

> It is difficult to realize the expanse and magnificence of this palace without seeing it...I have seen none in Hindustan that would surpass it in magnificence, or even would come near to it.[37]

If the great Jat ruler was as much fond of money as Wendel paints him to be, certainly he knew how to spend it munificently and wisely too. Though their plain and rustic habits—so characteristic of the Jat peasants—remained more or less unaffected, the Jat affluence, power and intercourse with the outside world left an imprint on their "costumes, dresses, edifices, language and in general everything." Whereas formerly only their chiefs knew about the royal splendour of Agra and Delhi, now even the commoners saw them veritably "in the midst of Deeg, Kumbher and Bharatpur."[38]

To conclude, Suraj Mal had found the Jats as petty *zamindars* but within a short span of time he raised them to "a reputation above Hindustan."[39]

---

37. *Memoires des Jats,* (Fr. Ms.), 44; See also *Dirgh* (Hindi Ms.), 1.
38. *Memoires des Jats,* (Fr. Ms.), 50-51.
39. *Memoires des Jats,* 67.

APPENDIX A

Side Light on the Character and Career of Muhkam Singh

Owing to the silence of our authorities, we are left to make conjectures regarding Muhkam's character. Though devoid of some of the good qualities of his father, Muhkam Singh seems to have shared Churaman's love of money and of predatory life. His fixing cash compensation for the release of the enemy soldiers, captured, in course of the fight with Nilkanth Nagar, is a unique example in this regard. His treatment of his father, younger brother, Zul Qaran, and cousin, Badan Singh reveals his rudeness, pugnacity, egoism, jealous disposition and contemptuous disregard of family affections. He was extremely ambitious and selfish too. Muhkam Singh's offer to embrace Islam to save his life, when a prisoner in Muhammad Shah's camp, and his panic flight during Jai Singh's invasion indicate that he lacked heroic fortitude and tenacity of purpose too. Yet, the credit of scoring, until then, the biggest ever victory over the imperial forces by a Jat leader, goes to him when he completely routed Nilkanth Nagar, the deputy governor of Agra.

Muhkam Singh's tenure in power was too short-lived to enable us to properly judge him as a leader. But in spite of it, his incapability in that capacity does not remain concealed to us. Imperious and self-indulgent, he was incapable of inspiring confidence in his own people. As a result, a sizable section of them headed by Badan Singh turned hostile to him, and helped the imperialists in defeating him, as disclosed above.

Unfortunately, we don't have complete and systematic information about his life, following his flight to Raja Ajit Singh (c. 8th November, 1722). Whatever scanty notices that we have about him in our sources, have yet not been brought to light. Even a recent historian of the Bharatpur Jats,[1] by referring to Muhkam Singh's meeting with Aqibat

---

1. Pande, *Bharatpur,* 34. The above incident is based on *Tarikh-i-Ahmad Shahi,* 94b, which Dr. Pande claims to have utilized. It is, however, surprising how its folios, 98b, 102b-103a, 103b, 106b, 107a, 131b, giving additional information on the point, escaped the attention of Dr. Pande.

Mahmud Khan (10th December, 1753) to regain his Raj, merely repeats what William Irvine[2] only causally made known to us about half a century ago.

Muhkam Singh's subsequent movements make it clear that the recapture of his patrimony remained his most captivating dream, almost till his death. To realize it, he entered into collusion with one or the other personage, to the obvious anxiety of Badan Singh and Suraj Mal. This must have influenced the latters' policy towards the personages concerned and vice versa. Incidentally, Wendel informs us that Suraj Mal did not like anybody giving any help to Muhkam to survive or even showing charity to him.[3]

A Marathi newsletter of 1725 alludes to one Muhkam Singh,[4] who was offered the governorship of Malwa. In absence of any clarification it is not possible for us to say definite if the person meant herein was the ex-Jat Raja or his namesake, Raja Muhkam Singh Khatri. *Maasir-ul-Umra* suggests that the dispossessed Jat chief, through the instrumentality of Muzaffar Khan, went to the Court and made unsuccessful efforts to seek its support (obviously sometime before the Khan's death in 1739).[5] We have a definite and contemporary evidence to show that in 1735 Muhkam Singh was still roaming hopelessly in search of allies to achieve his end.[6] Impliedly, it may prove that the Jodhpur Raja had turned a cold shoulder to him.[7]

The next reference ostensibly concerning him occurs in a yet another Marathi letter of 1750. It includes "Chura's son (Muhkam Singh)" among those killed in Safdar Jang's first Bangash war.[8] But the fact that it makes the Nawab Wazir, Safdar Jang, also perish therein, reflects the general unreliability of its contents, and thereby renders this vague reference useless for our purpose.

By far the most authentic as also significant information about Muhkam Singh's movements in 1753-54 is supplied to us by the Court historian of the reign of Ahmad Shah. The clever Jat perceived a golden

---

2. Irvine, *Later Mughals*, II, 124.
3. *Memoires des Jats* (Fr. Ms.) 1, footnote.
4. Qutoted by Dr. Raghubir Singh, *Malwa*, 172, footnote. Dr. Singh does not rule out the possibility of the man in question being the son of Churaman. Sukhvir Singh Gahlot (*Rajasthan Ke Itihas Ka Tithikram*, Jodhpur: 1967, 58) asserts, without any authority, that in 1732 the Jat was appointed *subahdar* of the province of Agra.
5. *M.U.*, I, 440. The subsequent portion of its version is ambiguous, wherein Muhkam Singh is apparently mistaken for Badan Singh.
6. *S.P.D.*, XXX, 134.
7. Contra see Pande, *Bharatpur*, 34.
8. *S.P.D.*, II, 23.

opportunity to realize his dream in Suraj Mal's mounting difficulties, consequent upon his defeat in the civil-war (1753) and resumption of Imad–Maratha offensive against him. On 11th December, 1753, (14th Safar), it was reported that Muhkam Singh met Aqibat Mahmud, the political adviser of Imad-ul-Mulk and requested for the restoration of his paternal *zamindari*.[9] On 24th December, (27th Safar), Muhkam Singh went to Imad's residence from his camp at Khizrabad.[10] Thereafter, he stayed on with the Mir Bakshi. He even offered to pay rupees two crores as *Peshkash,* if the *zamindari* were made over to him. Meanwhile, the regular payment of dues to the riotous soldiery had become a wrecking problem for the impoverished Mughal government. As a means to solve it, as also to wreck his vengeance upon Suraj Mal, Imad-ul-Mulk suggested to the Emperor to bestow Chura's *zamindari* upon his successor, Muhkam Singh (implying thereby that Suraj Mal should be dispossessed, who was prepared to pay rupees two crores). Ahmad Shah, however, demanded rupees five crores, in cash, apart from *jinsa.* In addition, Muhkam Singh was called upon to furnish an assurance that he would not raise collections from the *khalisa,* and would deposit in the royal exchequer "the revenue of his country, seven annas per rupee by way of 'nalbandi'.[11] Whether or not Muhkam accepted all these conditions, we cannot say. We, however, do find the Emperor ordering Imad-ul-Mulk to accomplish Muhkam's work,[12] and entertaining the hopes of getting rupees two crores.[13] Even though, in reality the attainment of this object was a far cry, the new deal seems to have aroused new hopes for the hitherto unsuccessful and despondent Muhkam. He energetically served Imad in his operations against his own brethren around Ballamgarh and Palwal. On 8th January, 1754 (13th Rabi' I, 1168 A.H.) Imad despatched him to Khandoji at Hodal.[14] He assisted Aqibat Mahmud in repressing the Jats of Mewat.[15]

We learn from Fransoo that having earlier entered the service of Malharrao Holkar, Muhkam had also won the favour of that leader.[16] As already related above, to assuage the feelings of the Jat Malharrao ploughed the site (former) of Thun with elephants and sowed pearls there in place of grains, during the Imad-Maratha invasion of Bharatpur

9. *TAH.*, 94b.
10. *Ibid.*, 98b.
11. *Ibid.*, 102b-103a.
12. *TAH.*, 103b.
13. cf. *TAH.*, 131b.
14. *Ibid.*, 106b.
15. *Ibid.*, 107a.
16. *Tawarikh-i-Hunud*, 19b; Also see *S.P.D.*, XXVII, 83.

(1754). However, Imad's (impliedly also of Holkar's) plan of re-installing their protege on the *gaddi* on Bharatpur, failed owing to their failure against Suraj Mal.

At last, getting despaired from all sides, the helpless Muhkam Singh stood a suppliant at the gate of his rival, Suraj Mal. Despite his persistent treacherous conduct, Suraj Mal displayed all courtesy and hospitality towards the moral enemy, now seeking his asylum. The Jat Raja fixed one rupee per village in all his talukas as the *'nazarana'* of Muhkam Singh, though, as Fransoo adds, the former forbade him the privilege of riding on horses, elephants and *palkies*. Instead, he could use '*charpai*' for the purpose. Thus, Muhkam accompanied by his followers, at the head of asses went to the villages, seated on a cot to realize his fixed money. After a long time had elapsed, Muhkam Singh during the reign of Rana Ranjit Singh called upon that Raja at '*phulbari*' (at Bharatpur) in Samvat 1840 (1783-1784 A.D.). Considering Muhkam's old age as also his own relationship with him, Ranjit Singh offered him an amount of money. After some time, Muhkam Singh went to Ajmer and died before Jiwa Ram Jat (the resident of Banjari)[XXV], the Mukhtar of Raja Suraj Mal.[17]

XXV. The correct name is Banchari which is situated beside Delhi-Agra highway. See U.N. Sharma, *Maharaja Jawahar Singh Aur Uttradhikari*, p. 1, 2.—Editor.

17. *Tawarikh-i-Hunud*, 19b-20a, 26a.

APPENDIX B
Paternity of Suraj Mal

Some controversy exists with regard to the paternity of this great Jat luminary. Accepting Wendel's testimony with approbation, Sir Jadunath Sarkar,[1] and following him Prof. H.R. Gupta[2] states that Suraj Mal was the adopted, and in no way the real son of Badan Singh. Keeping the above view in his mind, Dr. Pande conjectures that Badan Singh's brother, Rup Singh, was the father of Suraj Mal, whom Badan Singh, after the death of his brother, adopted as his son.[3] Professor Qanungo, disregards Wendel's testimony as based on hearsay and takes Suraj Mal to have been the offspring of Badan Singh.[4] But he cites no authority for it nor does he specifically mention his reasons for rejecting Wendel.

Wendel being involved in all the three views, referred to above, his version merits a closer attention. The French missionary claims that Suraj Mal was born of a beautiful woman (somebody else's wife) of an unknown caste, who, during a visit to her sister (one of the inmates of Jat Raja's harem) with the newly born, Suraj Mal in her lap, caught the fancy of Badan Singh. This lady, though not willing from the heart of her hearts, discovered the futility of resisting her lover. One positive consideration with her was that her sister was already well-established in Badan Singh's seraglio. She, thus, stayed on in his harem (serail) to become her new husband's most favourite queen and in the process her son got "all the fortune".[5]

The unauthenticity of this fanciful story is evident from more than one point. First, though Wendel does not specify it, the mention of "serail" reveals that Badan Singh, growing resourceful, had started keeping this royal institution well before the said episode, if at all it

---

1. Sarkar *Fall*, II, 433.
2. Gupta, *Panipat*, 44.
3. Pande, *Bharatpur*, 46.
4. Qanungo, *Jats*, 35 also 65.
5. *Memoires des Jats* (Fr. Ms.), 28.

occurred. At an earlier place, he points out that the maintenance of the harem demonstrated Badan Singh's "affluence" and "grandeur",[6] which obviously could be possible only after his assuming the leadership of the Jats in 1723. Its logical inference would be that the alleged woman, with the newly born baby in her lap, entered the Jat harem well after 1723. Thus, according to this version, Suraj Mal should have been born in or after 1723 and that his age at his death (1763) would have approximated to 40 years. But, this is contradicted by Wendel himself. In stating Suraj Mal to have been 55 year old at his death[7] (in (1763), he places his birth and the entrance of his alleged mother into Badan's harem in or about 1708. But by no stretch of imagination can Badan Singh be believed to have been affluent, great or a proud owner of a harem in 1708 or even in the following decade. This inconsistency in Wendel, somehow missed by the scholars, belies his completely unsupported account about Suraj Mal's paternity. Whether or not an alleged woman became Badan Singh's consort we cannot say, but certainly she could not be Suraj Mal's mother. In all probability, Wendel based his story on a mischievous rumour spread by Suraj Mal's opponents. One has only to turn the pages of his account to see that with all his qualities, Wendel was prone to mentioning approvingly such malicious gossips about the private affairs of the important Jat personage. He disputes the descent[8] of one distinguished Jat person, brands the other as devoid of filial love[9] and condemns yet another as a contemptible patricide.[10]

Stretching forward Wendel's notion, Dr. Pande propounds the view that Suraj Mal was the son of Badan Singh's brother, Rup Singh, from his wife "Deoki" and that after Rup Singh's death (which he places in or before 1722), his widow repaired to Badan Singh's harem along with the infant Suraj Mal in her arms.[11] In his support he cites the Jat practice

6. *Ibid.*, 23.
7. *Memoires des Jats,* (Fr. Ms.), 63.
8. Thus, he asserts (*Memoires des Jats,* 46) that Jawahar Singh was not the son of Suraj Mal as the latter was not that of Badan Singh.
9. For instance, he paints (*Memoires des Jats*) Suraj Mal as a heartless father, who instead of expressing his grief or arranging for medical relief for his severely wounded son, Jawahar Singh, repeatedly made greedy enquiries from him about the buried treasures.
10. Thus he accuses (*Memoires des Jats,* 1 footnote) Muhkam Singh of having murdered his father Churaman, even though we know that the latter had committed suicide.
11. Here he does not specifically mention about the baby or his approximate age. But this omission, if studied along with his acceptance of Wendel's story (see Pande, *Bharatpur,* 45) leads us to conclude that following that authority, he too belives Suraj Mal to have been an infant at this stage.

of "Dharenja" (marrying brother's wife) and the naming of one of the four tanks in Deeg's "Rup Sagar".[12] The details about Suraj Mal's parentages as conjectured by Dr. Pande are unsubstantiated and are contrary to the irrefutable contemporary evidence. *Sujan Charitra* contains a relevant passage wherein Safdar Jang unequivocably calls Rup Singh to be the "uncle"[13] and not the father of Suraj Mal. This decisive statement made by Suraj Mal's intimate friend and recorded with approval by his close companion and a native of Brij (Sudan) explodes the hypothetical reconstruction made by Dr. Pande. He puts Rup Singh's death in 1722, and thus, according to him, Suraj Mal was born in that year or a little earlier. But at the same time he agrees with Wendel that Suraj Mal was 55 years old[14] in 1763, without caring to resolve the inherent improbabilities of calculation. The two arguments advanced by him are not imperative. Rup Singh was the real brother of Badan Singh and their relations were by no means bad. Hence, Rup Singh, in his own right, deserved to be commemorated after his death by his family members. Such respectful dedication does not necessitate his being the father of Suraj Mal. Likewise, it is no doubt true that most of the Jat clans adhere to the practice of widow marriage or "Karewa". But Dr. Pande forgets that the proud Sinsinwaras, to prove their superiority over others, do not generally observe such customs.[15] It is to be noted that to maintain the high social dignity of his family, Badan Singh could go to the extent of killing all his daughters.[16] Such a dignity-conscious man had perhaps an added reason to refrain personally from the infamy of marrying a widow.

All the authorities other than Wendel, do not express any doubt whatsoever about the parentage of Suraj Mal. They clearly mention him as the son of Badan Singh. Sudan[17] and Somnath,[18] who had personal acquaintance with the Jat affairs, mention him as the eldest son of Badan Singh. Several other independent sources also confirm it. Thus, the author of *Tarikh-i-Ahmad Shahi*, also a contemporary of Suraj Mal,[19] mentions Badan Singh as the father of Suraj Mal. Giving full details, Fransoo, an authority weightier than Wendel, tells us that Suraj Mal was Badan Singh's

---

12. Pande, *Bharatpur*, 46.
13. *Sujan*, 60 also 54. Dr. Pande does not take note of this reference.
14. Pande, *Bharatpur*.
15. Ganga Singh, *op.cit.* 30-31.
16. See Appendix C.
17. *Sujan*, 4 and 6.
18. *Dirgh* (Hindi Ms.), 4; *Ras Peeushnidhi* and *Madhav Vinod* in Somnath, 4 and 318.
19. *TAH.* (Pers. Ms.), 43b.

eldest son, born of Rani Devki of a Jat family from Kama.[20] Ghulam Ali also describes Suraj Mal as his eldest son.[21] *Tarikh-i-Bharatpur*[22] and *Majma-ul-Akhbar*[23] are among the other sources, corroborating our view.

---

20. *Tawarikh-i-Hunud* (Pers. Ms.), 20a.
21. *Imad* (Pers. Ms.), 84. It is to be noted that Ghulam Ali records a scandalous story of the birth of Jawahar Singh. But he is totally silent about the version of Wendel regarding Suraj Mal's paternity.
22. *Tarikh-i-Bharatpur* (Pers. Ms.), 4b.
23. *Majma-ul-Akhbar* in Elliot, VIII, 362.

APPENDIX C

Sidelight on Badan Singh's Character

One glaring defect in Badan Singh's character, as directly or indirectly pointed out by the chroniclers and also transmitted to us by the popular tradition was his sexual weakness. The fact of his ever expanding harem (serail), uncharacterisitc of a man of his caste and customs,[1] also lends weightage to it. We learn that his harem consisted of extremely beautiful ladies each, "like a shining star" of all castes (Jats, Goree Rajput, Gujar and Ahir), some admitted by force while the rest by formal engagement. The number of inmates slowly rising touched a prodigious mark. While Wendel puts it at "150 if not more" Fransoo carries it to "nearly 400 Ranis as his wives".[2] In spite of the assertion to the contrary by Fransoo the last figure very likely included concubines and maid-servants as well, as is alluded to by Harsukh Rai.[3]

Though more than 30 sons[4] were born to Badan Singh, only 20 survived; the rest probably died in infancy. Out of his surviving sons those popular in history, besides the eldest Suraj Mal, included, Pratap Singh, Akhai Singh, Sobha Ram, Bhawani Singh, Balram, Sultan Singh, Ummed Singh, Devi Singh and Lal Singh.[5] All of his sons, except Suraj Mal and Pratap Singh who helped their father at Deeg, were made heads of villages.[6] Of these 18 sons, the descendants of 16, holding Watan *jagirs*, were known as Thakurs of "*Solah Kotaries* (sixteen houses)" while Pratap Singh with the title of "Raja" was later granted Wair[7] and Suraj Mal succeeded his father at Bharatpur. The number of his daughters was not less than that of his

---

1. *Memoires des Jats* (Fr. Ms.) 20, also 21 and 28.
2. *Memoires des Jats* (Fr. Ms.) 20; *Tawarikh-i-Hunud* (Pers. Ms.) 19a.
3. *Majma-ul-Akhbar* in Elliot, VIII, 361-362.
4. *Memoires des Jats* (Fr. Ms.) 20; *Somnath* (*Dirgh*, Hindi Ms. 4 and *Madhav Vinod* in *Somnath*, 318) speaks of "numerous sons", but like Wendel refers to Suraj Mal and Pratap Singh only.
5. *Tawarikh-i-Hunud* (Per. Ms.) 19a; *Sujan*, 5-6; *Majma-ul-Akhbar* in Elliot VIII, 362; Also see *Ganga Singh*, 110ff.
6. *Memoires des Jats*, (Fr. Ms.), 21.
7. Settlement Report quoted by Ganga Singh, 111-112.

sons. But Badan Singh put them to death fearing lest the Mughal Emperors should demand them as they previously did in case of the Rajput Rajas.[8]

It was commonly believed that in consequence of a large number of his offsprings coupled with a deterioration in his eyesight, Badan Singh found it difficult to recognize his children unless whoever, called on him, did not declare the name, age and residing place of his mother.[9]

---

8. *Tawarikh-i-Hunud* (Pers. Ms.), 19a; Also see *Memoires des Jats* (Fr. Ms.) 20.
9. *Memoires des Jat* (Pers. Ms.) 21; *Majma-ul-Akhbar* in Elliot, VIII, 362.

APPENDIX D

The Circumstances of Suraj Mal's Death

A lot of disagreement prevails among our authorities over the circumstances of Suraj Mal's death. We may briefly examine their versions to form an idea about the event. *Delhi Chronicle* narrates that in course of a sanguinary action entailing 1000 dead on both sides, Suraj Mal, with only 30 horsemen, charged the centre of the opponents and was slain. Mohammad Khan Billoch severed the head and a hand from his corpse. After retaining these with him for full two days he presented the same before Najib, only then the news of his death was believed.[1]

A Marathi news report (sent a couple of months after the incident) exactly reproducing the version of an envoy of a non-Jat Hindu King shows that one of Najib's confidants hatched a conspiracy with his connivance and treacherously assassinated the Jat Raja in course of an interview. It reads "Assuring Najib Khan (that he would execute the deed) somebody invited and killed Suraj Mal."[2]

The French historian of the Jats says that after skirmishes:

> "One day Suraj Mal, having been informed that a big party of the enemy had attacked Nahar Singh, his son and destined successor, who was in the expedition, he (Suraj Mal) marched in haste with a few thousand of cavalry to his succour. Unfortunately, in passing through a ditch, which the river (Hindan) had left there, he was taken (by surprise) on both sides by a part of the Rohilla infantry, which had formed an ambush there. By a furious volley of their muskets and by throwing, at the same time, a storm of arrows (which the Indians call *ban* and in which the Rohillas were highly skilled) on the Jats who were already in disorder, Suraj Mal, with all those who had accompanied him, lay either slain or wounded on the spot. There were scarcely a few who came back and brought the news to the camp in the rear that Suraj Mal was dead."[3]

---

1. *D.C.*
2. *S.P.D.*, XXIX, 79.
3. *Memoires des Jats* (Fr.Ms.) 61-62.

Alexander Dow, writing a few years later, refers to the legend that once the over confident Suraj Mal carelessly went for hunting. Najib getting the news, despatched under Siyyidu a body of soldiers who formed an ambush and eventually killed him.[4]

Nur-ud-Din says that after 3 p.m. Suraj Mal detached 5000 men and crossing the Hindan 4 miles upstream, fell upon the enemy rear. The rest of the Jat army (20,000) surrounded Najib on the other two sides. Thus, the fight raged on three sides. In the rear, after initial advantage, Suraj Mal and his troops were beaten and turned their back on the enemy. On receiving several wounds, Suraj Mal fell down from his horse. So also some of his servants. Meanwhile, Siyyidu and some other pursuers identified Suraj Mal and pierced their swords several times in his stomach. His head was also hacked to pieces. On the other hand, the main body of the Jat troops kept on fighting resolutely till 9 p.m., when both the sides drew back to their camps. The Jat Army decamped the same night. Najib, doubting Siyyidu's claim of having slain Suraj Mal, asked for some recognizable limb of his corpse. Next day, Siyyidu cut off an arm from the body of Suraj Mal and presented it before Sagar Mal and Karamullah. They confirmed that the sleeve around the arm was of the same chintz, of which Suraj Mal wore the tunic at the time of their meeting two days before and that the visible mark of the sore on the arm was of the boil that Suraj Mal had for three years. Thus, about 20 hours after the actual occurrence, the death of Suraj Mal was ascertained and Najib left the place next day (*i.e.* 27 December, 1763).[5]

Bayan-i-Waqa says that Suraj Mal led 6000 men in the attack and was killed. His corpse did not fall in the enemy's hands. Only when the Jats retreated at mid-night the news of his death was believed. Najib then returned to the Capital.[6]

Siyar describes that Suraj Mal had kept in reserve his 10,000 mounted matchlockmen, the best in India, in order to employ them at the opportune moment. He detached himself along with only a few friends and was riding up and down to examine the battlefield and decide where and when to deploy his select band. In the process, he stopped a while at a spot. From very close were passing some of Afzal Khan's troops which had been beaten by the Jat vanguard commanded by Mansa Ram,[7] Kalimullah and a few others pointed out more than once the impropriety of his remaining so

---

4. Dow, *Hindostan*, 342.
5. *Nur.*, 68a-70b.
6. *Bayan-i-Waqa* quoted by Qanungo, *Jats*, 153 and 158.
7. *Siyar*, IV, 31, 33.

near the enemy with only a few friends. But Suraj Mal was intent upon observing the enemy's movements. Meanwhile, Siyyidu was fleeing close by the Jat King with about 50 men. One of them recognized Suraj Mal and advised Siyyidu not to miss the golden opportunity. Suraj Mal was changing horses when Siyyidu turned and fell upon him. Another man smote him with his sabre and cut off one of his arms. In the meanwhile, two more rushed upon Suraj Mal, who was thus killed alongwith Saifullah, Amar Singh and two or three other men. The severed arm was carried to Najib but he continued to doubt if it was Suraj Mal's. Next day Yaqub Ali Khan affirmed it to be of Suraj Mal from its maimed appearance and from the sleeve which was of the same chintz of which Suraj Mal had put on a tunic in course of their meeting earlier. Thus, his death was ascertained.

Bihari Lal tells us that 30,000 Jats charged the "light force" of Najib from all the four sides. The Rohilla 'harangued' his men to show their valour. After six hours, the fighting ceased at sunset. Suraj Mal, who had attacked the rear, was slain by some unknown man. The Jats stood erect throughout the night. Next morning, his severed arm was brought to Najib but his head was missing. Then his favourite dark bay horse and attendants captured earlier were also brought and so his death was confirmed.[8]

Gulistan-i-Rahmat shows that after several days of engagements, one day, while Suraj Mal was inspecting one of the batteries near the entrenchments of Siyyidu Billoch, the enemy made a sally and shot him down.[9]

Gul-i-Rahmat describes the event in some details. According to it, Suraj Mal, with a big army and artillery, surrounded Najib's smaller numbers. An exchange of fire ensued which continued for several days. While pushing forward his batteries one day, Suraj Mal was passing with only 500 men near the entrenchments of the Billochis, when they noticed him and fired a volley of muskets at him. "As per fate" Suraj Mal was shot dead. His head was severed and carried away by the Billochi. Najib stayed there for three more days and then returned to Delhi.[10]

Fransoo touches the subject merely in passing and says that Suraj Mal was slain, fighting valiantly in the plains of Shahadara on Paush Badi 12th Samvat 1820 (31st December, 1763). His, corpse, however, could not be traced.[11]

---

8. Bihari lal Munshi's Life of Najib-ud-Daulah, trans J.N. Sarkar in *Islamic Culture*, X (October, 1936), 655.
9. *Gulistan*, 84.
10. *Gul*, 116-117.
11. *Tawarikh-i-Hunud* (Pers. Ms.), 22a.

Considerable divergence of views with regard to the manner of Suraj Mal's death is thus evident. The version of *Delhi Chronicle* has an importance of its own as entries in it were made following the occurrence of each particular incident. But the impetuoustly which it depicts is most uncharacteristic of the always extremely cautious Suraj Mal. Moreover, its contention that Siyyidu retained the head and the arm of the corpse for two full days does not stand to reason. Professor Qanungo, even though mainly depending upon *Delhi Chronicle*, does concede that the above claim "cannot be believed" and that "some of its details cannot bear common sense criticism."[12] On the other hand, the most bewildering point in Nur-ud-Din's narration is that the numbered Rohilla troops (less than 10,000)—by no means in a high morale, and also hampered by the illness of their leader—could succeed not only in containing the exultant 20,000 Jats on their two sides, but also in defeating and putting to flight the picked force of another 5000 under no less a general than Suraj Mal himself, in their rear.

Apparently, something is wrong with Nur-ud-Din's version also. All the authorities testify to it and Najib himself openly confessed the distinct superiority of the Jat prowess. Even if we ignore Siyar's emphatic remark that no troops in India could dare confront the Jat cavalry, it is certain that 5000 or 6000 horsemen, who are said to have attacked Najib rear, were the chosen band of the strongest man of the country. Hence, repulsing them must have required the exclusive attention of the major part, if not the whole, of Najib's available men on the spot. By implication it would mean that the fighting ceased on the other two sides and an overwhelming part of the Jat army remained idle throughout the conflict—a fact contradicted by Nur-ud-Din himself, leaving aside the common sense. Thus, it becomes certain that either Suraj Mal did not actually charge the rear or if he did, its ultimate result including the manner of his death was not that which Nur-ud-Din, *Bayan-i-Waqa* and Behari Lal would let us believe.

The contention of the Marathi news despatch that a plot was hatched and Suraj Mal was treacherously murdered in course of some interview, cannot by itself be safely accepted unless verified from some other source. If *Siyar* is to be relied upon, Yaqub Ali's insistence to Suraj Mal not to resolve upon any definite course of action till he returned the following day, may offer clue. The Marathi despatch looks relevant only to the extent that it suggests a surprise killing of the Jat Raja—a fact basically endorsed by Wendel, Siyar, *Gulistan-i-Rahmat*, *Gul-i-Rahmat*

12. Qanungo, *Jats*, 157.

and Dow, as also by the tradition. Nur-ud-Din also seems to support it in as much as he does not tell that Suraj Mal before he was finally killed had any occasion to hit back at his opponents. Thus, though agreeing on this important point, the sources differ on the preceding details and also on the actual background of the event. None of them gives a version wholly convincing and complete by itself. Dow's theory of hunting is too fanciful to deserve any serious attention, *Gul-i-Rahmat* expressly, and *Gulistan-i-Rahmat* by implication, overstretch the campaign to several days, which is incorrect.

Then again, *Gul-i-Rahmat's* claim that the head was cut off from Suraj Mal's body following his end is also untenable because if it were so, Suraj Mal's death could have been ascertained immediately, making it useless for Najib to stay there for three more days. *Siyar* speaks of Suraj Mal and five others being killed with the sabre thrusts without their offering any resistance whatsoever. This looks a little improbable, on the simple ground that unless somehow incapacitated, the five of them must have resisted and would not have allowed themselves to be overpowered so easily by a party of only four assailants. Moreover, how was it that Suraj Mal and his men were caught unawares when they were clearly seeing the enemy runaways passing close by. It seems that either Siyyidu and party first charged a volley of muskets and the used sabres to finish them up, or the actual number of the attackers was substantially more than four.

Of all the sources, Wendel was the most familiar with the Jat affairs. But even his account does not appear wholly convincing. He has altogether ignored Siyyidu's episode referred to by other authorities. Likewise, he says that nearly all of a "few thousand" accompanying Suraj Mal fell dead in the ambush, whereas the rest of the authorities suggest very few casualties alongwith Suraj Mal.

Thus, the actual circumstances of Suraj Mal's death remain obscure. What looks to be approximating to truth, is that at about sunset, while watching the movements of the troops, Suraj Mal happened to pass through a ditch of the Hindan with only a small retinue, when Siyyidu and party, that lay in ambush there, charged a volley of muskets at them. In the process Suraj Mal's head was either blown off or so badly mutilated that it became impossible to ascertain his death. For fear of being overpowered by the enemies, Siyyidu hurried away from the scene without even taking an arm of Suraj Mal with him, which, in the absence of the head, would have at once set at rest all doubts about his death. The fact that the Jat troops kept up the fight till they and their foes retired to their respective camps after 9 p.m., shows that none of Suraj Mal's attendants escaped to relate the gory tale. It was only after 9 p.m. that they somehow had the intelligence of the horrible tragedy that had befallen them.

APPENDIX E
Sidelight on Suraj Mal's Personality and Achievements

In appearance Suraj Mal was "taller than usual and robust, of a rather dark complexion and quite fat". He had "extremely twinkling" and "awe-inspiring eyes." "His whole physiognomy showed more of fire than what was noticeable in his conduct" which was amiable, gentle, generous and considerate.[1] He was a loving husband, a doting father, affectionate brother and an obedient son. Though he had several Queens, including the famous Rani Kishori and Rani Hansia,[2] he was not given to debauchery and dissipation. His noble act of honourable returning the Maratha ladies captured in a raid on the Holkar (1754), may show that he always preserved the modesty of women folk. Whether or not any daughter was born to him and immediately killed following the custom of his father (Badan Singh) we do not know, but his behaviour towards his sons,[3] including the intractable Jawahar, was affectionate.

---

1. *Memoires des Jats,* (Fr. Ms.), 63; *Dirgh* (Hindi Ms.) 4-6; *Madhav Vinod* in *Somnath,* 318; also *Siyar*, IV, 27.
2. Of the said 14 Queens of this King (see Ganga Singh, *op.cit.*, 256), the names of 6 have been authentically told to us by Fransoo (*Tawarikh-i-Hunud*, 22a-22b, 26b). He enumerates them as below: (i) Rani Kishori, the daughter of Chowdhari Kashi Ram Jat of Hodal. She was issueless. She personally went to the Deccan to procure the Maratha help later on. (ii) Rani Hansia, the daughter of Chowdhari Rati Ram Jat of Salempur. She died childless. Prof. Qanungo, (*Jats*, 75) and Dr. Pande (*Bharatpur,* 59) confusedly suppose Kishori and Hansia to be one and the same. (iii) Ganga Rani, she hailed from a village Bichawindi, and was the mother of Ranjit Singh. (iv) Kalyani Rani. She came from the village Nahani Jhansi and was the mother of Nahar Singh. (v) Rani Gauri, she originated from Gori Rajput clan of Amahand and was the mother of Jawahar and Ratan Singh. (vi) Rani Khattu, she was the *khas* wife of Suraj Mal. *Memoires des Jats* (Fr. Ms., 63) is incorrect that he had 4 wives only from whom he had four sons.[XXVI]

XXVI. See for details of wives and sons of Maharaja Suraj Mal, Upendra Nath Sharma, *Maharaja Jawahar Singh Aur Uttradhikari*, p. 1-4.—Editor.

3. History records 5 sons of Suraj Mal, namely Jawahar Singh, Ratan Singh, Nawal Singh, Ranjit Singh and Nahar Singh.

The way Suraj Mal unflinchingly stood beside Safdar Jang till the end is indicative of his devotion to his friends, while his treatment of Imad, Muhkam and Holkar suggests his heroic magnanimity towards his bitterest foes[4]—Musavi Khan being the lone exception in this regard. Like his father, Suraj Mal did not forget the good done to his own family by Jai Singh. Thus, inspite of his fabulous wealth and great strength, he continued to show his respect to the Jaipur ruler, Raja Madho Singh,[5] till the latter's collusion with Najib apparently made him suspect his motives.

So great and persistent was the popular trust in his benevolence and humane outlook that multitudinous people along with their valuables and families sought protection in his State in the face of recurrent threats. On one occasion (in 1761), the compassionate Jat spent as much as 10 lakhs of rupees from his pocket in looking after Maratha refugees.

He was a great builder and according to Wendel, spent "not lakhs but crores" on his magnificent edifices, such as, the "truly royal" and "superb" palace of Deeg and the gorgeous fort of Bharatpur, both incomparable in Hindustan.[6] He also displayed his grandeur by keeping a big herd of elephants and several thousand horses in his personal stables a number as Wendel says far in excess of that maintained by any other Raja in Hindustan.[7]

Suraj Mal seems to have been liberal in his religious views. It is said that Jawahar Singh's guru, Ram Krishna Mahant Bairagi (who often shared the charge of the vanguard in the battles)[8] was his guru also.[9] Suraj Mal is credited with building several tanks, arbours and temples in Govardharn, Mathura, Vrindaban and other religious places.[10] Besides, he spent lakhs of rupees in charitable deeds. Incidentally, all this militates against Wendel's charge[11] of Suraj Mal being exceedingly greedy. The Jat rulers would always be remembered for their important contribution to defence of the cultural places in the Brij. Numberous religious deeds were performed by them at different places in the Brij.

---

4. Somnath (*Dirgh*, Hindi Ms., 4-6, *Madhav Vinod* in *Somnath*, 318) gives exaggerated picture of Suraj Mal's sense of devotion to his friends.
5. *Memoires des Jats* (Fr. Ms.), 63.
6. *Memoires des Jats* (Fr. Ms.), 44.
7. *Ibid.*, 67.
8. *Nur.* 77a. He, however, does not speak of the above Mahant being the Guru of Suraj Mal also.
9. Danadhyaksh Family Papers, quoted by Ganga Singh, *op.cit.*, 263-264.
10. *Ibid.* One of his Queens Rani Kishori also laid out arbours and gardens in Mathura and Vrindaban. See *Tawarikh-i-Hunud* (Pers. Ms.), 22a. She and Nahar Singh showed great respect for the Brahmans. See *Memoires des Jats,* (Fr. Ms.), 46, footnote.
11. *Memoires des Jats,* (Fr. Ms.), 46, 64 footnote and 65.

Giriraj Gowardhan's importance increased under them and several artistic *chhataries* were built there along with other buildings.[12]

Born in a martial community, Suraj Mal was gifted with "a variety of military talents", which "vigorously supported his character in his many engagements."[13] No danger wavered his courage and resolutions as no success filled him with presumption or vanity. He was a gallant soldier, an excellent tactician and "a great captain", as his great adversary Najib-ud-Daulah himself admitted.[14] With "signs of boldness" visible at the very dawn of his career (early thirties), his military fame spread gradually far and wide and even the greatest in the land sought his powerful support. Along with bravery and courage he combined shrewdness, tact and calculation. He displayed a remarkable sense of realism, both in war and politics. He never acted on sudden impulse and set his hand to a task only after great deliberation.

At the time of his death, the standing army under him consisted of 15,000 cavalry, 25,000 infantry and 300 pieces of cannons.[15] He also possessed 63 (or 60) elephants and 5,000 horses in his stables.[16] Apart from it, considering the number of his forts, the garrison posted in them must not have been less than 25,000 soldiers, equipped with long and short range cannons and munition.

Suraj Mal was an ambitious and powerful man; but his ambition was tempered with caution and self-control. Gifted with an instinctive sagacity and strong sense of realism, Suraj Mal fully grasped the realities of the situation and then set his heart upon what was attainable in the field of war and administration. He could perceive the hazards of undue entanglement in far flung areas; so he scrupulously confined his activities to the nearby ethnic Jat areas only. Keeping an eye on the instincts and traditions of his people and combining persuasion with force, he proceeded cautiously to make them acquiesce in the institution of Kingship. Matrimonial relations with important families, grant of appanages to the members of the royal family[17] and lands to the other Jat grandees,[18] and the suppression of recalcitrant chiefs, may be

12. *Muttra Gaz* (Alld / 1911) 201.
13. *Siyar*, IV, 28.
14. *Nur*. 64b.
15. *Memoires des Jats*, (Fr. Ms.), 67.
16. *Ibid*. My Microfilm copy of this Ms. gives two different figures of the number of elephants kept by Suraj Mal. In the main body it is 60, while in the footnote, 63.
17. For example Wair was given first to Pratap Singh and then to his son Bahadur Singh (*Sujan*, 212, 223-224; *Memoires des Jats*, (Eng. ed. p.35); *Ras Peeushnidhi* in Somnath, 4) Mewat to Jawahar Singh (*TAL*., 114, Also *Nur*, 60b) Dholpur to Nahar Singh (Qanungo, *Jats*, 172) and Ghasira to Amar Singh (*Sujan*, 141).
18. For instance we learn from *Tawarikh-i-Hunud* (Pers. Ms. 21a) that Bhunda Ram was given a jagir worth rupees 3 lakhs. For the assignment of jagirs to the different Jat chieftains see Muttra Gazetteer, 201.

appreciated in this light. These Jagirdars remitted revenue to the State Treasury and helped the Raja in the defence of the realm. The stormy situation in northern India, which engrossed Suraj Mal's attention and his untimely death interrupted the process initiated by him. But what Suraj Mal followed, the rash Jawahar Singh could not. By his premature and violent attempt to switch over abruptly to an autocratic system, Jawahar Singh undid the solid work of his illustrious father.[19]

Several changes were effected in the land administration obtaining under Akbar. The pargana of Sahar was split into four parts—Sahar, Shergarh, Kosi and Shahpur. Mangotala was divided into Sonkh and Sonsa. Farah and possibly Mursan, Sahpau and Mant were made parganas about this time. Similar changes were made in several other districts of the kingdom.[20]

Unfortunately, the full details of Suraj Mal's administrative set-up have not come down to us. Below the King, who was the fountain-head, was probably the most powerful grandee, Balram Jat, (his brother-in-law) who held the post of Chief Minister.[21] Jiwa Ram held the office of *Diwan*.[22] As already told, Somnath was the *Danadhyaksh* (the head of the charity department). The management of the army seems to have been entrusted to several officers, each heading a sub-department. We know the names of two officers, Balram and Mohan Ram, who headed the cavalry and the artillery respectively. Balram was also the *faujdar* of the Capital.[23] This leads us to infer that there were other *faujdars* as well. This apart, the posts of *Mantri*, *Bakhshi*, *Kotwal* and *Qiladar* referred to in *Sujan Charitra* must have continued during the reign of Suraj Mal as well.[24]

Apart from the strongest band of troops, a network of fairly strong (three of them being impregnable) forts studded with beautiful buildings, richest treasures and a political system commensurate with the Jat instincts and traditions, the "Jat Plato" Suraj Mal handed down a Kingdom "well cultivated, peaceful and out of the danger of being suddenly attacked..."[25]

So long as he was alive Suraj Mal commanded the love, respect and admiration of his people.[26] Now even though more than two centuries have elapsed since his death, his memory is still alive and green in the heart of his people, who assemble every year (in a fair) at his *samadhi* at Shahdara to pay their homage to the great Jat hero.

---

19. Qanungo, *Jats*, 221-223.
20. Raghubir Singh, *Brij.*, p. 192-193.
21. Sarkar, *Fall*, II, 469; cf. *Memoires des Jats* (Fr. Ms.) 45 footnote, 68.
22. *Tawarikh-i-Hunud* (Pers. Ms.), 26a.
23. *Nur.*, 77a Qanungo, *Jats*, 172; Sarkar, *Fall*, II, 469.
24. *Sujan*, 55, 104, 112, 194, 219, 220.
25. *Memoires des Jats* (Fr. Ms.), 67
26. *Ibid.*, 67.

BIBLIOGRAPHY

Classification of Bibliography

I *Original Sources*

A. *PERSIAN*

1. Works dealing mainly with the Jat history
2. Works on the Mughal history under Aurangzeb and his successors
   - (a) General histories
     - i. MSS
     - ii. Published
     - iii. English Translations
   - (b) Documents, Letters, Farmans, Reports etc.
     - i. MSS
     - ii. Published
     - iii. English Translations

B. *MARATHI*

C. *HINDI*

1. MSS
2. Published

D. *FRENCH*

1. Ms
2. Translation

II *Sakhas*

III *Secondary Works*

A. *GENERAL*

1. English
2. Hindu
3. Urdu

B. *GAZETTEERS*

C. *SELECT ARTICLES*

I *Original Sources*

A. *PERSIAN*

(1) *Works dealing mainly with the Jat History*: (The following MSS. are being used for the first time).

1. *Tarikh-i-Bharatpur* by Anand Rai. Written 1247 A.H. *Khuda Bakhsha, VII, Nos. 602-154*,ff. 40. Though mainly the description of the siege of Bharatpur by Lord Lake (1804-05), it refers to the history of Churaman and after, and corroborates some known facts.

2. *Tawarikh-i-Hunud* by Frans Gottlieb Kuen, pen name Fransoo. *My personal microfilm copy made* from its only Ms. preserved in *British Museum,* London. Br. Mus. pers Add. 19, 501 folios, 66, with 15 lines to page. Fransoo (1777-1861), a German native of Poland, migrating to India entered the service of the famous captain Samru. Fransoo learnt Persian and Urdu and became an expert author, especially of poetry. The present Ms., written in elegant Persian for presentation to Captain Abraham Lockett, is the most valuable account of the Bharatpur Rajas upto 1826 A.D., based on the Hindu sources and the information derived from the Persian Munshis of the Bharatpur Court. Giving a geneology of the Sinsinwara chiefs from Raja Ràm (other than his name sake of the seventeenth century), the son of Sobhu Thakur of Bayana and Devsani of Sinsini, this Ms. throws a flood of light on the personality and achievements of Muhkam Singh, Badan Singh, Suraj Mal and the subsequent Jat Rajas. Thus, it fills up many gaps in the Jat history. However, quite a number of its earlier dates, Indian names and a few incidents (such as Khema Jats appointment as the governor of Agra and the Marathas' raising the siege of Kumbher immediately after the death of Khandoji) are incorrect.

3. *Waqa-i-Bharatpur* by Pt. Shankar Nath Nadir. Written in 1833 A.D., ff. 36. *Punjab University* Library, No. 179. It (ff. 1-2) gives an account of the happenings of Bharatpur in 1833 A.D. and the following year.

4. *Waqa-i-Jang-i-Bharatpur* by Maulavi Muhammad Fazl-i-Azim, "Azim" Written 1826 A.D. ff. 61. *Aligarh Muslim University* Library Ms. I, No. 476 (Salam 540/61). It is a masnavi on the operations against Durjan Sal of Bharatpur in 1825-26 A.D.

(2) *Works on the Mughal history under Aurangzeb and his successors.*

(a) General Histories—(i) Manuscripts

1. *Ahwal-i-Salatin-i-Mutakherin.* Anonymous. R.S.L. transcript from U.V.L. Ms. This work begins abruptly with Aurangzeb on his death-bed and goes down to the 30th year of the reign of Shah Alam (1789

A.D.). The reference about the Jats begin with Churaman (in 1129 A.H.). Here we find only a summarized account of the Jats upto the Civil war. After a gap of about seven years there is a passing reference to the Marathas occupying Delhi against the advice of Suraj Mal (1760). In its narrative on the Jats and other details it exactly follows *Mirat-i-Aftab-Numa.*

2. *Bahadur Shah Nama* by Niamat Ali. Rampur Library. A detailed official record of the first two years of Bahadur Shah's reign.

3. *Fatuhat-i-Alamgiri* by Ishwar Das Nagar. R.S.L. transcript from *J.N.S.* transcript in turn from Br. Mus. No. Add 23, 884. It gives comparatively detailed account of the rebellions under Gokul and Raja Rama and the subsequent suppression of the Jats by the imperialists. Its dates and names of persons at places are confusing which have been corrected with the help of the Court History. *Maasir-i-Alamgiri.*

4. *Ibratnama* by Faqir Khair-ud-Din Muhammad Allahabadi. *May own extract microfilm* copy from Br. Mus. Or. 1932. We have been able to use it upto folio 21a, which refers to Imad's flight to Suraj Mal. The subsequent folios are too dim to be clearly read. Its notices about the Jats during the reigns of Ahmad Shah and Alamgir Sani are too brief.

5. *Imad-us-Saadat* by Ghulam Ali Naqwi. *Banaras Hindu University Library* Ms. in bad shape. Page numbers marked by us. Though a later work (written: 1808 A.D.), it is useful for the early career of Churaman. Its references about the later activities of Suraj Mal are especially valuable because the informant of Ghulam Ali, Rao Radha Kishan was a close confidant of Suraj Mal.

XXVII. Its names of places and persons at places are confusing. For example it confuses Bharatpur with Thun.—Editor.

6. *Mirat-i-Aftab Numa* by Abdur Rahman entitled Shah Nawaz Khan. R.S.L. Ms. from the one of U.V.L. Completed in the 45th year of the reign of Shah Alam. Also see the entry under '1' above.

7. *Muntakhab-i-Khulasat-ul-Tawarikh* by Ram Parshad. Dr. G.D. Bhatnagar's (Reader in Med. History, B.H.U.) extract *microfilm copy* from Br. Mus. Or. 2057. Not an abridgement of *Khulasat-ut-Tawarikh* as the title might suggest.

8. *Roznamcha* (also known as *Ibratnama and Tarikh-Muhammad bin Mutamad Khan*) by Mirza Muhammad. R.S.L. Transcript from J.N.S. collection, in turn from Khuda Baksha Ms. An account of the first successors of Aurangzeb from the death of that Emperor to the death of Farrukh Siyar (1707-1719). This work takes a lenient view of the

activities of Churaman. It suggests that the alliance between the Sayyids and Churaman had its roots in Chhabela Ram's operations against the Jats.

9. *Safinat-ul-Aish* by Qurban Ali. Written c. 1728. Incomplete but the only extract copy in possession of Dr. G.D. Bhatnagar. Throws some light on the reign of Muhammad Shah. It is of no value for the Jat history.

10. *Sahifa-i-Iqba*. Anonymous. Written 1734. *A.M.U. History department Library.* Contains only incidental notices about the Jats, especially Churaman.

11. *Tarikh-i-Ahmad Shahi.* Anonymous history of the reign of Ahmad Shah. My personal microfilm copy from the Br. Mus. Library London. Br. Mus. Or. 2005. Generally a reliable contemporary source in which we find minute details about the Jat history from 1748 to 1754. Without it our knowledge about the Jats in this period would have been sadly incomplete. It throws valuable light especially on Suraj Mal's relations with Safdar Jang, Imad and Intizam and the career of Muhkam Singh during the period. It is, however, mistaken in recording that the Jats did not accompany Safdar Jang in his second Afghan expedition.

12. *Tarikh-i-Alamgir Sani.* Anonymous history of the reign of Alamgir Sani. R.S.L. Ms. copied from J.N.S. transcript in turn from Br. Mus. Or. 1749. It is one of the few Persian histories which takes a lenient view of the activities of Suraj Mal. This contemporary source gives *by far the fullest description of the Jat fortifications* and the Jat expansion during the period. It helps us in determining Suraj Mal's role in the imperial affairs. It advances our knowledge about the causes of the Abdali's return from the Jat country (1757 A.D.) and Suraj Mal's relations with the Wazir, Imad.

13. *Tarikh-i-Hind* (Also known as *Tarikh-i-Hindi*) by Rustam Ali. R.S.L. photostat copy from Br. Mus. Or 1628. General history of India down to 1740 A.D. contains only stray references about Churaman (between the battle of Hasanpur and the second siege of Thun) and the Jats of Mahaban.

14. *Tazkira-i-Shakir Khan* (also known as *Tarikh-i-Shakir Khani*) by Shakir Khan. R.S.L. copy from the transcript in J.N.S. collection. Shakir Khan says that from the accession of Muhammad Shah to that of Shah Alam he witnessed developments with his own eyes and recorded them in his work. But, his observations about the Jats, besides, being brief, are at places confusing (for instance, he mentions Suraj Mal in place of Balram in connection with an incident at Delhi between Safdar Jang and Javed Khan in 1752).

15. *Tazkirat-us-Salatin-i-Chaghtai* by Muhammad Hadi Kamwar Khan. R.S.L. transcript from U.V.L. in two vols. Its second volume going down to the 6th year of Muhammad Shah's reign (1724) is used here. Kamwar held various offices under Farrukh Siyar and his three successors and was thus an eye-witness of most of the things narrated in this book. Though his work contains references to the Jat activities during the reign of Aurangzeb, it is valuable for the period after that Emperor's death to the second siege of Thun by Jai Singh.

General Histories—(ii) Published.

1. *Gul-i-Rahmat* by Saadat Yar Khan. Lith. Agra, 1836. Composed in 1249 A.H. It is an expanded recension of *Gulistan-i-Rahmat.* Though it pays to read it, at places it ignores well known facts of the Jat history. For instance it does not speak of the participation of the Jats in the second Afghan expedition of Safdar Jang and the Civil war.

2. *Haqiqat-ul-Aqalim* by Qazi Murtaza Husain, Lith. Lucknow (Nawal Kishore). Written c. 1780 A.D. Though work on topography of the world, it is useful for the history also. It is the only source for the information that the Jats also participated in the battle of Manupur. References to the Jats of various places including those of Bharatpur and Gohad are no doubt brief, but are very valuable in as much as the author had personally visited the Jat country.

3. *Khazan-i-Amira* by Mir Ghulam Ali Khan Bilgrami, Azad Ptd. Kanpur (Nawal Kishore). Written 1762-63 A.D. It is a biographical sketch of Persian poets and some of the *Amirs*, who were contemporary to its author. In it is interwoven incidental references to the Bharatpur Jats from the first Pathan expedition of Safdar Jang onwards. It supplies valuable information on Suraj Mal's return from Bhau's camp (in 1760), although some of its contentions (such as that the Holkar appealed to Suraj Mal for help against the Abdali before the Maratha chief's rout at Sikandarabad) are incorrect.

4. *Maasir-i-Alamgiri* by Muhammad Saqi Mustaid Khan. Bib. Ind. Ser. Calcutta. A history of the reign of Aurangzeb. Its notices of the Jats are brief but valuable.

5. *Muntakhab-ul-Lubab* (Also known as *Tarikh-i-Khafi Khan*) by Muhammad Hashim, better known by the designation Khafi Khan, Vol.. II, Bib. Ind. Series, Calcutta. A general history which goes down to the fourteenth year of the reign of Muhammad Shah. "Brought up in Aurangzeb's service" and "employed by him" in different situations (Elliot, VII, 207), Khafi Khan shows distinct bias in his narrative against the Jats (especially Churaman).

6. *Shah Alam Nama* (Also known as *Ain-i-Alam Shah*) by Ghulam Ali Khan. Bib. Ind. Facs. I (to 1761 A.D.), 1912 A.D. ed. by Hari Nath De. Herein it takes notice of the Jats from the Abdali's invasion (1757) to Suraj Mal's departure from Bhau's camp (1760).

7. *Shahnama Munawwar Kalam* by Shivdas *Lakhanavi.* Written c. 1722 ed. by S.H. Askari Patna, 1968. A reliable and valuable source for the Jat history under *Churaman* from the first siege to the suicide of that chief and the campaign of Nilkanth Nagar against the Jats.

8. *Tarikh-i-Ahmad* or *Muharbat-i-Salatin-i-Durrania-o-Bhao-o-Jangu-o-Sikhaan* by Muhammad Abdul Karim. Written 1255 A.H. Pub. *Sultan-ul-Matabe,* 1266 A.H. Mere compilation from earlier sources.

9. *Waqa-i-Alam Shahi* by Prem Kishore Firaqi ed. by Imtiaz Ali, Arshi, Rampur, 1949.

General Histories—(iii) English Translations

1. Bihari Lal Munishi's *Life of Najib-ud-Daulah,* trans. by Sir Jadu Nath Sarkar in *Islamic Culture* (1936) entitled *Najib-ud-Daulah Ruhela chief.* Written 1787. Refers to Suraj Mal's struggle with Najib and the former's death.

2. *Delhi Chronicle.* Anonymous. *R.S.L.* copy of the abridged English translation by Sir Jadu Nath Sarkar of a rare Ms. (which he discovered at Patna) containing "detailed Chronology of Delhi events and reports received from 1738 to 1798 A.D." Following Sir Jadu Nath it is referred to as *Delhi Chronicle,* without citing the page number of the date of its entries.

3. *Dilkusha* (Also known as *Nushka-i-Dilkusha*) by Bhimsen. Abridged trans. by Jonathan Scott in *Ferishta's History of the Dekkan,* Vol. II, pt. III, Shrewsbury, 1794. Not useful for the Jat history.

4. Elliot and Dowson's. *History of India as told by its Own Historians,* Vols. I-VIII. (Kitab Mahal edition). Contains extract trans. of various works used by us.

5. *Ghulam Husain Samin's narrative.* Trans. by Sir William Irvine, entitled, "*Ahmad Shah Abdali and the Indian Wazir, Imad-ul-Mulk*", in Ind. Ant., 1907. Being an eye-witness's account, it is extremely valuable for the Abdali's Jat expedition (1757).

6. *Gulistan-i-Rahmat* by Nawab Muhammad Mustajab Khan. Written 1792-93. Abridged and translated by Charles Elliot, entitled, "*The Life of Hafizool-Moolk, Hafiz Rehmut Khan,*" London, 1831. It is on this work that *Gul-i-Rahmat* is based. See entry Published 1.

7. *Iqbalnama*. Anonymous. It covers the period from 1713 to 1750 A.D. Translated in full by Prof. S.H. Askari, who every kindly lent me his typed transcript. Its author (a Hindu) was a contemporary (eyewitness in some cases, such as the battle of Hasanpur and Sher Afghan's expedition against Kooch tribe in the early years of Muhammad Shah's reign) of the events described therein. It throws a good deal of light on the character and activities of Badan Singh during the invasion of Nadir Shah.

8. Kashi Raja's account of the battle of Panipat and the events leading to it. Trans. In parts by Sir Jadu Nath Sarkar in *I.H.Q.* 934, 1935. The part of this work covered in translation is not useful for our purpose.

9. *Khulasat-ut-Tawarikh* by Kalyan Singh, Trans. by Khan Bahadur Sarfaraz Husain Khan in parts in J.B.O.R.S., 1920.

10. *Maasir-ul-Umra* by Shah Nawaz Khan. Trans. by H. Beveridge and B. Prasad, Calcutta, Vols.I (1941), II (1952).

11. *Mirat-i-Ahmadi* by Ali Muhammad Khan. Written 1761. Trans. M.F. Lokhandwala. Gaekwad Oriental Series No. 146, Baroda, 1965. Though a history of Gujrat down to 1761, incidentally it gives valuable information about Delhi's affairs and in the process about the later activities of Suraj Mal.

12. Sayyid Nur-ud-Din Hasan's *Life of Najib-ud-Daulah* (*Br. Mus. Pers. Ms.* 24-410). Written c. 1772. Trans. by Sir Jadu Nath Sarkar in parts in *I.H.O. 1933* and *Islamic Culture,* 1933, Sh. Abdur Rashid has also translated it with an introduction and explanatory notes as *An Account of Najib-ud-Daulah* (Aligarh, 1952) and edited this account with an introduction and notes. "A fair and judicious" account, which, though devoted to the life of the Rohilla chief, contains a good deal of information about the Jats and their activities, especially during post-Panipat period. This is the only source telling us that Suraj Mal remitted the transit duty on grain in his State. Folio numbers of the Ms., as given by Prof. Sarkar, cited here.

13. *Siyar-ul-Mutakherin* by Ghulam Husain Khan Tabatabai. Written 1780 A.D. Trans. by Raymond or Haji Mustafa. Reprinted in 4 vols. from Calcutta, 1902; A second edition with introduction in 1926. Only Vols. III and IV of Haji Mustafa are used here. For earlier portion General Brigg's trans. (Vol. I, London, 1832) is cited which is better than the corresponding one by Haji Mustafa. *Siyar* covers in its narrative a long range of the Jat history but is invaluable for Suraj Mal's struggle with Salabat Khan and that chief's participation in Safdar Jang's two Afghan expeditions in which the historian's father, Hidayat Ali Khan

(in the second event) and uncle, Abdul Ali Khan (In the first and third events) were personally present. This work generally takes a lenient and sympathetic view of Suraj Mal and gives him due praise.

14. *Tarikh-i-Iradat Khan* by Iradat Khan Wazih. Abridged trans. by Jonathan Scott in Ferishta's *History of the Dekkan*, Vol. II, pt. 4

(b) Document, Letters, Farmans, Reports etc.—(i) Manuscripts

1. *Ahkam-i-Alamgiri* by B Inayatullah. R.S.L. Ms. in two vols., copied from the transcript in J.N.S. collection, in turn from the MS. in Rampur Library. A summarized collection of the orders issued by Aurangzeb to his secretary Inayatullah, for inclusion in the despatches. It refers to the last decade of that Emperor's reign. Very valuable for the Mughal-Jat clash over Sinsini during the period. But, as several letters contain no date and have not been arranged in chronological order, at places it becomes difficult to determine the exact timings of the events.

2. *Ajaib-ul-Afaq* R.S.L. Ms. copied from a photostat copy, from Br. Mus. Ms. No. 1776 (Rieu, III, 986a-b). A collection of letters written by Farrukh Siyar, Muhammad Shah and the chief Mughal officers to Raja Chhabela Ram, Girdhar Bahadur and his successors together with the answers of the latter. This collection is an extremely valuable contemporary source for Churaman's activities during the reign of Farrukh Siyar and the imperialists attempts to subdue him. Page numbers of the Ms. cited here.

3. *Jaipur Records* R.S.L. transcripts from the *Jaipur State archives.* "A miscellanceous collection of copies of letters, imperials *farmans*, *nishans, hasb-ul-hukums*, *Vakil* reports and the correspondence between the Amber rulers and the officials of the empire or those of their own State". (R. Singh), *A Handlist of Important Historical Manuscripts,* Sitamau: 1949, a17). The collections consist of the following series of volumes (i) Sarkar's collection series (vols. IV, VII, IX, X and XII utilized by us) (ii) Sitamau collection (Vol. I utilized), (iii) Additional series. *Akhbarat-i-Darbar-i-Mualla, Waqava* papers etc. (Vol. II covering 20th, 24th and 25th years of the reign of Aurangzeb, XXIII covering 5th, 9th and 15th years of the reign of Muhammad Shah, XXIV covering 25th and 26th years of the reign of latter and 4th and 5th years of that Ahmad Shah thoroughly screened by us). Being exactly contemporary, these documents stand out pre-eminently for the period covered by them. In particular, their importance lies in illustrating Aurangzeb's great concern over the renewed turbulence (during the next half of his reign) by the Jats and the kindred people in a greater part of the province of Agra and in providing minute details of the

refractory activities of various Jat catellancs and the persistent imperialists efforts to chastise them. Unless not indicated otherwise, page numbers of the Records cited here.

4. Letter (transcript from Bharatpur in fragments) by Nawab Safdar Jang addressed to Suraj Mal Jat (Letter given in the main thesis). In the possession of Mr. Mahendra Singh Varma, M.A., grand son of late Chowdhary Hukum Singh of the village, Libber Hedi (Distt. Saharanpur), President of Sarva-Khap Panchayat meeting held at village Shoram (Distt. Muzaffarnagar) in 1952. This letter enlightens us on the intimacy between the Wazir Safdar Jang and Suraj Mal and on the former's dependence on the latter.

Documents, Letters, Farmans, Reports etc.—(ii) Published

1. *Balmukund Nama.* Letters of Abdullah Khan to various personages and a few farmans. Ed. by Abdur Rashid, Department of History, Aligarh Muslim University.

2. *Daftar-i-Diwani-o-Mal-o-Mal-o-Mulki Sarkar-i-Ali* Nizam's government, Hyderabad, Deccan, 1357 A.H. Not useful for our purpose as it contains merely a passing reference to Nawal Singh and Ranjit Singh, the sons of Suraj Mal Jat.

3. *Shah Waliullah Dehlavi Ke Siyasi Maktubat.* Persian text and Urdu trans. by K.A. Nizami, Delhi, 1969. *Maktubat* are a very valuable source being exactly contemporary. They throw important light among other points on Najib-Suraj Mal relationship in post-Panipat period. Number of letters is cited here.

Documents, Letters, Farmans, Reports—(iii) English Translations

1. *An Anonymous Journal of Nadir Shah's Translations in India.* Translated by S.H. Askari in *Proc. I.H.C.,* (1947) entitled '*A Contemporary Correspondence Describing the Events at Delhi* at the time of Nadir Shah's "Invasions". It tends to demonstrate an attitude of resistance on the part of Badan Singh during Nadir Shah's stay at Delhi.

2. *Durrani–Rajput Relations: 1759-1761.* Correspondence between Madho Singh and the Abdali and others. Extract translation by S.H. Askari in *Proc. I.H.C.,* (1945).

3. *Two Historical Letters of the Great Asaf Jah I,* Persian text and English translation by Jadu Nath Sarkar in *Islamic Culture (1941).*

4. *Unpublished Correspondence Relating to Maharaja Madho Singh of Jaipur and some of his Contemporaries* by S.H. Askari, *Proc. I.H.C.,* (1948).

5. *Letters of a King Maker of the Eighteenth Century.* Eng. translation with Introduction and Notes of Balmukundnama by S. Chandra.

B. *MARATHI*

Number of letters is cited in each case

1. *Chandrachud Daftar.* ed. D.V. Apte, vol. I, Excepting letter 45 and 82, the others are useless for us.

2. *Marathanchya Itihasachin Sadhanen,* ed. V.K. Rajwade and others. Vols, I-XXI, of these Vols. I, III, and VI are extremely valuable.

3. *Purandare Daftar,* ed. K.V. Purandare, Vol. I.

4. *Selection from the Peshwas' Daftar.* ed. G.S. Sardesai. Vols. I-XXXXV. Of these Vols. II, XIII-XV-XXI-XXVII, XXIX and XXX are extremely valuable. Besides giving new information, these despatches supplement the one derived from other sources. The Marathi papers have made our knowledge of the Jats fuller.

5. *Selections from the Peshwas' Dafter,* New series Vol. I, ed. P.M. Joshi. Being used for the first time in the context of the Jat history.

C. *HINDI*—(i) Manuscripts

The MSS. under entry 1 and 3 below are being used for the first time here.

1. *Devdutta's untitled miscellaneous account of the Jats,* especially of the Doab and Haryana, running into 16 leaves written on both sides, size 12.5" x 5" composed in Samvat 1875, from earlier Sarva-Khap Panchayat (Doab) records. It enlightens us about the social, religious and political practices of the Jats and other groups of the Doab and Haryana during the medieval period. On ff. 12-14 (sidenotes) it makes a passing reference to Samarth Guru Ram Das's exhortation to Gokul for rebellion, a fact pointed out by the persistent local tradition among the Jats. The Ms. is in the possession of Chowdhary Qabul Singh of Shoram (Muzaffarnagar, U.P.).

2. *Pt. Kanha Ram's untitled Pothi.* (In possession of Chowdhary Qabul Singh, Muzaffarnagar) Containing wrongly bound 16 leaves written on both sides. The number of lines in a leaf and the size of letters are not uniform. Size 12.5" x 5". The first leaf, though mutilated, mentions Samvat 1840. The visible difference in ink and size of letters suggests its gradual compilation. Even if begun in 1840, it was completed at a later date. Its author, Kanha Ram is said to have been a person of local repute, was a resident of village Shoram, Dist. Muzaffarnagar. His descendants, whom I had the occasion to meet, still live there.

This MS. written in bad Hindi, is an unconnected compilation mostly from the earlier but now untraceable Pothis and partly from the author's own observations, showing the activities of the Jats and other local people especially of the Doab and Haryana, during medieval times.

Its earlier portion (leaves 3a-11a) refers to the meetings, along with their resolutions, of the Sarva Khap Panchayat (Doab) held in Samvat 1252, 1254 (in a jungle near Baraut), 1256, 1305, 1312 (Bhokharhedi) 1317 (Libberhedi), 1344 (Shikarpur), 1383 (Sisauli), 1408 (in a jungle near Sisaul Bhanaura), 1455 (in a jungle of *Chagama*), 1460 (Sikarpur), 1547 (in a jungle near Baraut), 1560 (Mauza Bavali), 1584, 1597 (Kairana) 1613 (Nisarh) 1621 (Shoram), 1665 (Khekaram) 1686 (Nisarh) 1718 (Chhaprauli), 1727, 1764 (Bhaisewal) 1766 (Karnol) and 1817 (Sisauli). The latter part of the Pothi (leaves 11b-16b) bound reversely, enumerates the social customs of the Jats and other people and the nature, scope, formation and functioning of the Sarva Khap Panchayat. This compilation is worthy of our attention as giving some important facts about the Jats, known only to the local people and supported by the persistent tradition. However, an attempt to find their corroboration in the writings of the contemporary historians, may prove futile as in most cases the latter could have neither access to, nor evince interest in the local happenings of historically less important people of relatively obscure and distant place. And yet its testimony needs to be handled with utmost caution; the dates in some cases are incorrect and the numbers of participants in the Panchayat meetings and of local militia raised for any battle seem to be highly inflated.

3. *Somnath's works.* Somnath was the great grandson of Narottam Mishra, who hailed from Mathura. Somnath has given his family table which shows that he belonged to a family of learned Brahmans who worked as Priests of various chiefs. He enjoyed the patronage of Suraj Mal for some time and then lived at the Court of Suraj Mal's brother, Pratap Singh and nephew, Bahadur Singh at Wair. The colophons of most of his works known to us, clearly mention that they were composed at the instance of one of these three Jat chiefs. The Kashi Nagari pracharini Sabha is bringing out a collection of his works as *Somnath Granthawali* of which the first part is shortly to be released. I have consulted the press copy. Other works of Somnath, (i) Nawabollas (Incomplete, having four stanzas only; devoted to Nawab "Ghazi Azam Khan", probably a mistake for Nawab Ghazi-ud-Din Imad ul-mulk, who lived for long as a refugee at the Jat court); (ii) *Sangram Darpan* (pp. 26. composed in Samvat 1786); (iii) *Brijendra Vinod* (pp. 212,

copied from the original in Jyeshtha Samvat, 1837 by Bhaskaran Kashmiri Pandit for Raja Ranjit Singh Jat); (iv) *Ram Charitra Ratnakar* and (v) *Ram Kaladhar* (typed copy pp. 48) are in the form of MSS. in the Sabha Library copied from the originals at Bharatpur. Of his works some are on poetics, while others are translations of standard Sanskrit texts including the Puranas and Epics. These works show the literary activities going on in the Jat Kingdom and serve as a corrective to the common impression that the Jats had little interest in the literary pursuits. They give us an idea of the social and cultural life in the Jat Kingdom. The only work having any historical value is *Dirgh Nagar Varnan* (Ms., it runs into seven pages and ends abruptly). It describes the layout of Deeg palaces etc., and gives the geneological list of the Sinisinwara chiefs. The characterization of the chiefs, besides being highly exaggerated in the worst traditions of the Riti poetry, is stereo typed and only occassionally gives us an insight into their individual traits. For political history these works (barring to some extent *Dirgh Nagar Varnan*) are without any utility.

Hindi—(ii) Published

1. *Somnath Granthawali.* Vol. I (in press). Being edited by Sudhakar Pande, Kashi, 1971. Collection of the Poems of the same Somnath. I have consulted the press copy. (See entry under *Hindi, MSS.,* 3). The work includes *Ras Peeushnidhi* (pp. 1—224). (Composed in Jyestha, Somnath, 1794), *Madhav Vinod* (pp. 317-498. composed in Ashwin, Samvast 1809), *Ras Panchadhavi* (composed in Agahan, Samvat 1800), and *(Shringar Vilas.* The first two (*Ras Peeushnidhi,* pp. 2-8; *Madhav Vinod,* pp. 317-320) generally follow the contents of *Dirgh Nagar Varnan* (Hindi Ms. described above). The remaining two works and the others being brought out in this volume are devoid of any historical value.

2. *Sujan Charitra by Sudan.* Written c. 1784, Ist edition Kashi. I came across its three neatly written manuscripts in Bharatpur, two of them in the private collection of Somnath Chaturvedi (near Lakshman Temple, Bharatpur City). It gives an account of the exploits of Suraj Mal from 1745, to the beginning of 1754, besides casual references to the history of the Jats before that period. With the exception of Prof. A.L. Srivastava (*First two Nawabs of Oudh,* p. 294) earlier scholars have not given due importance to this text. A comparative study* reveals that its

* Our article, "Ghasira Ke Yudha Ka Aitihasik Paryalochan" appears in *Nagari Pracharini Patrika,* Commemoration volume, Samvat 2024. A second article, 'Chronology in the Sujan Charitra' has been accepted for publication in the *Journal of the Bihar Research Society.*

details, including dates, are generally authentic. In some cases (for example Ghasira's campaign) it gives fuller details than are to be found elsewhere. Moreover, information available in other sources is supported and thus confirmed by Sudan (for example, Wendel's statement that Jawahar Singh received the highest honours from the Mughal Emperor Ahmad Shah is supported by Sudan). The great merit of the work is that Sudan, a native of Mathura and a close companion of Suraj Mal, had access to information not available to outsiders. It is written in the literary style, characteristic of the Riti poetry and hence at places it has to be assessed after making due allowance to Sudan's desire to create literary embellishments which, however, do not affect the core of historical facts. If he praises his patron he cleverly alludes to his shortcomings also. His generally balanced approach is apparent from his due praise of the opponents of Suraj Mal (such as Bahadur Singh and Asad Khan).

D. *FRENCH*—(i) Manuscript

Memores de L' origine, accroissement et etat present de puissance des Jats dans L' Indostan, II de Partie, suite des Memoires des Pattans. My personal microfilm copy made from the Ms. in India Office Library, London. L.O.L. Orme Collection, O.V. 216, No. 2. The MS. appears to be the original, sent by Father Francis Xzvier Wendel with a covering letter to an unknown addressee, may be to Robert Orme himself who left India in 1759. The MS. forms the second of the four parts, in a leather bound volume lettered MSS., Vol. 30 x 22 cm. (i) 122. Part I, pp. 1-26 is in the form of an unsigned letter. Part II, pp. 29-114, consists of the present MS. Part III, pp. 115-118 and Part IV pp. 119-122. The last one contains the letter dated: Agra, 27th October, 1769 from F.X. Wendel. R. Orme notes at the end that he read it in June, 1772 and again in 1777.

The fact that the last letter signed by Wendel is in the same handwriting to be seen in parts I to III, supports S.C. Hill's suggestion that the present MS., though nowhere specified as such, was written by F.X. Wendel who was in India from 1751 *until his death in 1803*, at Lucknow. He was in Agra between 1766 and 1771, supplying secret information to the English especially about the Jats. From a reference in the Ms. (p. 64, footnote) pertaining to the year 1760, it is clear that for some time at least he resided at the Jat Court, at Bharatpur, during the life time of Raja Suraj Mal also. Dr. R.J. Bingle of India Office Library has very kindly enclosed with his personal letter dated 10th February, 1971, the Xerox copies of extracts concerning Wendel's activities in India in (i) *Jesuit missionaries in Northern India and*

Inscriptions on their Tombs, Agra, pp. 41-42 by Rev. Henri Hosten, S.J. (Calcutta: 1907) and (ii) *List of inscriptions on Christian Tombs and Tablets of Historical interest in the United Provinces of Agra and Oudh,* p. 53, by E.A.H. Blunt (Allahabad: 1911).

My copy visibly shows two types of page numbers; the first indicates the number running through all the four parts of the volume according to which the Ms. begins at p. 29 and ends at p. 115; the second gives separate numbering to the present Ms., *i.e.* pp. 1-86. I have cited the latter numbers as they look more appropriate. With the help of Miss Asha of Mauritius we have made the full translation of this valuable source.

French—(ii) Translations

1. *Le Journal Du Voyage du Bengale a Delhy* (Paris Ms.) by L.L. Dolisy De Modave. Extracts of this eyewitness account have been translated by Jadu Nath Sarkar entitled, 'The Delhi Empire A century after Bernier, in *Islamic Culture* XI, 1937.

2. *Travels in Mogul Empire* by Bernier. Trans. A. Constable, S. Chand & Co., 1968.

3. *Storia Do Mogor* by Noccolao Manucci. Trans. Sir William Irvine, Vols. I (1906), III (1907), London, II (1966), Calcutta. (At different times Manucci wrote besides French in Portuguese and Italian. The text which Irvine translated was largely in Portuguese and partly in French).

II. Sakhas

Verses in the Jataki dialect dealing with notable events of Medieval Indian history, especially concerning the Jats. I heard and collected several Sakhas in course of my visit to parts of Haryana, Western U.P. and Rajasthan. Mr. Jagdev Singh Sidhanti (Prop. Samrat Press, Delhi) having tape recorded one Sakha on Suraj Mal, and Bhau before Panipat, in the voice of Imad-ud-Din and party of Haryana, has very kindly sent to me its typed copy. Sakhas, a sort of Ballads, though composed much earlier, probably not long after the date of occurrence of the event narrated by them—are in unwritten form. They are, however, still fresh in the memory of the Jogis—a class of professional rural singers—who generation after generation have earned their bread by reciting them to rural folk. At places the note of exaggeration in the delineation of the events is discernible. The number of fighters in battles, as given in them, is also understandably inflated. Nevertheless, they have importance of their own in so far as they constitute floating evidence of the seamy side of history.

III. *Secondary Works*

A. *GENERAL*

(1) English

Ali, M. Athar — *The Mughal Nobility under Aurangzeb*, Asia Publishing House, 1966.

Beams, John — (ed.) H.M. Elliots *Memoirs of Races of North Western Provinces of India* Vol. I, London.

Beveridge, H. — *The Comprehensive History of India, Civil Military and Social*, Vol. II, London.

Chandra, S. — *Parties and Politics at the Mughal Court*, Aligarh, 1959.

Chatterji. N.L. — *Mir Qasim*, Allahabad, 1935.

Chopra, P.N. — *Society and Culture during Mughal Age*, Agra, 1963.

Dow, Alexander — *The History of Hindostan*, translated from Persian, Vol. II, London, 1812.

Duff, J.C.G. — *A History of the Marathas*, Vol. I, Oxford, 1921.

Erskine, William — *The History of India under the first Two Sovereigns of the House of Taimur, Babar and Humayun*, Vols. I & II, London, 1854.

Elliot & Dowson — *History of India*, Vols. I-VIII, Kitab Mahal edition.

Elliot, H.M. — *History of India*, Vol. II, Calcutta, 1901.

Faruki, Zahir-ud-Din — *Aurangzeb and His Times*, Bombay, 1935.

Franklin, W. — *The History of the Reign of Shah Aulum*, London, 1798.

Fraser, James — *The History of Nadir Shah*, Panini Office, Allahabad.

Growse, F.S. — *Mathura: A District Memoir*, Allahabad, 1883.

Gupta, H.R. — *Studies in the Later Mughal History of the Panjab*, Lahore, 1944.

— (ed.) *Marathas and Panipat*, Chandigarh, 1961.

Habib, Irafan — *The Agrarian System of Mughal India (1556-1707)* Bombay; 1963.

Husain, Mahmud — (ed.) *A History of the Freedom Movement*, Vols. I (1957), II, (1960) Karachi.

Husain, Yusuf — *The First Nizam*, Bombay, 1963.

Hutton, J.H. — *Caste in India*, Cambridge, 1946.

Ibbetson, Denzil — *The Panjab Castes*, Lahore Government Printing Press, 1916.

Irvine, William — *The Later Mughals*, Vols. I & II Calcutta.

Keene, H.G. — *The Moghul Empire*, London 1866.

Lanepool, Stanely — *Medieval India under Muhammadan Rule*, London, 1923.

Latif, S.M. — *Agra, Historical and Descriptive*, Calcutta, 1896.

Majumdar, D.N. — *Races and Cultures of India*, Bombay, 1965.

Majumdar, R.C. — *Corporate Life in Ancient India*, Calcutta, 1918.

— (ed.) *Classical Accounts of India*; Calcutta, 1960.

Malik, Z. — *Muhammad Shah*, Unpublished thesis. A.M.U. Library.

Moreland, W.H. — *From Akbar to Aurangzeb*, London 1923.

Owen, Sidney J. — *The Fall of the Mogul Empire*, London, 1912.

Pande, A.B — *Later Medieval India*, Allahabad, 1963.

Pande, Ram — *Bharatpur upto 1826*, Jaipur, May, 1970.

Pradhan, M.C. — *The Political System of the Jats of Northern India*, Oxford, 1966.

Prasad, Beni — *History of Jahangir*, London, 1930.

Prasad, Ishwari — *A Short History of Muslim Rule in India*, Allahabad Ist edition.

Qanungo, K.R. — *History of the Jats*, Vol. I, Calcutta, 1925.

— *Studies in Rajput History*, Delhi 1960.

Risley, Herbert — *The people of India*, Calcutta, 1908.

Russel, R.V — *The Tribes and Castes of the Central Provinces of India*, Vol. III, London, 1916.

Saksena, B.P. — *History of Shah Jahan of Delhi*, Allahabad, 1938.

Sardesai, G.S. — *New History of the Marathas*, Vol. II Bombay, 1958.

Sarkar, J.N. — *Anecdotes of Aurangzib and other Historical Essays*, edition 1925.

— *Fall of the Mughal Empire*, Calcutta, Vol. I (1932), II (1934).

— *History of Aurangzib*, Calcutta—Vols. I (1912), II (1912), III (1928), IV (1930), V (1924).

— *India of Aurangzib*, Sanyal and Co. Printers, 1901.

—	*Mughal Administration*, Calcutta 1924.
—	*Studies in Mughal India*, Calcutta, 1919.
Scott, Jonathan	*Ferishta's History of the Dekkan*, Vol. II, Shrewsbury, 1794.
Sharma, Sri Ram	*A Bibliography of Mughal India*, Bombay, 1932.
—	*The Religious Policy of the Mughal Emperors*, Bombay, 1962.
—	*Studies in Medieval Indian History*, Sholapur, 1956.
Shejwalkar, T.S	*Panipat*: 1761, Poona, 1946.
Srivastava, A.L.	*The First Two Nawabs of Oudh*, Lucknow, 1933.
—	*Shuja-ud-Daulah*, Vol. I, Agra, 1961.
Singh, Ganda	*Ahmad Shah Durrani*, Bombay, 1959.
Sinha, H.N.	*Rise of the Peshwas*, Allahabad, 1931.
Tod, James	*The Annals and Antiquities of Rajasthan*, ed. by W. Crooks, 3 Vols.
Tripathi, R.P.	*Some Aspects of Muslim Administration*, Allahabad, 1959.
Upadhyaya, V.	*The Socio-Religious Conditions of North India*, Varanasi, 1964
Vaidya, C.V.	*History of Medieval Hindu India*, Vol. I, Poona, 1921.

(2) Hindi

Bhargava, V.S.	*Rajasthan Ke Itihas Ka Sarvekshna*, Jaipur., 1971.
Bhatnagar, V.S.	*Sawai Jai Singh, Jaipur*, 1972.
Chandra, S.	*Uttar Mughal Kalin Bharat Ka Itihas*, Meerut, 1972.
Desh Raj, Thakur	*Jat Itihas*, Kanti Press, 1938.
—	*Marwar Ka Jat Itihas*, Nagore, 1954.
Dikshit, G.C.	*Brajendra Vansha Bhaskar*, Agra, Samvat 1983.
Gahlot, Jagdish Singh	*Rajputana Ka Itihas*, Vol. III, Jodhpur, 1966.
Gahlot, S.S.	*Rajasthan Ke Itihas Ka Tithikram*, Jodhpur, 1967.
Jaiswal, K.P.	*Andhkar Yugin Bharat* (trans. Ram Chandra Varma), Kashi, Samvat 2014.
Mitra, M.	*Maharaja Ajit Singh Aur Unka Yug*, Jaipur, 1973.
Prasad, Beni	*Jaton Ki Utpatti Aur Itihas.*

Ranawat, M.S.	*Bharatpur Maharaja Jawahar Singh Jat*, Jodhpur, 1973.
Saran, P.	*Mughalon Ka Prantiya Shashan*, Lucknow, 1970.
Sharma, M.L.	*Kota Rajya Ka Itihas.*
Sharma, U.N.	*Jaton Ka Navin Itihas*, Jaipur, 1977.
Singh, Ganga	*Yadu Vansha*, Vol. I, Bharatpur, 1967.
Singh, Raghubir	*Malwa Main Yugantar*, Purvakal, Indore, 1938.
—	*Brij Ka Itihas*, I
Srivastava, A.L.	*Awadh Ke Pratham Do Nawab*, Agra, 1957.
Shastri, Y.P.	*Prachin Rajya Vansh Evam Jat Kshatriya Itihas*, Hardwar, 1944.
Tomar Tikam Singh	*Hindi Veer Kavya*, Hindustani Academy, Allahabad, 1954.
Vidyalankar, J.C.	*Bhartiya Itihas Ki Ruprekha*, Vol. I, Hindustani Academy, Allahabad, 1933.

(3) Urdu

Khalidi, A.N.	*Taqwim Hijari-o-Iswari*, Karachi, 1952.
Mitra, K.	*Khalisa Shahidon Ka Balidan*, Lahore.
Numani, Maulana Shibh	*Aurangzeb Alamgir.*
Paramanandji, Bhai	*Tarikh-i-Panjab*, Lahore.
Saiyid, Ahmad	*Tarikh-i-Agra*, Agra, 1931.
Saiyid, M.M.	*Omra-i-Hinud*, Kanpur, 1910.

(B). GAZETTEERS

1. *District Gazetteers of the United Provincess.*
2. *Imperial Gazetteer of India* (Provincial series for U.P., Agra and Oudh), 2 Vols. Calcutta, 1908.
3. *The Imperial Gazetteer of India*, New edition, Oxford, 1908 (relevant volumes).
4. *Delhi Gazetteer.*
5. *Bombay Gazetteer*, Vol. IX, 1931.
6. *Muttra Gazetter*, 1911.

C. SELECT ARTICLES

This list does not include the articles already referred to above.

(a) *Deccan Geographer*

Mukerji, A.B.	*The Jats of the Upper Ganga-Jamuna Doab*, Vol. VI, 1968.

(b) *Indian Historical Quarterly*

Dhar, S.N. — *The Arab Conquest of Sind,* Vol. XVI, 1940.

(c) *Islamic Culture*

Gupta, H.R. — *Mughalani Begam, the Governor of Lahore,* Vol. XIV, 1940.

Habib, M. — *The Arab Conquest of Sind,* Vol. III, 1929.

Hashimi, Syed — *The Arab Rule in Sind,* Vol. I, 1927.

Heras, J. — *Durrani Influence in Northern India,* Vol. XI, 1937.

Husain, Yusuf — *Nizam-ul-Mulk Asaf Jah I,* Vols. VIII-IX, 1934-35.

Jaffar, S.M. — *Arab Administration of Sind,* 1943.

Khulusi, S.A. — (Extract trans.) *An account of Nadir Shah in an Eighteenth Century* Ms. Vol. XXV, 1951.

Sarkar, J.N. — *Ahmad Shah Abdali in India,* 1748, Vol. VI, 1932.

Shah, Abdul Rashid — (Extract trans.) *Insha-i--Mahru or Tarassul-i-Ain-ul-Mulki,* Vol. XVI, 1942.

Smith, W.C. — *Lower Class Uprisings in the Mughal Empire,* Vol. XX, 1946.

(d) *Journal of Asiatic Society of Bengal*

Irvine, William — *Nadir Shah and Muhammad Shah,* 1897.

— *The Bangash Nawabs of Farrukhabad,* Vol. XLVIII, Part I, 1879.

(e) *Journal of Bihar and Orissa Research Society*

Sarkar, J.N. — *A Correct Chronology of the Delhi History,* 1739-1754, Vol. XVIII, Part I, 1932.

(f) *Journal of India History*

Srivastava, A.L. — *Akbar's Theory of Kingship,* 1962.

(g) *Modern Review*

Sarkar, J.N. — *The Breaking-up of the Mughal Empire: Jat and Gujars,* October, 1923

— *The End of Nadir Shah,* May, 1929.

(h) *Nagari Pracharini Patrika* (Hindi)

Dwivedi, G.C. — *Ghasira Ke Yudha Ka Aitihasik Paryalochan,* Commemoration volume, Samvat 2024.

(i) *Proceedings of Indian History Congress*

Agaskar, M.S. *Mahadji Sindhia in the Battle of Panipat*, 1953.

Banga, Indu *Ahmad Shah Abdali's Designs over the Panjab*, 1968.

Chandra, Satish *Jiziyah in the Post-Aurangzeb Period*, 1946.

— *Raja Jai Singh Sawai's Contribution to Imperial Politics*, 1948.

Mahajan, D.B. *The Battle of Sakhar Khelda and the part played by Raghoji Jadhava of Sindh Khed*, 1951.

Pande, Ram *Raja Bishan Singh's Campaign against the Jats*, 1968.

— *Relations between Badan Singh and Sawai Raja Jai Singh*, 1969.

Qanungo, K.R. *Some Side-Lights on the career of Raja Bishan Singh Kachhwah of Amber*, 1948.

Rao, V.R. *Panipat and the Nizam*, 1950.

Sangar, S.P. *Political Offences in Aurangazeb's India*, 1950.

Siddiqi, Zameeruddin. *The Wizarat of Safdar Jang*, 1968.

Tikkimal, H.C. *Sawai Jai Singh and the Marwar Affairs in the reign of Emperor, Muhammad Shah*, 1970.

(j) *Proceedings of Indian Historical Records Commission*

Khare, G.H. *Some New Records on the Maratha-Jaipur Relations*, Vol. XXIV, 1948.

Puntambekar, S.V. *The Political and Religious Policy of the First Two Peshwas in the North*, Vol. XXII, 1945.

(k) *Uplabdhi* (*Hindi*)

Dwivedi, G.C. *Badan Singh Ke Kal Main Bharatpur Ka Pradeshik Vistar*, Samvat 2025.

Index